I AM BATMAN

VOL. 1

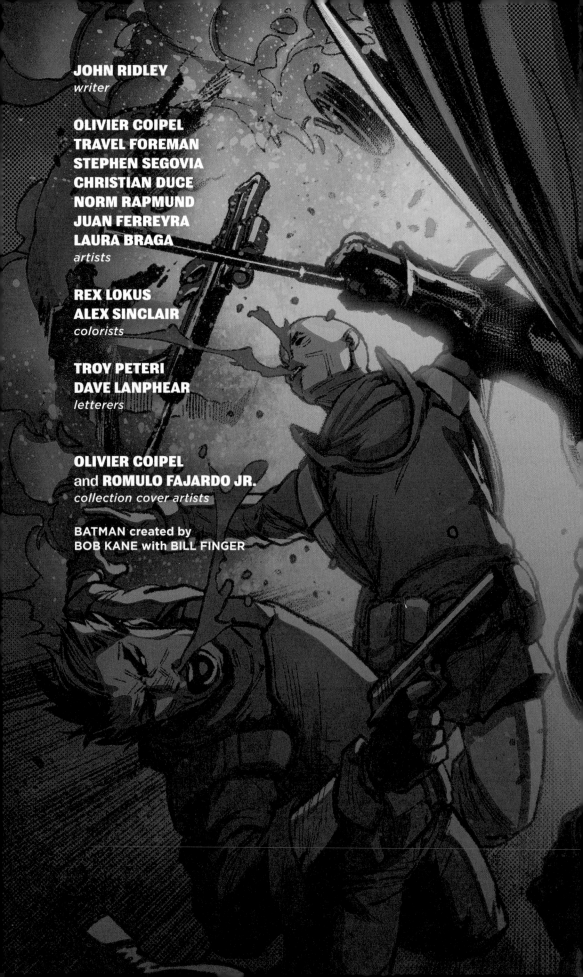

JOHN RIDLEY
writer

OLIVIER COIPEL
TRAVEL FOREMAN
STEPHEN SEGOVIA
CHRISTIAN DUCE
NORM RAPMUND
JUAN FERREYRA
LAURA BRAGA
artists

REX LOKUS
ALEX SINCLAIR
colorists

TROY PETERI
DAVE LANPHEAR
letterers

OLIVIER COIPEL
and **ROMULO FAJARDO JR.**
collection cover artists

BATMAN created by
BOB KANE with BILL FINGER

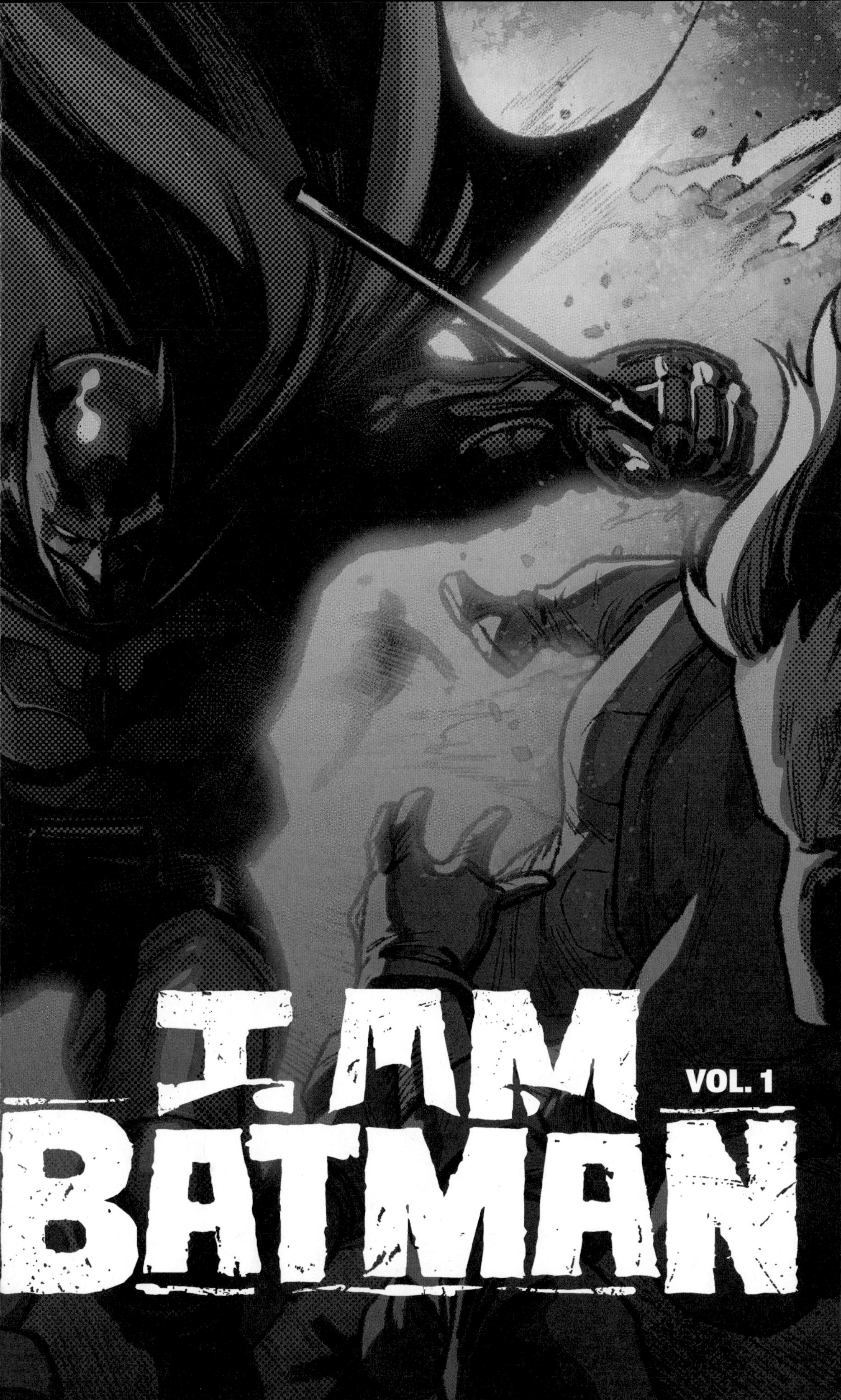
I AM
BATMAN
VOL. 1

Ben Abernathy Editor – Original Series & Collected Edition
Dave Wielgosz Associate Editor – Original Series
Steve Cook Design Director – Books
Megen Bellersen Publication Design
Ryane Lynn Hill Production Editor

Marie Javins Editor-in-Chief, DC Comics

Anne DePies Senior VP – General Manager
Jim Lee Publisher & Chief Creative Officer
Don Falletti VP – Manufacturing Operations & Workflow Management
Lawrence Ganem VP – Talent Services
Alison Gill Senior VP – Manufacturing & Operations
Jeffrey Kaufman VP – Editorial Strategy & Programming
Nick J. Napolitano VP – Manufacturing Administration & Design
Nancy Spears VP – Revenue

I AM BATMAN VOL. 1

DC Comics, 2900 West Alameda Ave., Burbank, CA 91505
Printed by Transcontinental Interglobe, Beauceville, QC, Canada.
7/15/2022.
ISBN: 978-1-77951-661-9

Library of Congress Cataloging-in-Publication Data is available.

PEFC Certified
This product is
from sustainably
managed forests and
controlled sources
PEFC/01-31-106   www.pefc.org

I Am Batman #0
cover art by Travel Foreman
and Rex Lokus

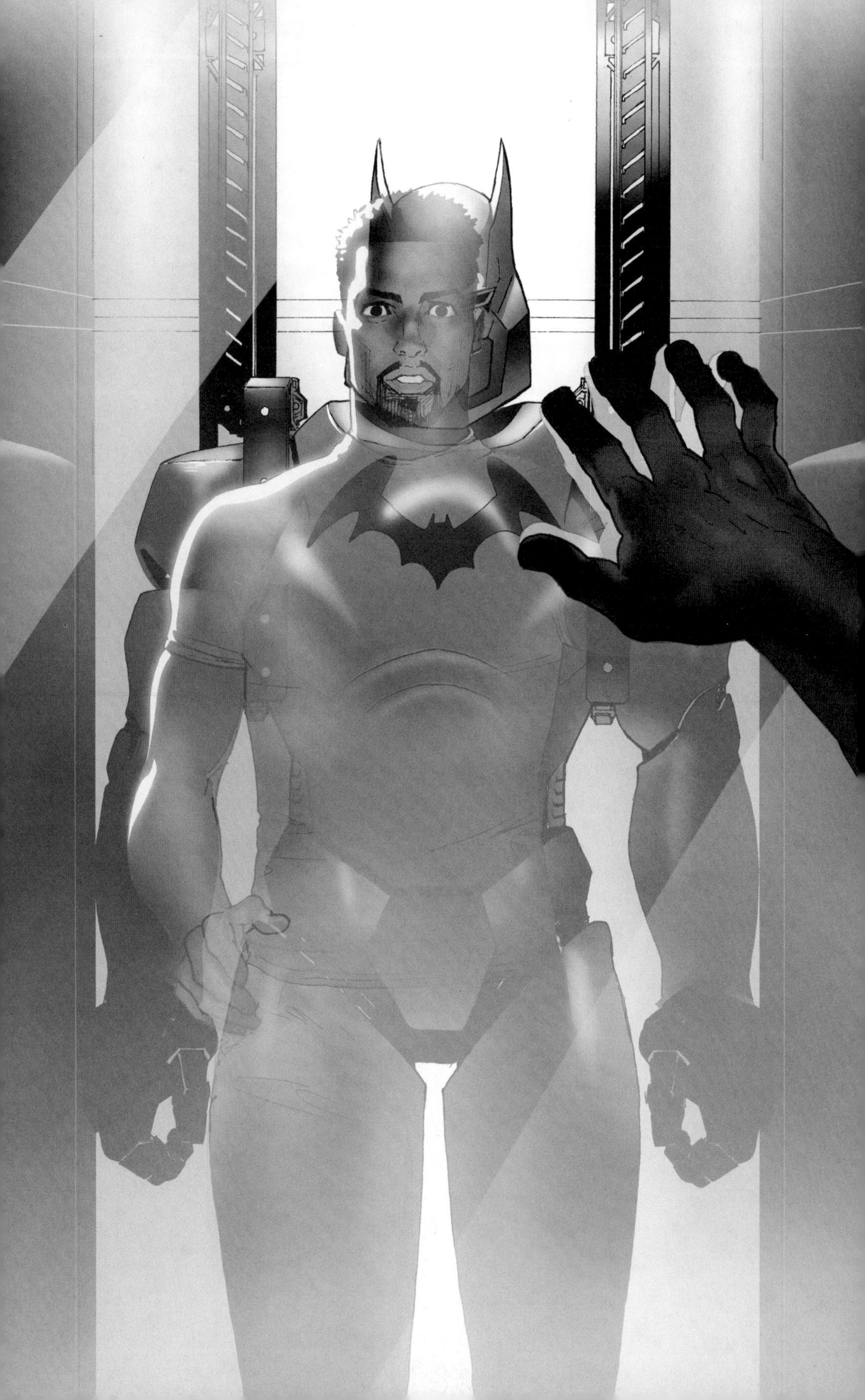

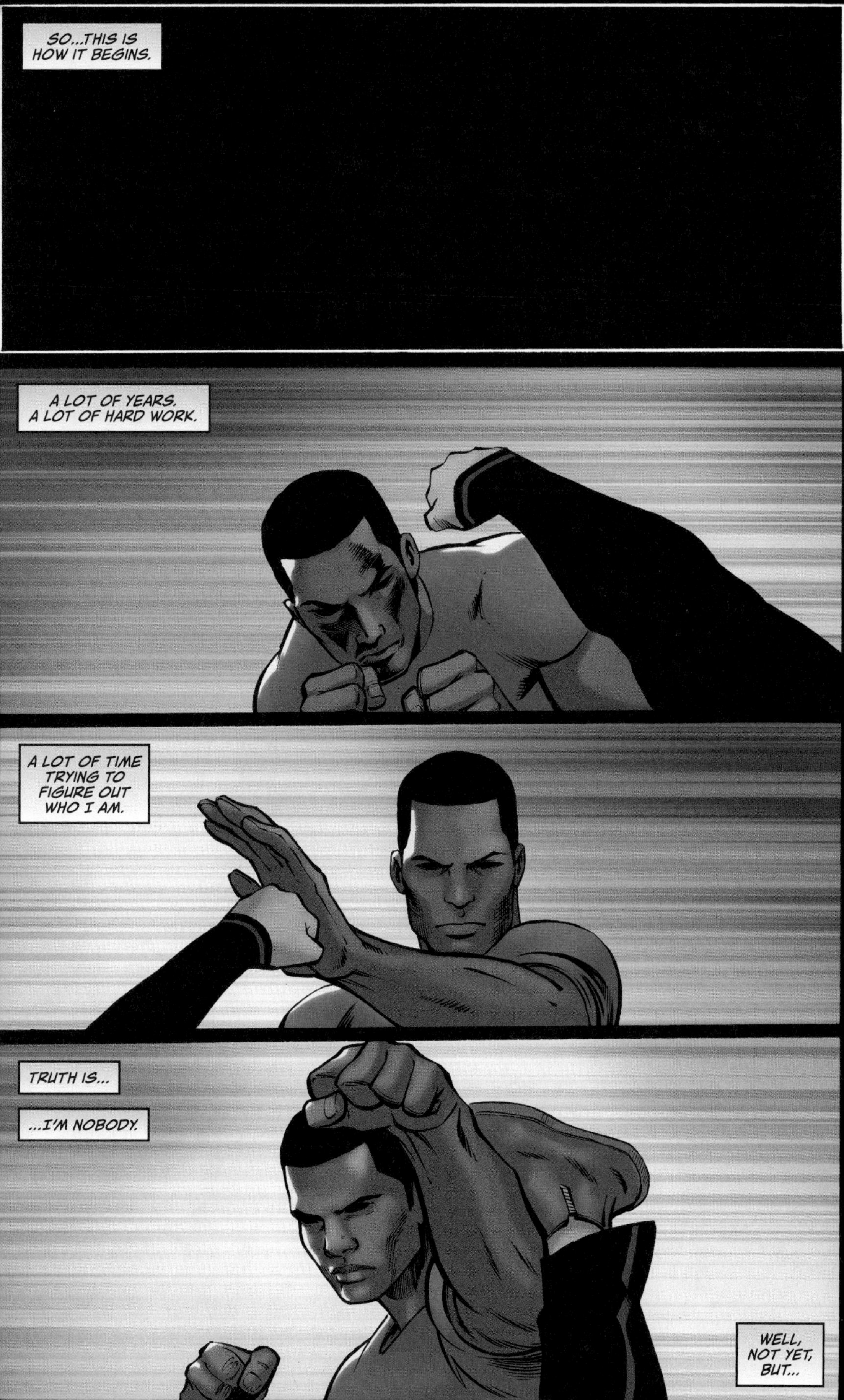
SO...THIS IS HOW IT BEGINS.
A LOT OF YEARS. A LOT OF HARD WORK.
A LOT OF TIME TRYING TO FIGURE OUT WHO I AM.
TRUTH IS...
...I'M NOBODY.
WELL, NOT YET, BUT...

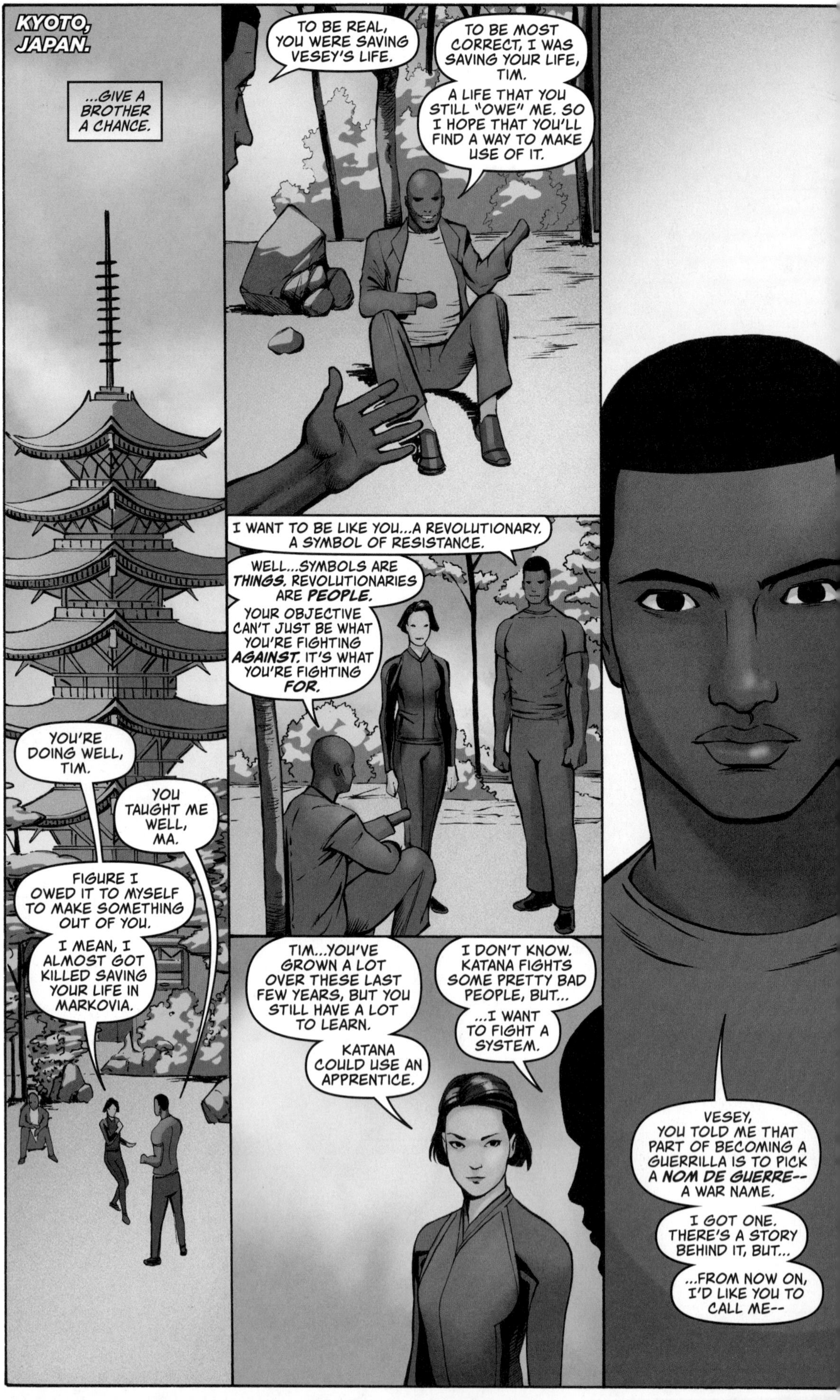
KYOTO, JAPAN.
...GIVE A BROTHER A CHANCE.
YOU'RE DOING WELL, TIM.
YOU TAUGHT ME WELL, MA.
FIGURE I OWED IT TO MYSELF TO MAKE SOMETHING OUT OF YOU.
I MEAN, I ALMOST GOT KILLED SAVING YOUR LIFE IN MARKOVIA.
TO BE REAL, YOU WERE SAVING VESEY'S LIFE.
TO BE MOST CORRECT, I WAS SAVING YOUR LIFE, TIM.
A LIFE THAT YOU STILL "OWE" ME. SO I HOPE THAT YOU'LL FIND A WAY TO MAKE USE OF IT.
I WANT TO BE LIKE YOU...A REVOLUTIONARY. A SYMBOL OF RESISTANCE.
WELL...SYMBOLS ARE THINGS. REVOLUTIONARIES ARE PEOPLE.
YOUR OBJECTIVE CAN'T JUST BE WHAT YOU'RE FIGHTING AGAINST. IT'S WHAT YOU'RE FIGHTING FOR.
TIM...YOU'VE GROWN A LOT OVER THESE LAST FEW YEARS, BUT YOU STILL HAVE A LOT TO LEARN.
KATANA COULD USE AN APPRENTICE.
I DON'T KNOW. KATANA FIGHTS SOME PRETTY BAD PEOPLE, BUT...
...I WANT TO FIGHT A SYSTEM.
VESEY, YOU TOLD ME THAT PART OF BECOMING A GUERRILLA IS TO PICK A NOM DE GUERRE--A WAR NAME.
I GOT ONE. THERE'S A STORY BEHIND IT, BUT...
...FROM NOW ON, I'D LIKE YOU TO CALL ME--

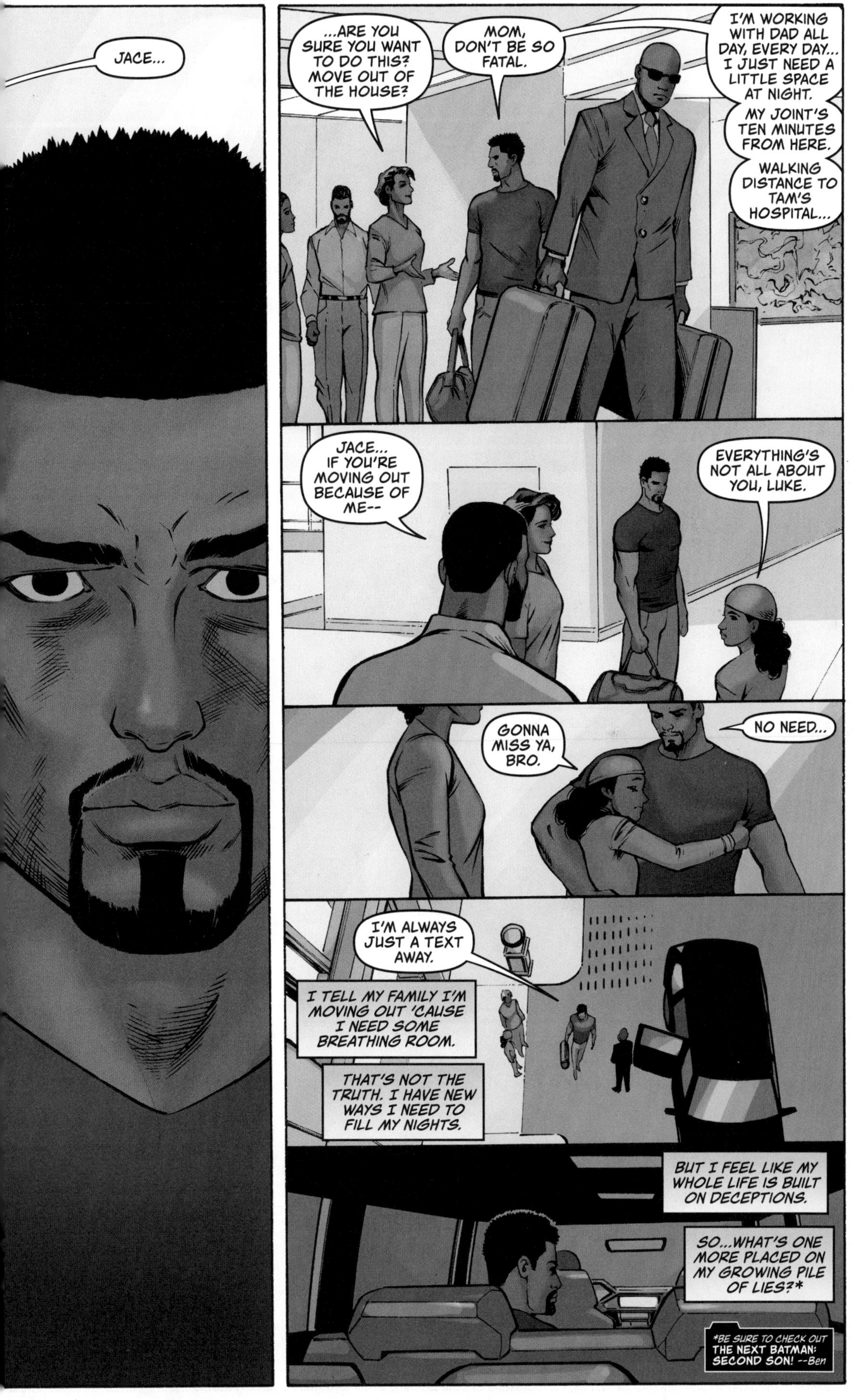
JACE...
...ARE YOU SURE YOU WANT TO DO THIS? MOVE OUT OF THE HOUSE?
MOM, DON'T BE SO FATAL.
I'M WORKING WITH DAD ALL DAY, EVERY DAY... I JUST NEED A LITTLE SPACE AT NIGHT.
MY JOINT'S TEN MINUTES FROM HERE.
WALKING DISTANCE TO TAM'S HOSPITAL...
JACE... IF YOU'RE MOVING OUT BECAUSE OF ME--
EVERYTHING'S NOT ALL ABOUT YOU, LUKE.
GONNA MISS YA, BRO.
NO NEED...
I'M ALWAYS JUST A TEXT AWAY.
I TELL MY FAMILY I'M MOVING OUT 'CAUSE I NEED SOME BREATHING ROOM.
THAT'S NOT THE TRUTH. I HAVE NEW WAYS I NEED TO FILL MY NIGHTS.
BUT I FEEL LIKE MY WHOLE LIFE IS BUILT ON DECEPTIONS.
SO...WHAT'S ONE MORE PLACED ON MY GROWING PILE OF LIES?*
*BE SURE TO CHECK OUT THE NEXT BATMAN: SECOND SON! --Ben

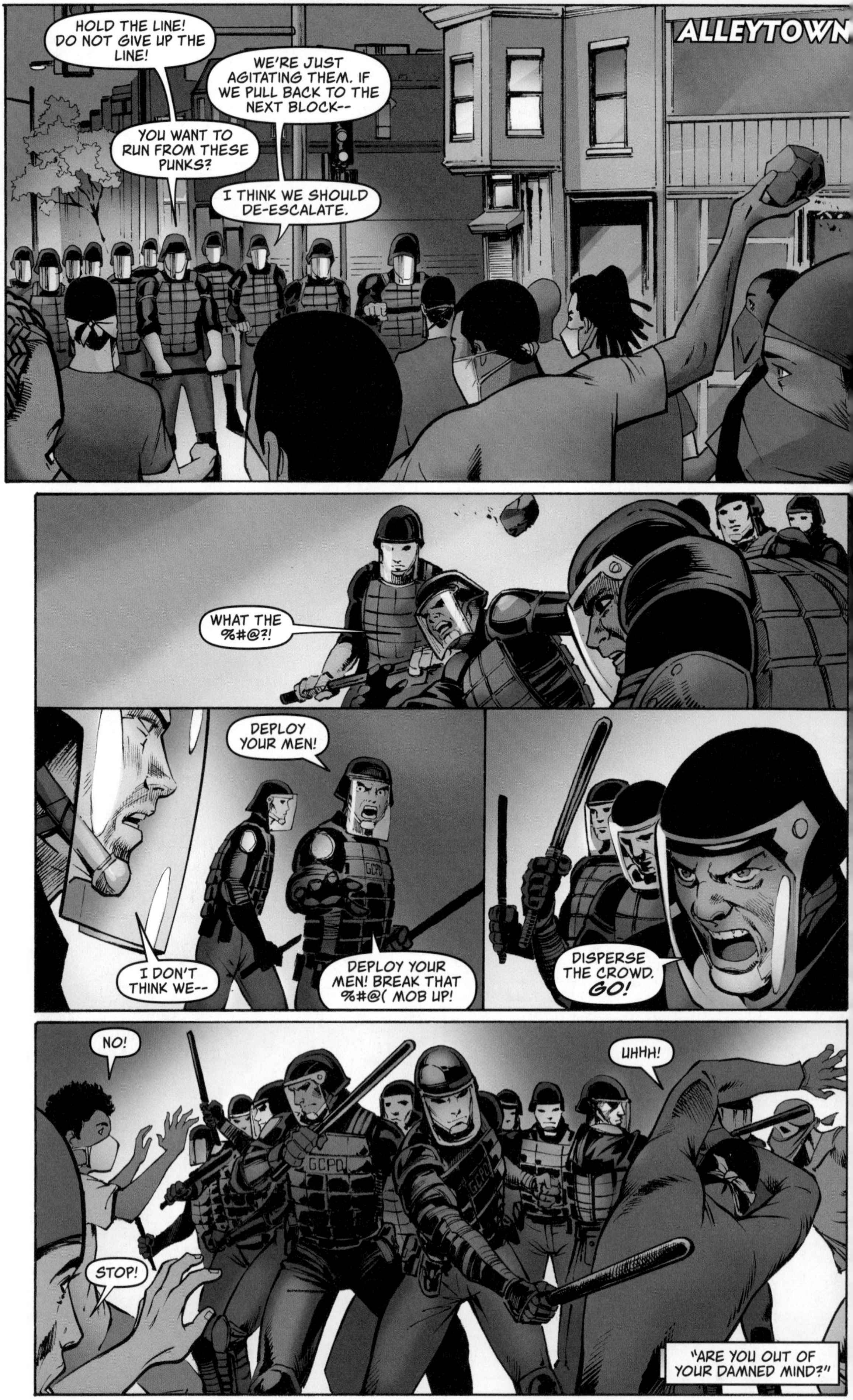
ALLEYTOWN
HOLD THE LINE! DO NOT GIVE UP THE LINE!
YOU WANT TO RUN FROM THESE PUNKS?
WE'RE JUST AGITATING THEM. IF WE PULL BACK TO THE NEXT BLOCK--
I THINK WE SHOULD DE-ESCALATE.
WHAT THE %#@?!
DEPLOY YOUR MEN!
I DON'T THINK WE--
DEPLOY YOUR MEN! BREAK THAT %#@(MOB UP!
DISPERSE THE CROWD. GO!
NO!
UHHH!
STOP!
"ARE YOU OUT OF YOUR DAMNED MIND?"

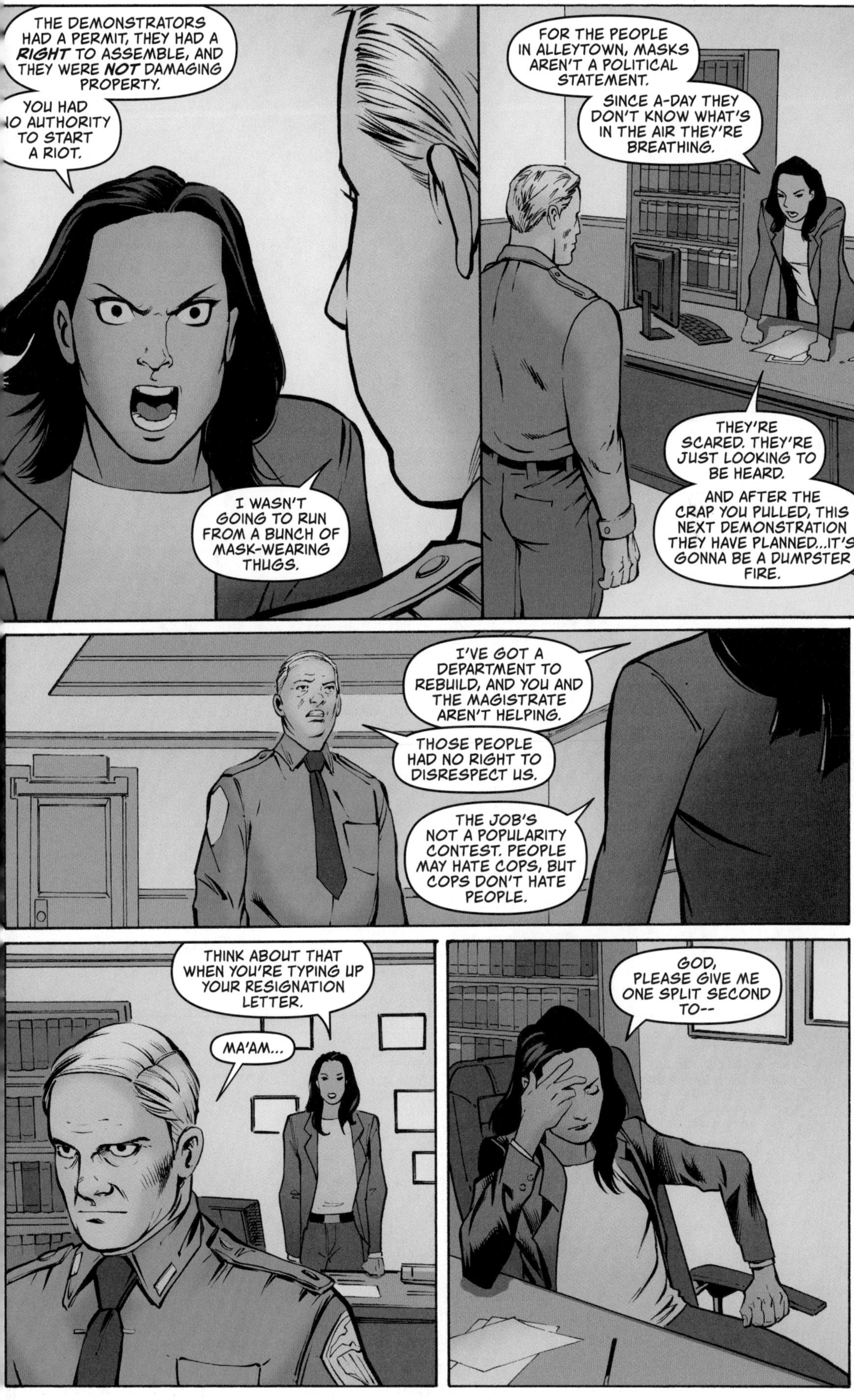
THE DEMONSTRATORS HAD A PERMIT, THEY HAD A **RIGHT** TO ASSEMBLE, AND THEY WERE **NOT** DAMAGING PROPERTY.
YOU HAD NO AUTHORITY TO START A RIOT.
I WASN'T GOING TO RUN FROM A BUNCH OF MASK-WEARING THUGS.
FOR THE PEOPLE IN ALLEYTOWN, MASKS AREN'T A POLITICAL STATEMENT.
SINCE A-DAY THEY DON'T KNOW WHAT'S IN THE AIR THEY'RE BREATHING.
THEY'RE SCARED. THEY'RE JUST LOOKING TO BE HEARD.
AND AFTER THE CRAP YOU PULLED, THIS NEXT DEMONSTRATION THEY HAVE PLANNED...IT'S GONNA BE A DUMPSTER FIRE.
I'VE GOT A DEPARTMENT TO REBUILD, AND YOU AND THE MAGISTRATE AREN'T HELPING.
THOSE PEOPLE HAD NO RIGHT TO DISRESPECT US.
THE JOB'S NOT A POPULARITY CONTEST. PEOPLE MAY HATE COPS, BUT COPS DON'T HATE PEOPLE.
THINK ABOUT THAT WHEN YOU'RE TYPING UP YOUR RESIGNATION LETTER.
MA'AM...
GOD, PLEASE GIVE ME ONE SPLIT SECOND TO--

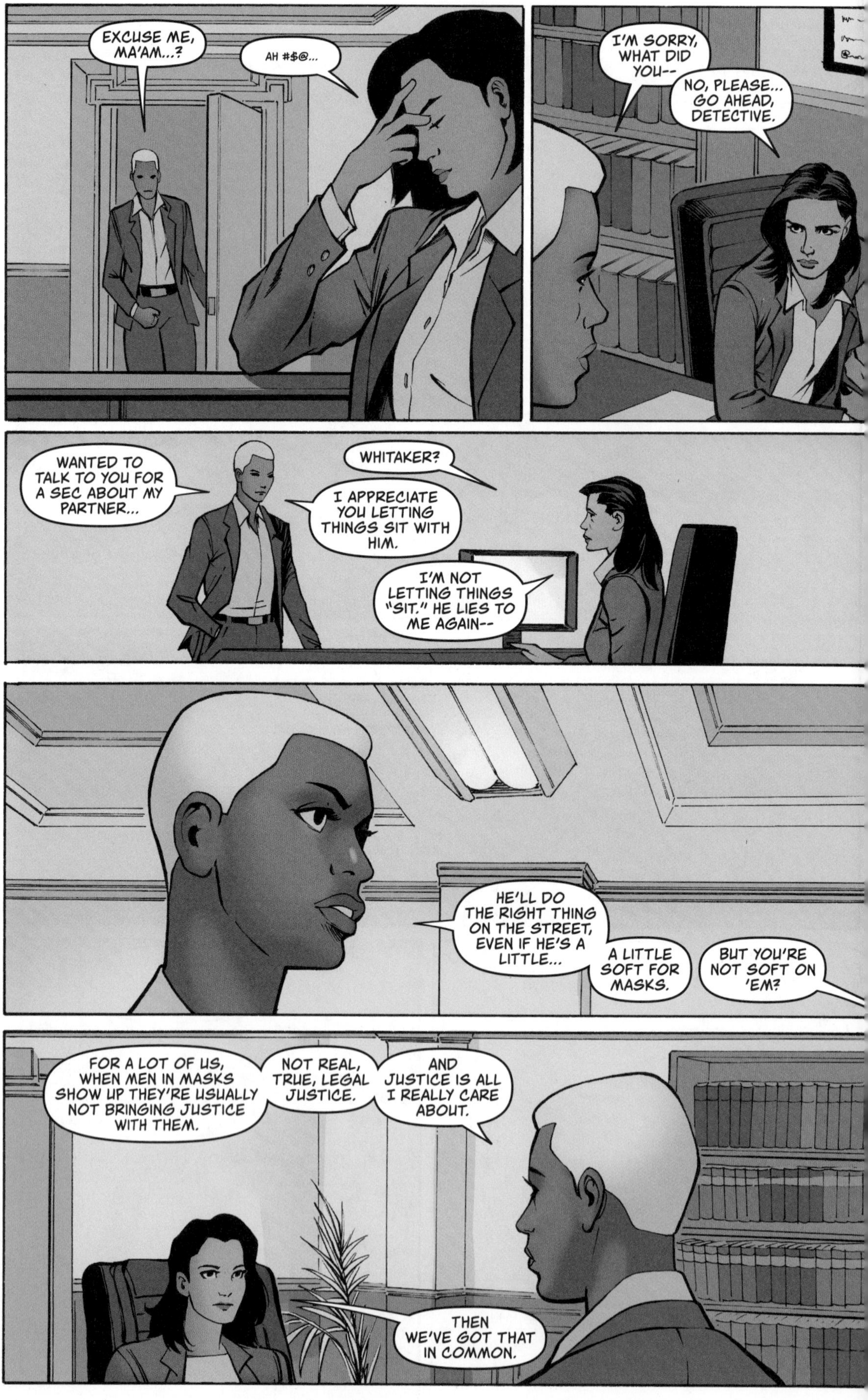
EXCUSE ME, MA'AM...?
AH #$@...
I'M SORRY, WHAT DID YOU--
NO, PLEASE... GO AHEAD, DETECTIVE.
WANTED TO TALK TO YOU FOR A SEC ABOUT MY PARTNER...
WHITAKER?
I APPRECIATE YOU LETTING THINGS SIT WITH HIM.
I'M NOT LETTING THINGS "SIT." HE LIES TO ME AGAIN--
HE'LL DO THE RIGHT THING ON THE STREET, EVEN IF HE'S A LITTLE...
A LITTLE SOFT FOR MASKS.
BUT YOU'RE NOT SOFT ON 'EM?
FOR A LOT OF US, WHEN MEN IN MASKS SHOW UP THEY'RE USUALLY NOT BRINGING JUSTICE WITH THEM.
NOT REAL, TRUE, LEGAL JUSTICE.
AND JUSTICE IS ALL I REALLY CARE ABOUT.
THEN WE'VE GOT THAT IN COMMON.

CAN I ASK YOU A QUESTION? YOU SPENT YOUR CAREER AROUND MASKS. WHERE DO YOU LAND ON THEM?

I LAND RIGHT WHERE THE LAW TELLS ME.

I DON'T MEAN AS COMMISSIONER. I MEAN AS RENEE MONTOYA.

I'M SORRY, MA'AM. DIDN'T MEAN TO GET PERSONAL.

NO. YOU'RE NOT. IT'S JUST...

LOOK, I'M, UH, ONLY GUESSING, BUT MASKS...

SOMETIMES ANONYMITY ALLOWS YOU TO BE THE PERSON YOU REALLY ARE.

IT'S LIKE AN ONLINE THREAD. WHEN YOU CAN HIDE YOUR IDENTITY YOU CAN BE DEEP, OR YOU CAN BE A TROLL.

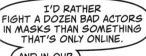

I'D RATHER FIGHT A DOZEN BAD ACTORS IN MASKS THAN SOMETHING THAT'S ONLY ONLINE.

AND IN OUR HEADS.

YEAH. WELL. I'M FINE FIGHTING BOTH.

GOOD. 'CAUSE THIS NEXT DEMONSTRATION IN ALLEYTOWN...

...YOU AND WHITAKER ARE GOING TO BE THE OFFICERS IN CHARGE.

DON'T LET ME DOWN.

"YOU DON'T HAVE ANYTHING TO PROVE."

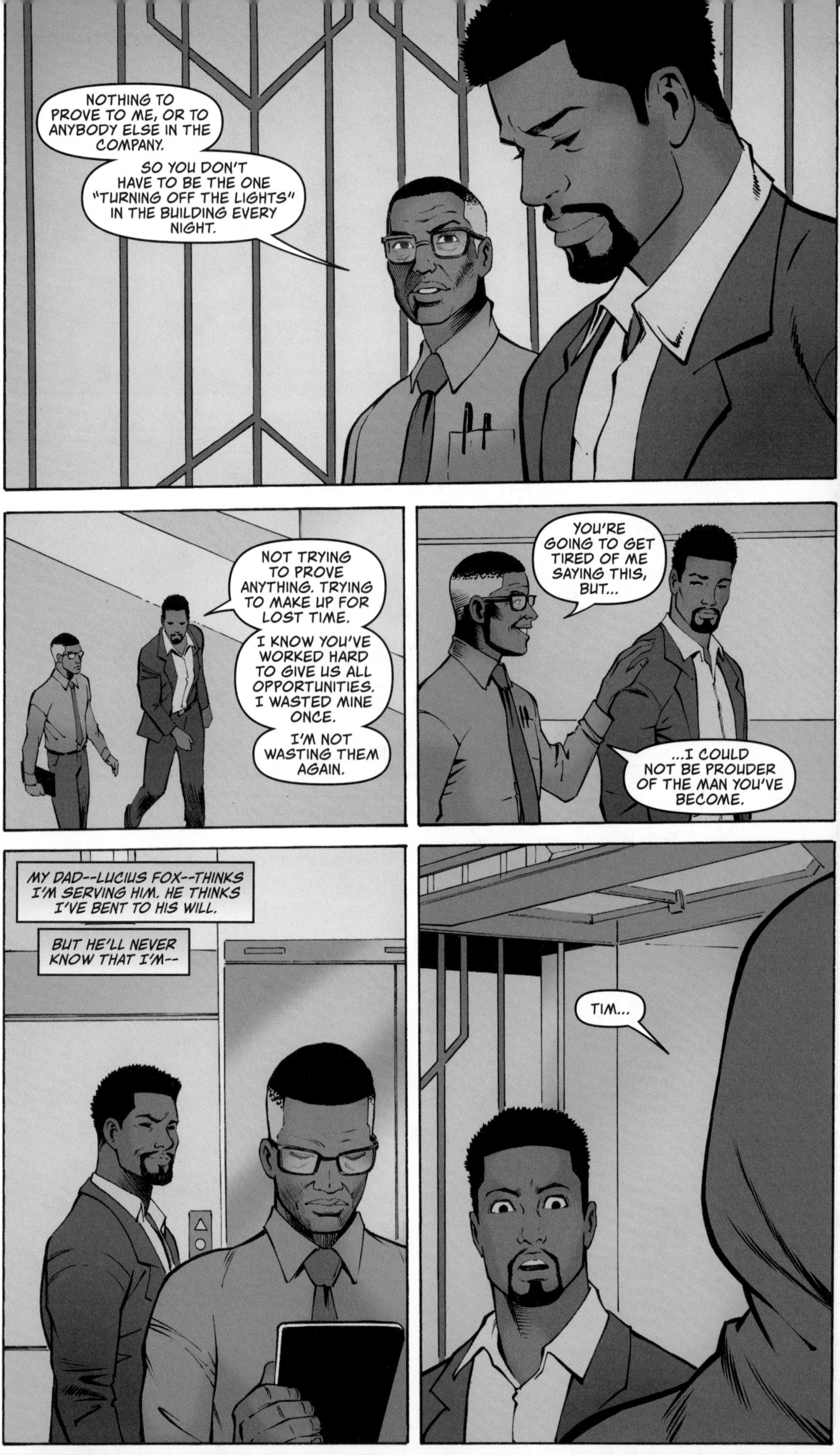
NOTHING TO PROVE TO ME, OR TO ANYBODY ELSE IN THE COMPANY.
SO YOU DON'T HAVE TO BE THE ONE "TURNING OFF THE LIGHTS" IN THE BUILDING EVERY NIGHT.
NOT TRYING TO PROVE ANYTHING. TRYING TO MAKE UP FOR LOST TIME.
I KNOW YOU'VE WORKED HARD TO GIVE US ALL OPPORTUNITIES. I WASTED MINE ONCE.
I'M NOT WASTING THEM AGAIN.
YOU'RE GOING TO GET TIRED OF ME SAYING THIS, BUT...
...I COULD NOT BE PROUDER OF THE MAN YOU'VE BECOME.
MY DAD--LUCIUS FOX--THINKS I'M SERVING HIM. HE THINKS I'VE BENT TO HIS WILL.
BUT HE'LL NEVER KNOW THAT I'M--
TIM...

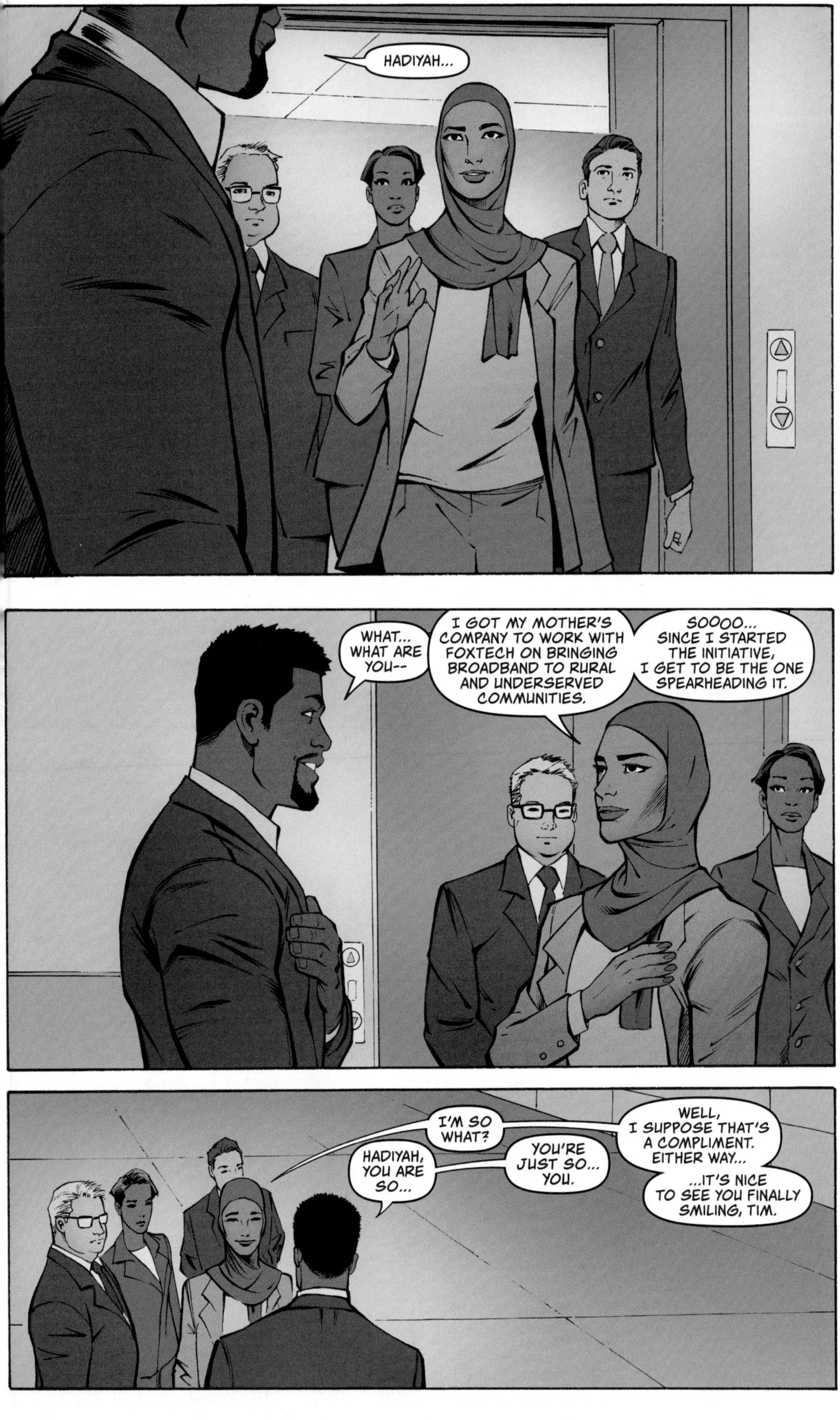
HADIYAH...
WHAT... WHAT ARE YOU--
I GOT MY MOTHER'S COMPANY TO WORK WITH FOXTECH ON BRINGING BROADBAND TO RURAL AND UNDERSERVED COMMUNITIES.
SOOOO... SINCE I STARTED THE INITIATIVE, I GET TO BE THE ONE SPEARHEADING IT.
HADIYAH, YOU ARE SO...
I'M SO WHAT?
YOU'RE JUST SO... YOU.
WELL, I SUPPOSE THAT'S A COMPLIMENT. EITHER WAY...
...IT'S NICE TO SEE YOU FINALLY SMILING, TIM.

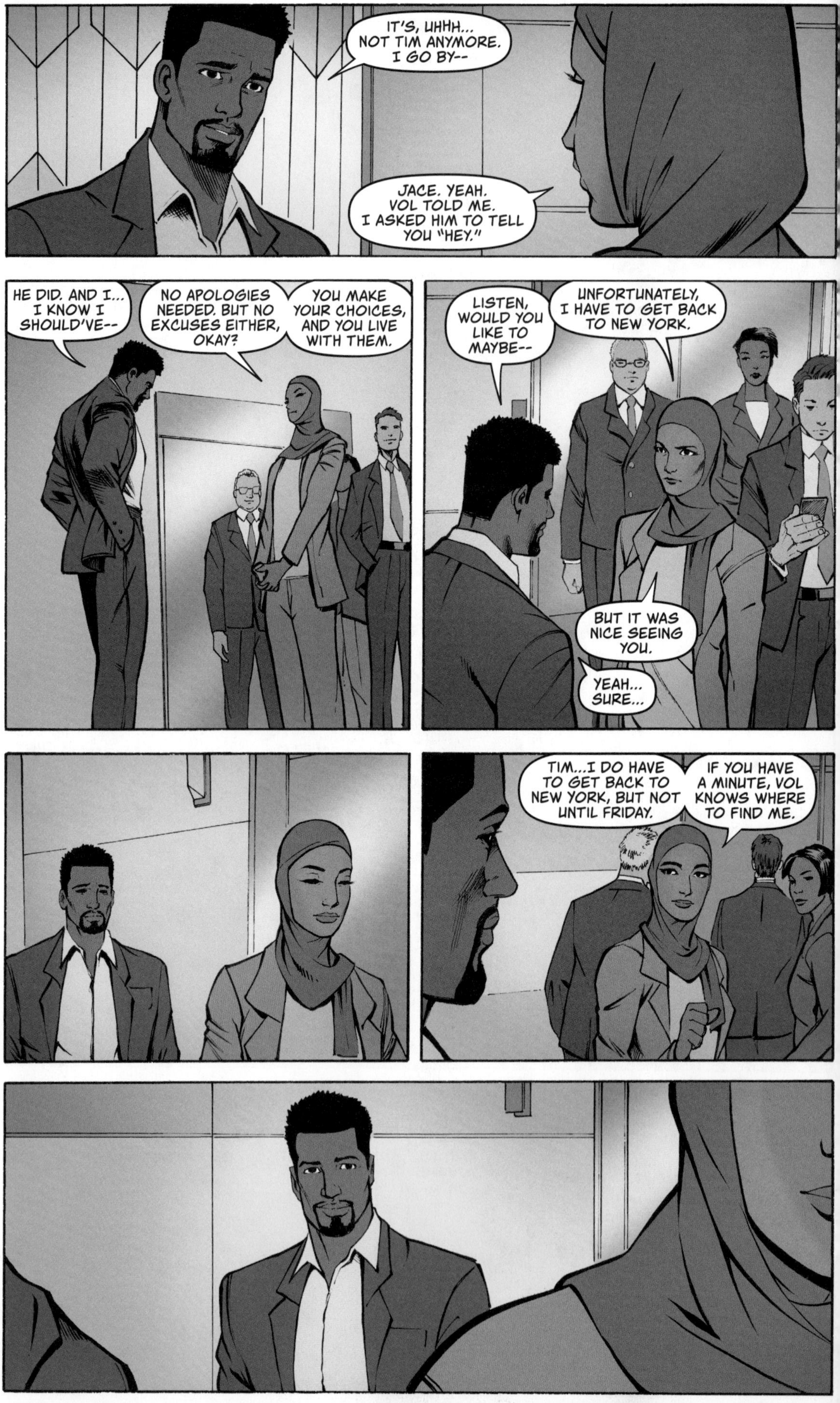
IT'S, UHHH... NOT TIM ANYMORE. I GO BY--
JACE. YEAH. VOL TOLD ME. I ASKED HIM TO TELL YOU "HEY."
HE DID. AND I... I KNOW I SHOULD'VE--
NO APOLOGIES NEEDED. BUT NO EXCUSES EITHER, OKAY?
YOU MAKE YOUR CHOICES, AND YOU LIVE WITH THEM.
LISTEN, WOULD YOU LIKE TO MAYBE--
UNFORTUNATELY, I HAVE TO GET BACK TO NEW YORK.
BUT IT WAS NICE SEEING YOU.
YEAH... SURE...
TIM...I DO HAVE TO GET BACK TO NEW YORK, BUT NOT UNTIL FRIDAY.
IF YOU HAVE A MINUTE, VOL KNOWS WHERE TO FIND ME.

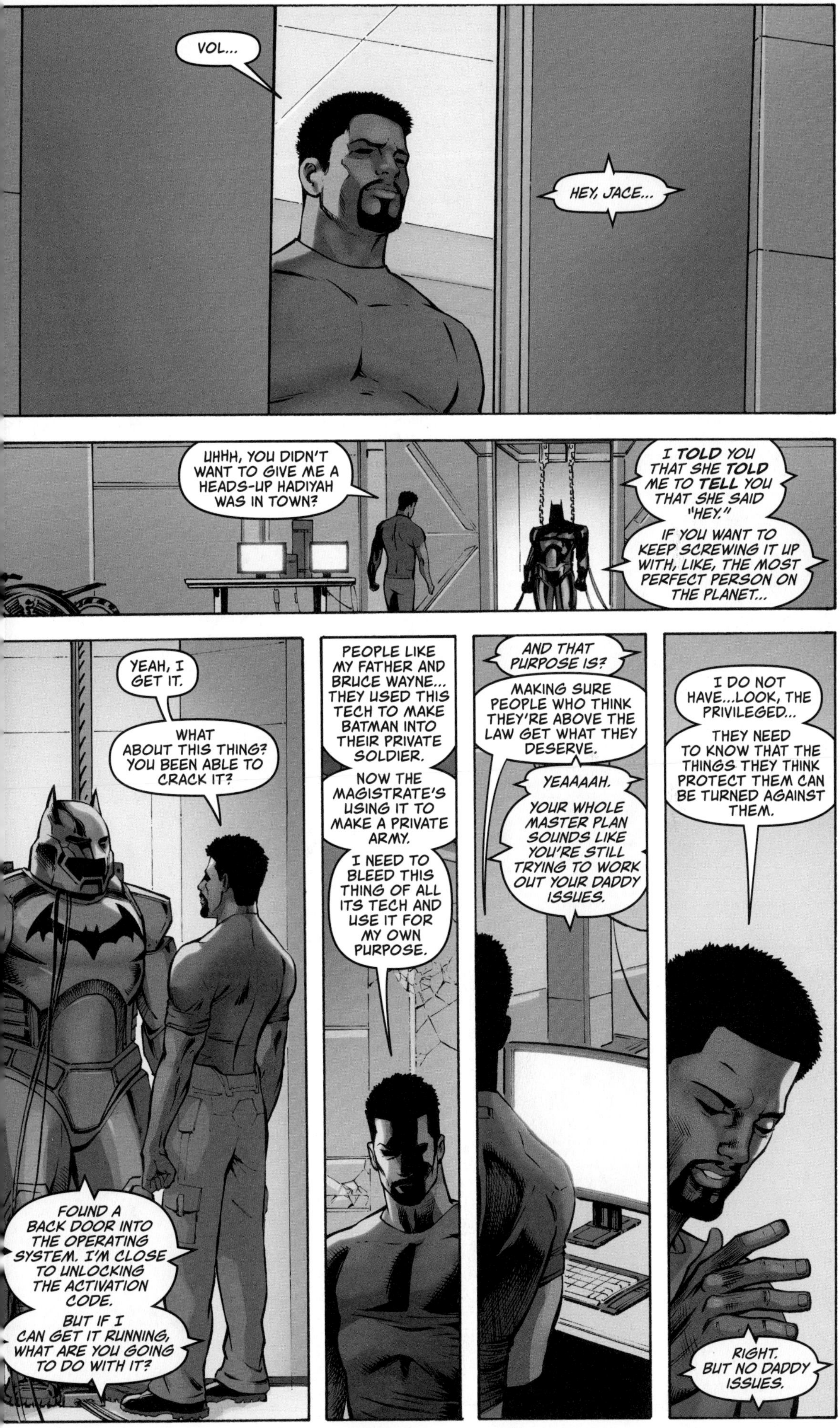
VOL...
HEY, JACE...
UHHH, YOU DIDN'T WANT TO GIVE ME A HEADS-UP HADIYAH WAS IN TOWN?
I **TOLD** YOU THAT SHE **TOLD** ME TO **TELL** YOU THAT SHE SAID "HEY."
IF YOU WANT TO KEEP SCREWING IT UP WITH, LIKE, THE MOST PERFECT PERSON ON THE PLANET...
YEAH, I GET IT.
WHAT ABOUT THIS THING? YOU BEEN ABLE TO CRACK IT?
FOUND A BACK DOOR INTO THE OPERATING SYSTEM. I'M CLOSE TO UNLOCKING THE ACTIVATION CODE.
BUT IF I CAN GET IT RUNNING, WHAT ARE YOU GOING TO DO WITH IT?
PEOPLE LIKE MY FATHER AND BRUCE WAYNE... THEY USED THIS TECH TO MAKE BATMAN INTO THEIR PRIVATE SOLDIER.
NOW THE MAGISTRATE'S USING IT TO MAKE A PRIVATE ARMY.
I NEED TO BLEED THIS THING OF ALL ITS TECH AND USE IT FOR MY OWN PURPOSE.
AND THAT PURPOSE IS?
MAKING SURE PEOPLE WHO THINK THEY'RE ABOVE THE LAW GET WHAT THEY DESERVE.
YEAAAAH.
YOUR WHOLE MASTER PLAN SOUNDS LIKE YOU'RE STILL TRYING TO WORK OUT YOUR DADDY ISSUES.
I DO NOT HAVE...LOOK, THE PRIVILEGED...
THEY NEED TO KNOW THAT THE THINGS THEY THINK PROTECT THEM CAN BE TURNED AGAINST THEM.
RIGHT. BUT NO DADDY ISSUES.

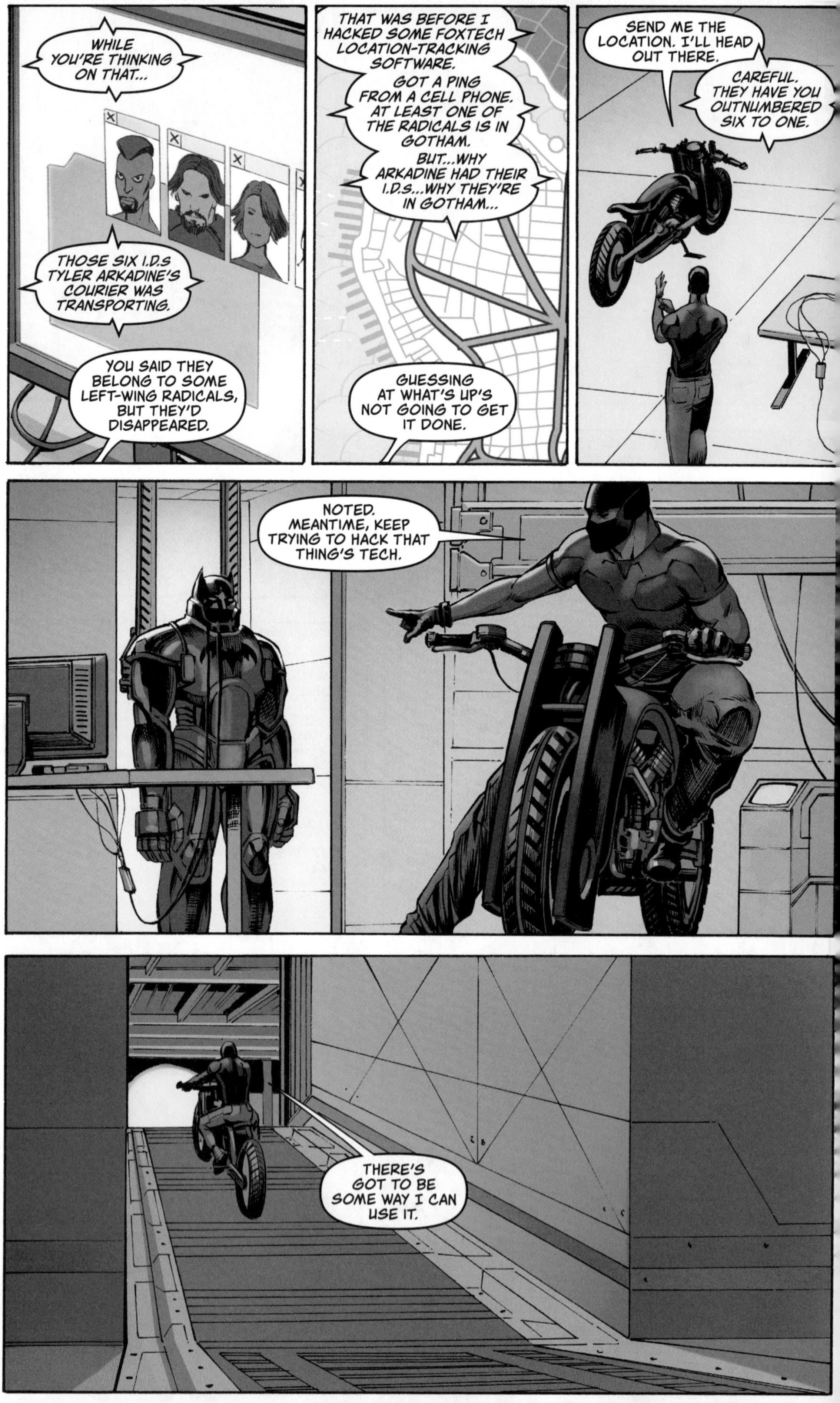
WHILE YOU'RE THINKING ON THAT...
THOSE SIX I.D.S TYLER ARKADINE'S COURIER WAS TRANSPORTING.
YOU SAID THEY BELONG TO SOME LEFT-WING RADICALS, BUT THEY'D DISAPPEARED.
THAT WAS BEFORE I HACKED SOME FOXTECH LOCATION-TRACKING SOFTWARE.
GOT A PING FROM A CELL PHONE. AT LEAST ONE OF THE RADICALS IS IN GOTHAM.
BUT...WHY ARKADINE HAD THEIR I.D.S...WHY THEY'RE IN GOTHAM...
GUESSING AT WHAT'S UP'S NOT GOING TO GET IT DONE.
SEND ME THE LOCATION. I'LL HEAD OUT THERE.
CAREFUL. THEY HAVE YOU OUTNUMBERED SIX TO ONE.
NOTED. MEANTIME, KEEP TRYING TO HACK THAT THING'S TECH.
THERE'S GOT TO BE SOME WAY I CAN USE IT.

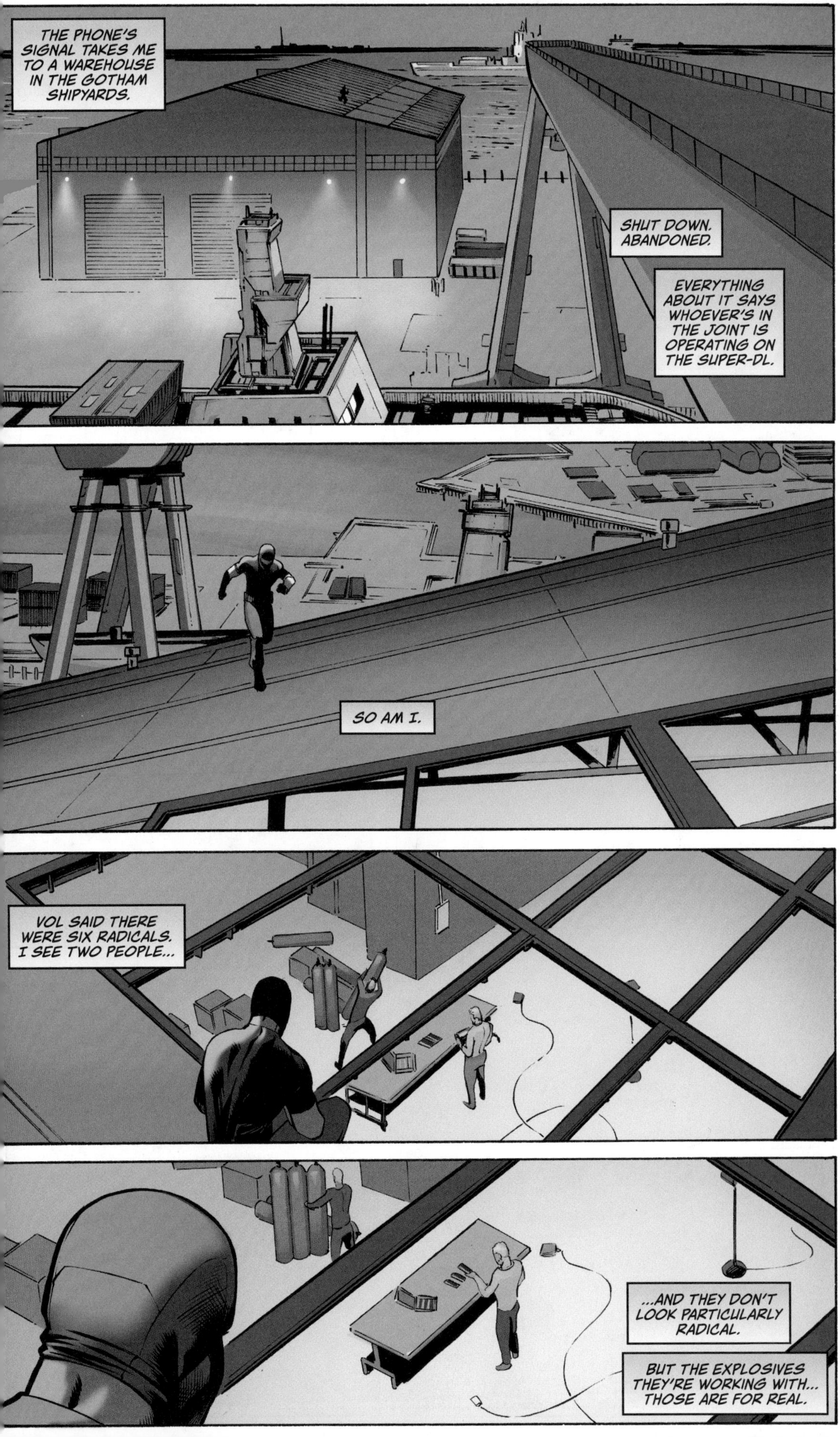
THE PHONE'S SIGNAL TAKES ME TO A WAREHOUSE IN THE GOTHAM SHIPYARDS.
SHUT DOWN. ABANDONED.
EVERYTHING ABOUT IT SAYS WHOEVER'S IN THE JOINT IS OPERATING ON THE SUPER-DL.
SO AM I.
VOL SAID THERE WERE SIX RADICALS. I SEE TWO PEOPLE...
...AND THEY DON'T LOOK PARTICULARLY RADICAL.
BUT THE EXPLOSIVES THEY'RE WORKING WITH... THOSE ARE FOR REAL.

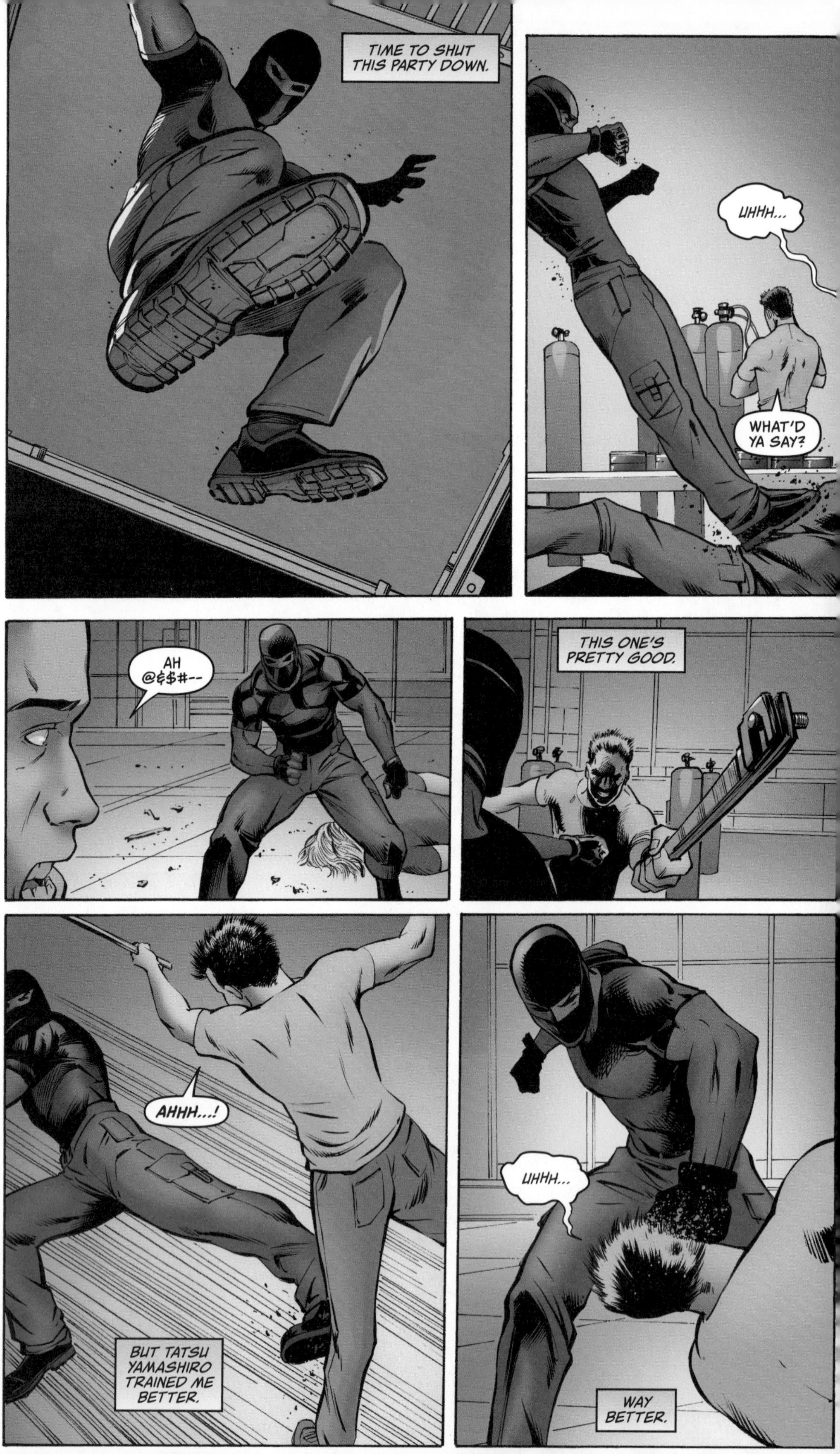
TIME TO SHUT THIS PARTY DOWN.
UHHH...
WHAT'D YA SAY?
AH @&$#--
THIS ONE'S PRETTY GOOD.
AHHH...!
BUT TATSU YAMASHIRO TRAINED ME BETTER.
UHHH...
WAY BETTER.

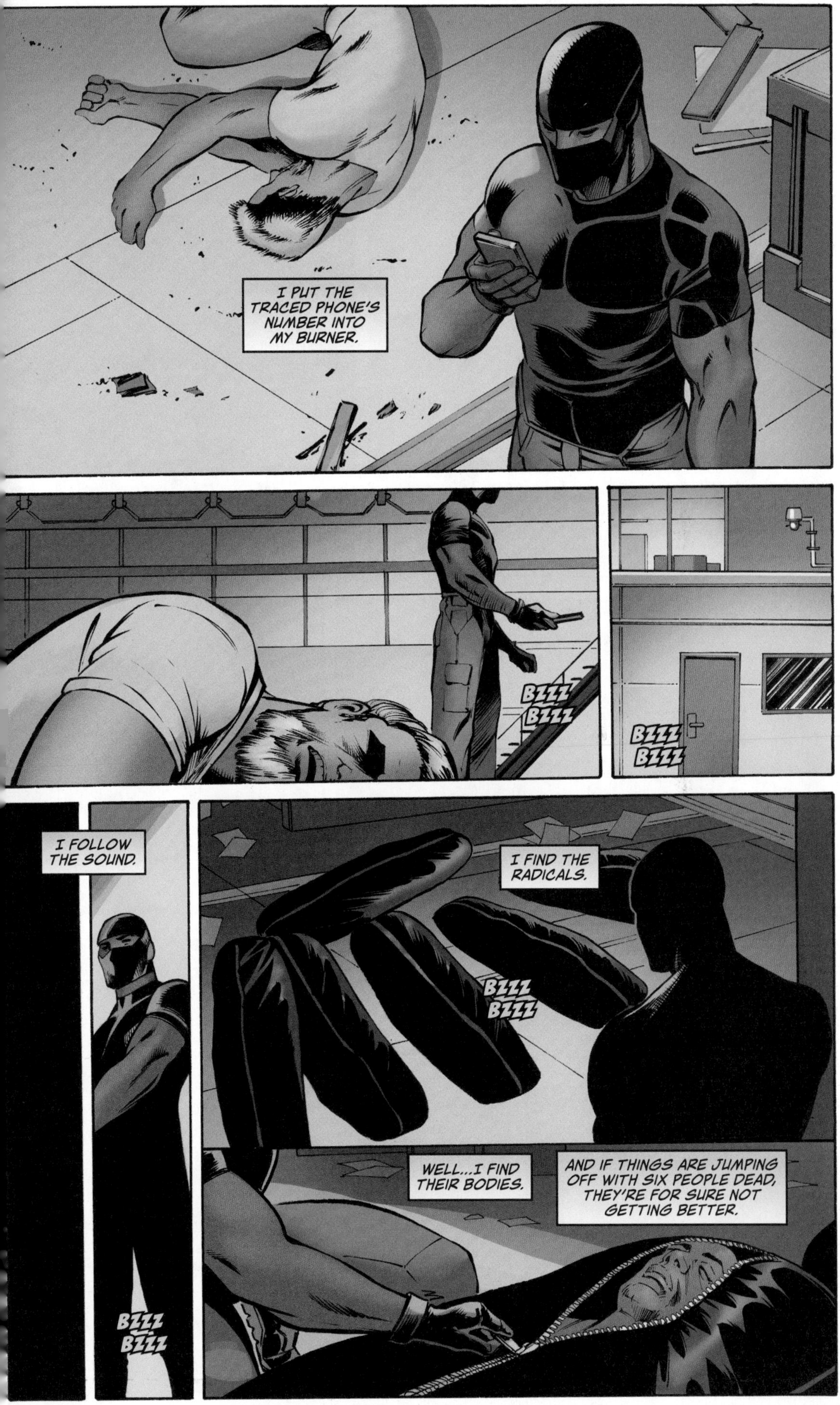
I PUT THE TRACED PHONE'S NUMBER INTO MY BURNER.
BZZZ BZZZ
BZZZ BZZZ
I FOLLOW THE SOUND.
BZZZ BZZZ
I FIND THE RADICALS.
BZZZ BZZZ
WELL...I FIND THEIR BODIES.
AND IF THINGS ARE JUMPING OFF WITH SIX PEOPLE DEAD, THEY'RE FOR SURE NOT GETTING BETTER.

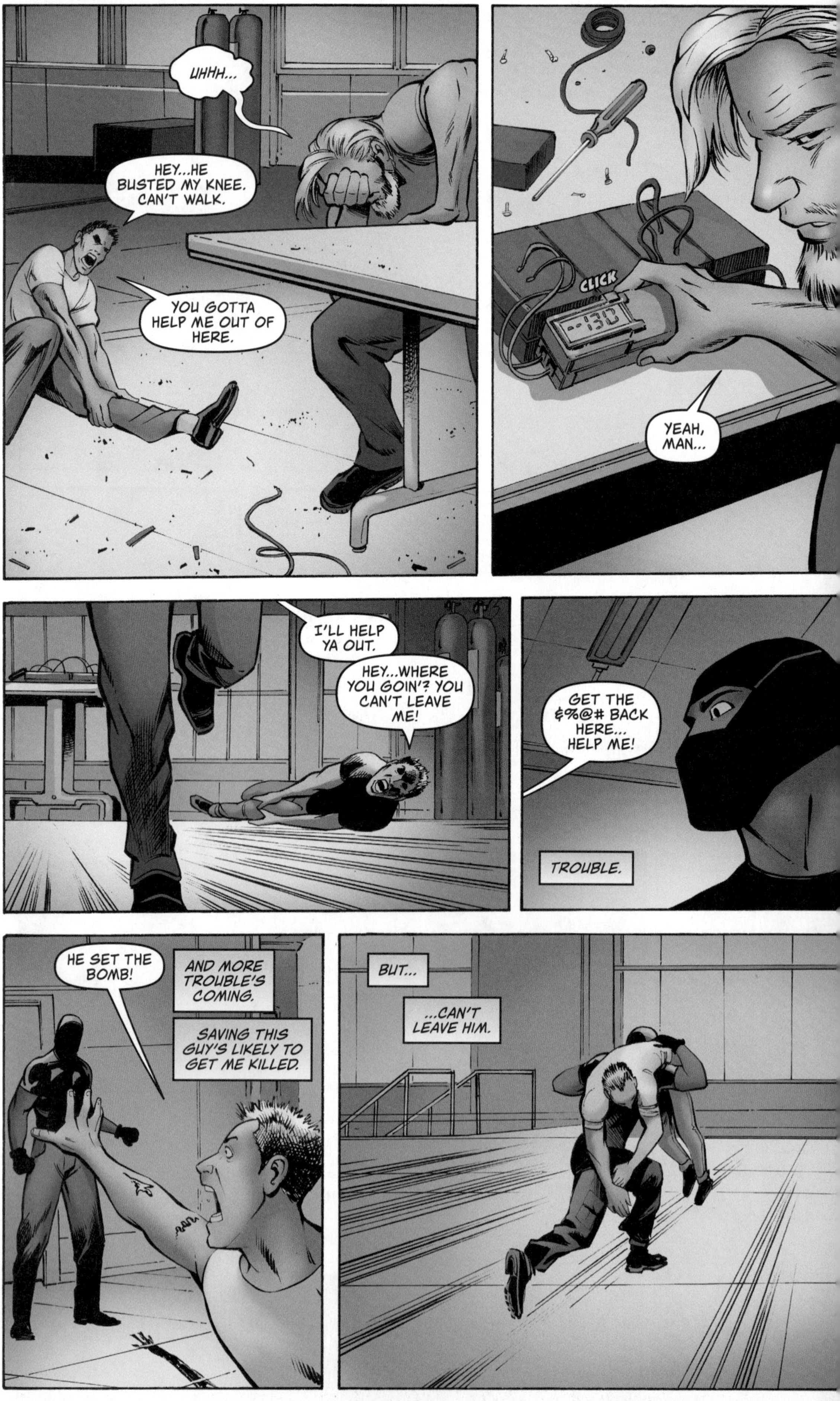
UHHH...
HEY...HE BUSTED MY KNEE. CAN'T WALK.
YOU GOTTA HELP ME OUT OF HERE.
CLICK
YEAH, MAN...
I'LL HELP YA OUT.
HEY...WHERE YOU GOIN'? YOU CAN'T LEAVE ME!
GET THE $%@# BACK HERE... HELP ME!
TROUBLE.
HE SET THE BOMB!
AND MORE TROUBLE'S COMING.
SAVING THIS GUY'S LIKELY TO GET ME KILLED.
BUT...
...CAN'T LEAVE HIM.

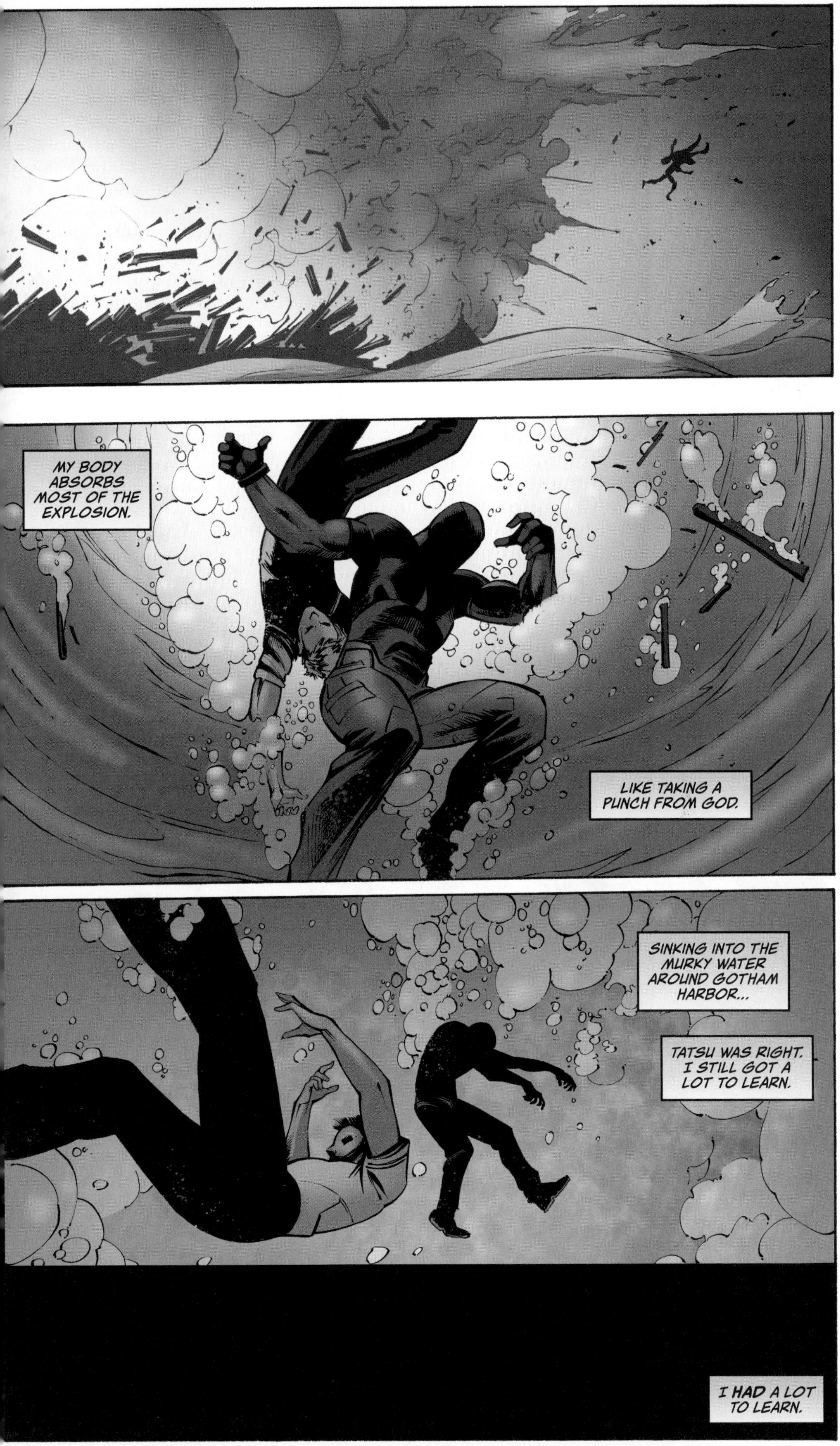
MY BODY ABSORBS MOST OF THE EXPLOSION.
LIKE TAKING A PUNCH FROM GOD.
SINKING INTO THE MURKY WATER AROUND GOTHAM HARBOR...
TATSU WAS RIGHT. I STILL GOT A LOT TO LEARN.
I HAD A LOT TO LEARN.

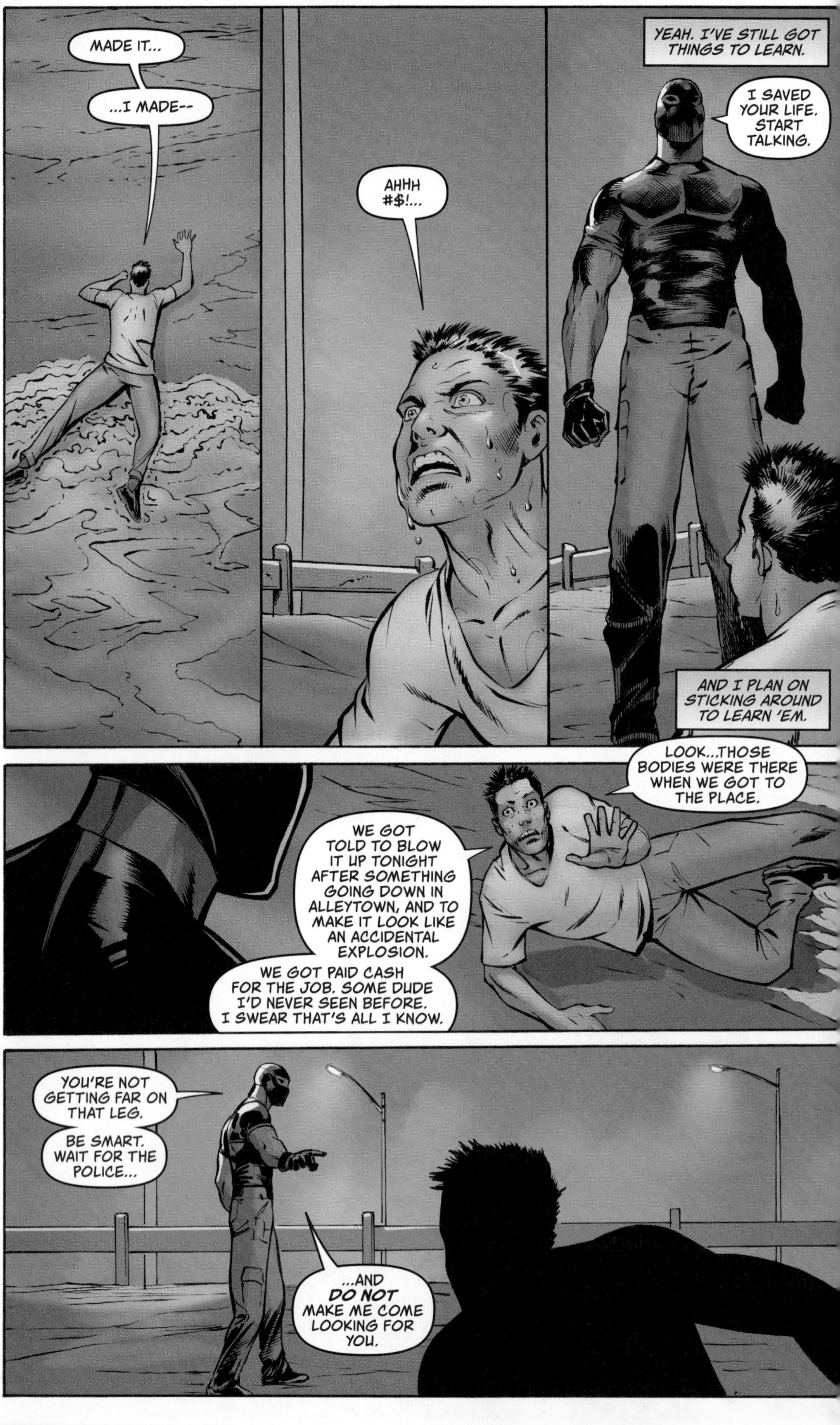

MADE IT...
...I MADE--
AHHH #$!...
YEAH. I'VE STILL GOT THINGS TO LEARN.
I SAVED YOUR LIFE. START TALKING.
AND I PLAN ON STICKING AROUND TO LEARN 'EM.
LOOK...THOSE BODIES WERE THERE WHEN WE GOT TO THE PLACE.
WE GOT TOLD TO BLOW IT UP TONIGHT AFTER SOMETHING GOING DOWN IN ALLEYTOWN, AND TO MAKE IT LOOK LIKE AN ACCIDENTAL EXPLOSION.
WE GOT PAID CASH FOR THE JOB. SOME DUDE I'D NEVER SEEN BEFORE. I SWEAR THAT'S ALL I KNOW.
YOU'RE NOT GETTING FAR ON THAT LEG.
BE SMART. WAIT FOR THE POLICE...
...AND DO NOT MAKE ME COME LOOKING FOR YOU.

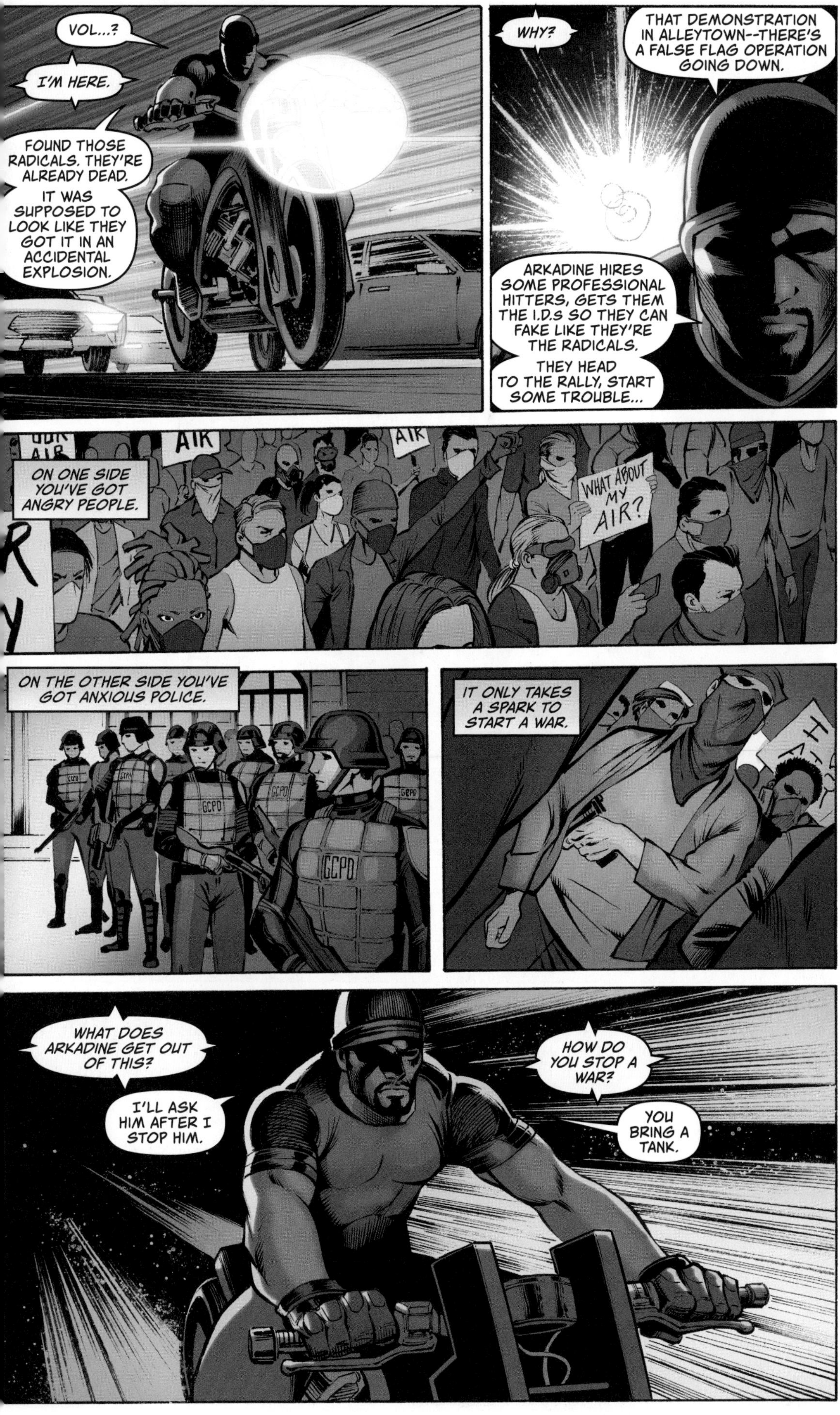
VOL...?
I'M HERE.
FOUND THOSE RADICALS. THEY'RE ALREADY DEAD.
IT WAS SUPPOSED TO LOOK LIKE THEY GOT IT IN AN ACCIDENTAL EXPLOSION.
WHY?
THAT DEMONSTRATION IN ALLEYTOWN--THERE'S A FALSE FLAG OPERATION GOING DOWN.
ARKADINE HIRES SOME PROFESSIONAL HITTERS, GETS THEM THE I.D.S SO THEY CAN FAKE LIKE THEY'RE THE RADICALS.
THEY HEAD TO THE RALLY, START SOME TROUBLE...
ON ONE SIDE YOU'VE GOT ANGRY PEOPLE.
AIR
AIR
WHAT ABOUT MY AIR?
ON THE OTHER SIDE YOU'VE GOT ANXIOUS POLICE.
GCPD
IT ONLY TAKES A SPARK TO START A WAR.
WHAT DOES ARKADINE GET OUT OF THIS?
I'LL ASK HIM AFTER I STOP HIM.
HOW DO YOU STOP A WAR?
YOU BRING A TANK.

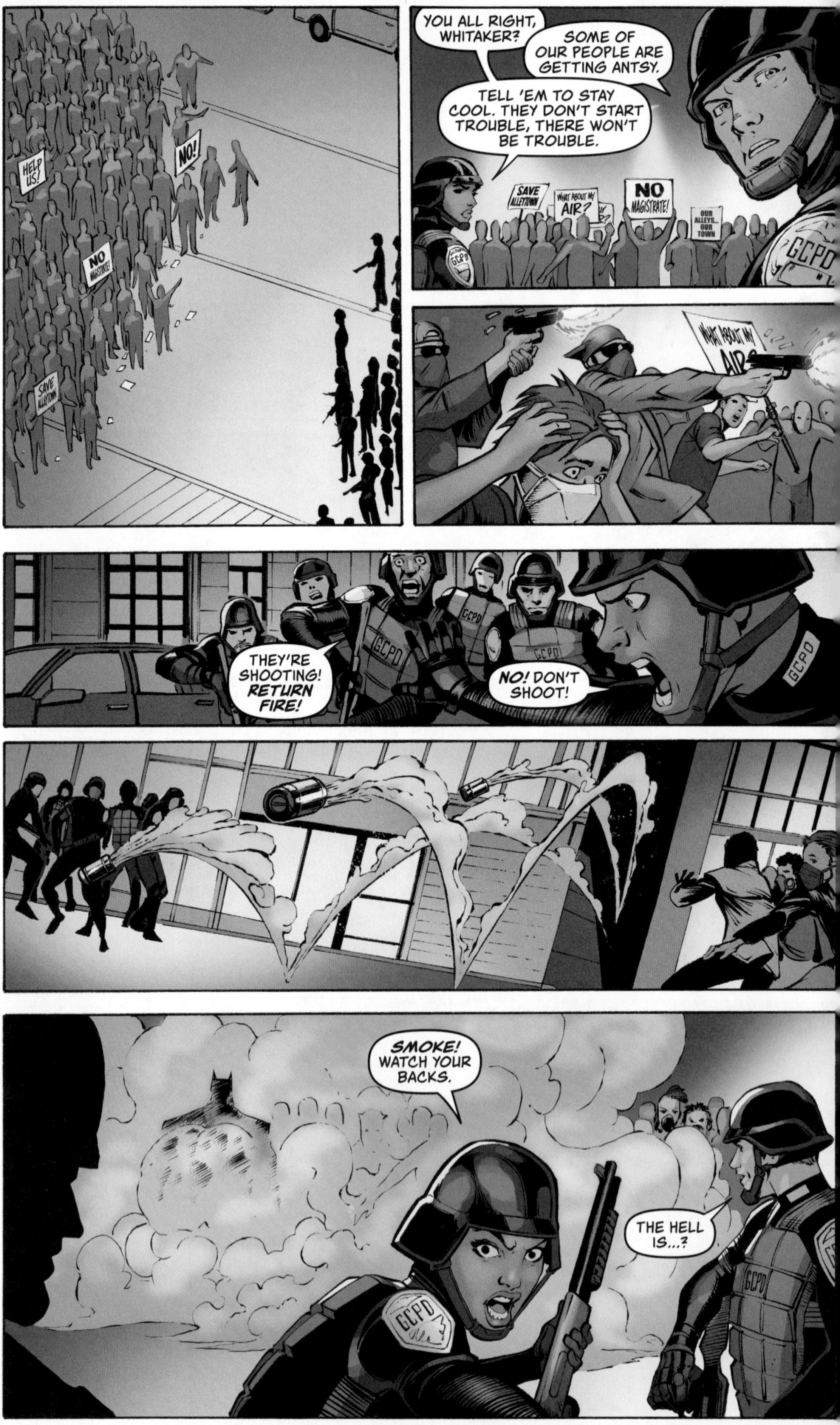
HELP US!
NO!
NO MAGISTRATE!
SAVE ALLEYTOWN
YOU ALL RIGHT, WHITAKER?
SOME OF OUR PEOPLE ARE GETTING ANTSY.
TELL 'EM TO STAY COOL. THEY DON'T START TROUBLE, THERE WON'T BE TROUBLE.
SAVE ALLEYTOWN
WHAT ABOUT MY AIR?
NO MAGISTRATE!
OUR ALLEYS... OUR TOWN
GCPD
THEY'RE SHOOTING! RETURN FIRE!
NO! DON'T SHOOT!
GCPD
SMOKE! WATCH YOUR BACKS.
THE HELL IS...?
GCPD

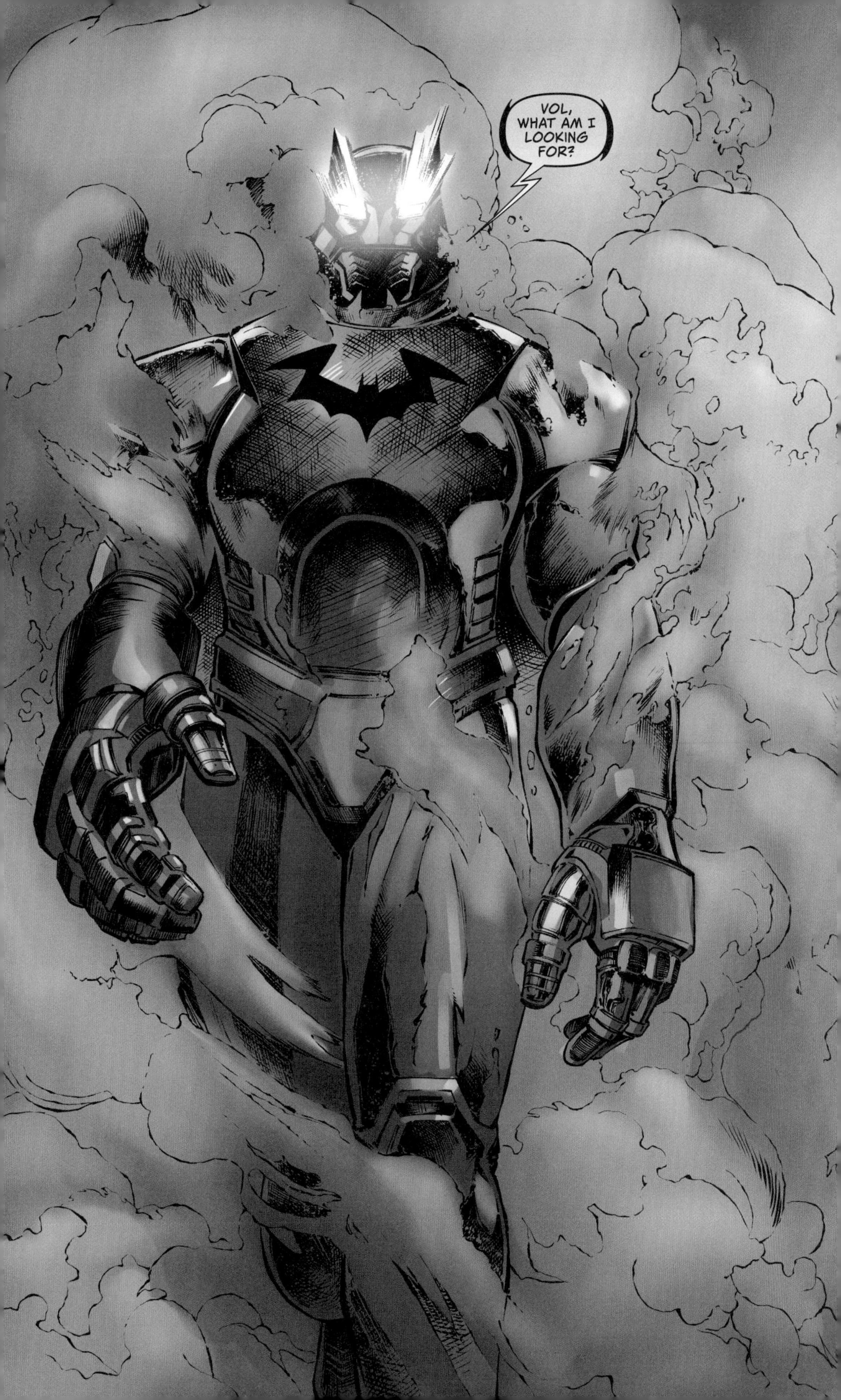
VOL, WHAT AM I LOOKING FOR?

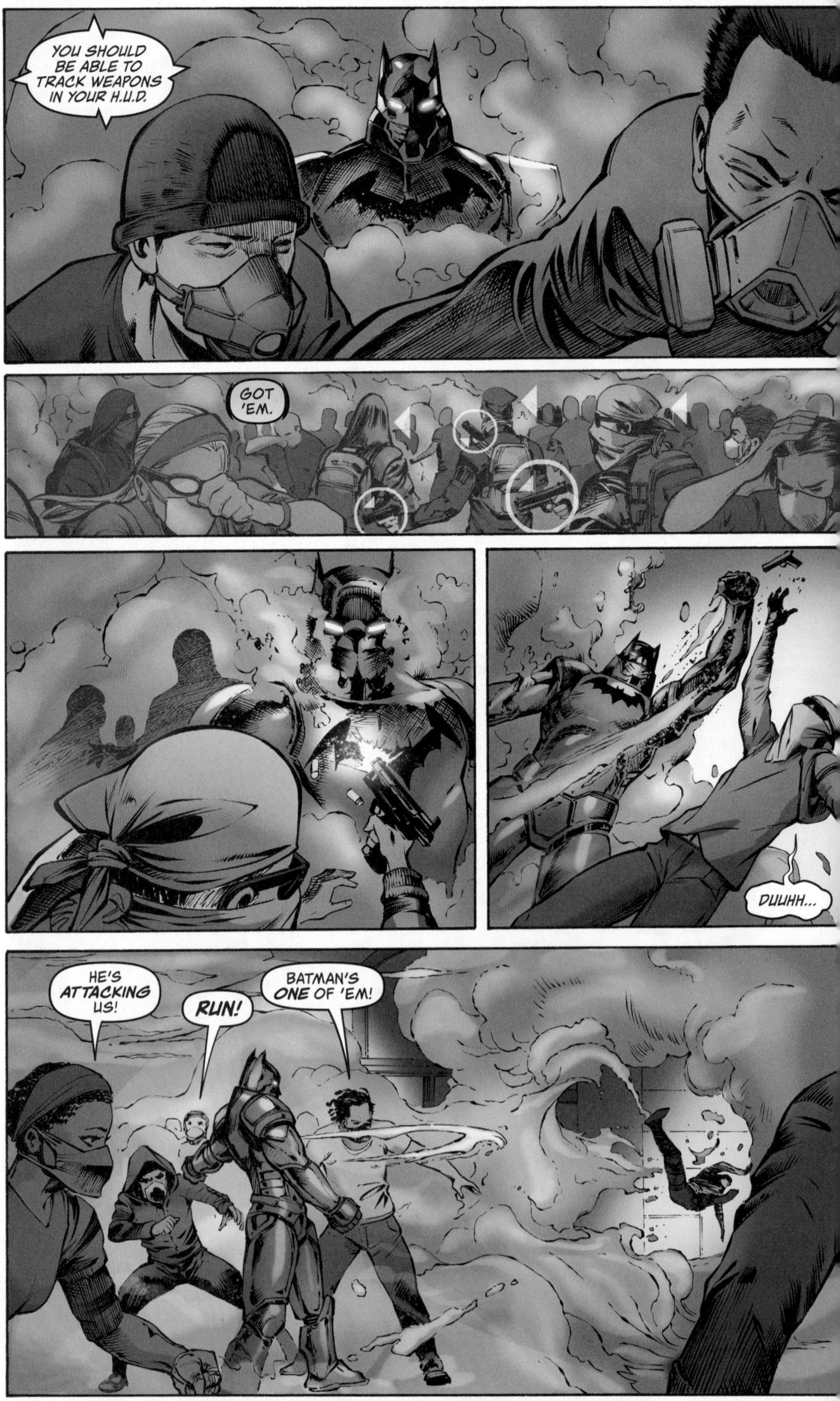
YOU SHOULD BE ABLE TO TRACK WEAPONS IN YOUR H.U.D.
GOT 'EM.
DUUHH...
HE'S ATTACKING US!
RUN!
BATMAN'S ONE OF 'EM!

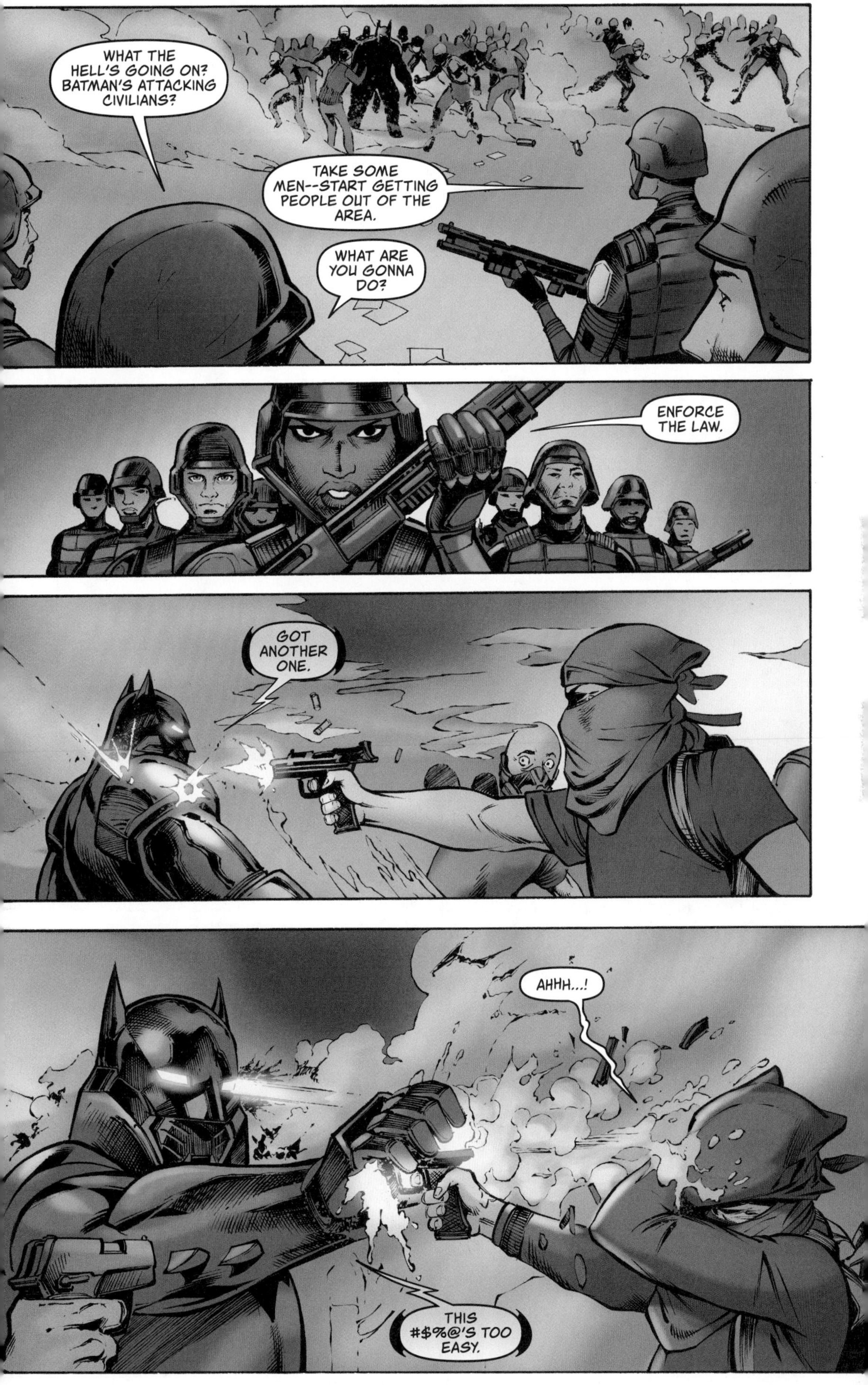
WHAT THE HELL'S GOING ON? BATMAN'S ATTACKING CIVILIANS?
TAKE SOME MEN--START GETTING PEOPLE OUT OF THE AREA.
WHAT ARE YOU GONNA DO?
ENFORCE THE LAW.
GOT ANOTHER ONE.
AHHH...!
THIS #$%@'S TOO EASY.

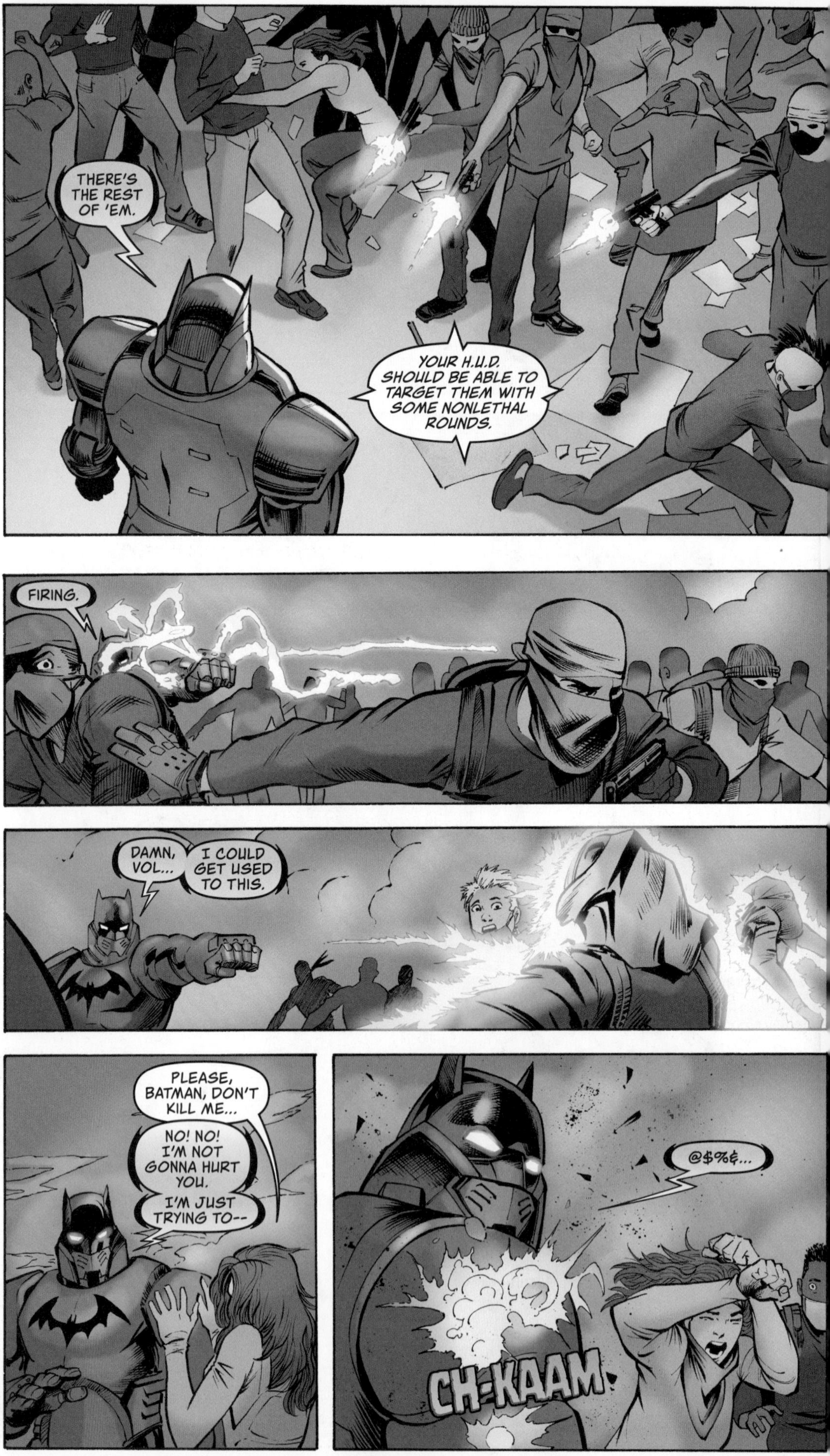
THERE'S THE REST OF 'EM.
YOUR H.U.D. SHOULD BE ABLE TO TARGET THEM WITH SOME NONLETHAL ROUNDS.
FIRING.
DAMN, VOL...
I COULD GET USED TO THIS.
PLEASE, BATMAN, DON'T KILL ME...
NO! NO! I'M NOT GONNA HURT YOU.
I'M JUST TRYING TO--
@$%&...
CH-KAAM

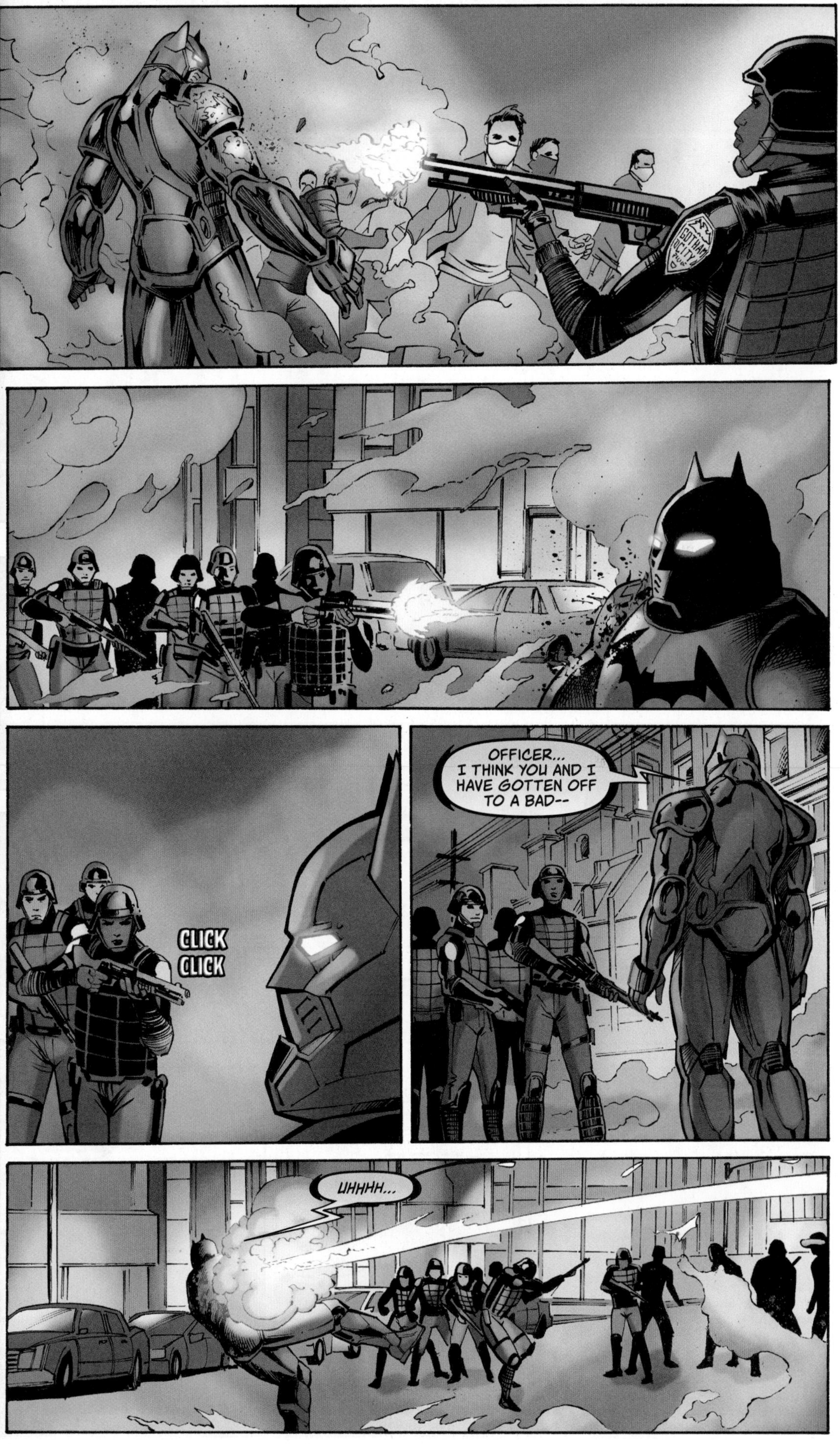
CLICK
CLICK
OFFICER... I THINK YOU AND I HAVE GOTTEN OFF TO A BAD--
UHHHH...

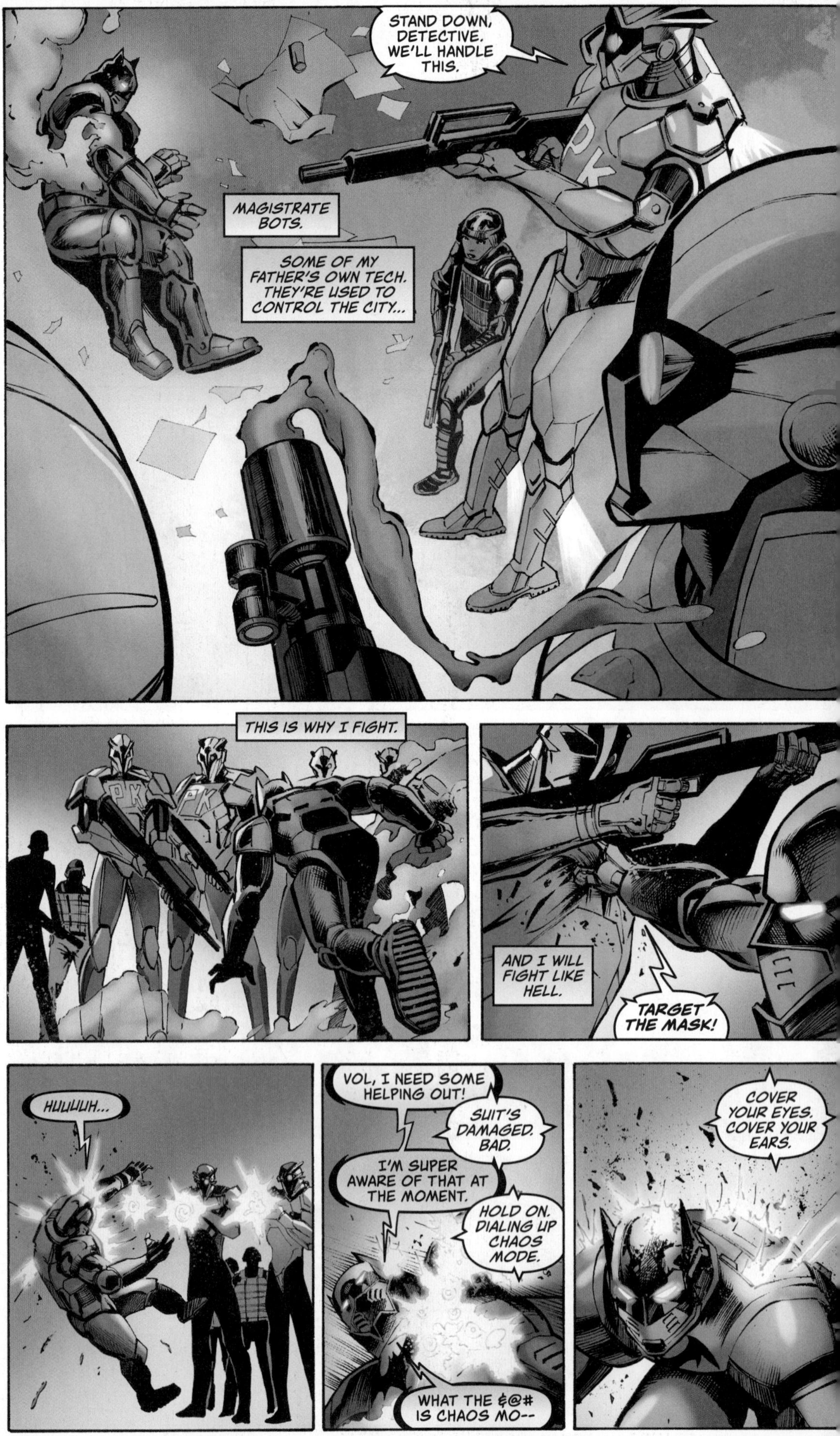
STAND DOWN, DETECTIVE. WE'LL HANDLE THIS.
MAGISTRATE BOTS.
SOME OF MY FATHER'S OWN TECH. THEY'RE USED TO CONTROL THE CITY...
THIS IS WHY I FIGHT.
AND I WILL FIGHT LIKE HELL.
TARGET THE MASK!
HUUUUH...
VOL, I NEED SOME HELPING OUT!
SUIT'S DAMAGED. BAD.
I'M SUPER AWARE OF THAT AT THE MOMENT.
HOLD ON. DIALING UP CHAOS MODE.
WHAT THE &@# IS CHAOS MO--
COVER YOUR EYES. COVER YOUR EARS.

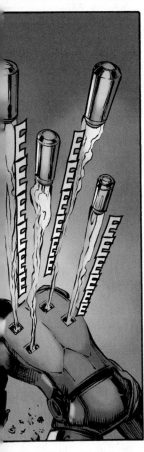

AHHH...

SHOOT IT!

EEEEEE EEEEEE EEEEEE

HOLD YOUR FIRE.

IT'S EMPTY.

GET SOME REINFORCEMENTS DOWN HERE. FIND WHOEVER WAS IN THAT THING!

DO ME A FAVOR...

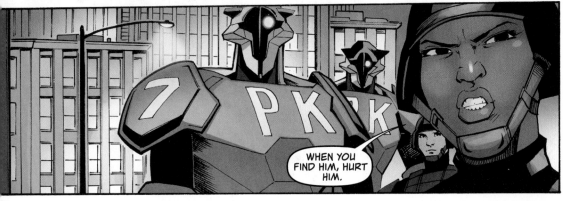

WHEN YOU FIND HIM, HURT HIM.

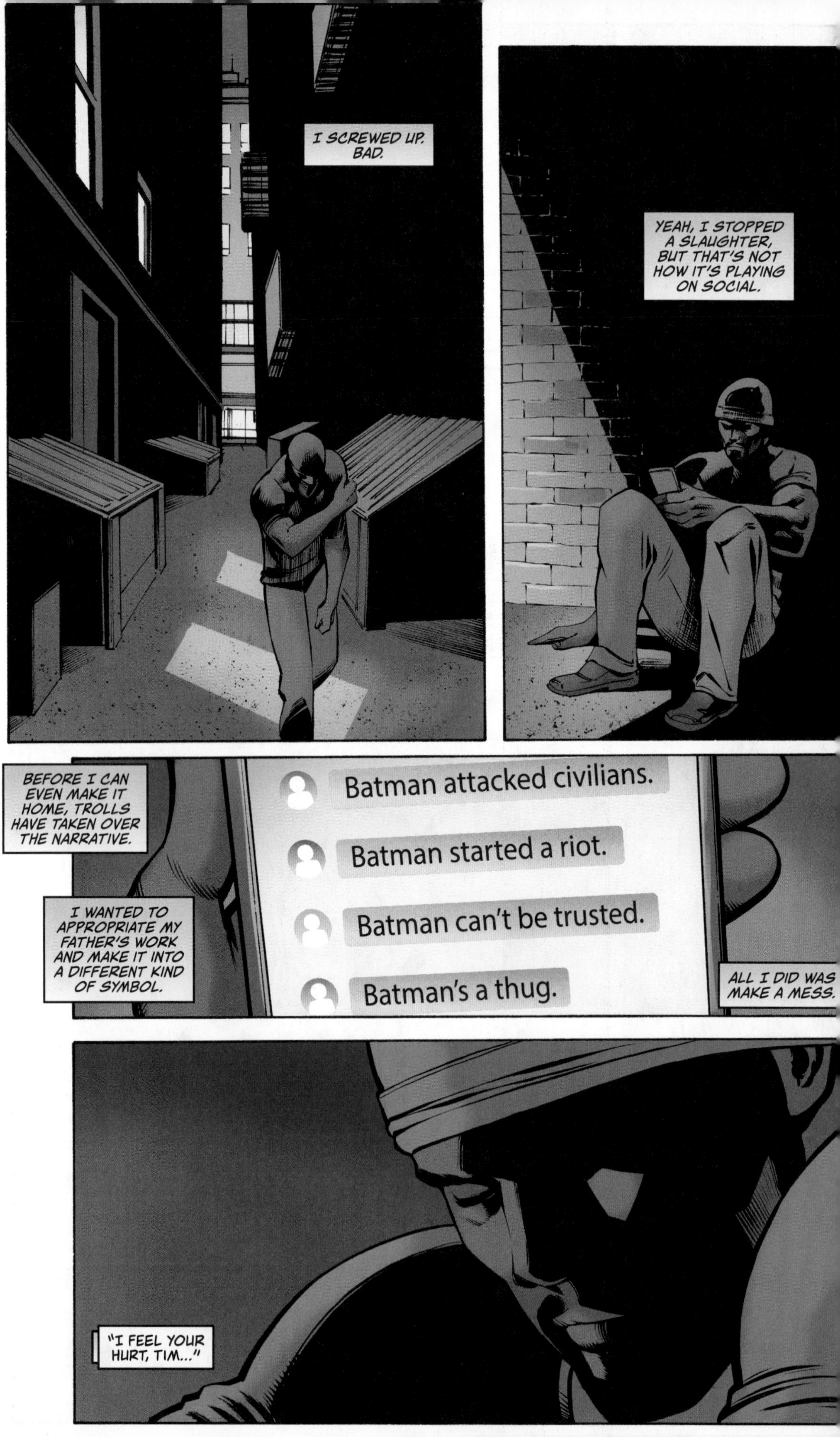
I SCREWED UP. BAD.
YEAH, I STOPPED A SLAUGHTER, BUT THAT'S NOT HOW IT'S PLAYING ON SOCIAL.
BEFORE I CAN EVEN MAKE IT HOME, TROLLS HAVE TAKEN OVER THE NARRATIVE.
Batman attacked civilians.
Batman started a riot.
I WANTED TO APPROPRIATE MY FATHER'S WORK AND MAKE IT INTO A DIFFERENT KIND OF SYMBOL.
Batman can't be trusted.
Batman's a thug.
ALL I DID WAS MAKE A MESS.
"I FEEL YOUR HURT, TIM..."

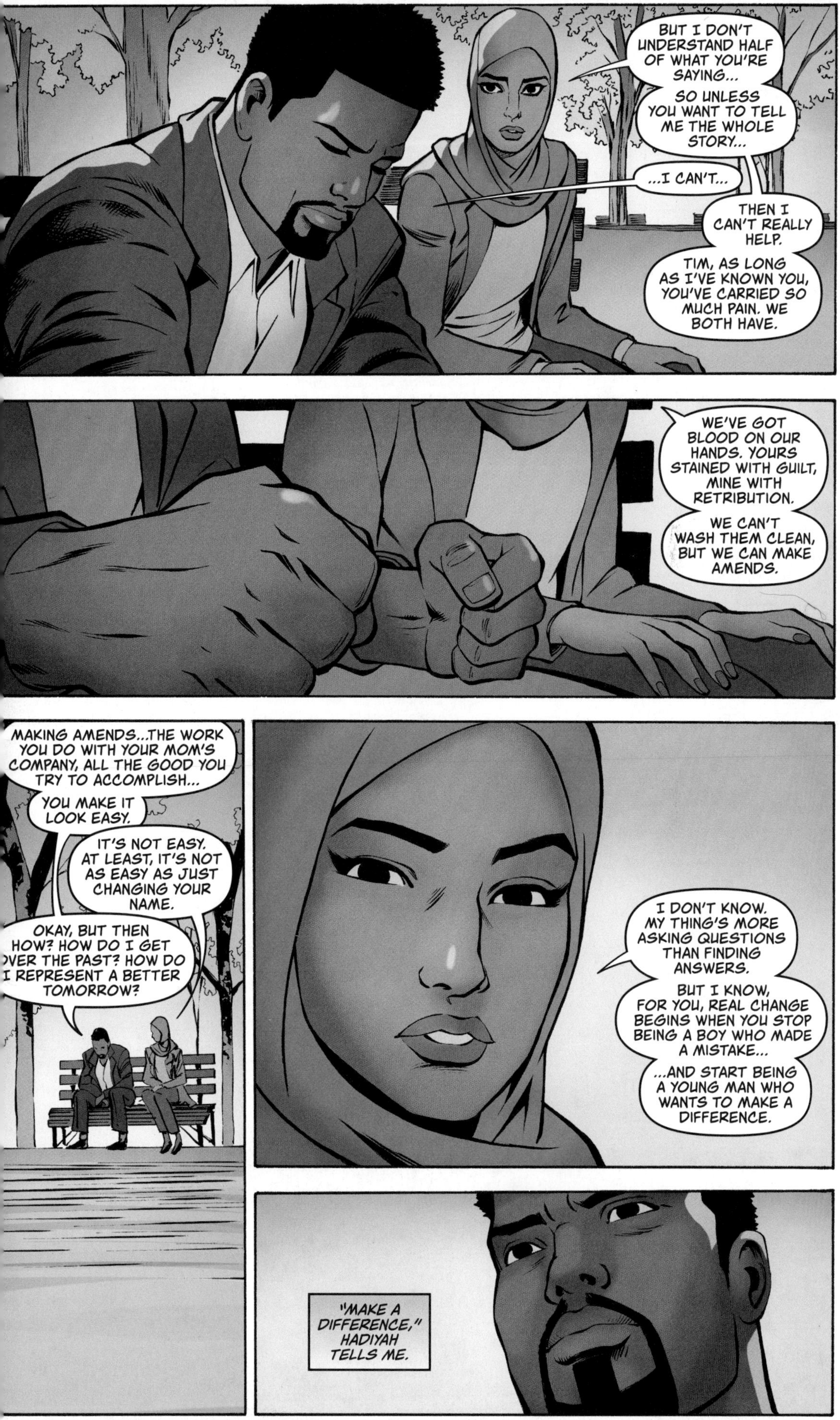

BUT I DON'T UNDERSTAND HALF OF WHAT YOU'RE SAYING...
SO UNLESS YOU WANT TO TELL ME THE WHOLE STORY...
...I CAN'T...
THEN I CAN'T REALLY HELP.
TIM, AS LONG AS I'VE KNOWN YOU, YOU'VE CARRIED SO MUCH PAIN. WE BOTH HAVE.
WE'VE GOT BLOOD ON OUR HANDS. YOURS STAINED WITH GUILT, MINE WITH RETRIBUTION.
WE CAN'T WASH THEM CLEAN, BUT WE CAN MAKE AMENDS.
MAKING AMENDS...THE WORK YOU DO WITH YOUR MOM'S COMPANY, ALL THE GOOD YOU TRY TO ACCOMPLISH...
YOU MAKE IT LOOK EASY.
IT'S NOT EASY. AT LEAST, IT'S NOT AS EASY AS JUST CHANGING YOUR NAME.
OKAY, BUT THEN HOW? HOW DO I GET OVER THE PAST? HOW DO I REPRESENT A BETTER TOMORROW?
I DON'T KNOW. MY THING'S MORE ASKING QUESTIONS THAN FINDING ANSWERS.
BUT I KNOW, FOR YOU, REAL CHANGE BEGINS WHEN YOU STOP BEING A BOY WHO MADE A MISTAKE...
...AND START BEING A YOUNG MAN WHO WANTS TO MAKE A DIFFERENCE.
"MAKE A DIFFERENCE," HADIYAH TELLS ME.

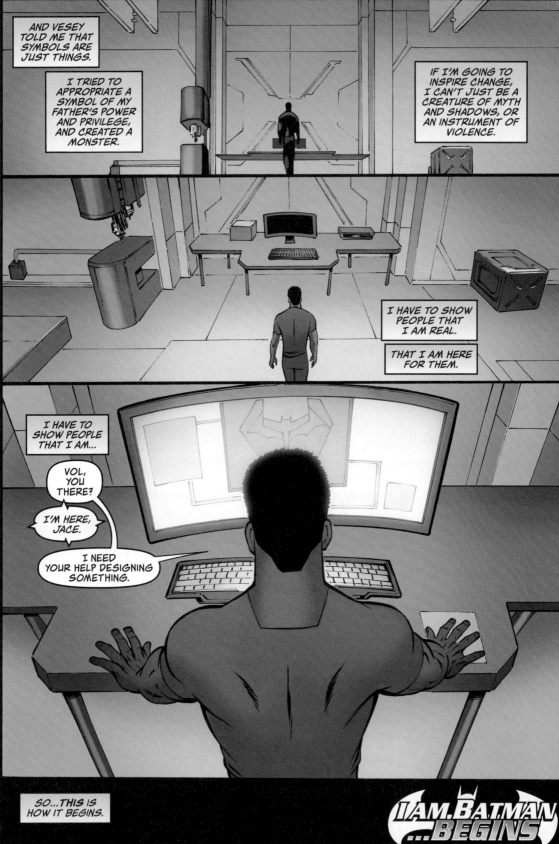

AND VESEY TOLD ME THAT SYMBOLS ARE JUST THINGS.

I TRIED TO APPROPRIATE A SYMBOL OF MY FATHER'S POWER AND PRIVILEGE, AND CREATED A MONSTER.

IF I'M GOING TO INSPIRE CHANGE, I CAN'T JUST BE A CREATURE OF MYTH AND SHADOWS, OR AN INSTRUMENT OF VIOLENCE.

I HAVE TO SHOW PEOPLE THAT I AM REAL.

THAT I AM HERE FOR THEM.

I HAVE TO SHOW PEOPLE THAT I AM...

VOL, YOU THERE?

I'M HERE, JACE.

I NEED YOUR HELP DESIGNING SOMETHING.

SO...THIS IS HOW IT BEGINS.

I AM. BATMAN ...BEGINS

WRITTEN BY
JOHN RIDLEY

PENCILLED BY
TRAVEL FOREMAN

INKED BY
NORM RAPMUND

COLORED BY
REX LOKUS

LETTERED BY ALW'S DAVE LANPHEAR
MAIN COVER BY FOREMAN & LOKUS
VARIANT COVERS BY
DAVE WILKINS, DERRICK CHEW & RICCARDO FEDERICI
EDITED BY BEN ABERNATHY
BATMAN CREATED BY BOB KANE WITH BILL FINGER

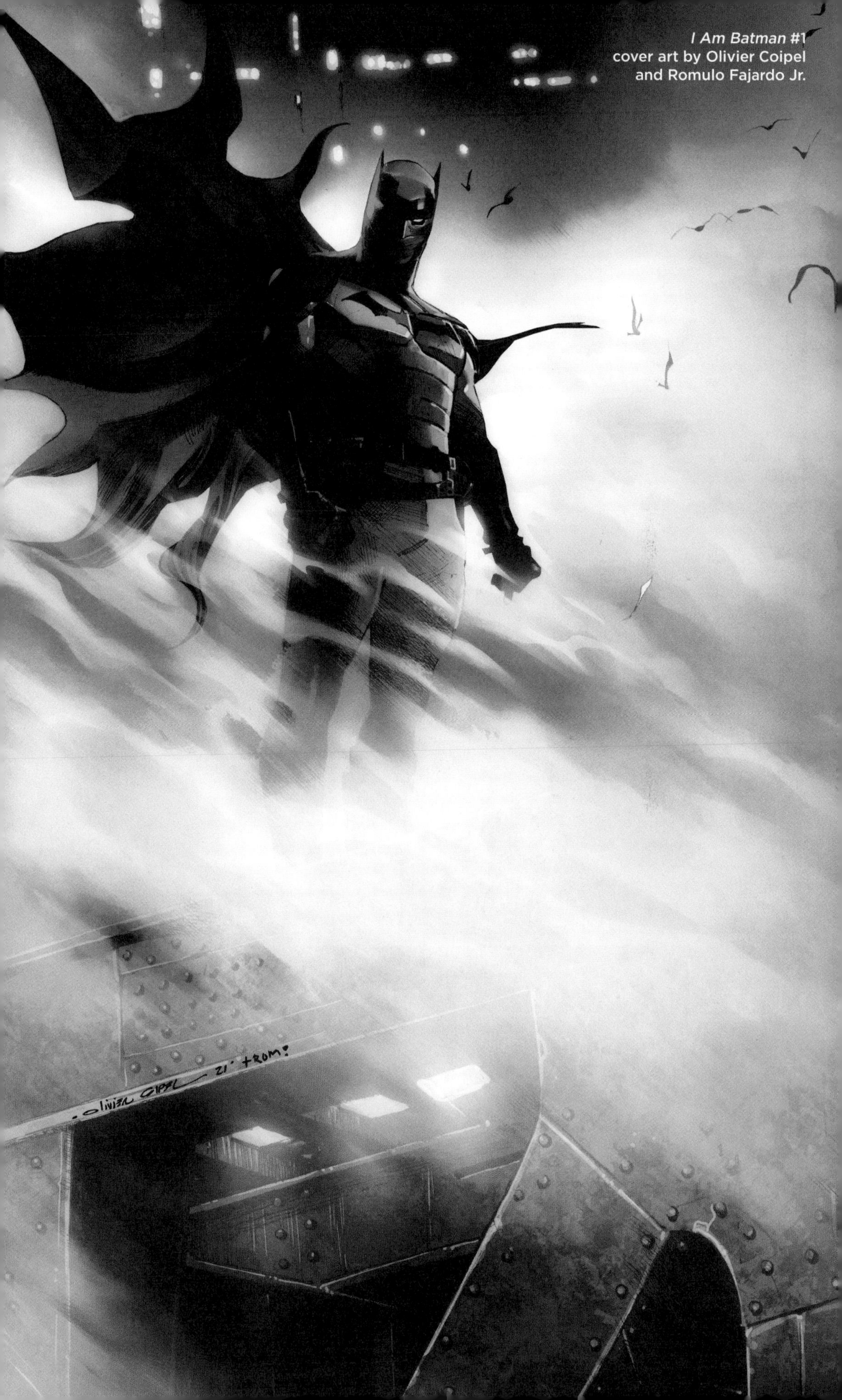

I Am Batman #1
cover art by Olivier Coipel
and Romulo Fajardo Jr.

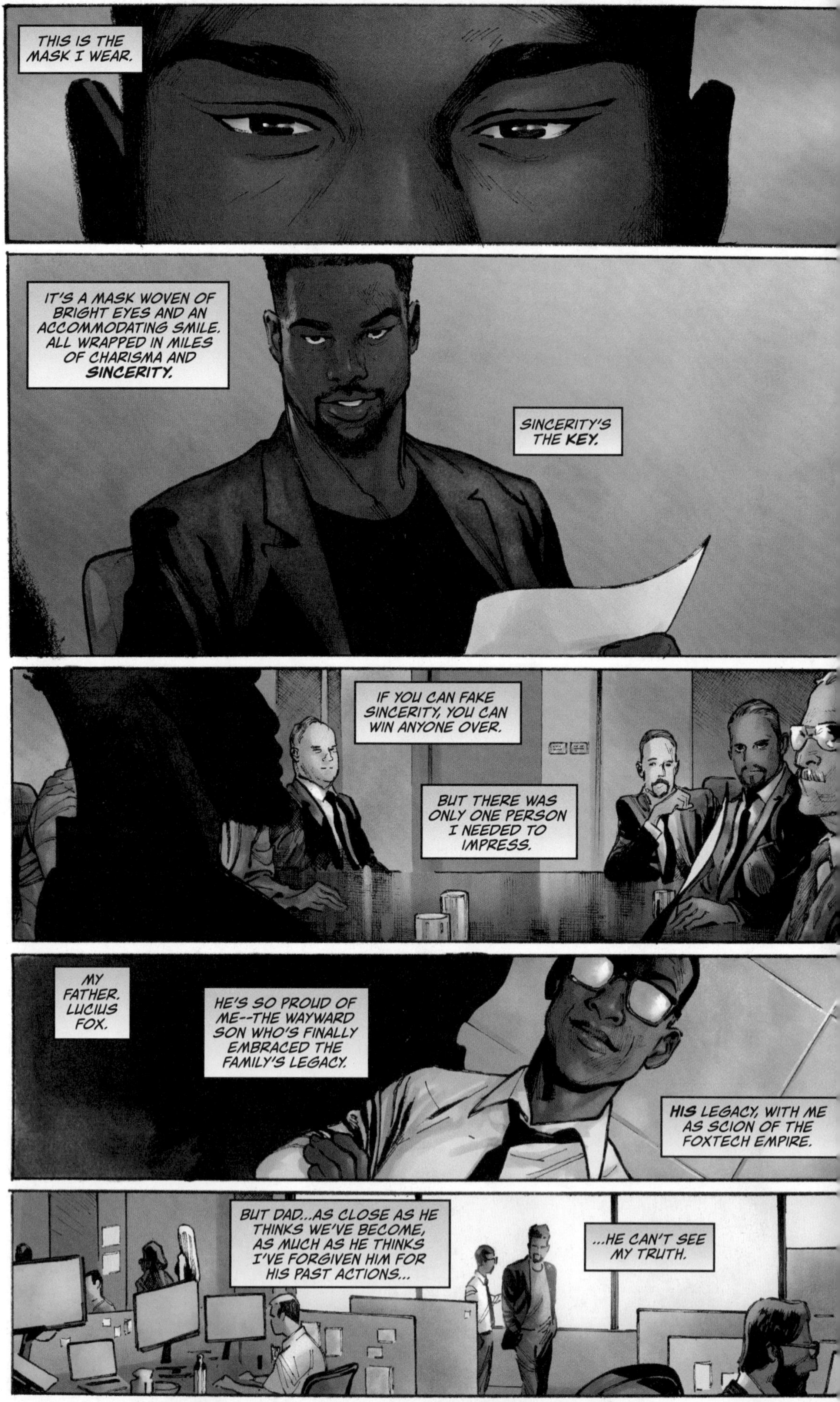

THIS IS THE MASK I WEAR.
IT'S A MASK WOVEN OF BRIGHT EYES AND AN ACCOMMODATING SMILE. ALL WRAPPED IN MILES OF CHARISMA AND SINCERITY.
SINCERITY'S THE KEY.
IF YOU CAN FAKE SINCERITY, YOU CAN WIN ANYONE OVER.
BUT THERE WAS ONLY ONE PERSON I NEEDED TO IMPRESS.
MY FATHER. LUCIUS FOX.
HE'S SO PROUD OF ME--THE WAYWARD SON WHO'S FINALLY EMBRACED THE FAMILY'S LEGACY.
HIS LEGACY, WITH ME AS SCION OF THE FOXTECH EMPIRE.
BUT DAD...AS CLOSE AS HE THINKS WE'VE BECOME, AS MUCH AS HE THINKS I'VE FORGIVEN HIM FOR HIS PAST ACTIONS...
...HE CAN'T SEE MY TRUTH.

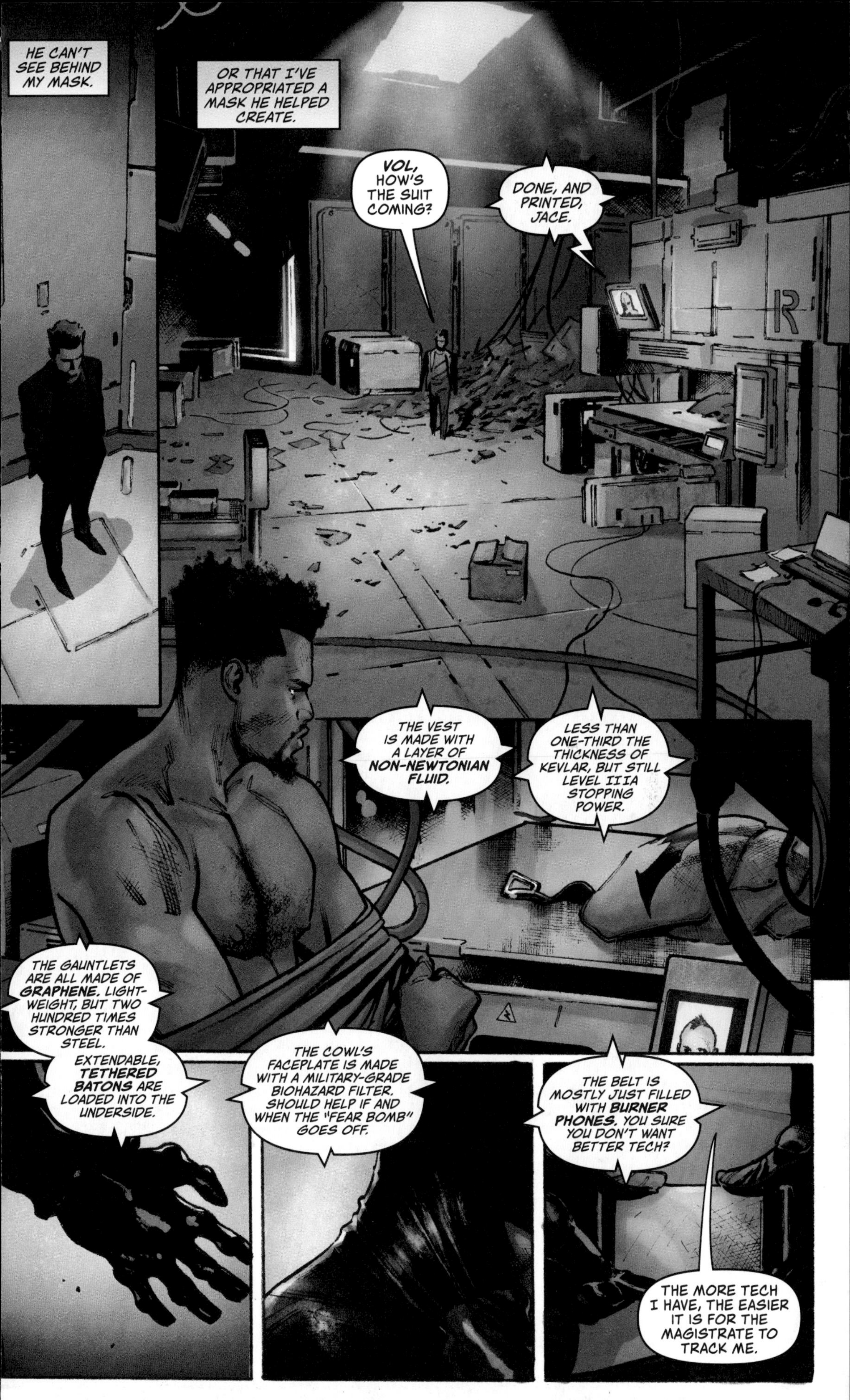
HE CAN'T SEE BEHIND MY MASK.
OR THAT I'VE APPROPRIATED A MASK HE HELPED CREATE.
VOL, HOW'S THE SUIT COMING?
DONE, AND PRINTED, JACE.
THE VEST IS MADE WITH A LAYER OF NON-NEWTONIAN FLUID.
LESS THAN ONE-THIRD THE THICKNESS OF KEVLAR, BUT STILL LEVEL IIIA STOPPING POWER.
THE GAUNTLETS ARE ALL MADE OF GRAPHENE. LIGHT-WEIGHT, BUT TWO HUNDRED TIMES STRONGER THAN STEEL.
EXTENDABLE, TETHERED BATONS ARE LOADED INTO THE UNDERSIDE.
THE COWL'S FACEPLATE IS MADE WITH A MILITARY-GRADE BIOHAZARD FILTER. SHOULD HELP IF AND WHEN THE "FEAR BOMB" GOES OFF.
THE BELT IS MOSTLY JUST FILLED WITH BURNER PHONES. YOU SURE YOU DON'T WANT BETTER TECH?
THE MORE TECH I HAVE, THE EASIER IT IS FOR THE MAGISTRATE TO TRACK ME.

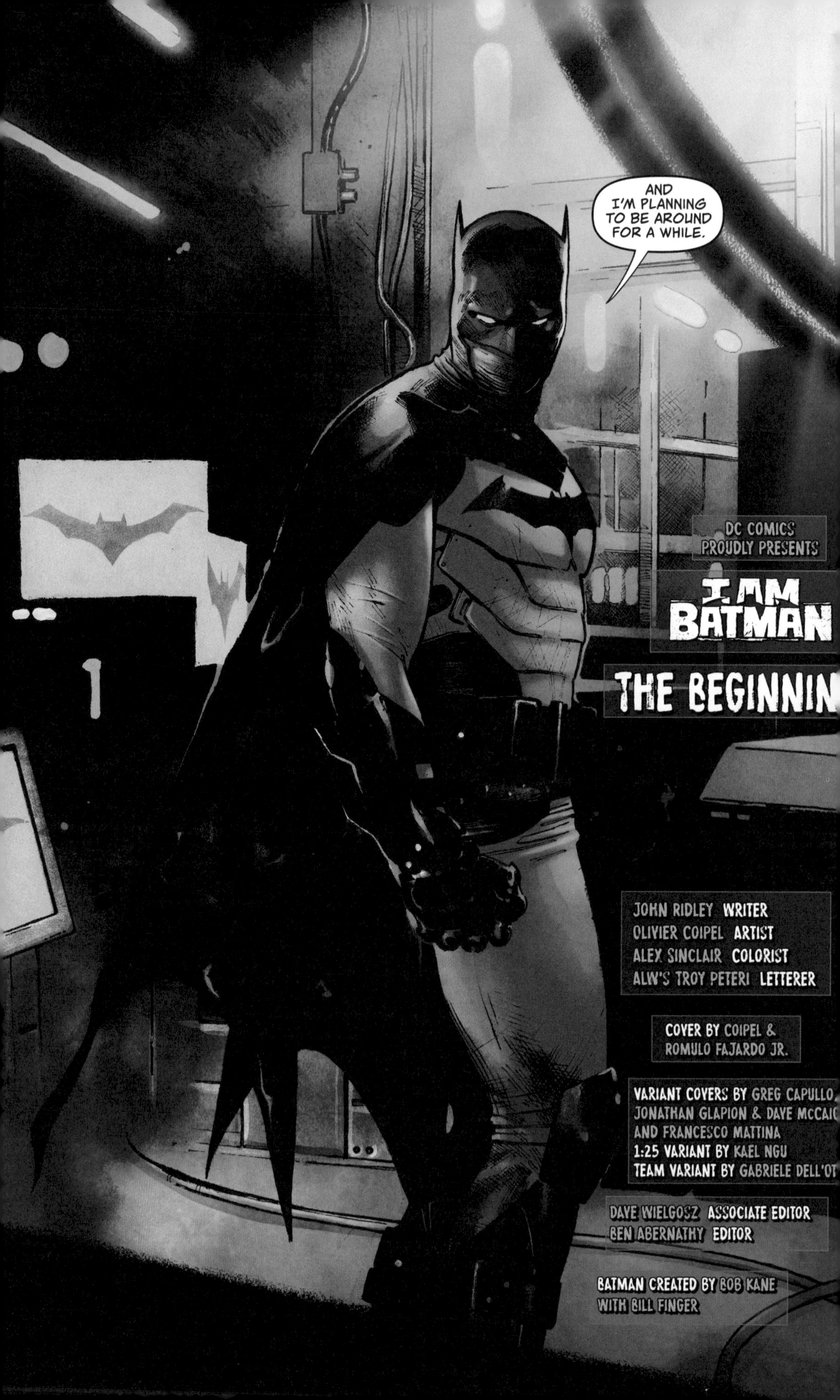

AND I'M PLANNING TO BE AROUND FOR A WHILE.
DC COMICS PROUDLY PRESENTS
I AM BATMAN
THE BEGINNIN
JOHN RIDLEY WRITER
OLIVIER COIPEL ARTIST
ALEX SINCLAIR COLORIST
ALW'S TROY PETERI LETTERER
COVER BY COIPEL & ROMULO FAJARDO JR.
VARIANT COVERS BY GREG CAPULLO,
JONATHAN GLAPION & DAVE MCCAI
AND FRANCESCO MATTINA
1:25 VARIANT BY KAEL NGU
TEAM VARIANT BY GABRIELE DELL'OT
DAVE WIELGOSZ ASSOCIATE EDITOR
BEN ABERNATHY EDITOR
BATMAN CREATED BY BOB KANE WITH BILL FINGER

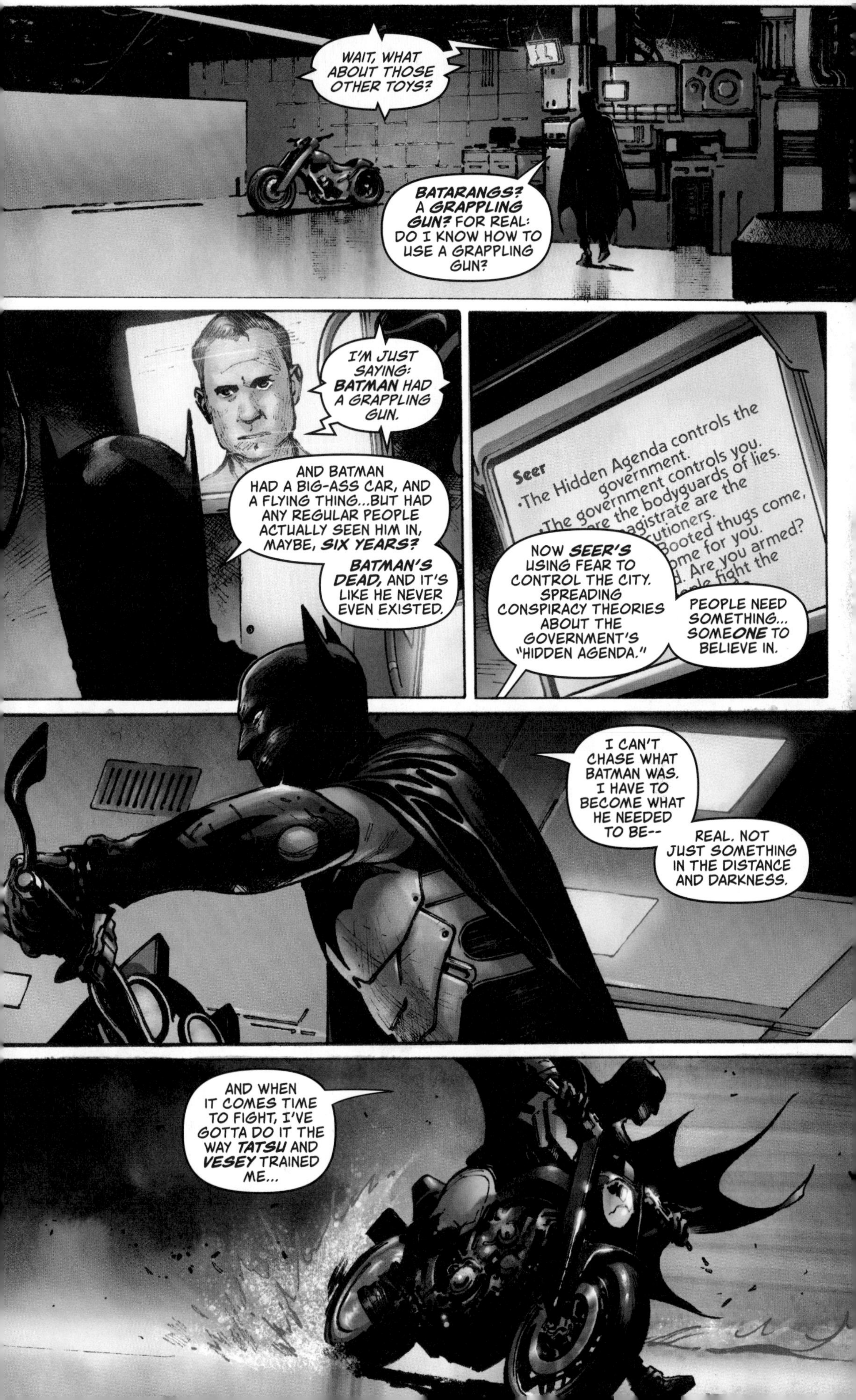
WAIT, WHAT ABOUT THOSE OTHER TOYS?
BATARANGS? A GRAPPLING GUN? FOR REAL: DO I KNOW HOW TO USE A GRAPPLING GUN?
I'M JUST SAYING: BATMAN HAD A GRAPPLING GUN.
AND BATMAN HAD A BIG-ASS CAR, AND A FLYING THING...BUT HAD ANY REGULAR PEOPLE ACTUALLY SEEN HIM IN, MAYBE, SIX YEARS?
BATMAN'S DEAD, AND IT'S LIKE HE NEVER EVEN EXISTED.
Seer
•The Hidden Agenda controls the government.
•The government controls you.
NOW SEER'S USING FEAR TO CONTROL THE CITY. SPREADING CONSPIRACY THEORIES ABOUT THE GOVERNMENT'S "HIDDEN AGENDA."
PEOPLE NEED SOMETHING... SOMEONE TO BELIEVE IN.
I CAN'T CHASE WHAT BATMAN WAS. I HAVE TO BECOME WHAT HE NEEDED TO BE--
REAL. NOT JUST SOMETHING IN THE DISTANCE AND DARKNESS.
AND WHEN IT COMES TIME TO FIGHT, I'VE GOTTA DO IT THE WAY TATSU AND VESEY TRAINED ME...

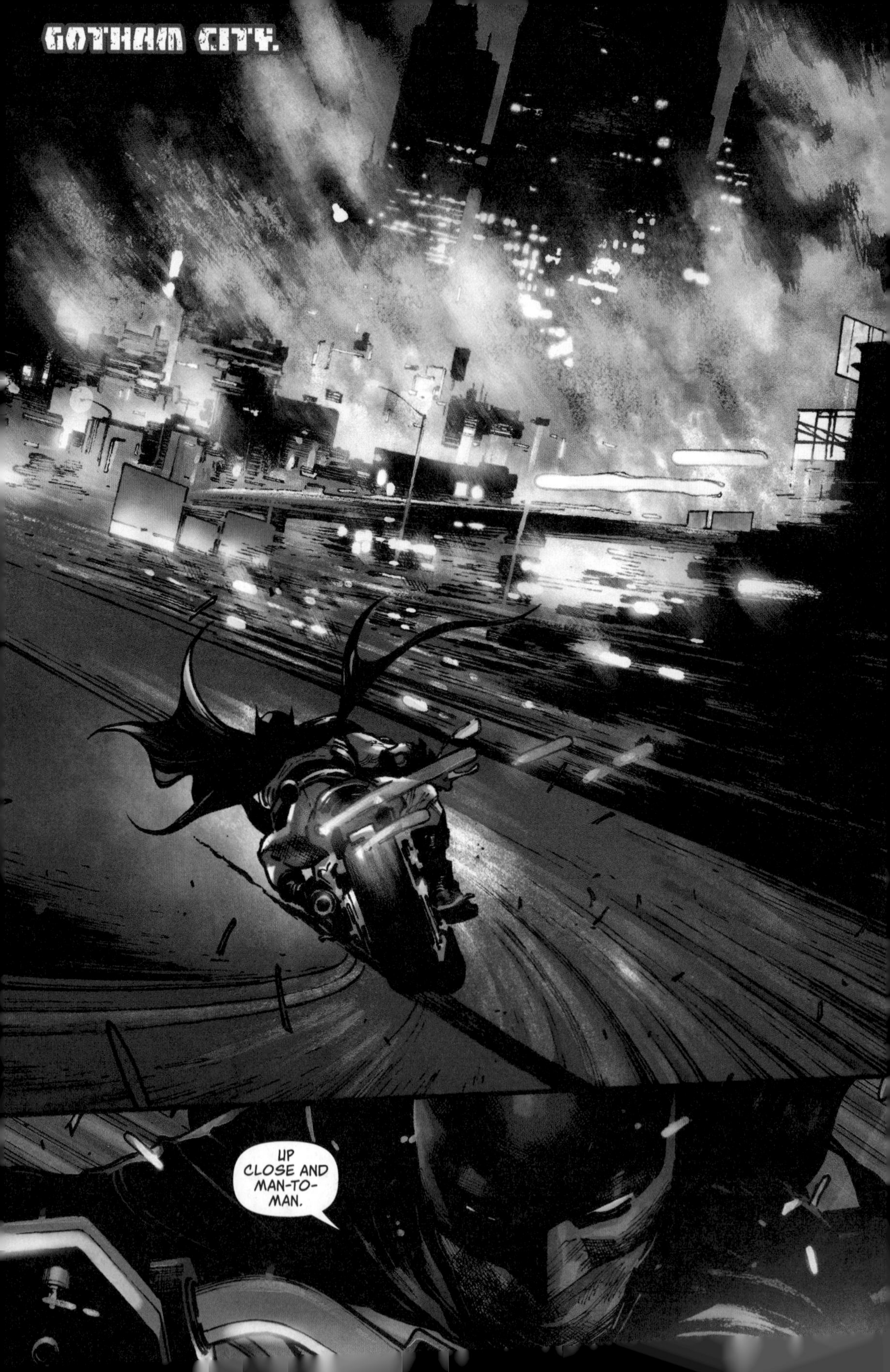
GOTHAM CITY.
UP CLOSE AND MAN-TO-MAN.

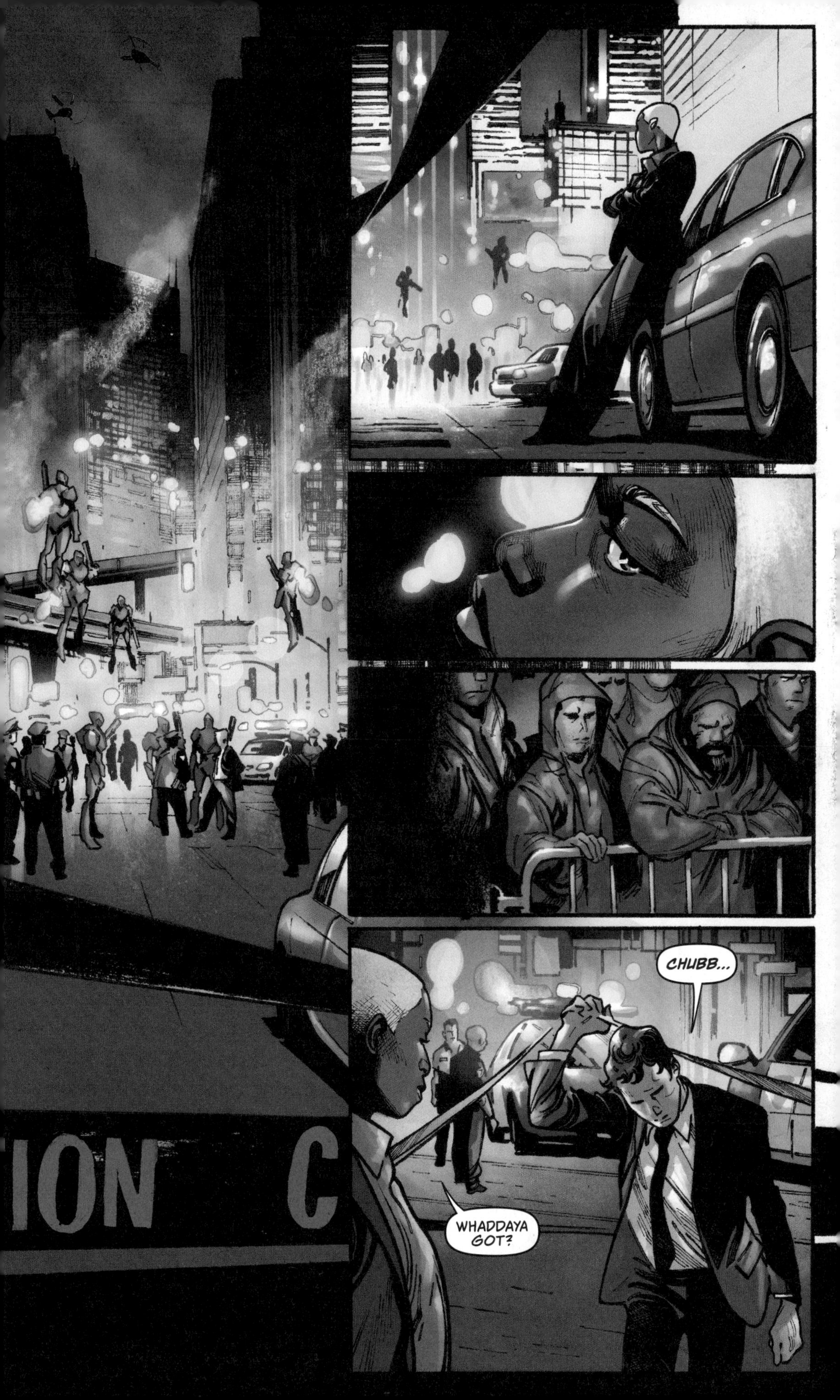

ION C
CHUBB...
WHADDAYA GOT?

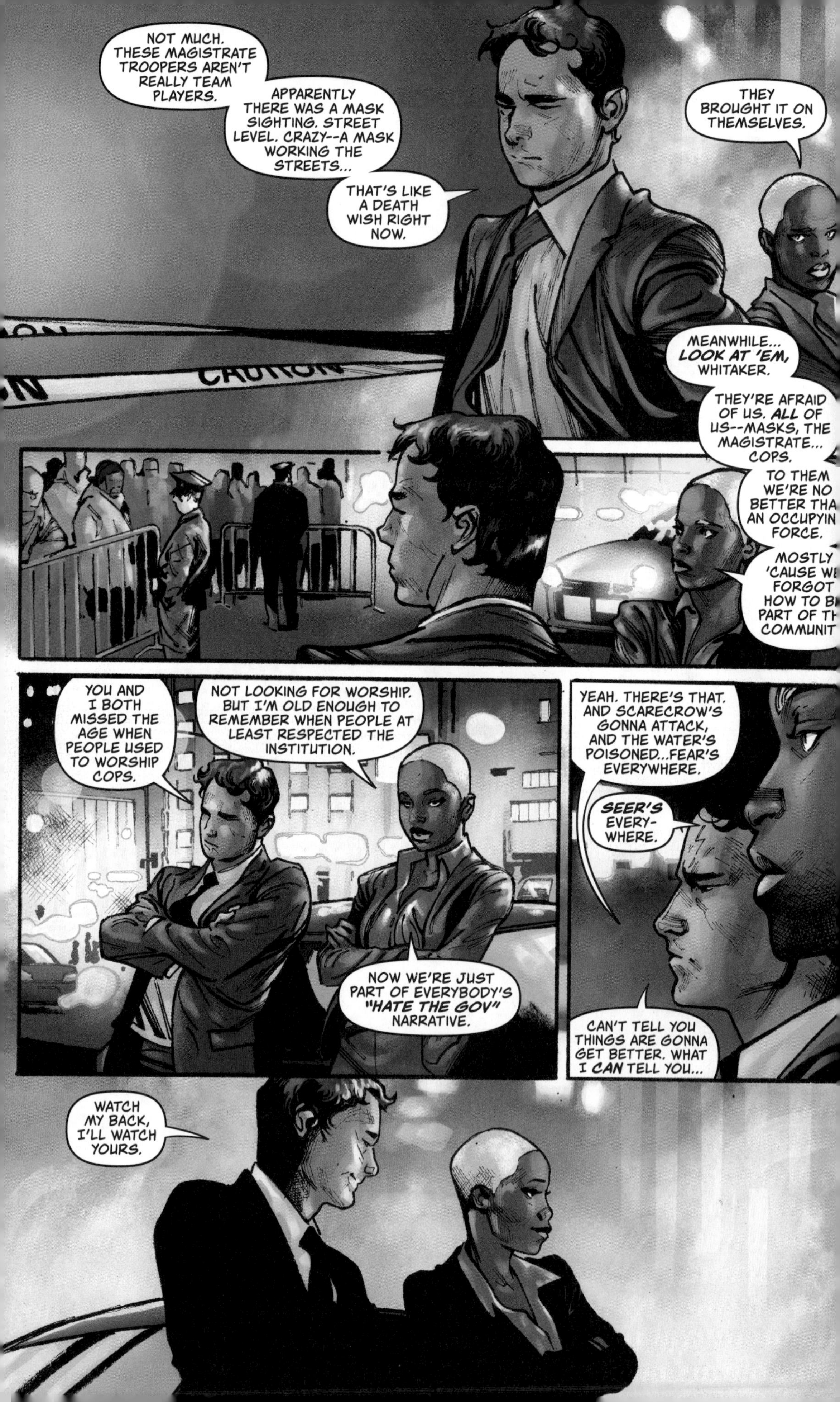

NOT MUCH. THESE MAGISTRATE TROOPERS AREN'T REALLY TEAM PLAYERS.
APPARENTLY THERE WAS A MASK SIGHTING. STREET LEVEL. CRAZY--A MASK WORKING THE STREETS...
THAT'S LIKE A DEATH WISH RIGHT NOW.
THEY BROUGHT IT ON THEMSELVES.
CAUTION
MEANWHILE... LOOK AT 'EM, WHITAKER.
THEY'RE AFRAID OF US. ALL OF US--MASKS, THE MAGISTRATE... COPS.
YOU AND I BOTH MISSED THE AGE WHEN PEOPLE USED TO WORSHIP COPS.
NOT LOOKING FOR WORSHIP. BUT I'M OLD ENOUGH TO REMEMBER WHEN PEOPLE AT LEAST RESPECTED THE INSTITUTION.
NOW WE'RE JUST PART OF EVERYBODY'S "HATE THE GOV" NARRATIVE.
YEAH. THERE'S THAT. AND SCARECROW'S GONNA ATTACK, AND THE WATER'S POISONED...FEAR'S EVERYWHERE.
SEER'S EVERY-WHERE.
CAN'T TELL YOU THINGS ARE GONNA GET BETTER. WHAT I CAN TELL YOU...
WATCH MY BACK, I'LL WATCH YOURS.

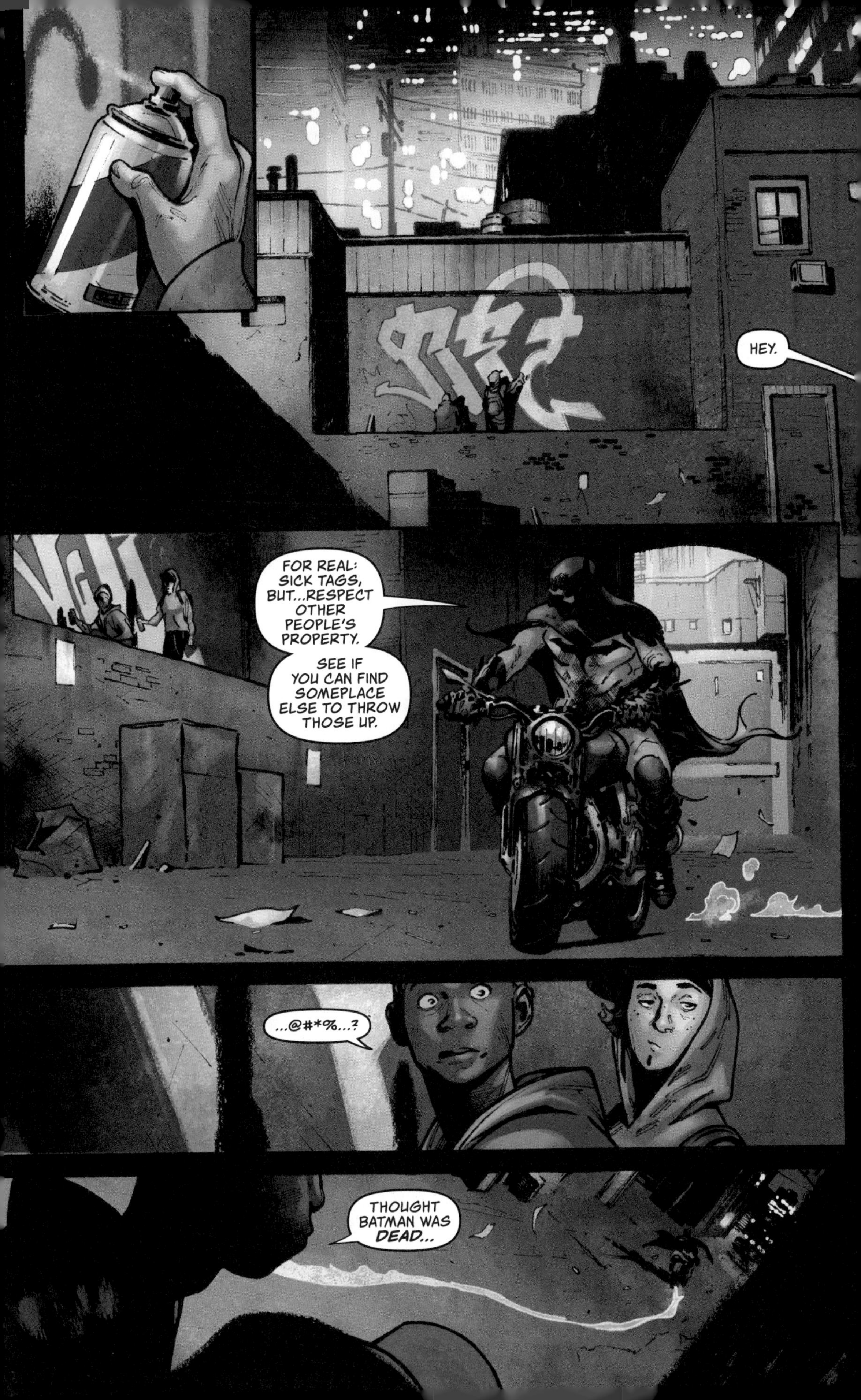
HEY.
FOR REAL: SICK TAGS, BUT...RESPECT OTHER PEOPLE'S PROPERTY.
SEE IF YOU CAN FIND SOMEPLACE ELSE TO THROW THOSE UP.
...@#*%...?
THOUGHT BATMAN WAS *DEAD*...

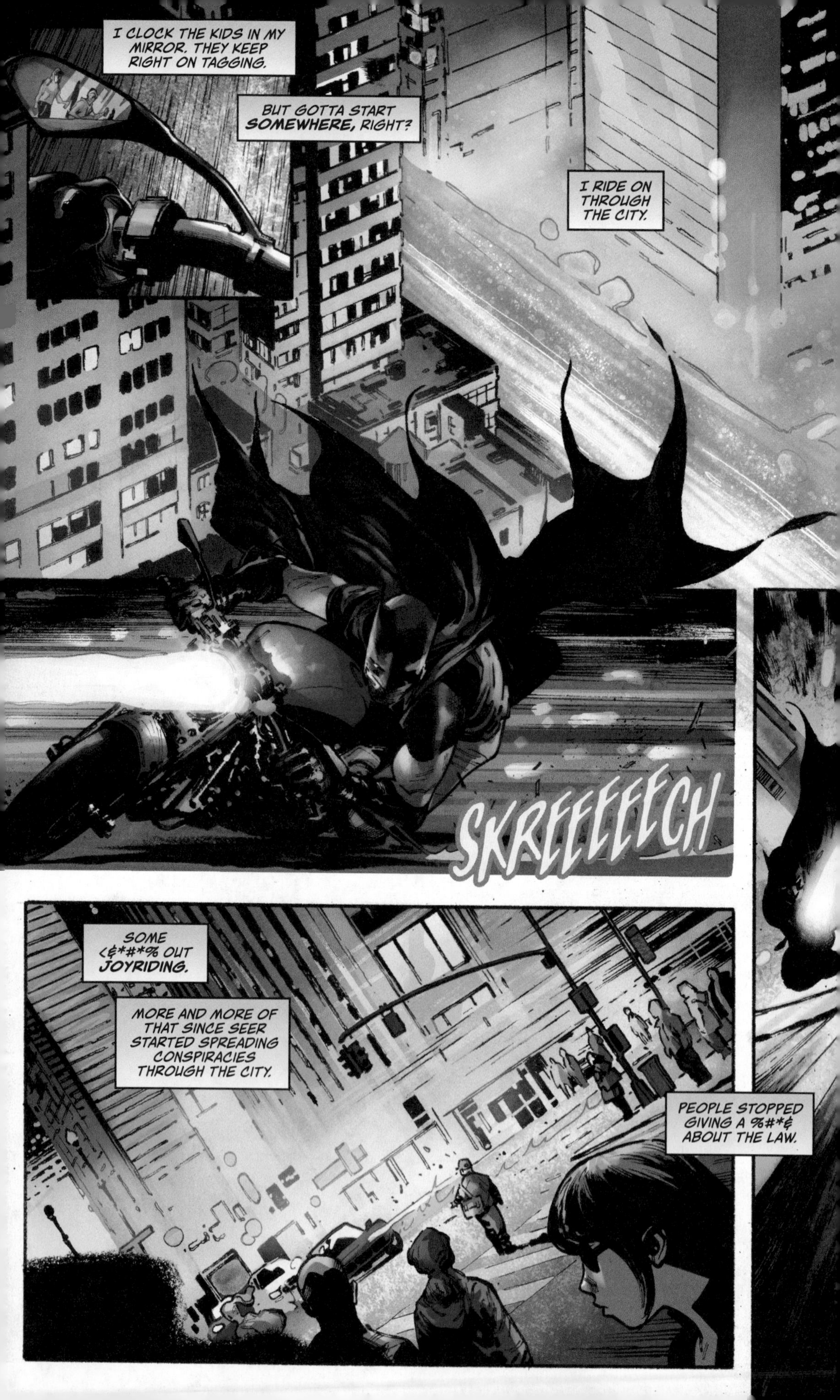
I CLOCK THE KIDS IN MY MIRROR. THEY KEEP RIGHT ON TAGGING.
BUT GOTTA START SOMEWHERE, RIGHT?
I RIDE ON THROUGH THE CITY.
SKREEEEECH
SOME <$*#*% OUT JOYRIDING.
MORE AND MORE OF THAT SINCE SEER STARTED SPREADING CONSPIRACIES THROUGH THE CITY.
PEOPLE STOPPED GIVING A %#*$ ABOUT THE LAW.

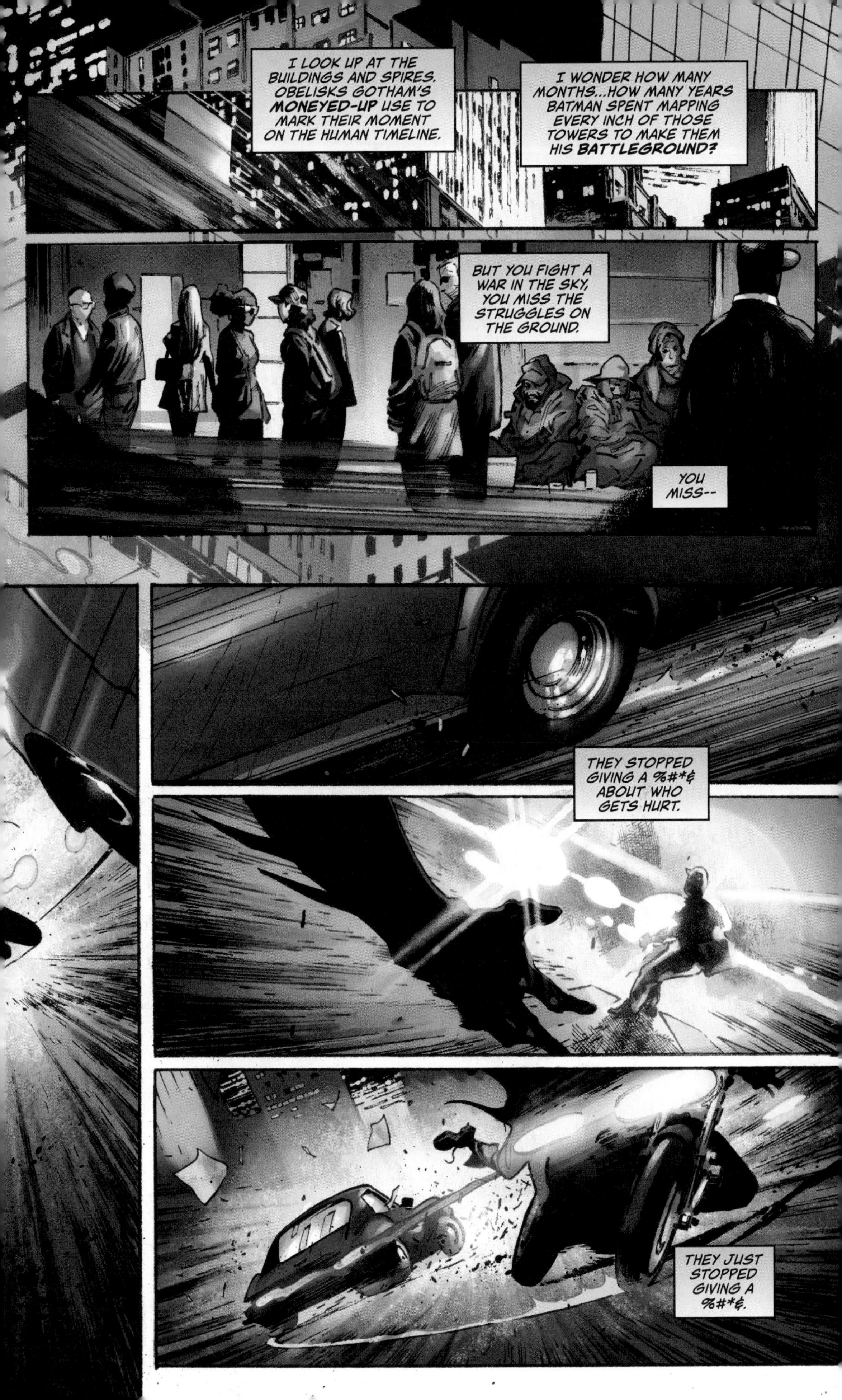
I LOOK UP AT THE BUILDINGS AND SPIRES. OBELISKS GOTHAM'S MONEYED-UP USE TO MARK THEIR MOMENT ON THE HUMAN TIMELINE.
I WONDER HOW MANY MONTHS...HOW MANY YEARS BATMAN SPENT MAPPING EVERY INCH OF THOSE TOWERS TO MAKE THEM HIS BATTLEGROUND?
BUT YOU FIGHT A WAR IN THE SKY, YOU MISS THE STRUGGLES ON THE GROUND.
YOU MISS--
THEY STOPPED GIVING A %#*& ABOUT WHO GETS HURT.
THEY JUST STOPPED GIVING A %#*&.

...THANK YOU...
THE GUY'S OKAY. I'M NOT.
RAGE. BITTERNESS. A DESIRE FOR PUNISHMENT. I FEEL IT FOR THE DRIVER OF THE CAR.
MAYBE.
OR MAYBE I JUST FEEL IT TOWARD MYSELF.
WHO DOES THE DRIVER REMIND ME OF?
CAN'T TELL IF THE GUY IS DRUNK, HIGH, OR JUST AN @&#*#%.

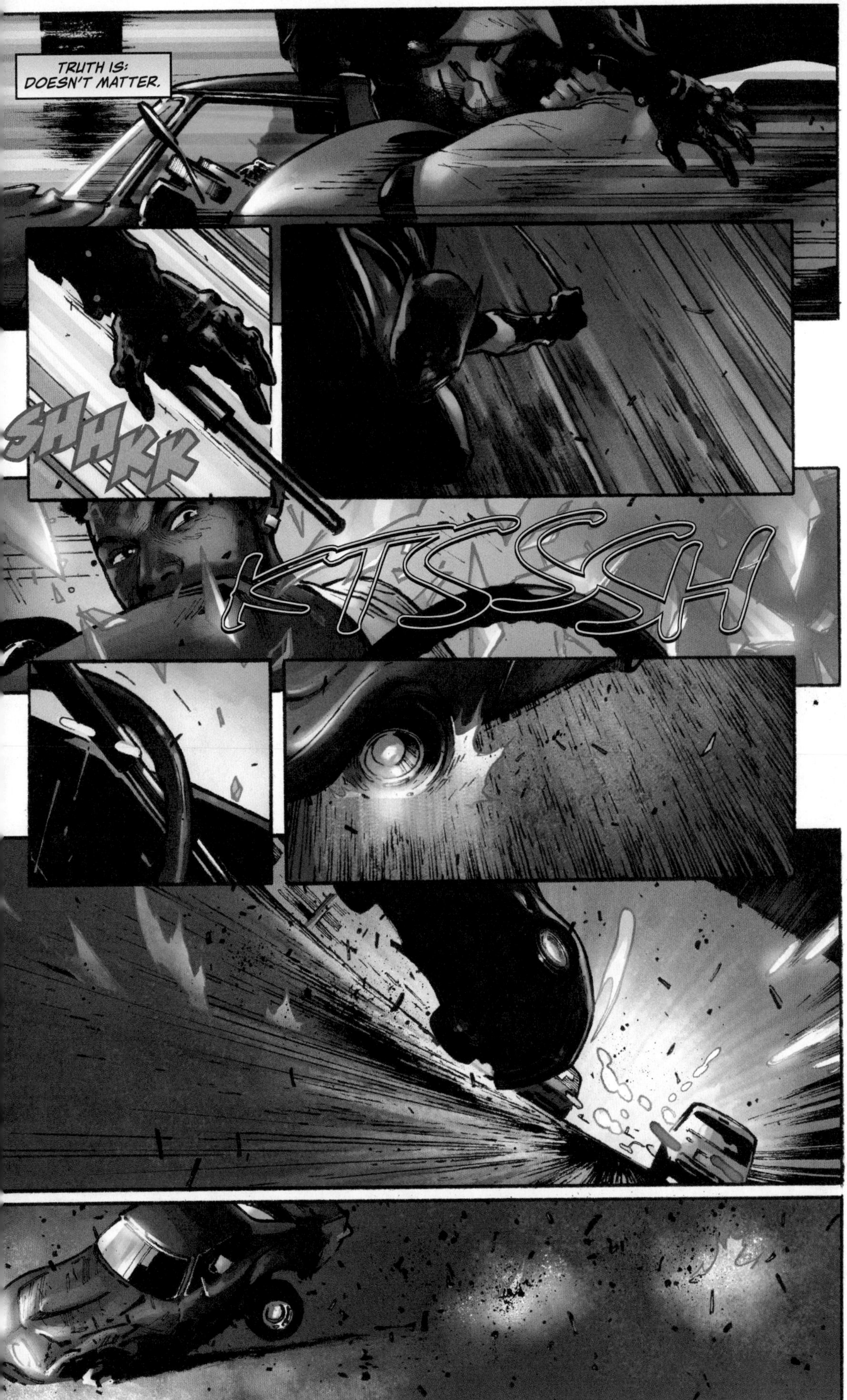
TRUTH IS:
DOESN'T MATTER.
SHHKK
KTSSSH

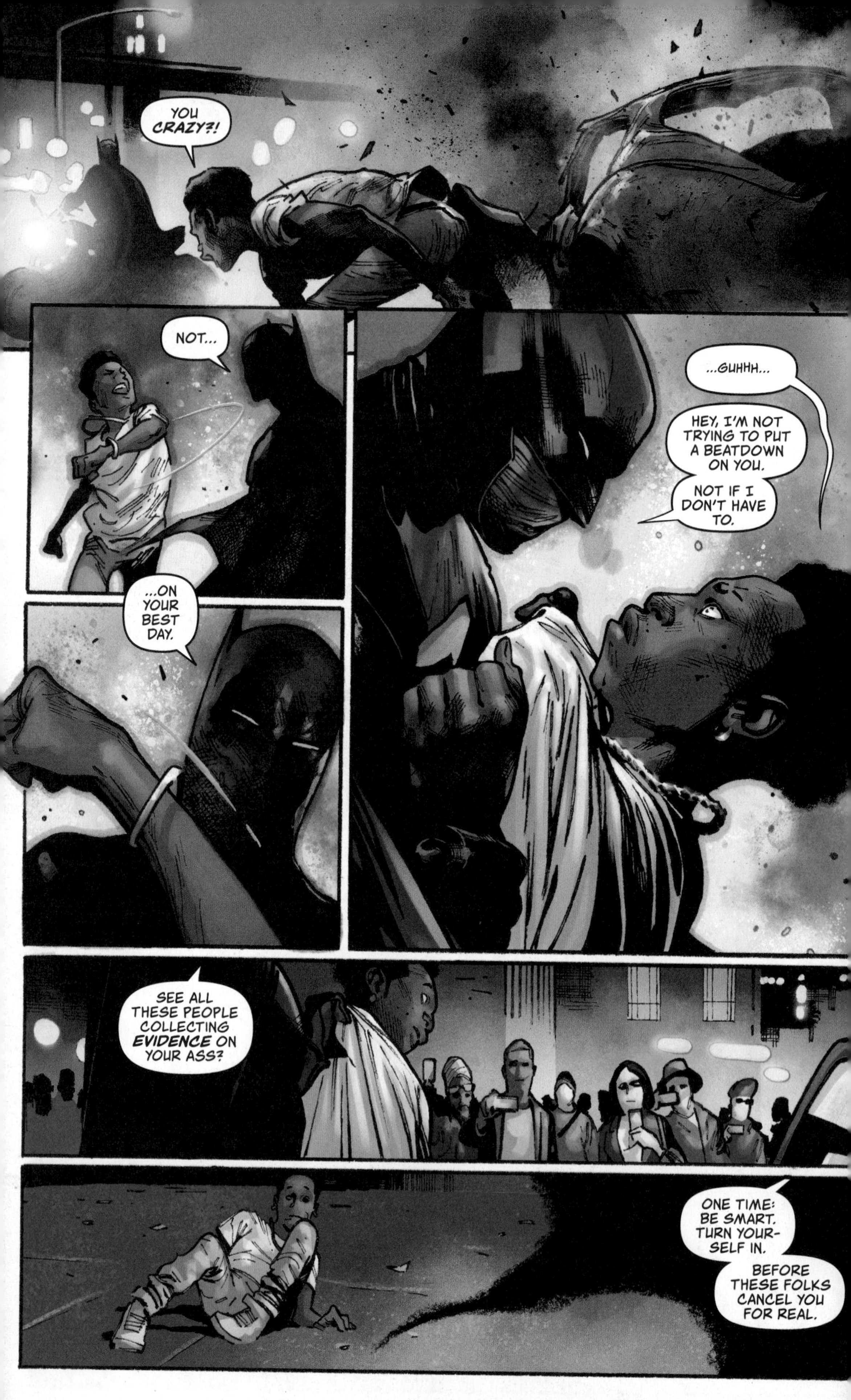
YOU CRAZY?!
NOT...
...ON YOUR BEST DAY.
...GUHHH...
HEY, I'M NOT TRYING TO PUT A BEATDOWN ON YOU.
NOT IF I DON'T HAVE TO.
SEE ALL THESE PEOPLE COLLECTING EVIDENCE ON YOUR ASS?
ONE TIME: BE SMART. TURN YOURSELF IN.
BEFORE THESE FOLKS CANCEL YOU FOR REAL.

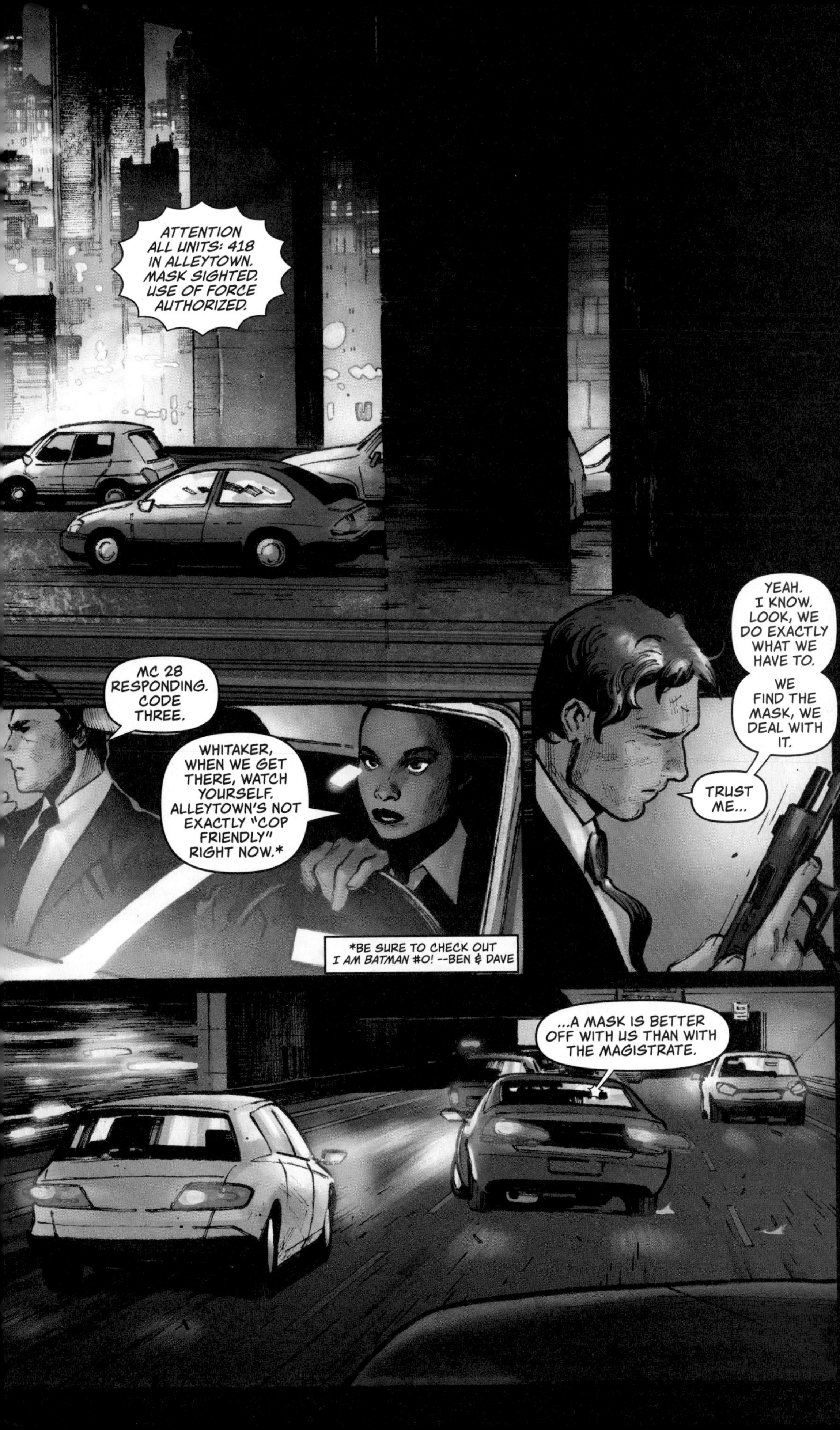

ATTENTION ALL UNITS: 418 IN ALLEYTOWN. MASK SIGHTED. USE OF FORCE AUTHORIZED.
MC 28 RESPONDING. CODE THREE.
WHITAKER, WHEN WE GET THERE, WATCH YOURSELF. ALLEYTOWN'S NOT EXACTLY "COP FRIENDLY" RIGHT NOW.*
*BE SURE TO CHECK OUT I AM BATMAN #0! --BEN & DAVE
YEAH. I KNOW. LOOK, WE DO EXACTLY WHAT WE HAVE TO.
WE FIND THE MASK, WE DEAL WITH IT.
TRUST ME...
...A MASK IS BETTER OFF WITH US THAN WITH THE MAGISTRATE.

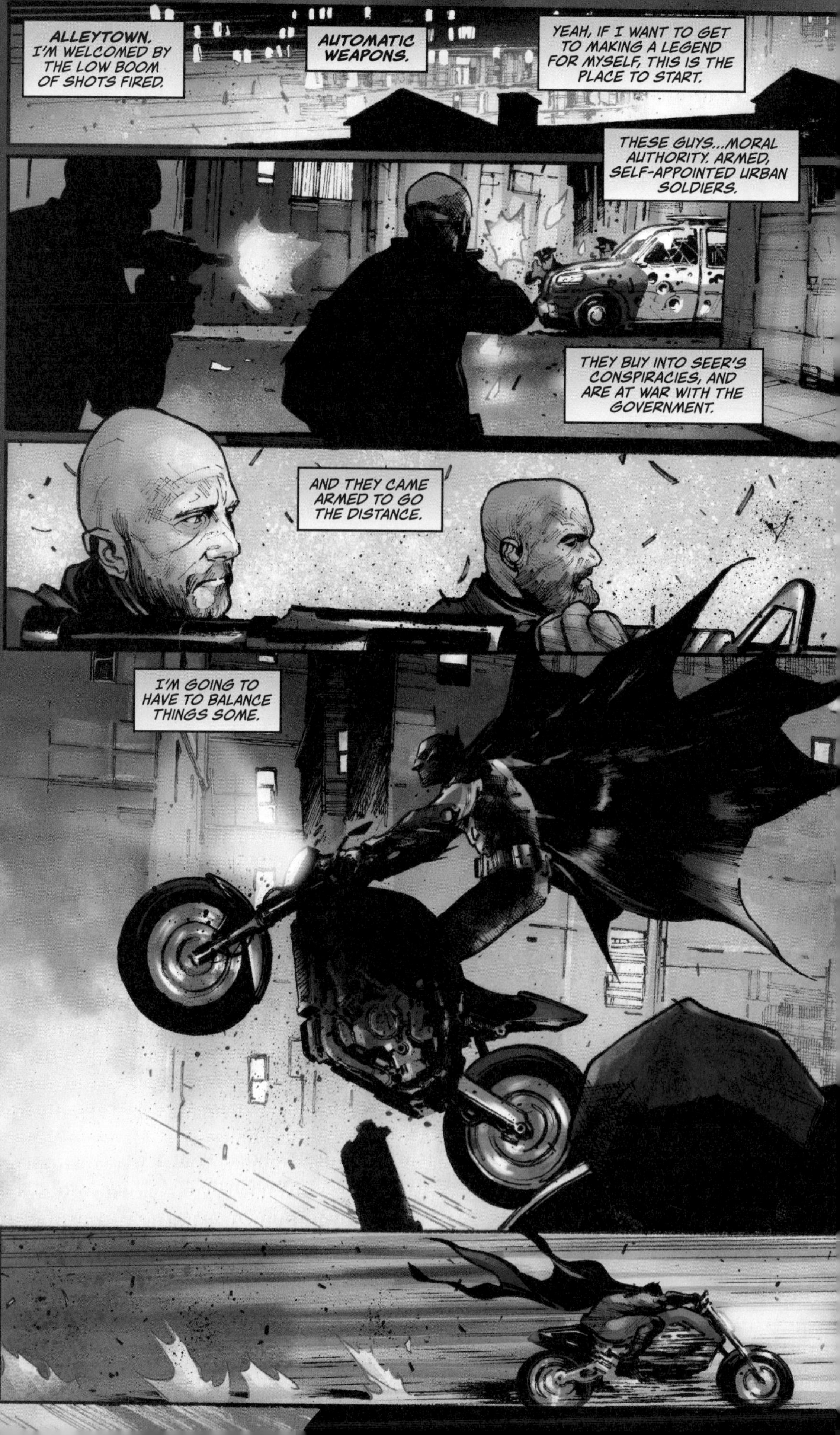
ALLEYTOWN. I'M WELCOMED BY THE LOW BOOM OF SHOTS FIRED.
AUTOMATIC WEAPONS.
YEAH, IF I WANT TO GET TO MAKING A LEGEND FOR MYSELF, THIS IS THE PLACE TO START.
THESE GUYS...MORAL AUTHORITY. ARMED, SELF-APPOINTED URBAN SOLDIERS.
THEY BUY INTO SEER'S CONSPIRACIES, AND ARE AT WAR WITH THE GOVERNMENT.
AND THEY CAME ARMED TO GO THE DISTANCE.
I'M GOING TO HAVE TO BALANCE THINGS SOME.

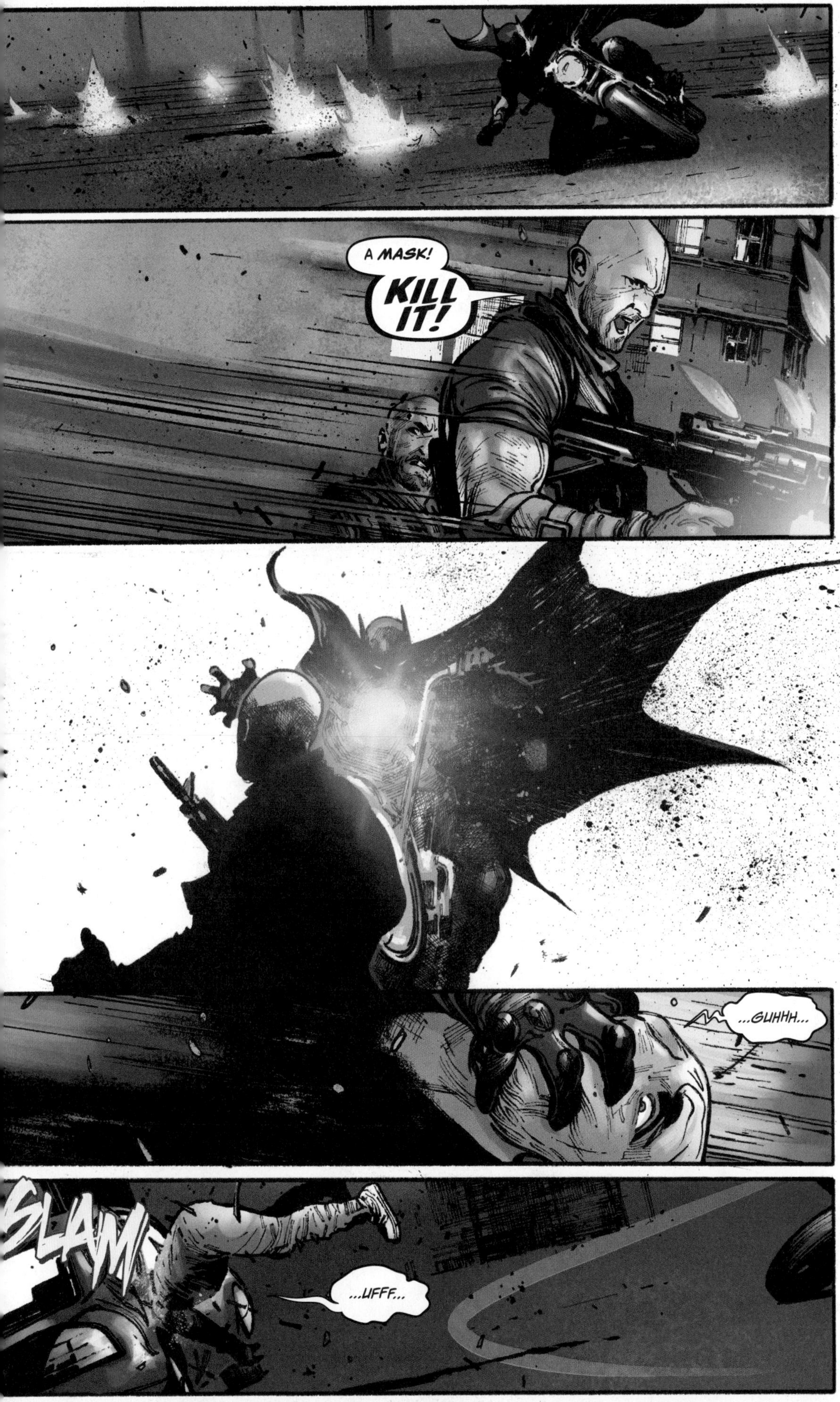
A MASK!
KILL IT!
...GUHHH...
SLAM
...UFFF...

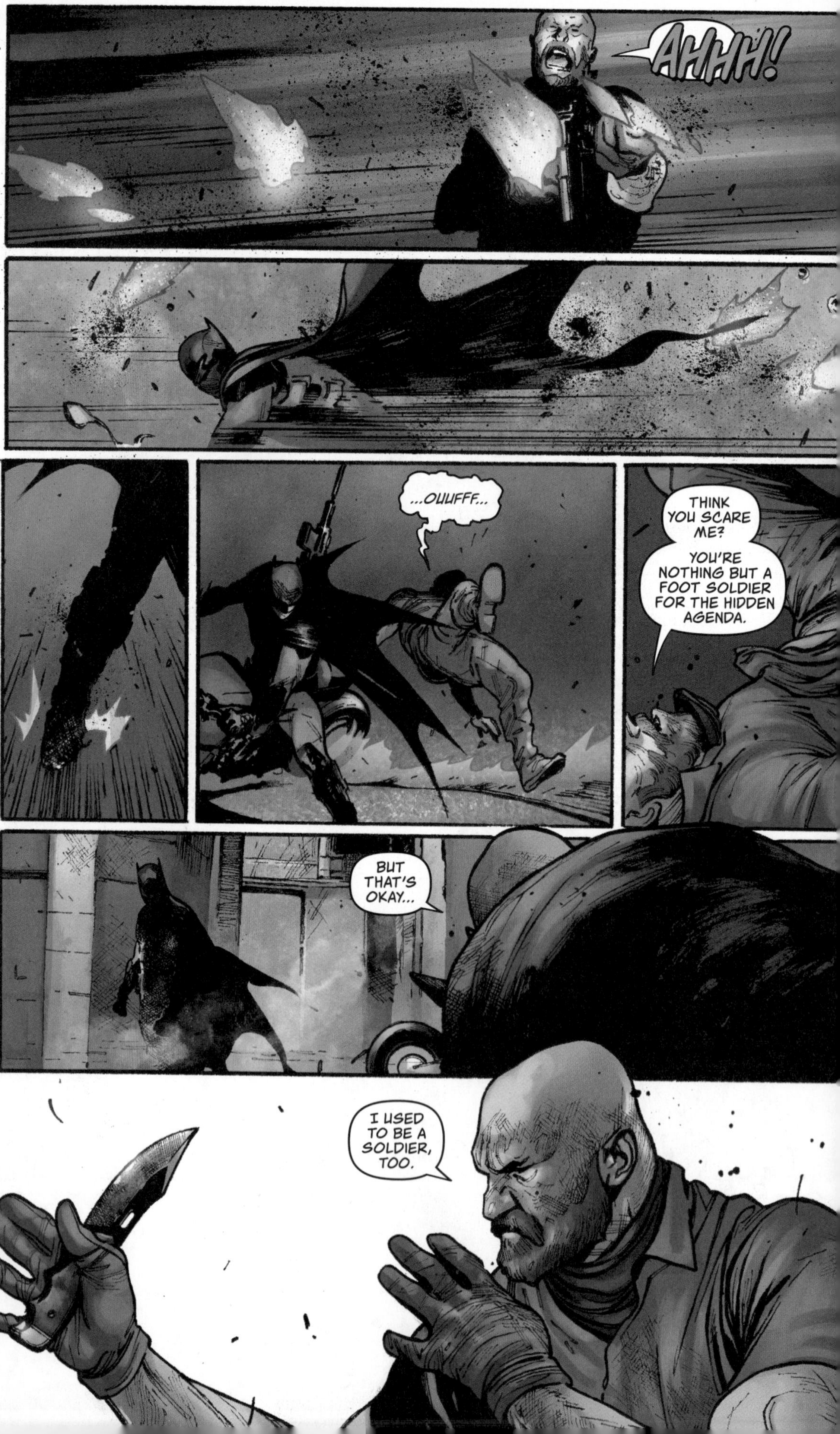
AHHH!
...OUUFFF...
THINK YOU SCARE ME?
YOU'RE NOTHING BUT A FOOT SOLDIER FOR THE HIDDEN AGENDA.
BUT THAT'S OKAY...
I USED TO BE A SOLDIER, TOO.

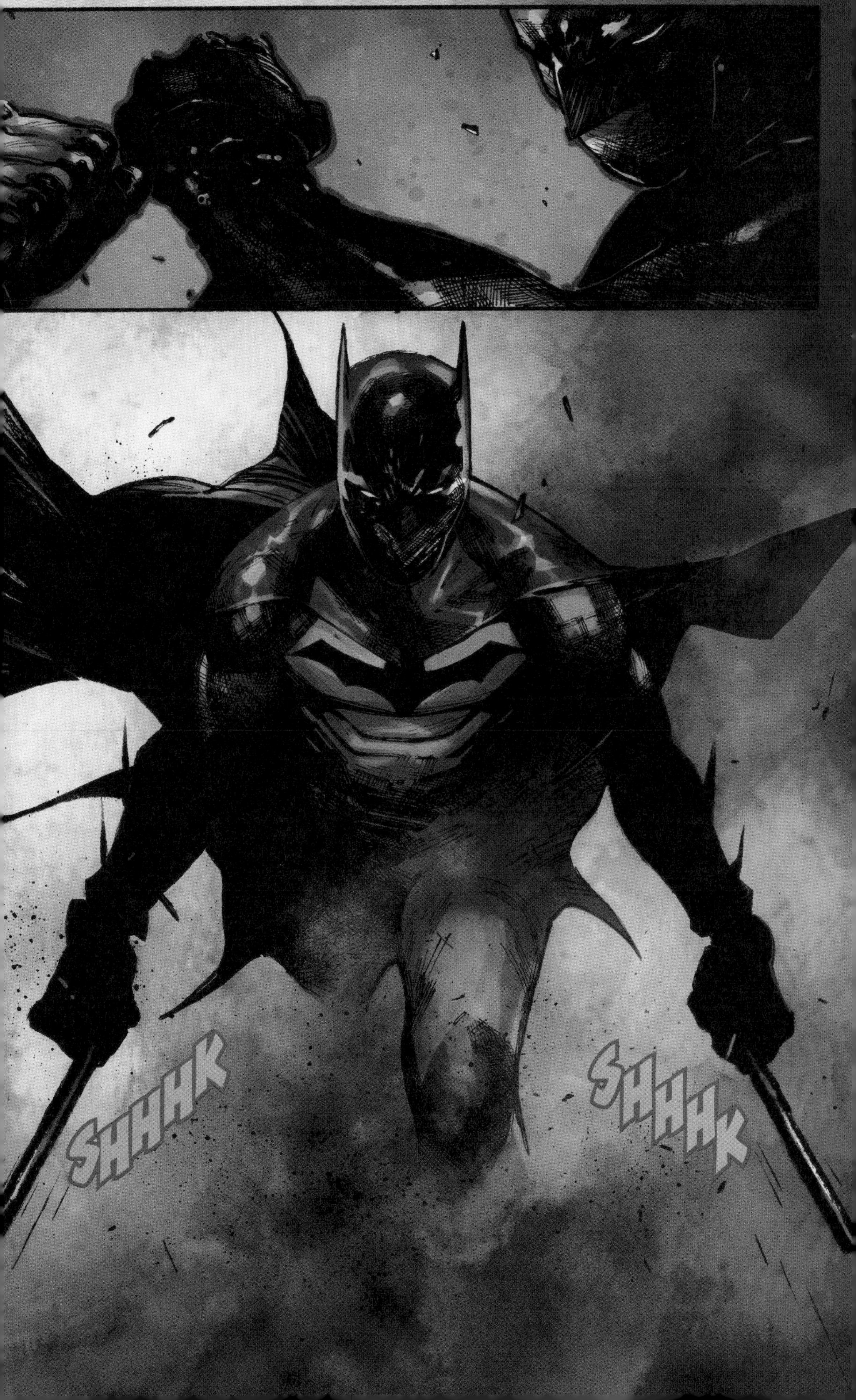
SHHHK
SHHHK

OOOFFFF...
NUHHH...
UHHHH...
AHHH!
NUH-UH. LEAVE IT.

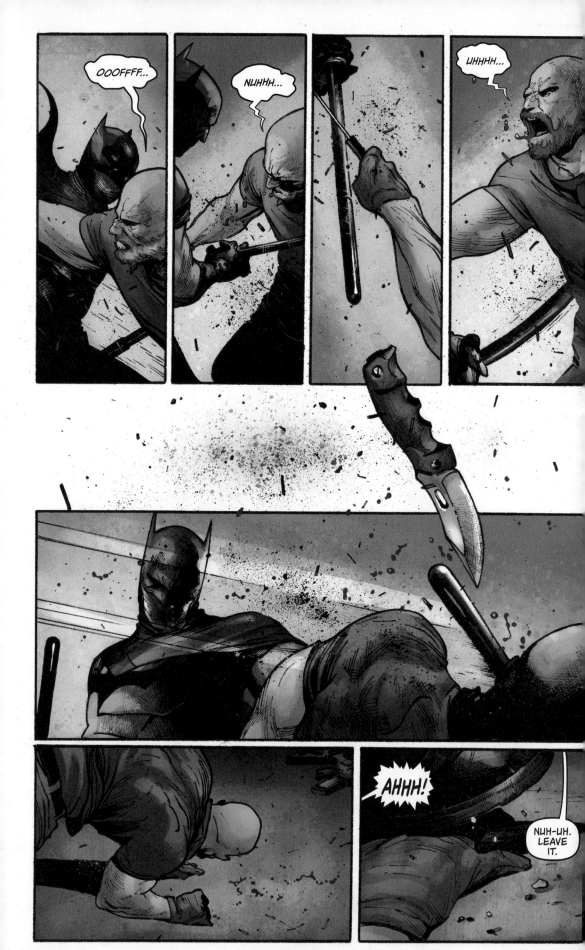

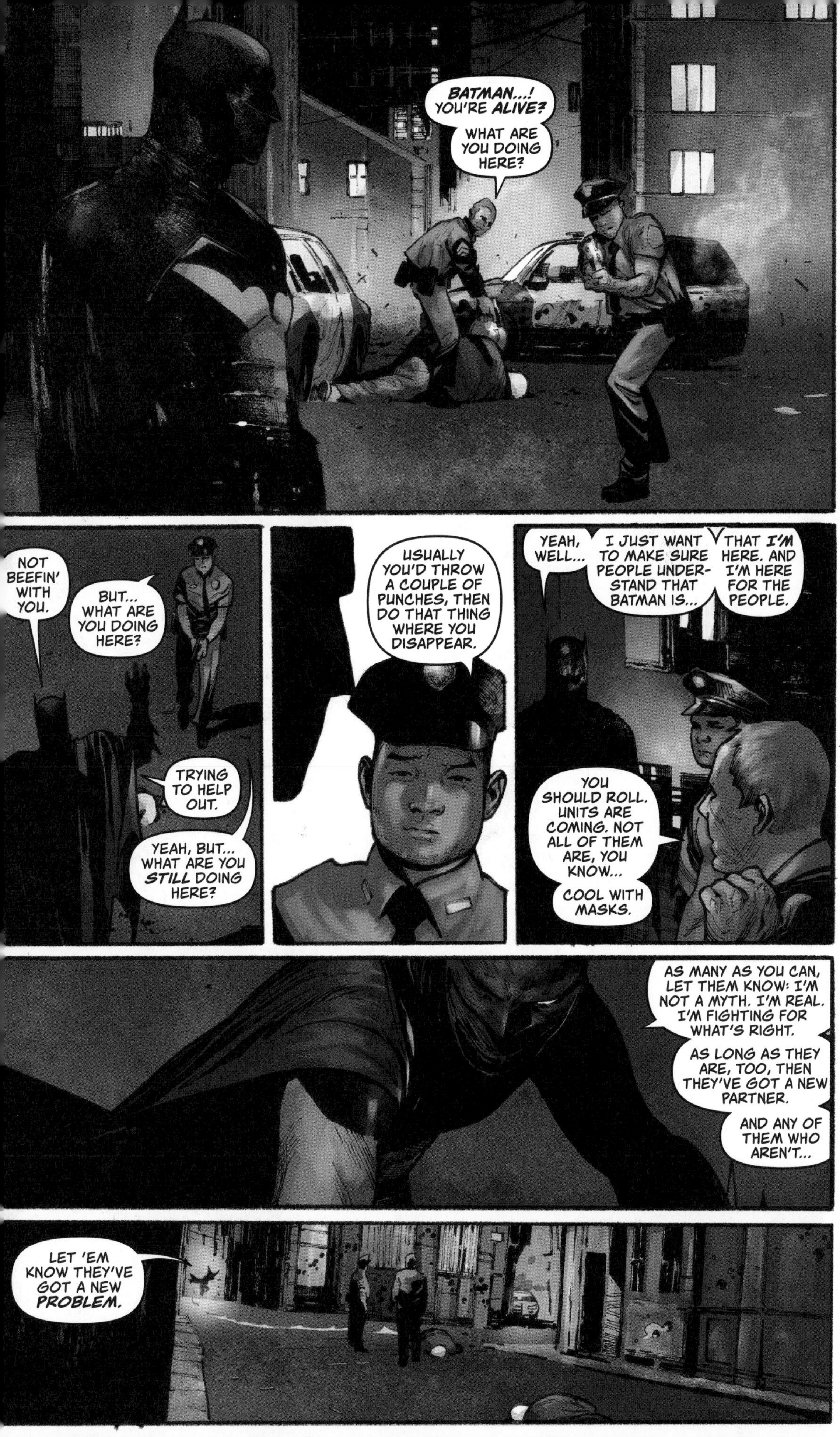

BATMAN...! YOU'RE ALIVE?
WHAT ARE YOU DOING HERE?
NOT BEEFIN' WITH YOU.
BUT... WHAT ARE YOU DOING HERE?
TRYING TO HELP OUT.
YEAH, BUT... WHAT ARE YOU STILL DOING HERE?
USUALLY YOU'D THROW A COUPLE OF PUNCHES, THEN DO THAT THING WHERE YOU DISAPPEAR.
YEAH, WELL...
I JUST WANT TO MAKE SURE PEOPLE UNDER-STAND THAT BATMAN IS...
THAT I'M HERE. AND I'M HERE FOR THE PEOPLE.
YOU SHOULD ROLL. UNITS ARE COMING. NOT ALL OF THEM ARE, YOU KNOW...
COOL WITH MASKS.
AS MANY AS YOU CAN, LET THEM KNOW: I'M NOT A MYTH. I'M REAL. I'M FIGHTING FOR WHAT'S RIGHT.
AS LONG AS THEY ARE, TOO, THEN THEY'VE GOT A NEW PARTNER.
AND ANY OF THEM WHO AREN'T...
LET 'EM KNOW THEY'VE GOT A NEW PROBLEM.

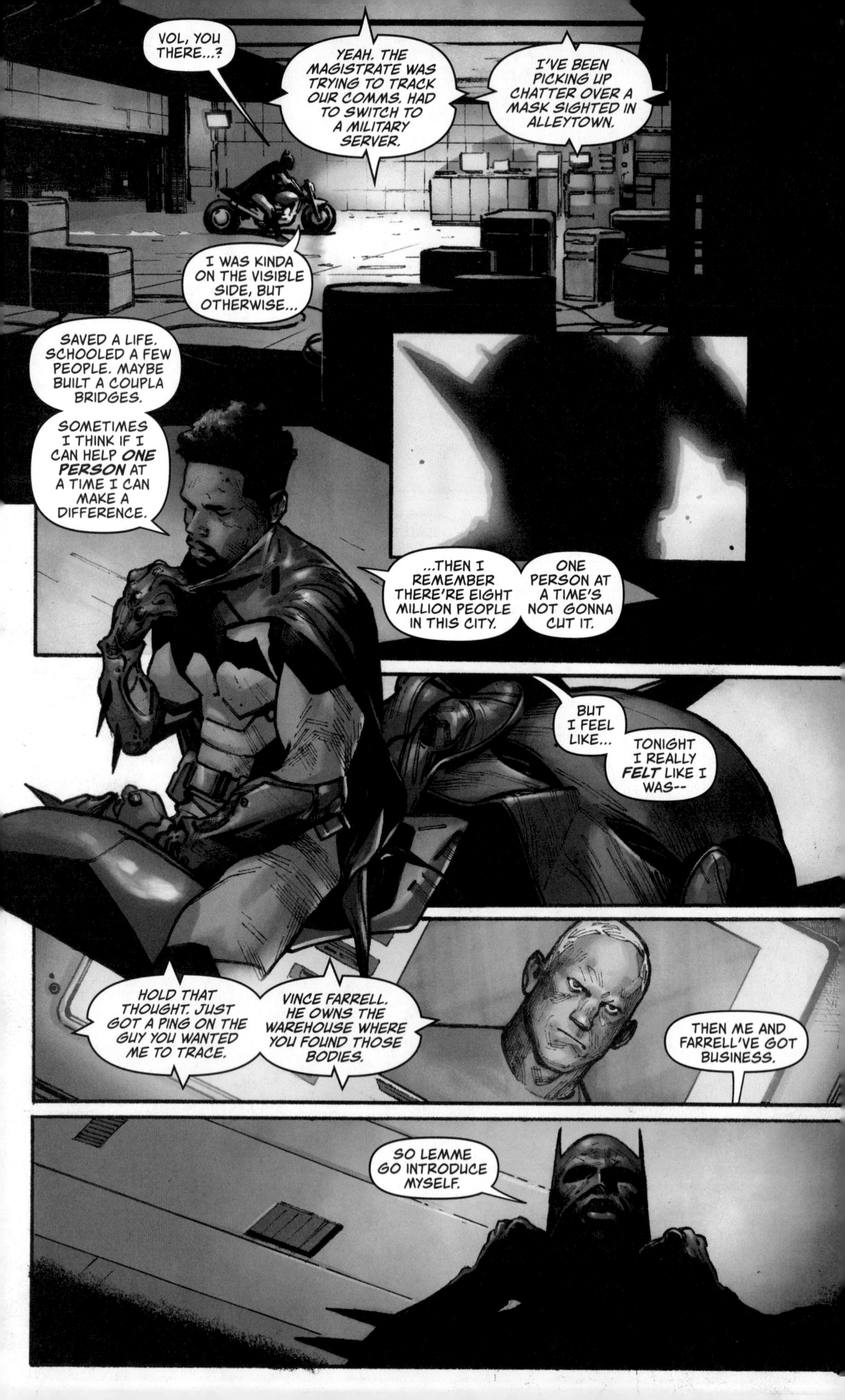
VOL, YOU THERE...?
YEAH. THE MAGISTRATE WAS TRYING TO TRACK OUR COMMS. HAD TO SWITCH TO A MILITARY SERVER.
I'VE BEEN PICKING UP CHATTER OVER A MASK SIGHTED IN ALLEYTOWN.
I WAS KINDA ON THE VISIBLE SIDE, BUT OTHERWISE...
SAVED A LIFE. SCHOOLED A FEW PEOPLE. MAYBE BUILT A COUPLA BRIDGES.
SOMETIMES I THINK IF I CAN HELP ONE PERSON AT A TIME I CAN MAKE A DIFFERENCE.
...THEN I REMEMBER THERE'RE EIGHT MILLION PEOPLE IN THIS CITY.
ONE PERSON AT A TIME'S NOT GONNA CUT IT.
BUT I FEEL LIKE...
TONIGHT I REALLY FELT LIKE I WAS--
HOLD THAT THOUGHT. JUST GOT A PING ON THE GUY YOU WANTED ME TO TRACE.
VINCE FARRELL. HE OWNS THE WAREHOUSE WHERE YOU FOUND THOSE BODIES.
THEN ME AND FARRELL'VE GOT BUSINESS.
SO LEMME GO INTRODUCE MYSELF.

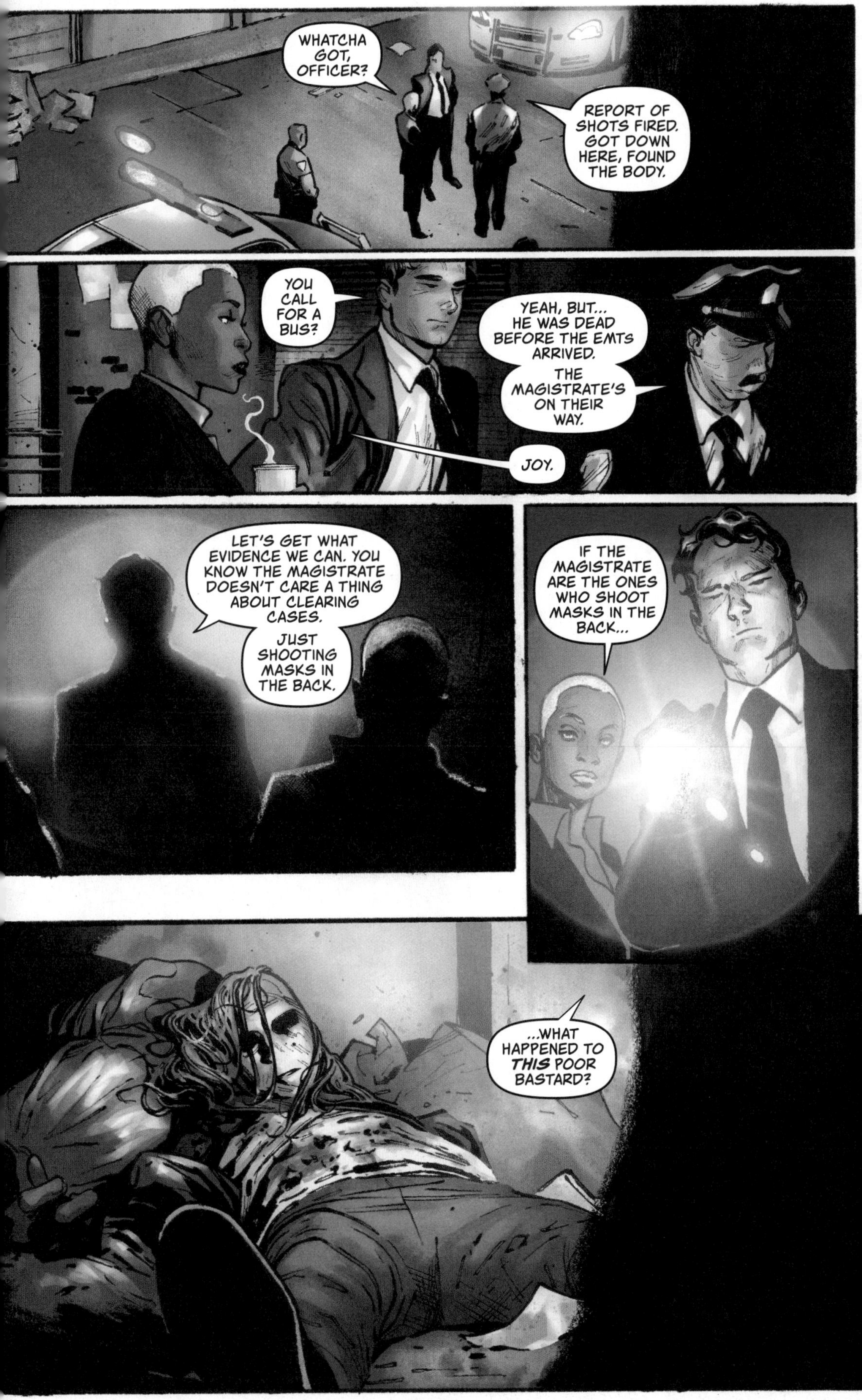
WHATCHA GOT, OFFICER?
REPORT OF SHOTS FIRED. GOT DOWN HERE, FOUND THE BODY.
YOU CALL FOR A BUS?
YEAH, BUT... HE WAS DEAD BEFORE THE EMTS ARRIVED.
THE MAGISTRATE'S ON THEIR WAY.
JOY.
LET'S GET WHAT EVIDENCE WE CAN. YOU KNOW THE MAGISTRATE DOESN'T CARE A THING ABOUT CLEARING CASES.
JUST SHOOTING MASKS IN THE BACK.
IF THE MAGISTRATE ARE THE ONES WHO SHOOT MASKS IN THE BACK...
...WHAT HAPPENED TO *THIS* POOR BASTARD?

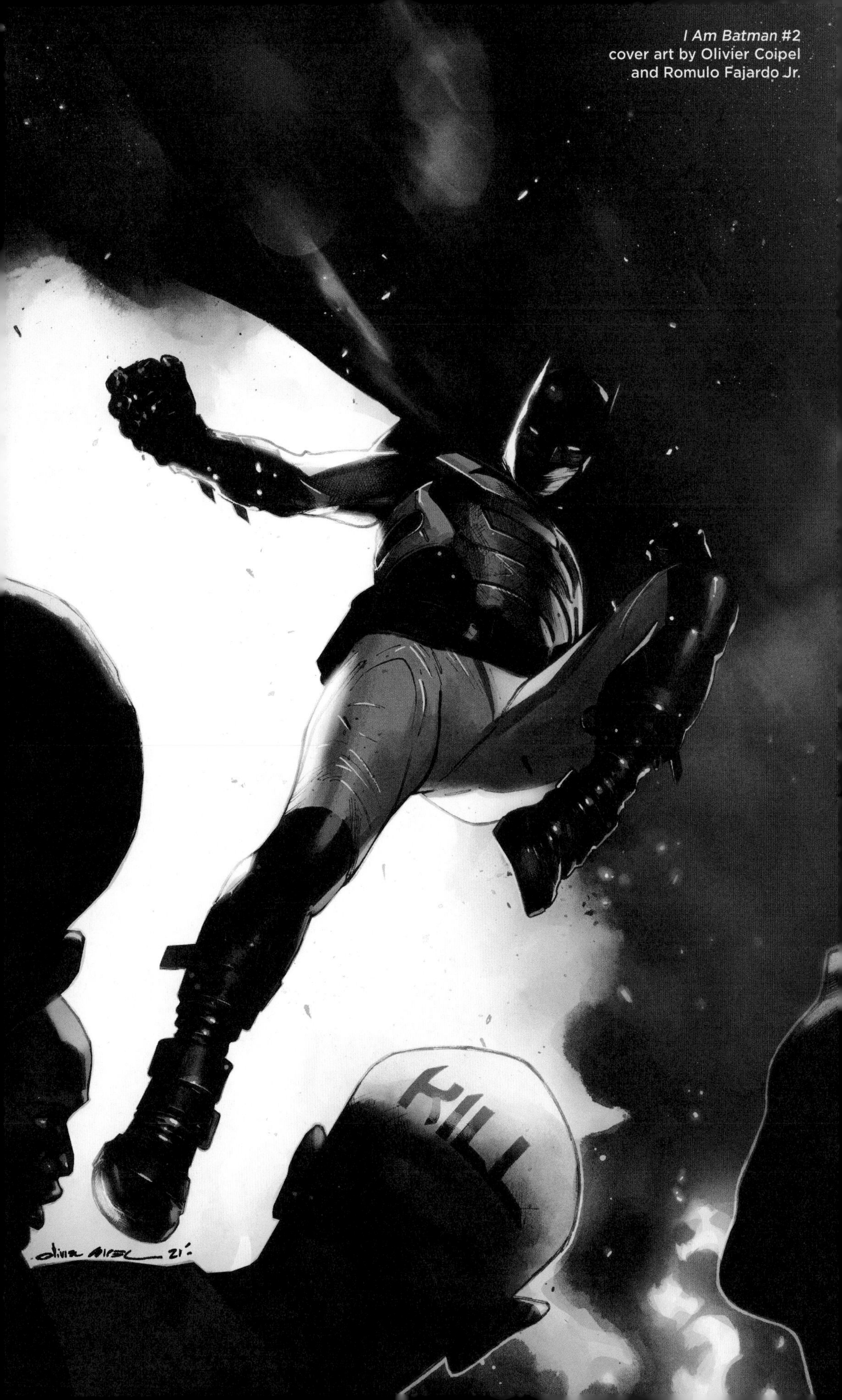
KILL

I Am Batman #2
cover art by Olivier Coipel
and Romulo Fajardo Jr.

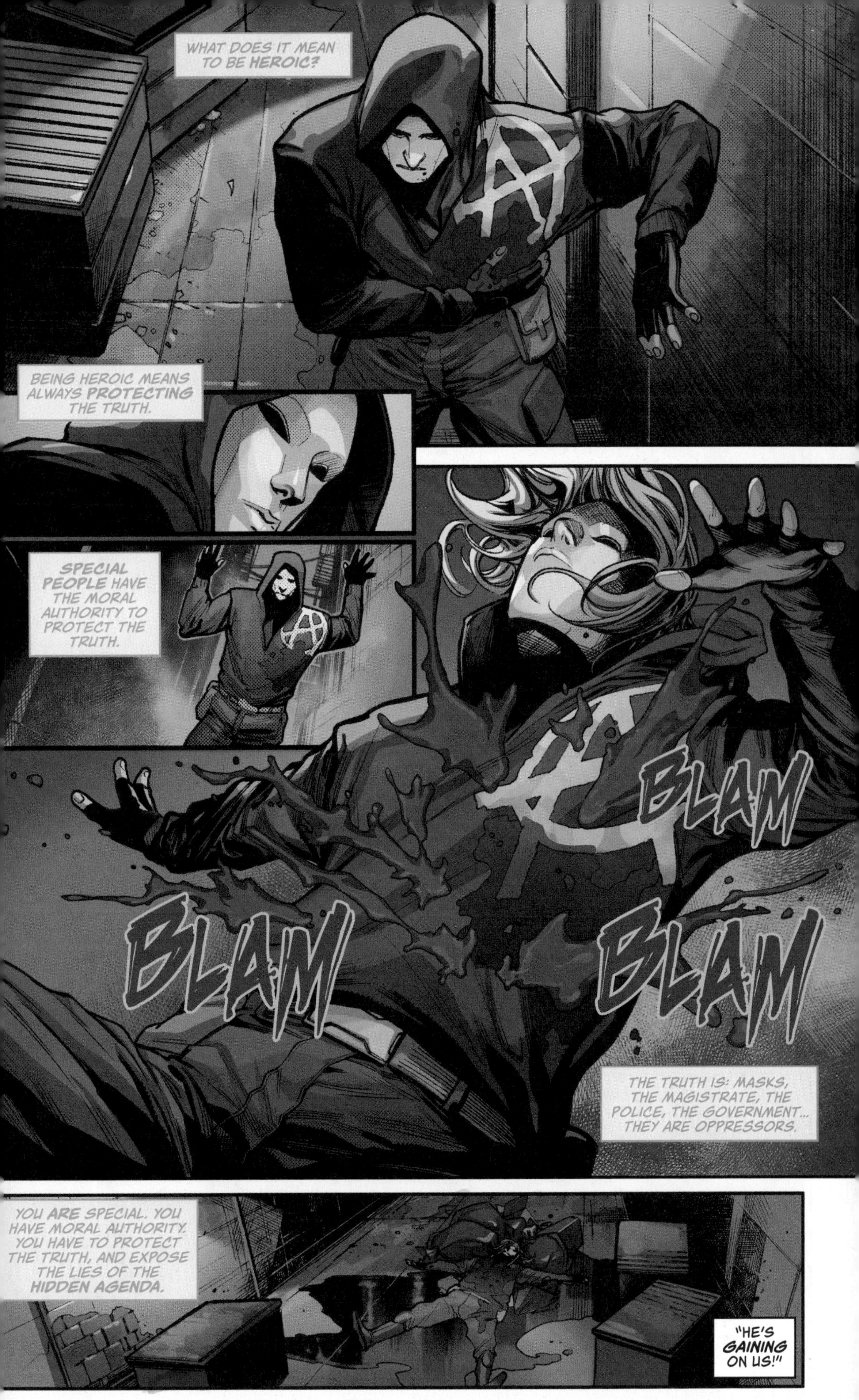
WHAT DOES IT MEAN TO BE HEROIC?
BEING HEROIC MEANS ALWAYS PROTECTING THE TRUTH.
SPECIAL PEOPLE HAVE THE MORAL AUTHORITY TO PROTECT THE TRUTH.
BLAM
BLAM
BLAM
THE TRUTH IS: MASKS, THE MAGISTRATE, THE POLICE, THE GOVERNMENT... THEY ARE OPPRESSORS.
YOU ARE SPECIAL. YOU HAVE MORAL AUTHORITY. YOU HAVE TO PROTECT THE TRUTH, AND EXPOSE THE LIES OF THE HIDDEN AGENDA.
"HE'S GAINING ON US!"

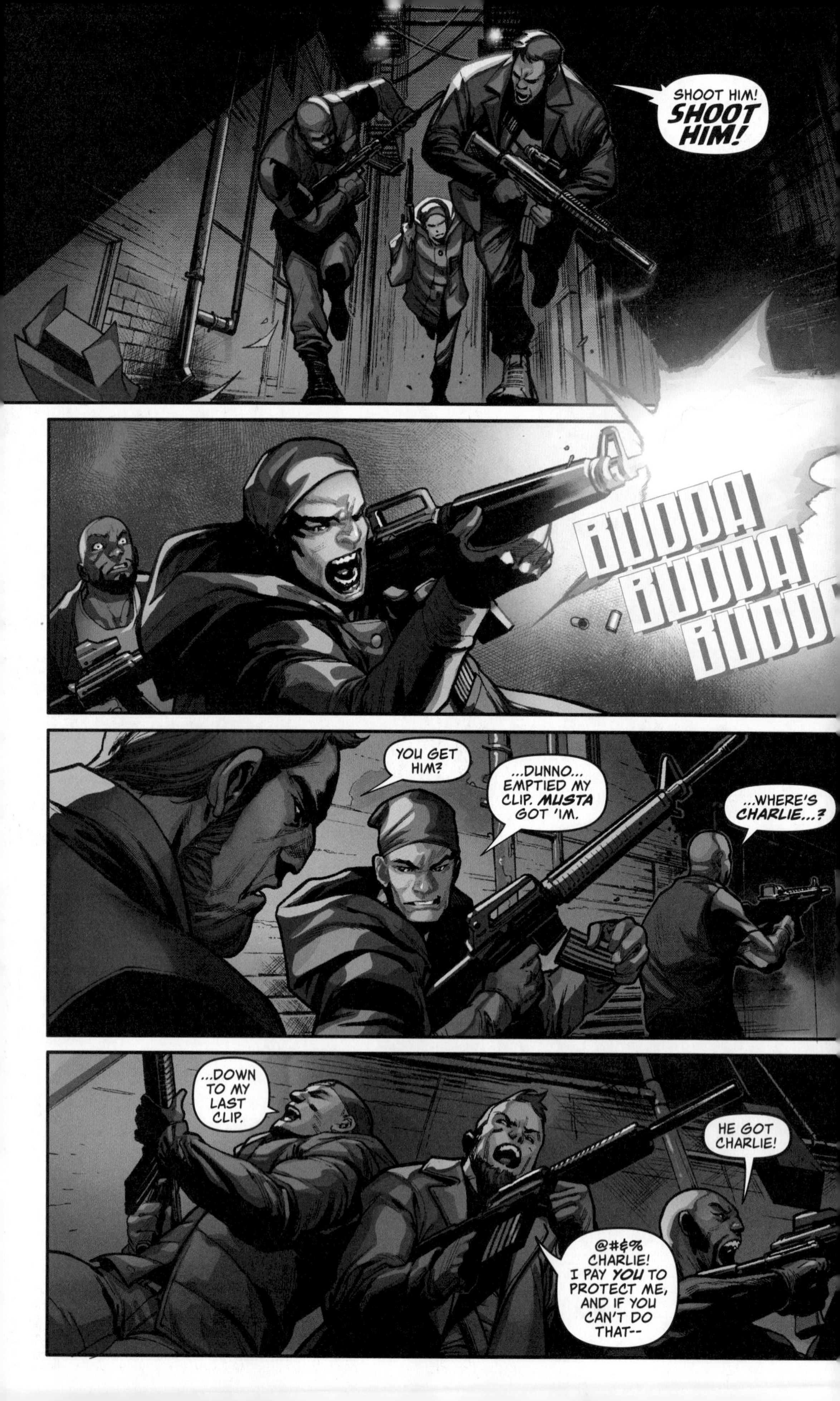

SHOOT HIM! SHOOT HIM!
BUDDA BUDDA BUDD
YOU GET HIM?
...DUNNO... EMPTIED MY CLIP. MUSTA GOT 'IM.
...WHERE'S CHARLIE...?
...DOWN TO MY LAST CLIP.
HE GOT CHARLIE!
@#&% CHARLIE! I PAY YOU TO PROTECT ME, AND IF YOU CAN'T DO THAT--

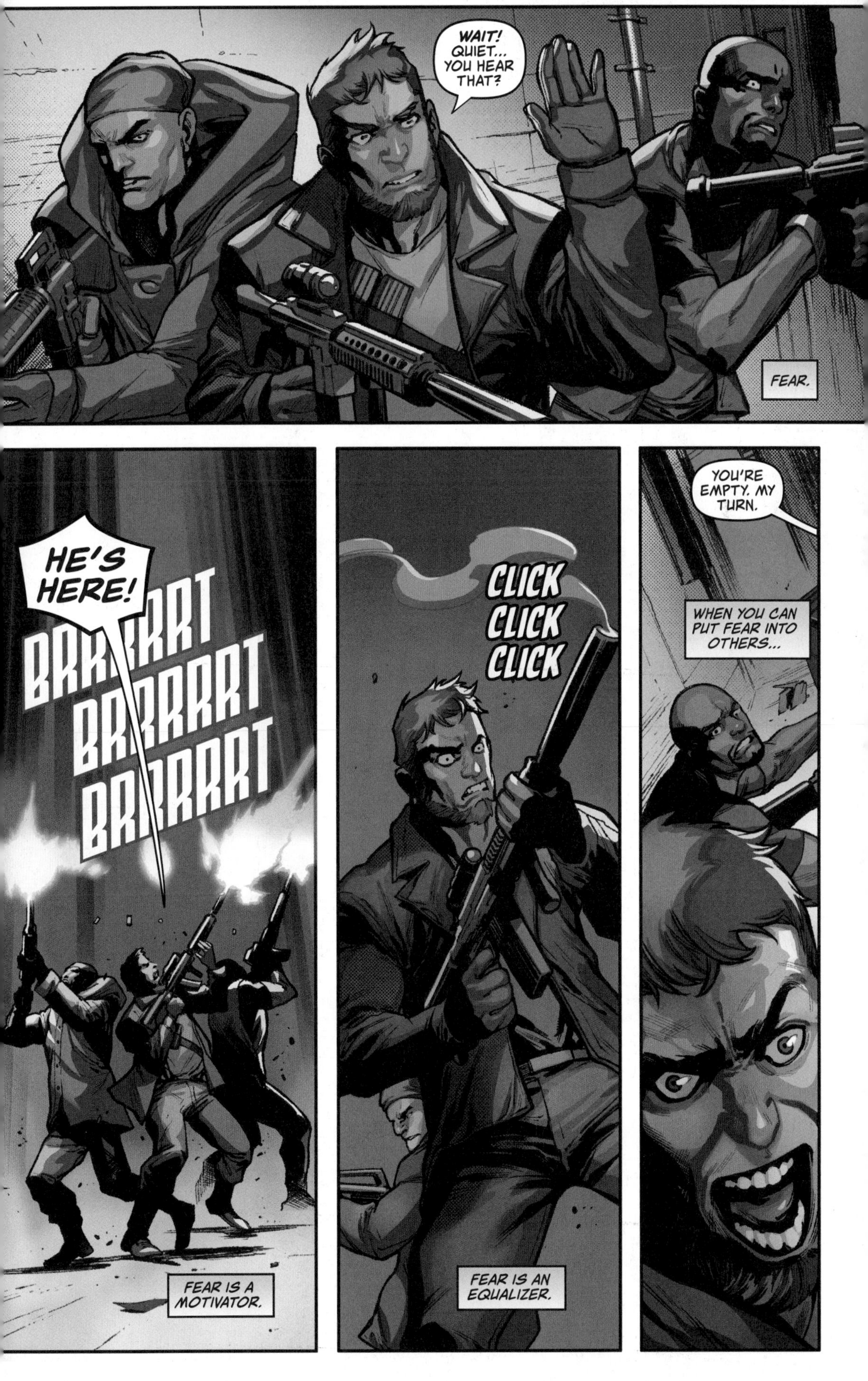
WAIT! QUIET... YOU HEAR THAT?
FEAR.
HE'S HERE!
BRRRRRT BRRRRRT BRRRRRT
FEAR IS A MOTIVATOR.
CLICK CLICK CLICK
FEAR IS AN EQUALIZER.
YOU'RE EMPTY. MY TURN.
WHEN YOU CAN PUT FEAR INTO OTHERS...

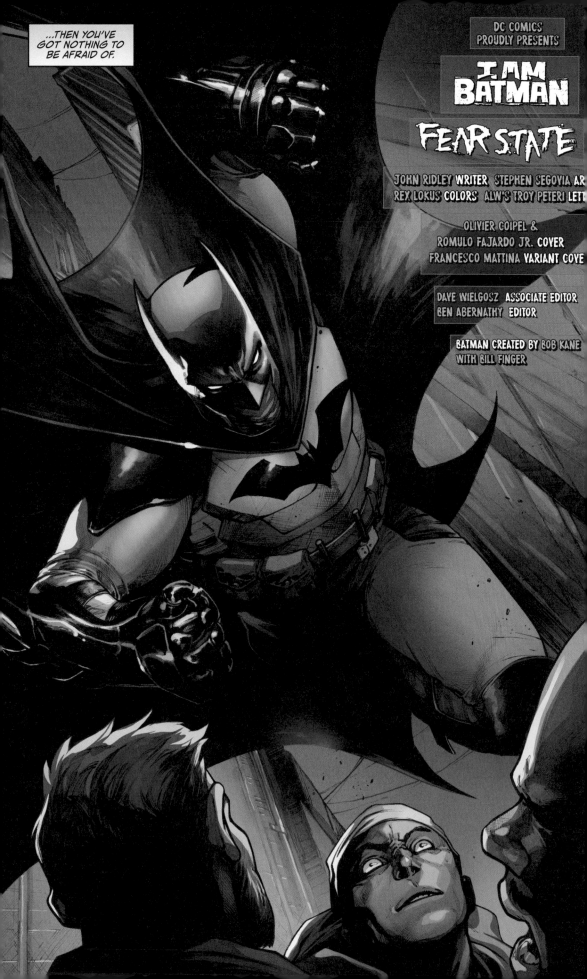

...THEN YOU'VE GOT NOTHING TO BE AFRAID OF.

DC COMICS PROUDLY PRESENTS

I AM BATMAN

FEAR STATE

JOHN RIDLEY WRITER STEPHEN SEGOVIA AR
REX LOKUS COLORS ALW'S TROY PETERI LETT

OLIVIER COIPEL &
ROMULO FAJARDO JR. COVER
FRANCESCO MATTINA VARIANT COVE

DAVE WIELGOSZ ASSOCIATE EDITOR
BEN ABERNATHY EDITOR

BATMAN CREATED BY BOB KANE
WITH BILL FINGER

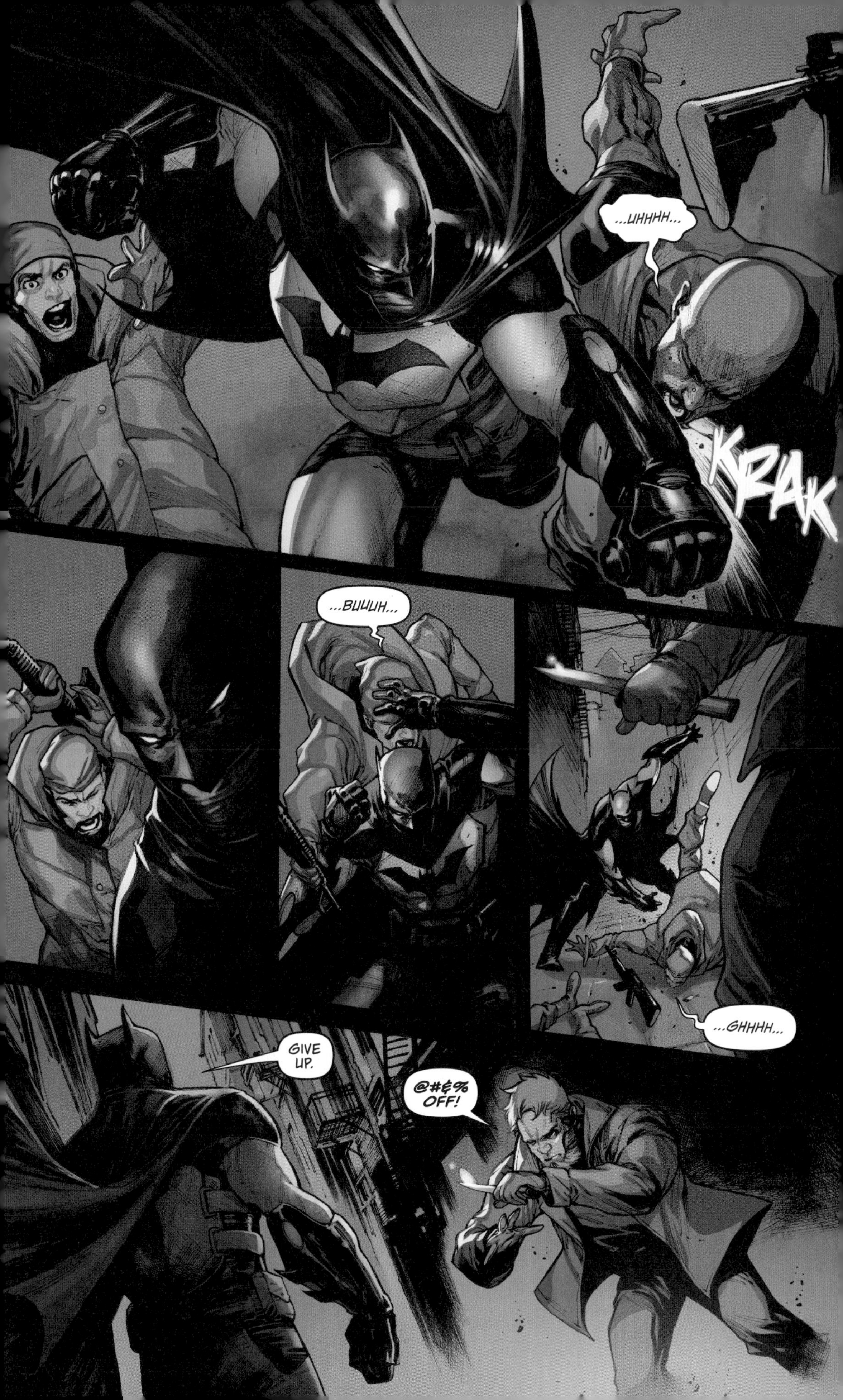
...UHHHH...
KRAK
...BUUUH...
...GHHHH...
GIVE UP.
@#&% OFF!

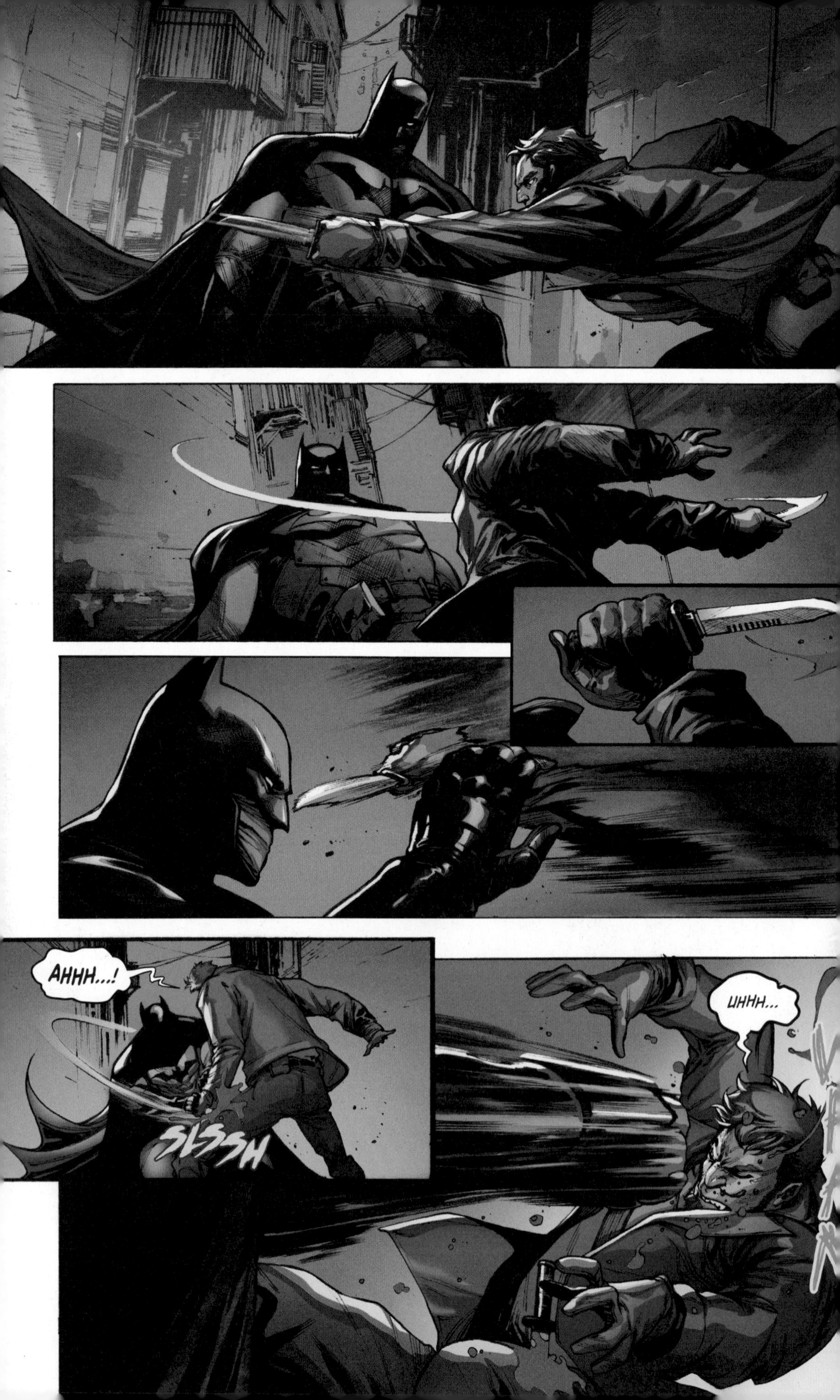
AHHH...!
SLSSH
UHHH...

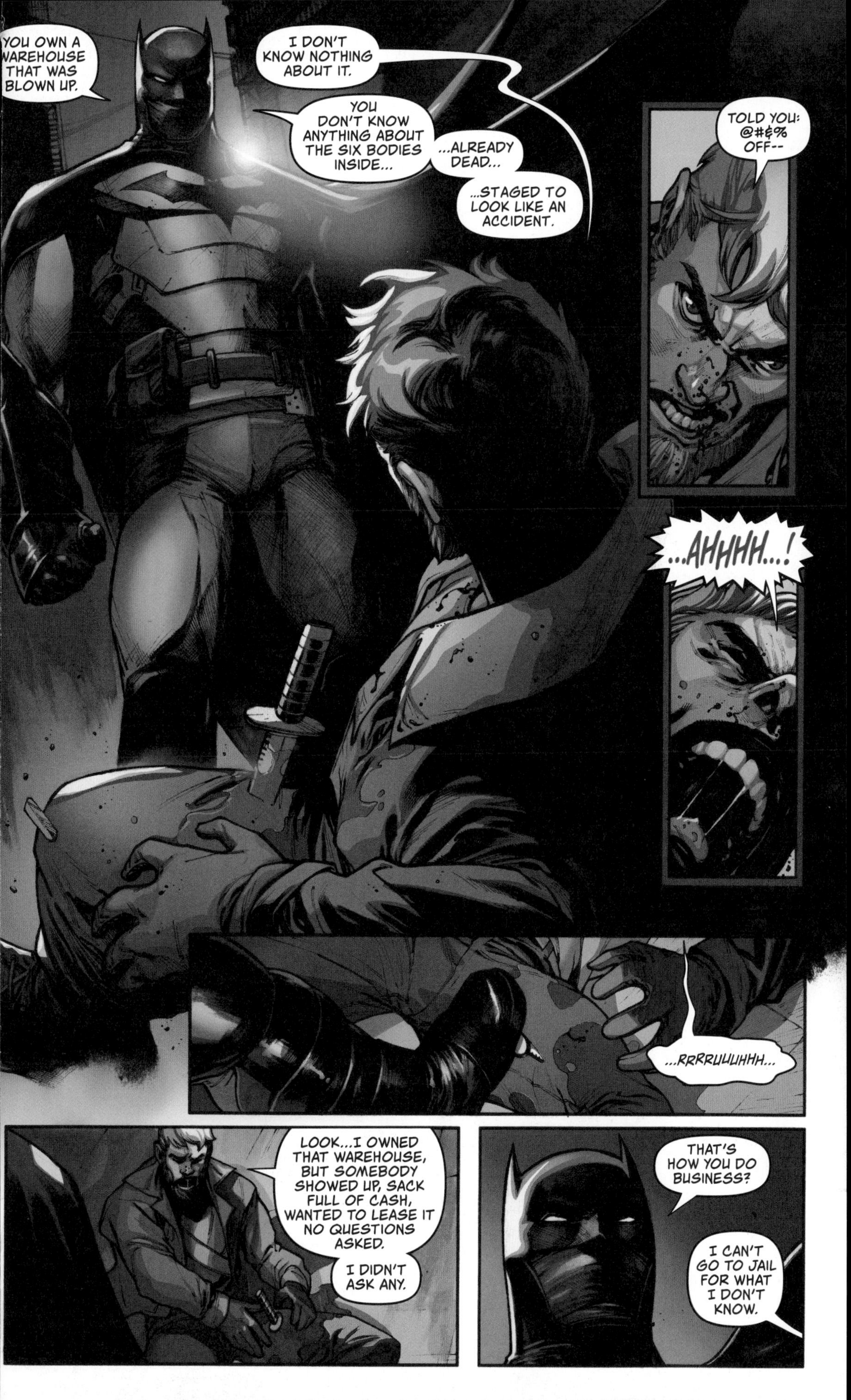
YOU OWN A WAREHOUSE THAT WAS BLOWN UP.
I DON'T KNOW NOTHING ABOUT IT.
YOU DON'T KNOW ANYTHING ABOUT THE SIX BODIES INSIDE...
...ALREADY DEAD...
...STAGED TO LOOK LIKE AN ACCIDENT.
TOLD YOU: @#&% OFF--
...AHHHH...!
...RRRRUUUHHH...
LOOK...I OWNED THAT WAREHOUSE, BUT SOMEBODY SHOWED UP, SACK FULL OF CASH, WANTED TO LEASE IT NO QUESTIONS ASKED.
I DIDN'T ASK ANY.
THAT'S HOW YOU DO BUSINESS?
I CAN'T GO TO JAIL FOR WHAT I DON'T KNOW.

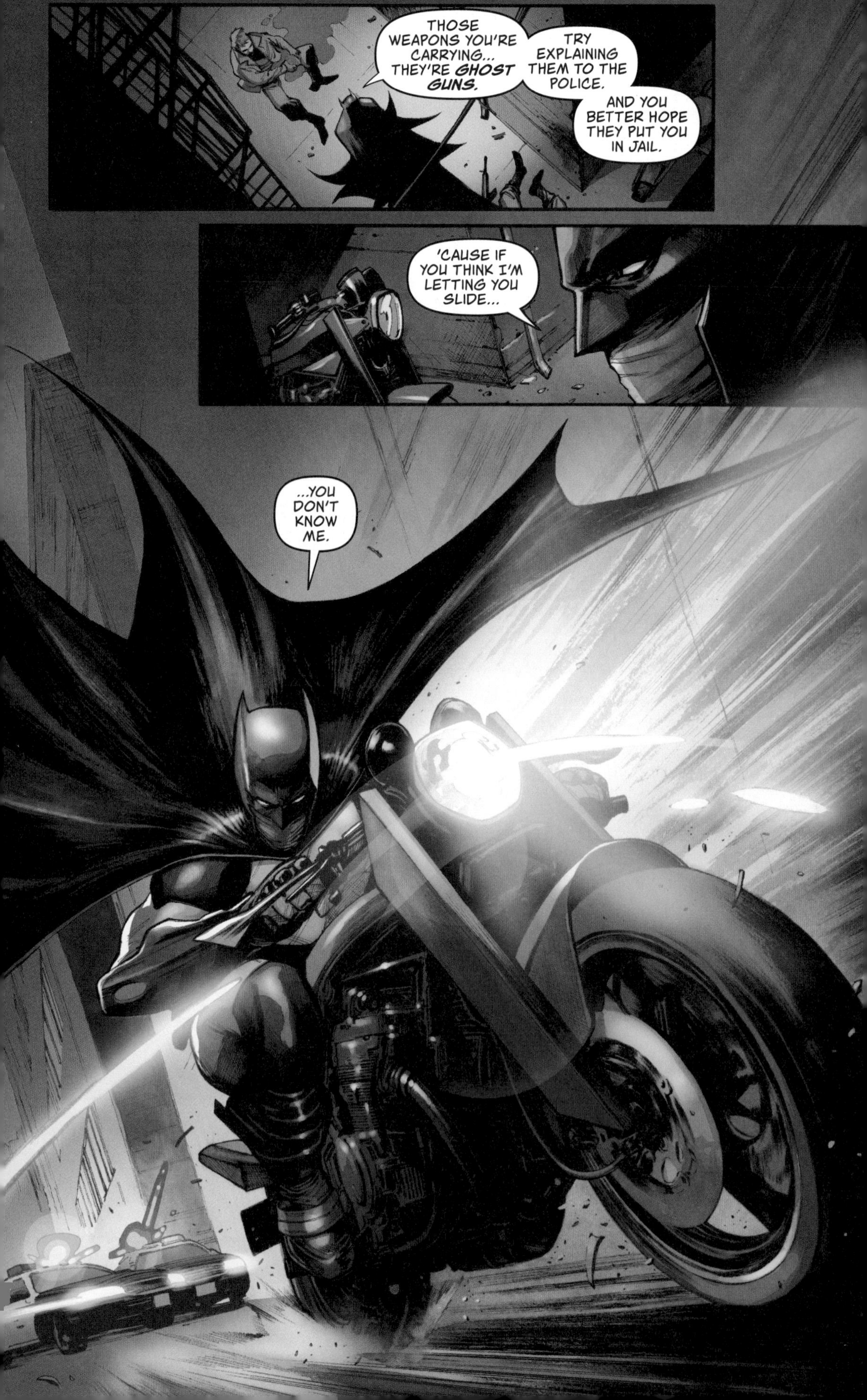
THOSE WEAPONS YOU'RE CARRYING... THEY'RE GHOST GUNS.
TRY EXPLAINING THEM TO THE POLICE.
AND YOU BETTER HOPE THEY PUT YOU IN JAIL.
'CAUSE IF YOU THINK I'M LETTING YOU SLIDE...
...YOU DON'T KNOW ME.

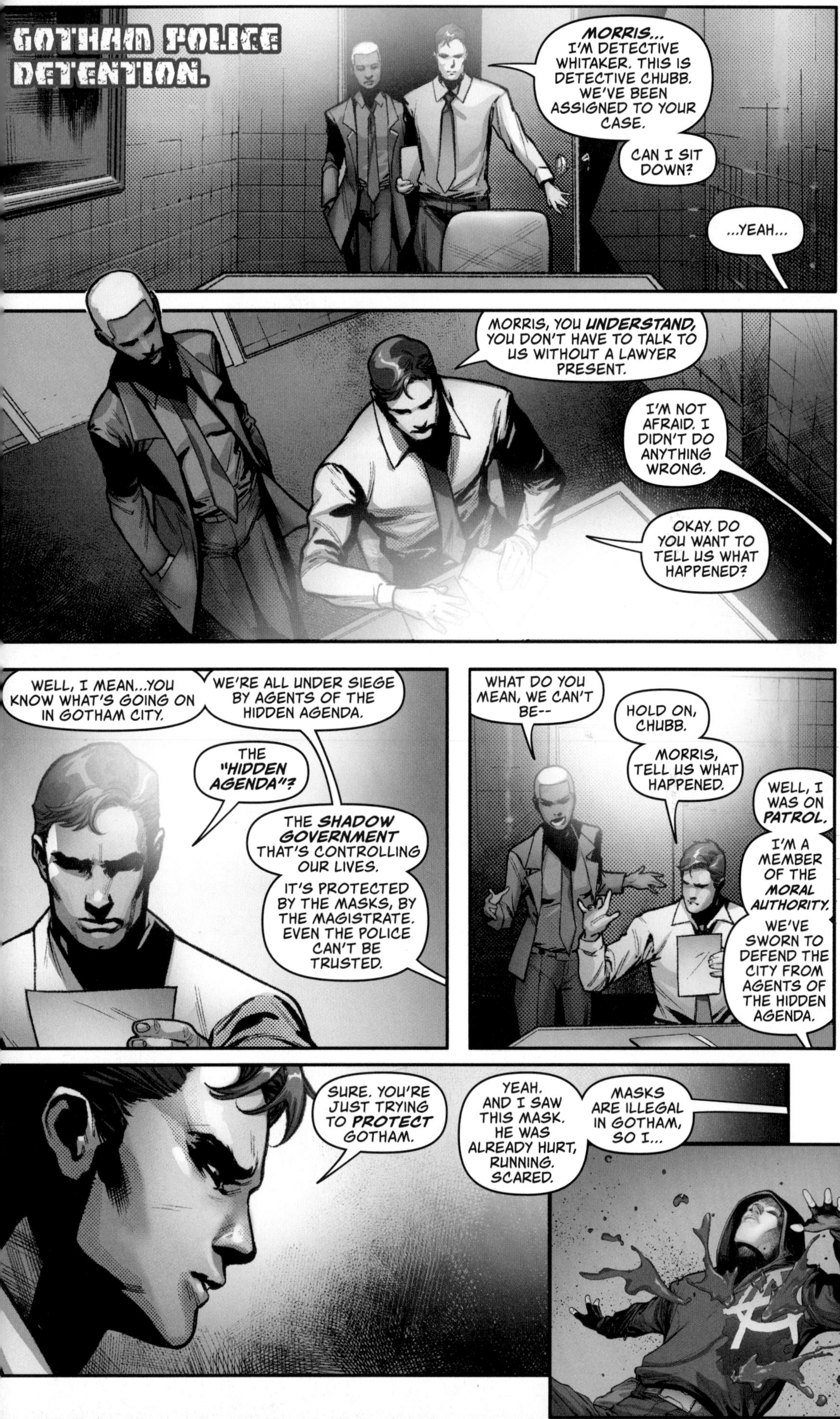
GOTHAM POLICE DETENTION.
MORRIS... I'M DETECTIVE WHITAKER. THIS IS DETECTIVE CHUBB. WE'VE BEEN ASSIGNED TO YOUR CASE.
CAN I SIT DOWN?
...YEAH...
MORRIS, YOU UNDERSTAND, YOU DON'T HAVE TO TALK TO US WITHOUT A LAWYER PRESENT.
I'M NOT AFRAID. I DIDN'T DO ANYTHING WRONG.
OKAY. DO YOU WANT TO TELL US WHAT HAPPENED?
WELL, I MEAN...YOU KNOW WHAT'S GOING ON IN GOTHAM CITY.
WE'RE ALL UNDER SIEGE BY AGENTS OF THE HIDDEN AGENDA.
THE "HIDDEN AGENDA"?
THE SHADOW GOVERNMENT THAT'S CONTROLLING OUR LIVES.
IT'S PROTECTED BY THE MASKS, BY THE MAGISTRATE. EVEN THE POLICE CAN'T BE TRUSTED.
WHAT DO YOU MEAN, WE CAN'T BE--
HOLD ON, CHUBB.
MORRIS, TELL US WHAT HAPPENED.
WELL, I WAS ON PATROL.
I'M A MEMBER OF THE MORAL AUTHORITY.
WE'VE SWORN TO DEFEND THE CITY FROM AGENTS OF THE HIDDEN AGENDA.
SURE. YOU'RE JUST TRYING TO PROTECT GOTHAM.
YEAH. AND I SAW THIS MASK. HE WAS ALREADY HURT, RUNNING. SCARED.
MASKS ARE ILLEGAL IN GOTHAM, SO I...

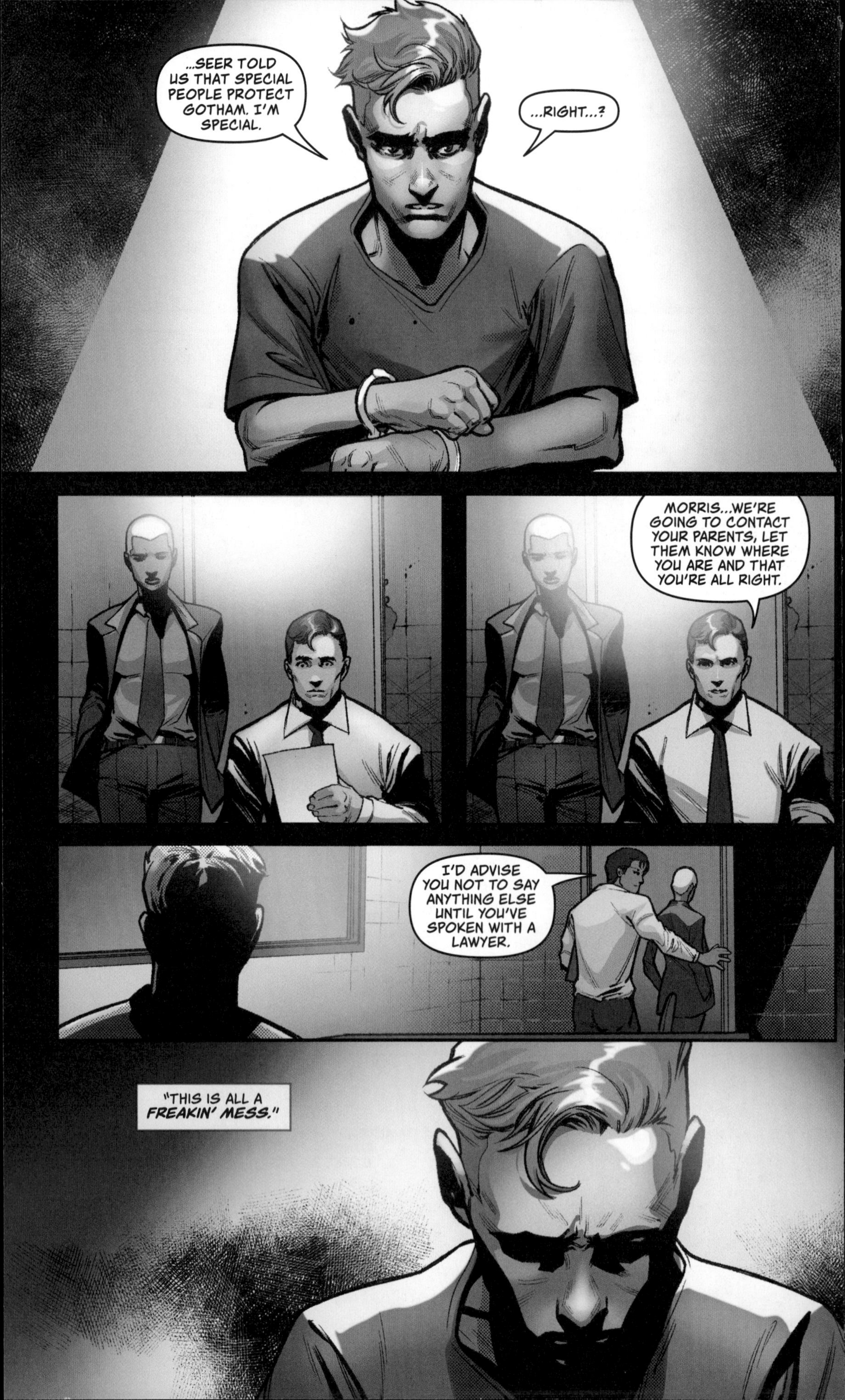

...SEER TOLD US THAT SPECIAL PEOPLE PROTECT GOTHAM. I'M SPECIAL.
...RIGHT...?
MORRIS...WE'RE GOING TO CONTACT YOUR PARENTS, LET THEM KNOW WHERE YOU ARE AND THAT YOU'RE ALL RIGHT.
I'D ADVISE YOU NOT TO SAY ANYTHING ELSE UNTIL YOU'VE SPOKEN WITH A LAWYER.
"THIS IS ALL A *FREAKIN' MESS.*"

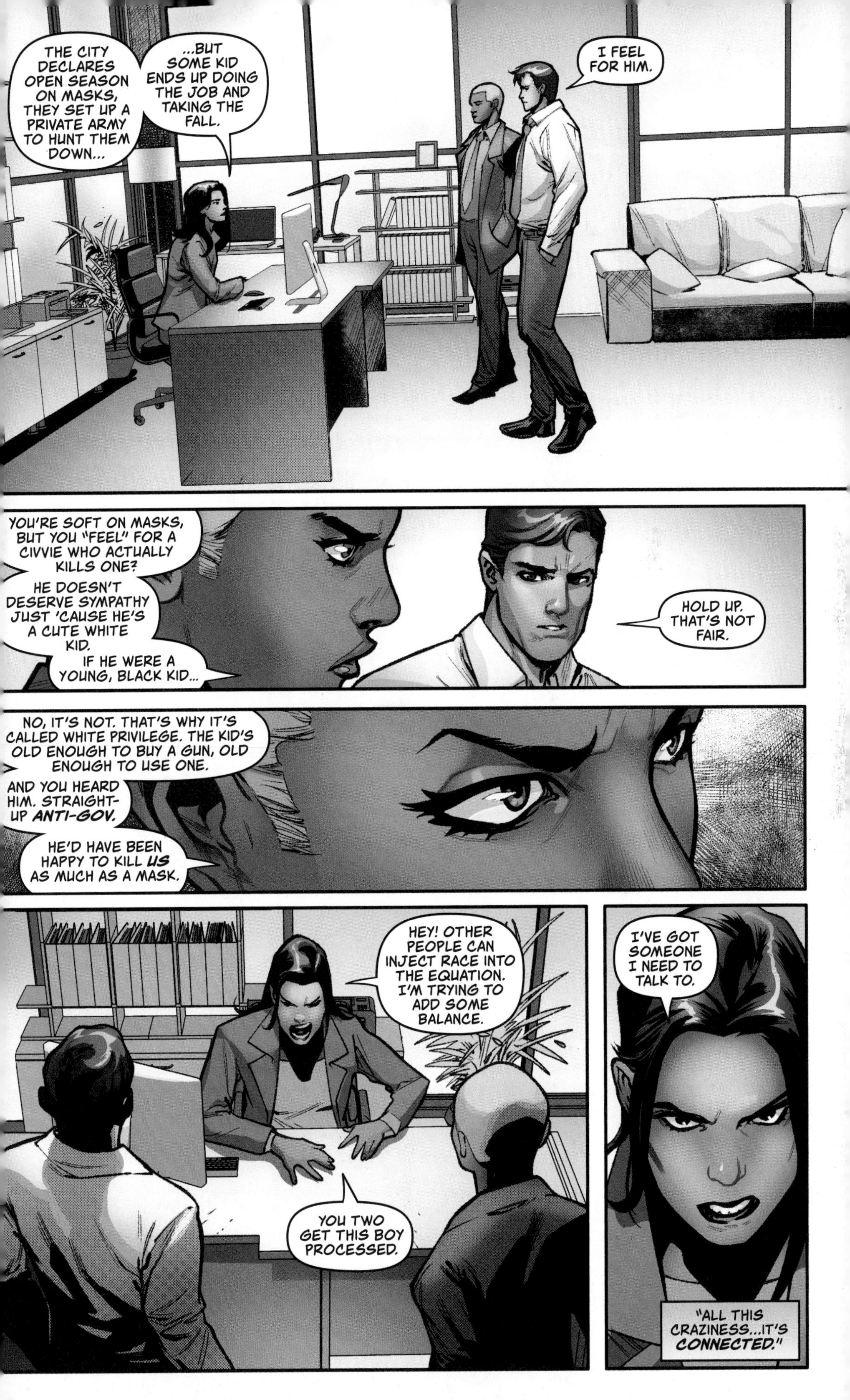

THE CITY DECLARES OPEN SEASON ON MASKS, THEY SET UP A PRIVATE ARMY TO HUNT THEM DOWN...
...BUT SOME KID ENDS UP DOING THE JOB AND TAKING THE FALL.
I FEEL FOR HIM.
YOU'RE SOFT ON MASKS, BUT YOU "FEEL" FOR A CIVVIE WHO ACTUALLY KILLS ONE?
HE DOESN'T DESERVE SYMPATHY JUST 'CAUSE HE'S A CUTE WHITE KID.
IF HE WERE A YOUNG, BLACK KID...
HOLD UP. THAT'S NOT FAIR.
NO, IT'S NOT. THAT'S WHY IT'S CALLED WHITE PRIVILEGE. THE KID'S OLD ENOUGH TO BUY A GUN, OLD ENOUGH TO USE ONE.
AND YOU HEARD HIM. STRAIGHT-UP *ANTI-GOV.*
HE'D HAVE BEEN HAPPY TO KILL *US* AS MUCH AS A MASK.
HEY! OTHER PEOPLE CAN INJECT RACE INTO THE EQUATION. I'M TRYING TO ADD SOME BALANCE.
YOU TWO GET THIS BOY PROCESSED.
I'VE GOT SOMEONE I NEED TO TALK TO.
"ALL THIS CRAZINESS...IT'S *CONNECTED.*"

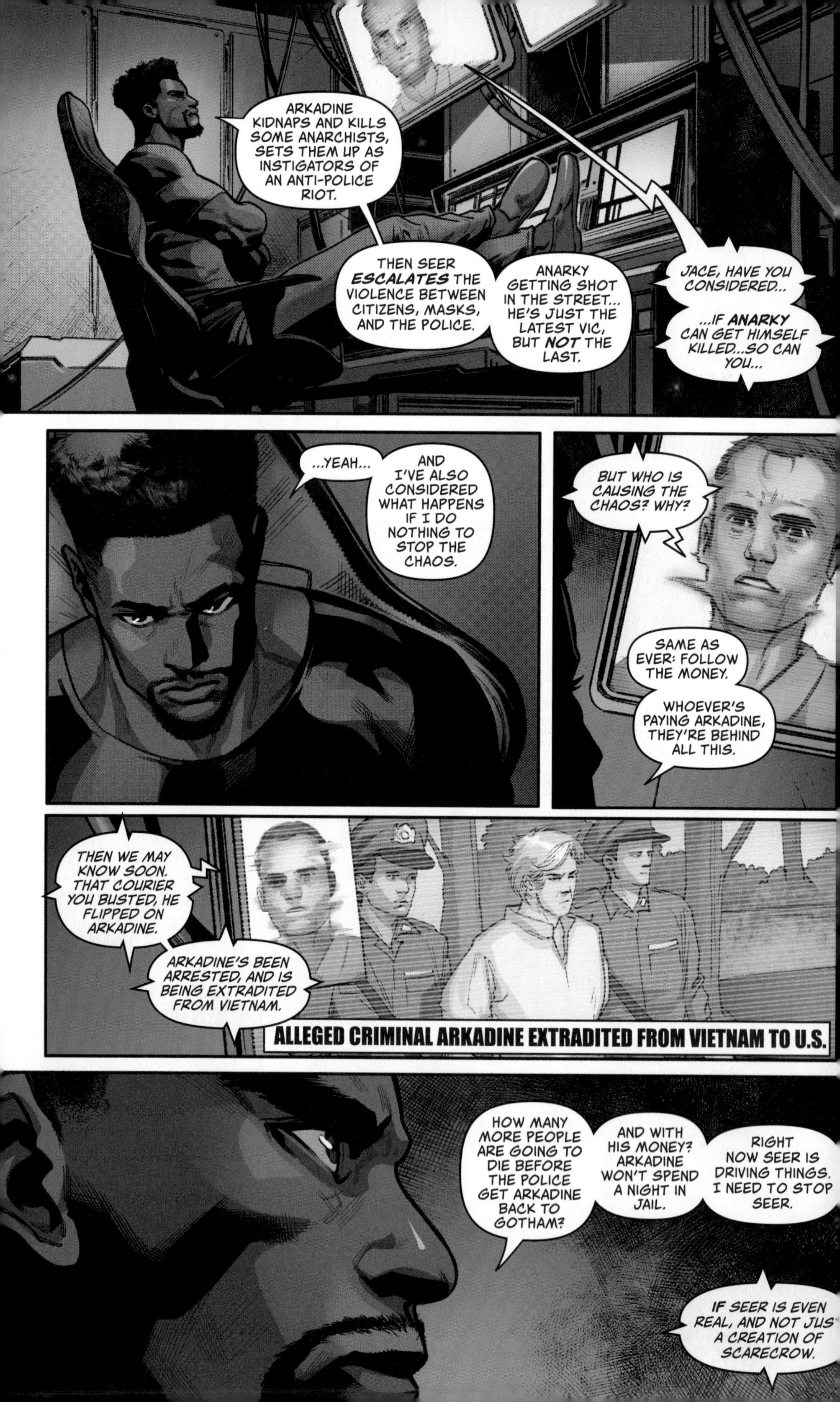
ARKADINE KIDNAPS AND KILLS SOME ANARCHISTS, SETS THEM UP AS INSTIGATORS OF AN ANTI-POLICE RIOT.
THEN SEER ESCALATES THE VIOLENCE BETWEEN CITIZENS, MASKS, AND THE POLICE.
ANARKY GETTING SHOT IN THE STREET... HE'S JUST THE LATEST VIC, BUT NOT THE LAST.
JACE, HAVE YOU CONSIDERED...
...IF ANARKY CAN GET HIMSELF KILLED...SO CAN YOU...
...YEAH...
AND I'VE ALSO CONSIDERED WHAT HAPPENS IF I DO NOTHING TO STOP THE CHAOS.
BUT WHO IS CAUSING THE CHAOS? WHY?
SAME AS EVER: FOLLOW THE MONEY.
WHOEVER'S PAYING ARKADINE, THEY'RE BEHIND ALL THIS.
THEN WE MAY KNOW SOON. THAT COURIER YOU BUSTED, HE FLIPPED ON ARKADINE.
ARKADINE'S BEEN ARRESTED, AND IS BEING EXTRADITED FROM VIETNAM.
ALLEGED CRIMINAL ARKADINE EXTRADITED FROM VIETNAM TO U.S.
HOW MANY MORE PEOPLE ARE GOING TO DIE BEFORE THE POLICE GET ARKADINE BACK TO GOTHAM?
AND WITH HIS MONEY? ARKADINE WON'T SPEND A NIGHT IN JAIL.
RIGHT NOW SEER IS DRIVING THINGS. I NEED TO STOP SEER.
IF SEER IS EVEN REAL, AND NOT JUS A CREATION OF SCARECROW.

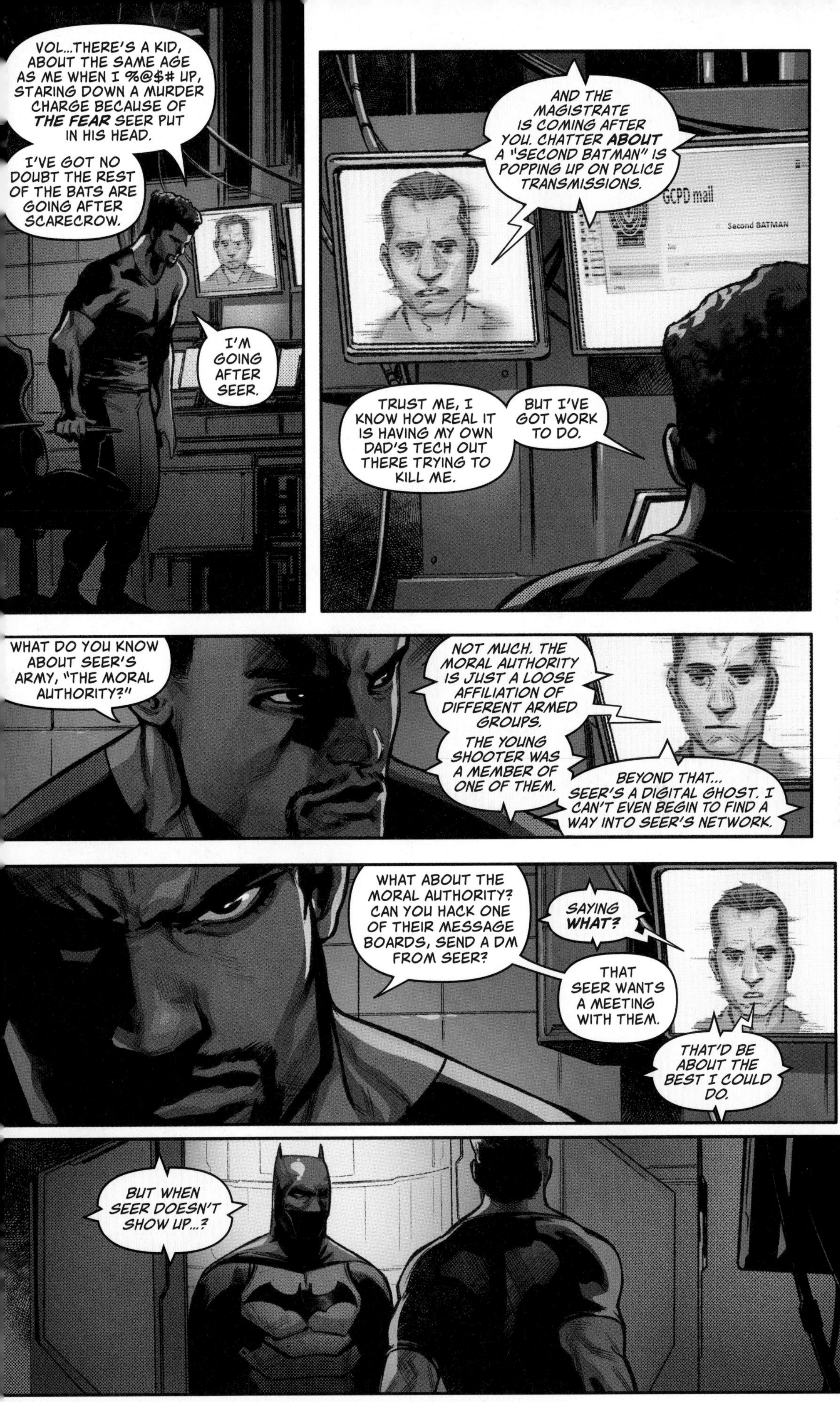
VOL...THERE'S A KID, ABOUT THE SAME AGE AS ME WHEN I %@$# UP, STARING DOWN A MURDER CHARGE BECAUSE OF THE FEAR SEER PUT IN HIS HEAD.
I'VE GOT NO DOUBT THE REST OF THE BATS ARE GOING AFTER SCARECROW.
I'M GOING AFTER SEER.
AND THE MAGISTRATE IS COMING AFTER YOU. CHATTER ABOUT A "SECOND BATMAN" IS POPPING UP ON POLICE TRANSMISSIONS.
GCPD mail
Second BATMAN
TRUST ME, I KNOW HOW REAL IT IS HAVING MY OWN DAD'S TECH OUT THERE TRYING TO KILL ME.
BUT I'VE GOT WORK TO DO.
WHAT DO YOU KNOW ABOUT SEER'S ARMY, "THE MORAL AUTHORITY?"
NOT MUCH. THE MORAL AUTHORITY IS JUST A LOOSE AFFILIATION OF DIFFERENT ARMED GROUPS.
THE YOUNG SHOOTER WAS A MEMBER OF ONE OF THEM.
BEYOND THAT... SEER'S A DIGITAL GHOST. I CAN'T EVEN BEGIN TO FIND A WAY INTO SEER'S NETWORK.
WHAT ABOUT THE MORAL AUTHORITY? CAN YOU HACK ONE OF THEIR MESSAGE BOARDS, SEND A DM FROM SEER?
SAYING WHAT?
THAT SEER WANTS A MEETING WITH THEM.
THAT'D BE ABOUT THE BEST I COULD DO.
BUT WHEN SEER DOESN'T SHOW UP...?

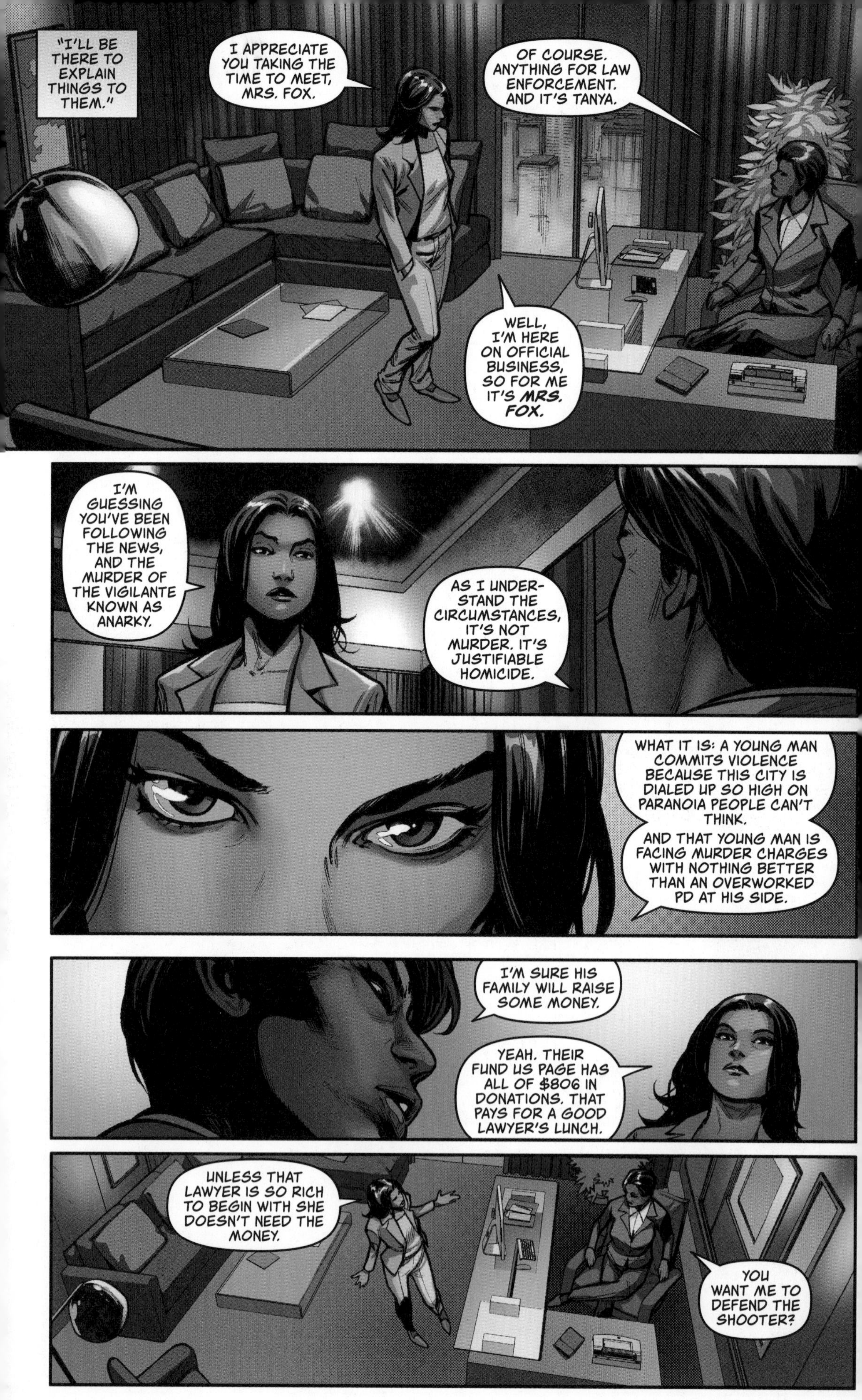
"I'LL BE THERE TO EXPLAIN THINGS TO THEM."
I APPRECIATE YOU TAKING THE TIME TO MEET, MRS. FOX.
OF COURSE. ANYTHING FOR LAW ENFORCEMENT. AND IT'S TANYA.
WELL, I'M HERE ON OFFICIAL BUSINESS, SO FOR ME IT'S ***MRS. FOX.***
I'M GUESSING YOU'VE BEEN FOLLOWING THE NEWS, AND THE MURDER OF THE VIGILANTE KNOWN AS ANARKY.
AS I UNDER-STAND THE CIRCUMSTANCES, IT'S NOT MURDER. IT'S JUSTIFIABLE HOMICIDE.
WHAT IT IS: A YOUNG MAN COMMITS VIOLENCE BECAUSE THIS CITY IS DIALED UP SO HIGH ON PARANOIA PEOPLE CAN'T THINK.
AND THAT YOUNG MAN IS FACING MURDER CHARGES WITH NOTHING BETTER THAN AN OVERWORKED PD AT HIS SIDE.
I'M SURE HIS FAMILY WILL RAISE SOME MONEY.
YEAH. THEIR FUND US PAGE HAS ALL OF $806 IN DONATIONS. THAT PAYS FOR A GOOD LAWYER'S LUNCH.
UNLESS THAT LAWYER IS SO RICH TO BEGIN WITH SHE DOESN'T NEED THE MONEY.
YOU WANT ME TO DEFEND THE SHOOTER?

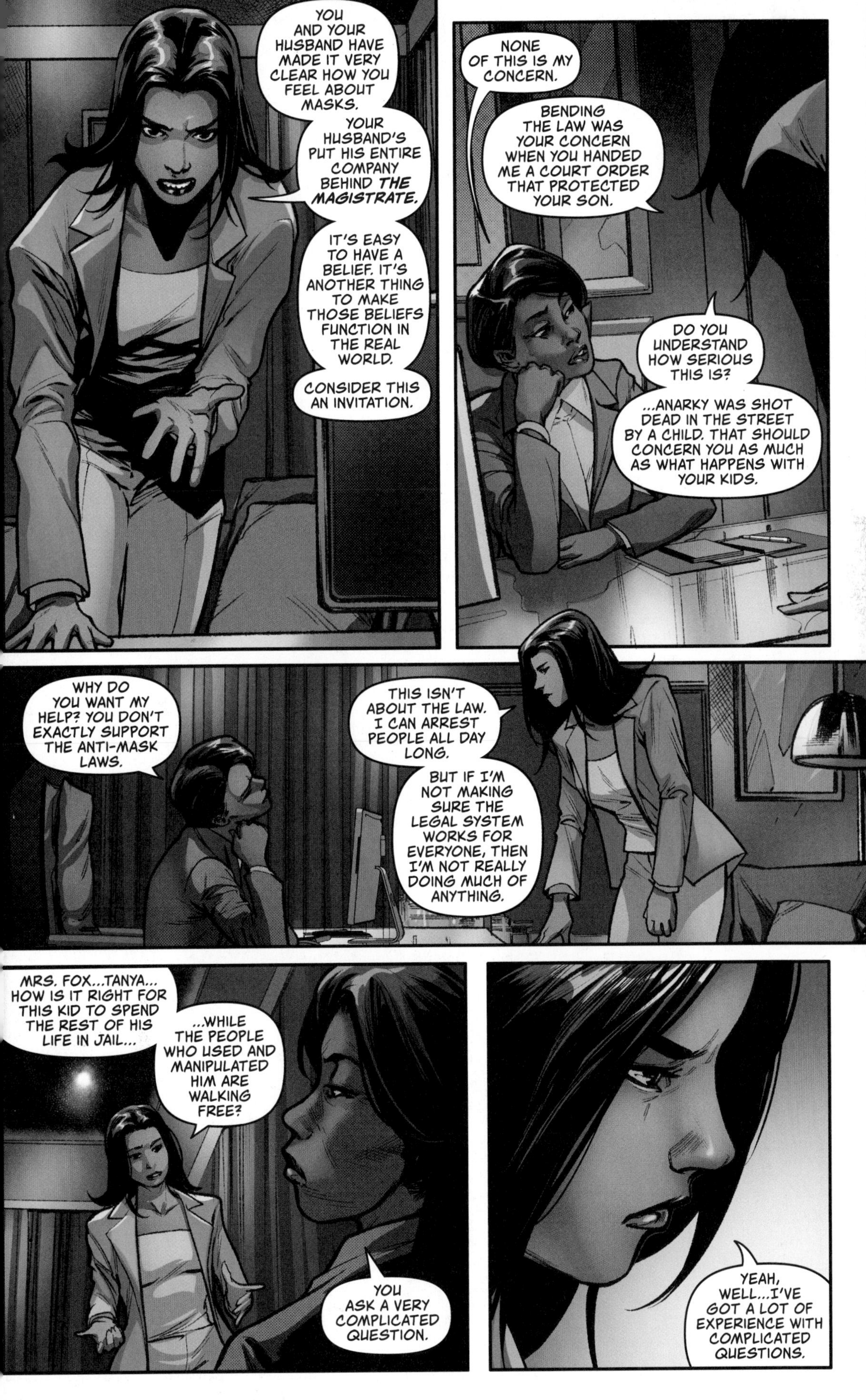

YOU AND YOUR HUSBAND HAVE MADE IT VERY CLEAR HOW YOU FEEL ABOUT MASKS.
YOUR HUSBAND'S PUT HIS ENTIRE COMPANY BEHIND *THE MAGISTRATE.*
IT'S EASY TO HAVE A BELIEF. IT'S ANOTHER THING TO MAKE THOSE BELIEFS FUNCTION IN THE REAL WORLD.
CONSIDER THIS AN INVITATION.
NONE OF THIS IS MY CONCERN.
BENDING THE LAW WAS YOUR CONCERN WHEN YOU HANDED ME A COURT ORDER THAT PROTECTED YOUR SON.
DO YOU UNDERSTAND HOW SERIOUS THIS IS?
...ANARKY WAS SHOT DEAD IN THE STREET BY A CHILD. THAT SHOULD CONCERN YOU AS MUCH AS WHAT HAPPENS WITH YOUR KIDS.
WHY DO YOU WANT MY HELP? YOU DON'T EXACTLY SUPPORT THE ANTI-MASK LAWS.
THIS ISN'T ABOUT THE LAW. I CAN ARREST PEOPLE ALL DAY LONG.
BUT IF I'M NOT MAKING SURE THE LEGAL SYSTEM WORKS FOR EVERYONE, THEN I'M NOT REALLY DOING MUCH OF ANYTHING.
MRS. FOX...TANYA... HOW IS IT RIGHT FOR THIS KID TO SPEND THE REST OF HIS LIFE IN JAIL...
...WHILE THE PEOPLE WHO USED AND MANIPULATED HIM ARE WALKING FREE?
YOU ASK A VERY COMPLICATED QUESTION.
YEAH, WELL...I'VE GOT A LOT OF EXPERIENCE WITH COMPLICATED QUESTIONS.

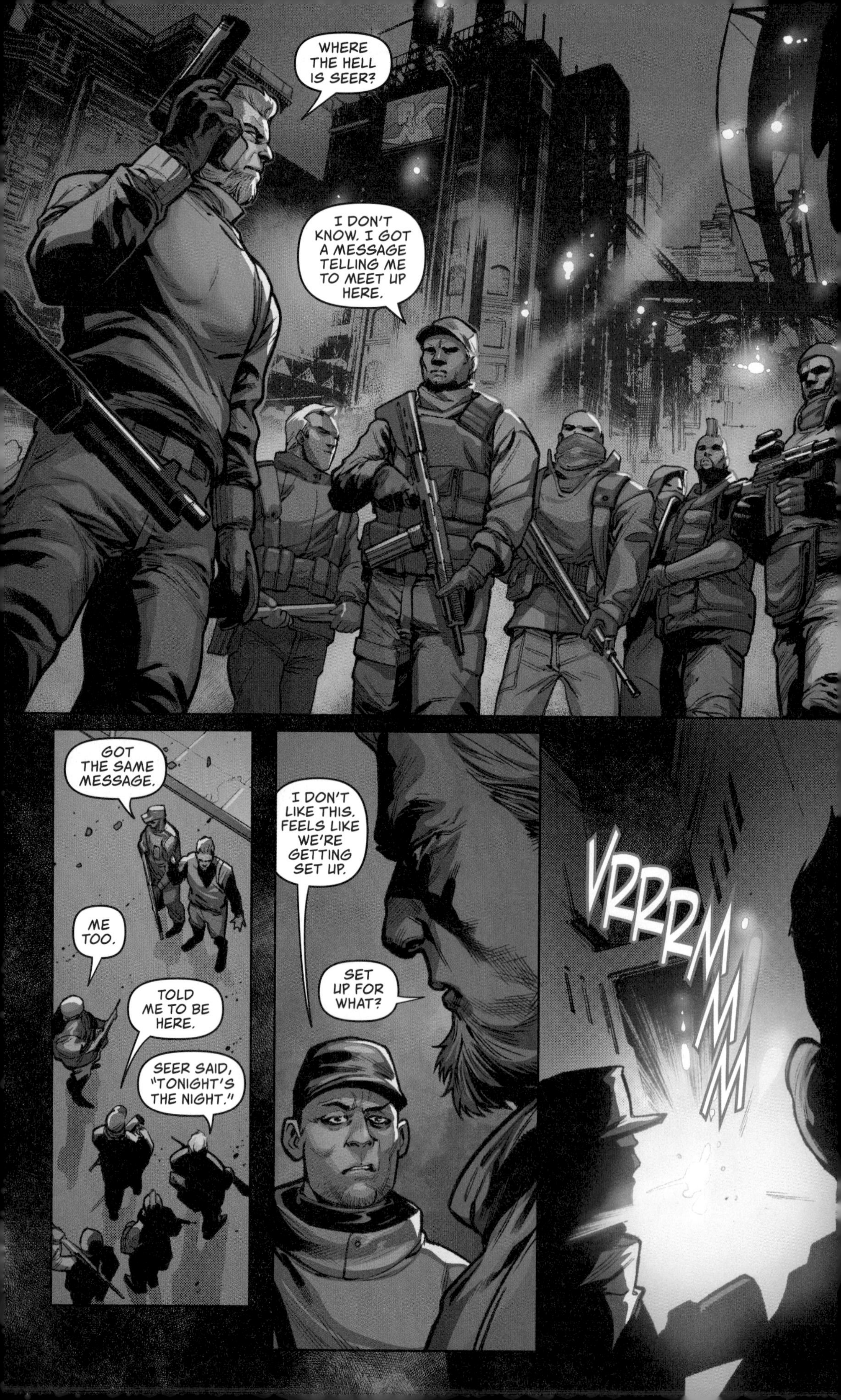
WHERE THE HELL IS SEER?
I DON'T KNOW. I GOT A MESSAGE TELLING ME TO MEET UP HERE.
GOT THE SAME MESSAGE.
ME TOO.
TOLD ME TO BE HERE.
SEER SAID, "TONIGHT'S THE NIGHT."
I DON'T LIKE THIS. FEELS LIKE WE'RE GETTING SET UP.
SET UP FOR WHAT?
VRRRMMMM

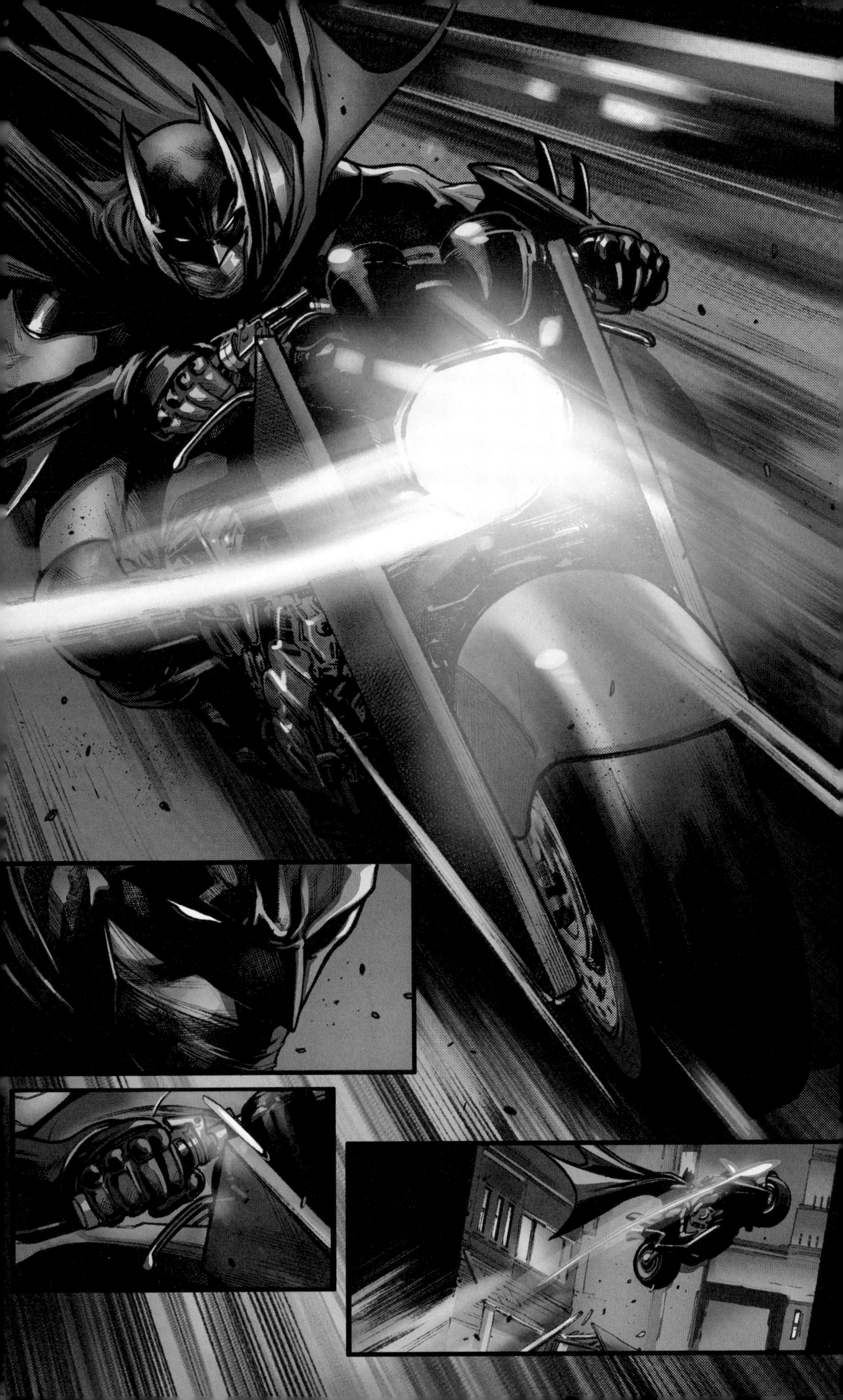

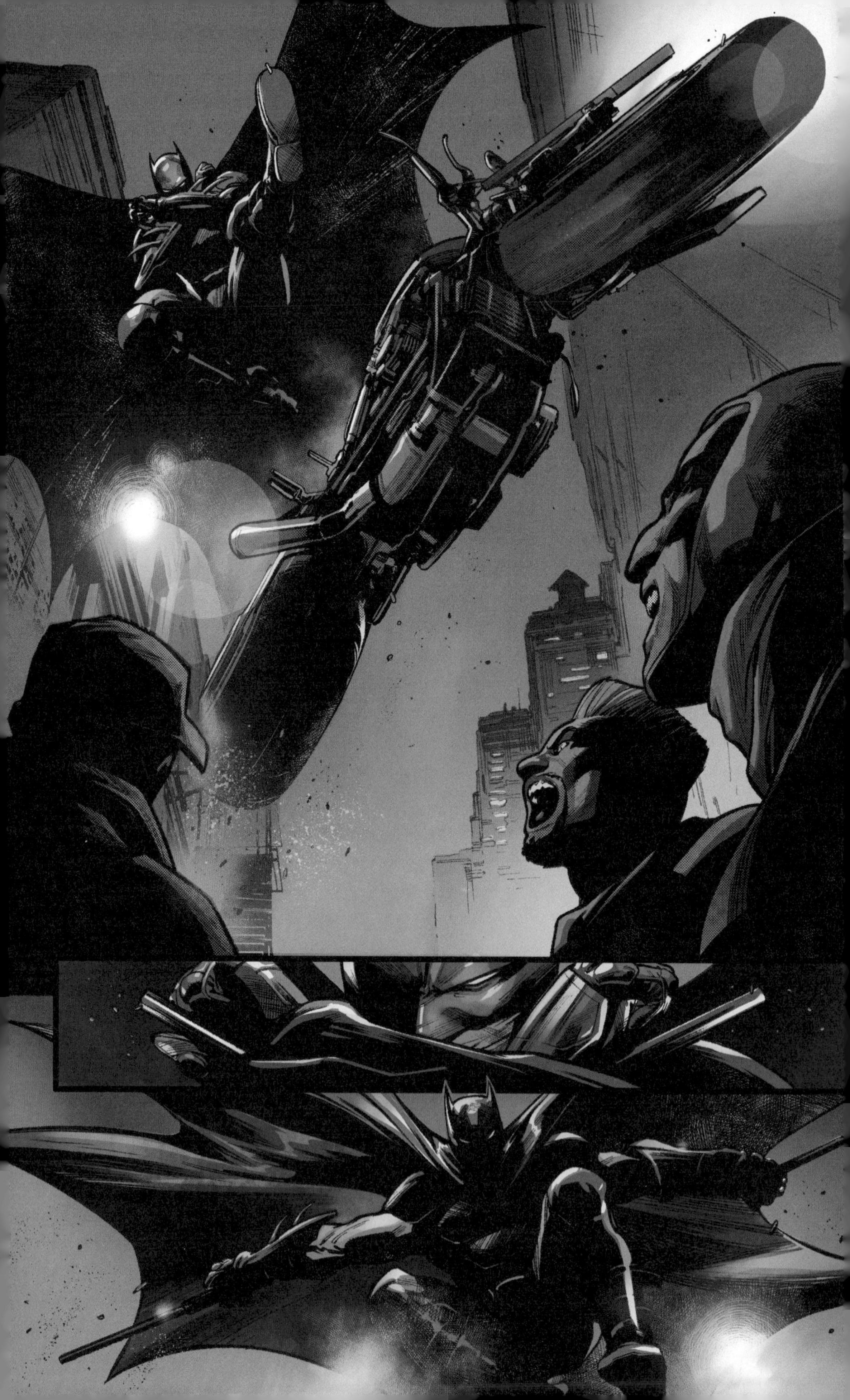

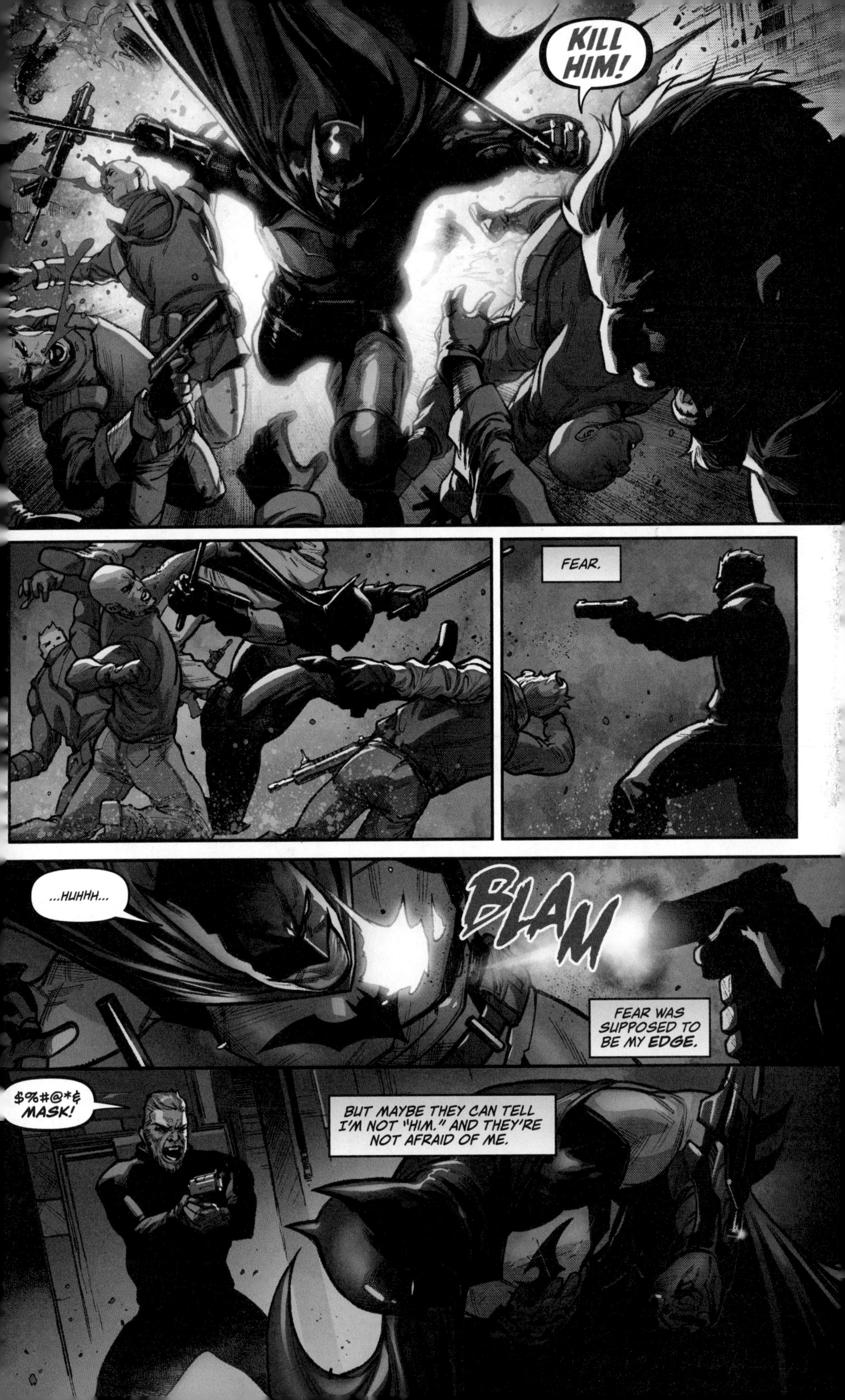
KILL HIM!
FEAR.
...HUHHH...
BLAM
FEAR WAS SUPPOSED TO BE MY EDGE.
$%#@*& MASK!
BUT MAYBE THEY CAN TELL I'M NOT "HIM." AND THEY'RE NOT AFRAID OF ME.

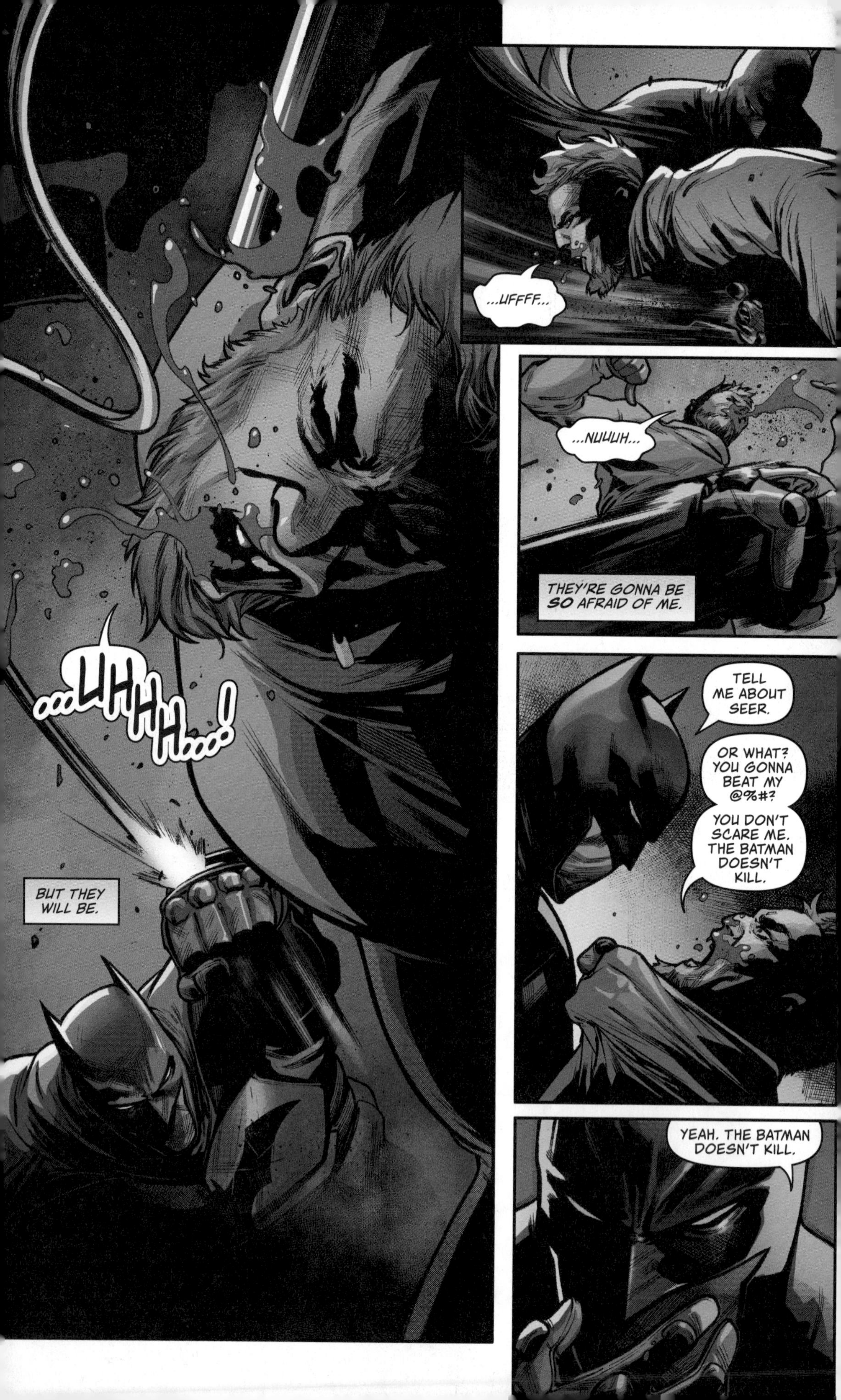
...UHHHHHooo!
BUT THEY WILL BE.
...UFFFF...
...NUUUH...
THEY'RE GONNA BE **SO** AFRAID OF ME.
TELL ME ABOUT SEER.
OR WHAT? YOU GONNA BEAT MY @%#?
YOU DON'T SCARE ME. THE BATMAN DOESN'T KILL.
YEAH. THE BATMAN DOESN'T KILL.

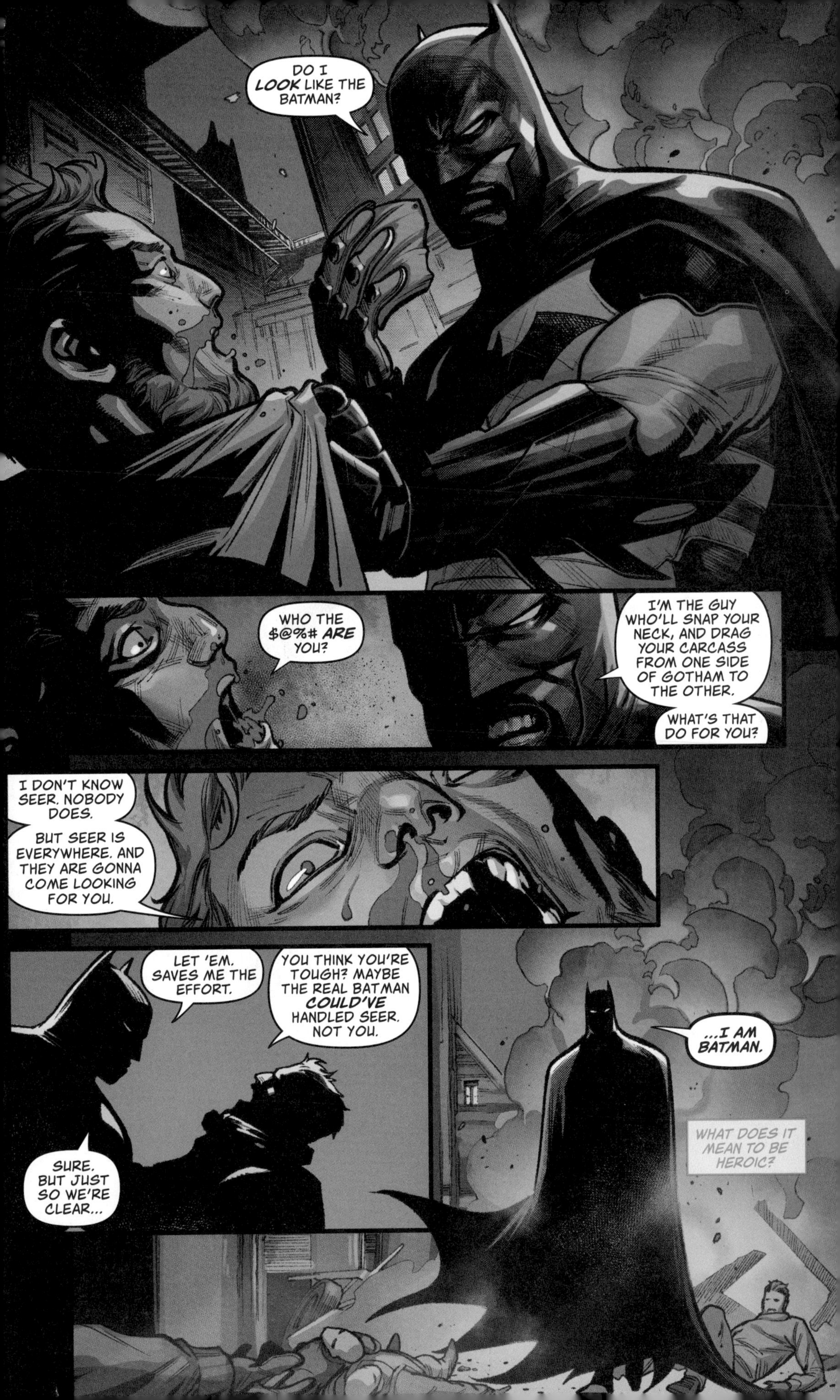

DO I LOOK LIKE THE BATMAN?
WHO THE $@%# ARE YOU?
I'M THE GUY WHO'LL SNAP YOUR NECK, AND DRAG YOUR CARCASS FROM ONE SIDE OF GOTHAM TO THE OTHER.
WHAT'S THAT DO FOR YOU?
I DON'T KNOW SEER. NOBODY DOES.
BUT SEER IS EVERYWHERE. AND THEY ARE GONNA COME LOOKING FOR YOU.
LET 'EM. SAVES ME THE EFFORT.
YOU THINK YOU'RE TOUGH? MAYBE THE REAL BATMAN COULD'VE HANDLED SEER. NOT YOU.
SURE. BUT JUST SO WE'RE CLEAR...
...I AM BATMAN.
WHAT DOES IT MEAN TO BE HEROIC?

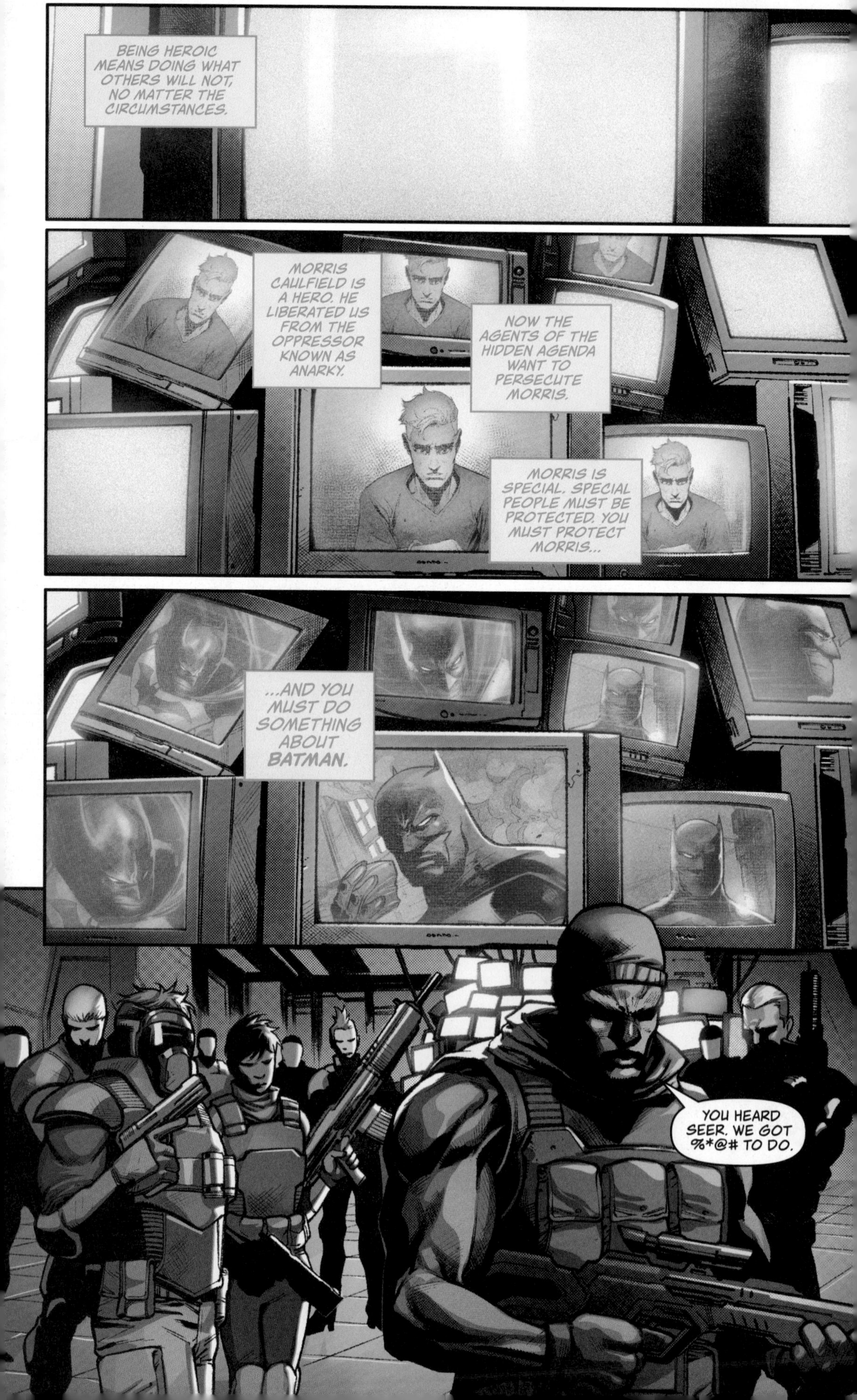
BEING HEROIC MEANS DOING WHAT OTHERS WILL NOT, NO MATTER THE CIRCUMSTANCES.
MORRIS CAULFIELD IS A HERO. HE LIBERATED US FROM THE OPPRESSOR KNOWN AS ANARKY.
NOW THE AGENTS OF THE HIDDEN AGENDA WANT TO PERSECUTE MORRIS.
MORRIS IS SPECIAL. SPECIAL PEOPLE MUST BE PROTECTED. YOU MUST PROTECT MORRIS...
...AND YOU MUST DO SOMETHING ABOUT BATMAN.
YOU HEARD SEER. WE GOT %*@# TO DO.

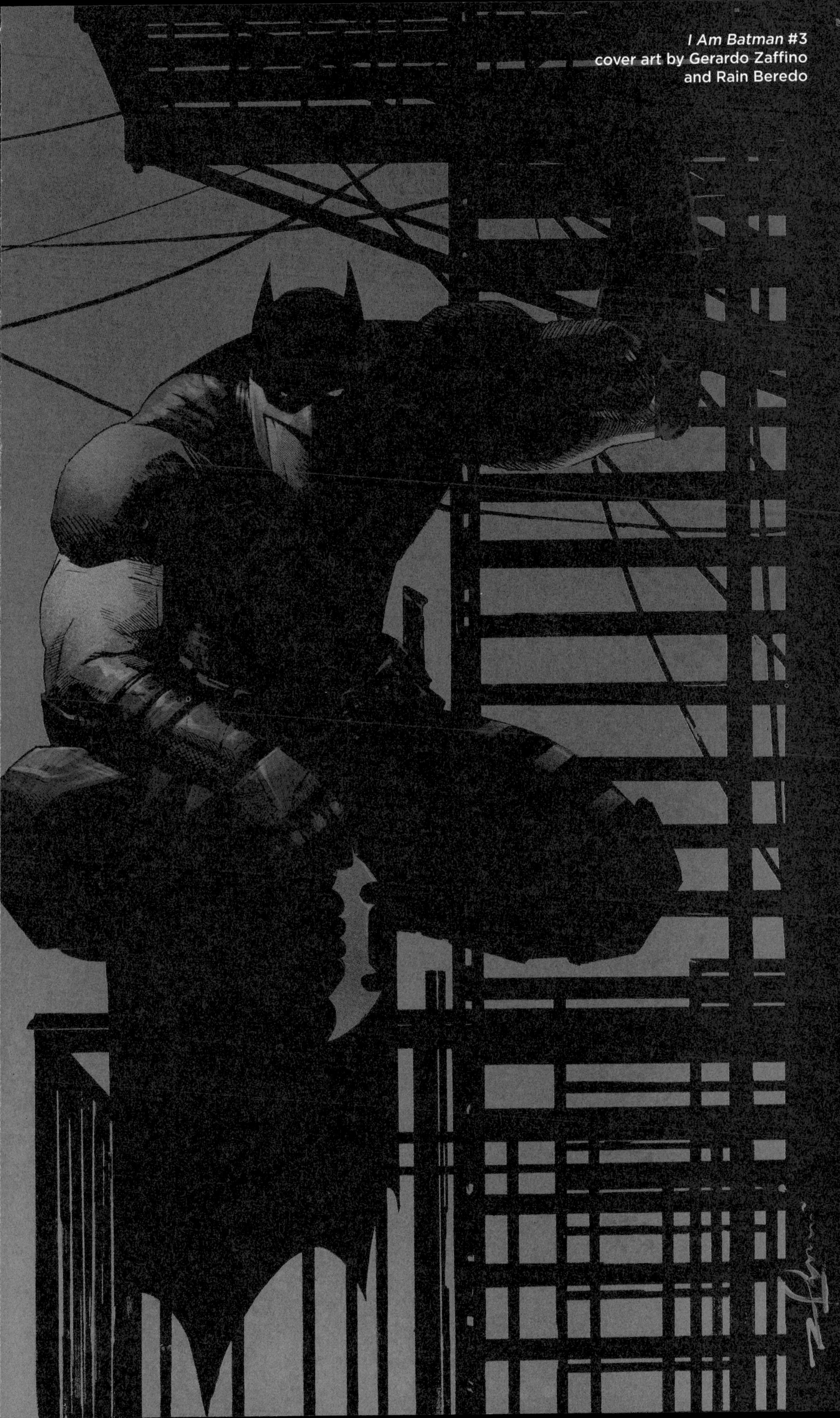

I Am Batman #3
cover art by Gerardo Zaffino
and Rain Beredo

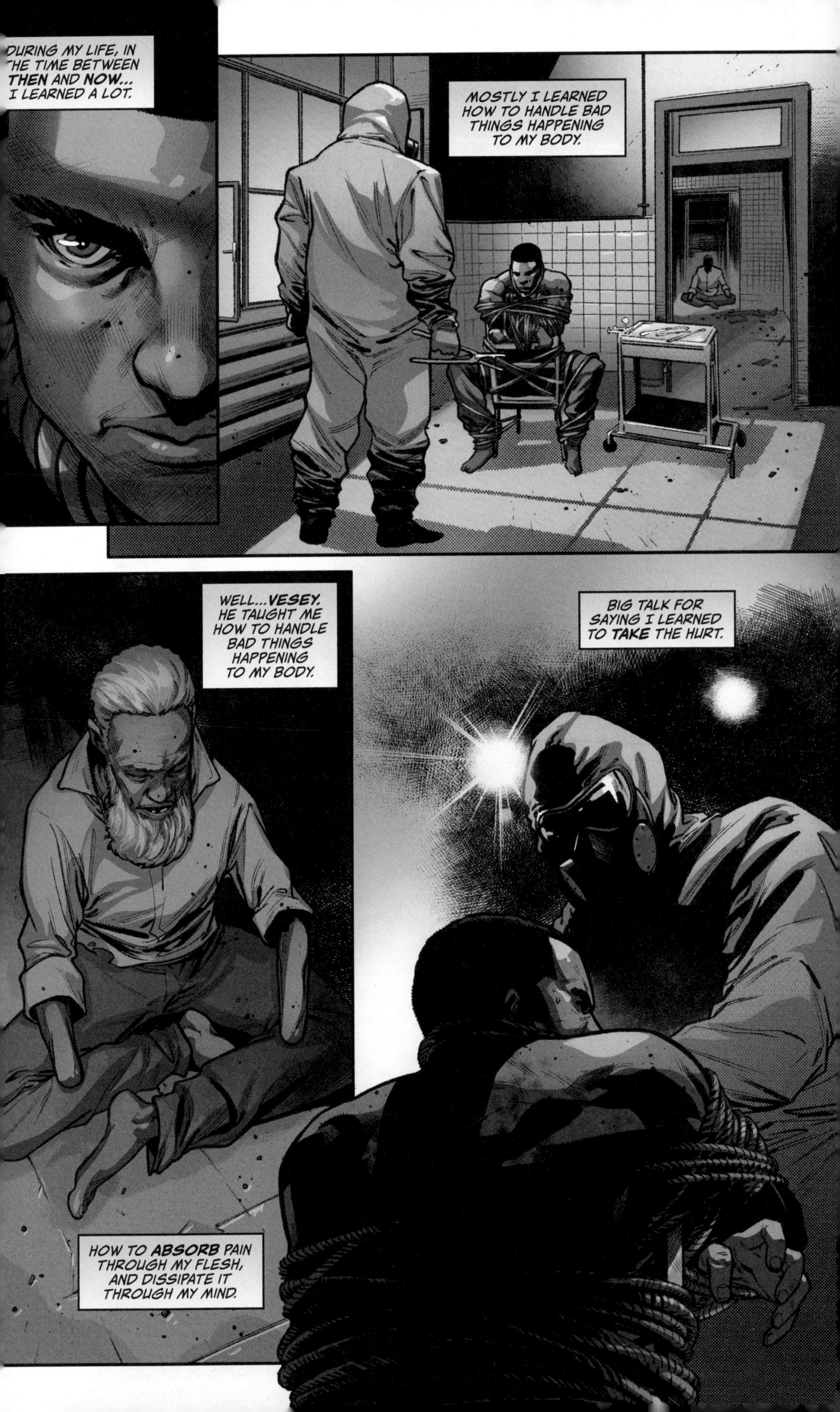
DURING MY LIFE, IN THE TIME BETWEEN THEN AND NOW... I LEARNED A LOT.
MOSTLY I LEARNED HOW TO HANDLE BAD THINGS HAPPENING TO MY BODY.
WELL...VESEY. HE TAUGHT ME HOW TO HANDLE BAD THINGS HAPPENING TO MY BODY.
HOW TO ABSORB PAIN THROUGH MY FLESH, AND DISSIPATE IT THROUGH MY MIND.
BIG TALK FOR SAYING I LEARNED TO TAKE THE HURT.

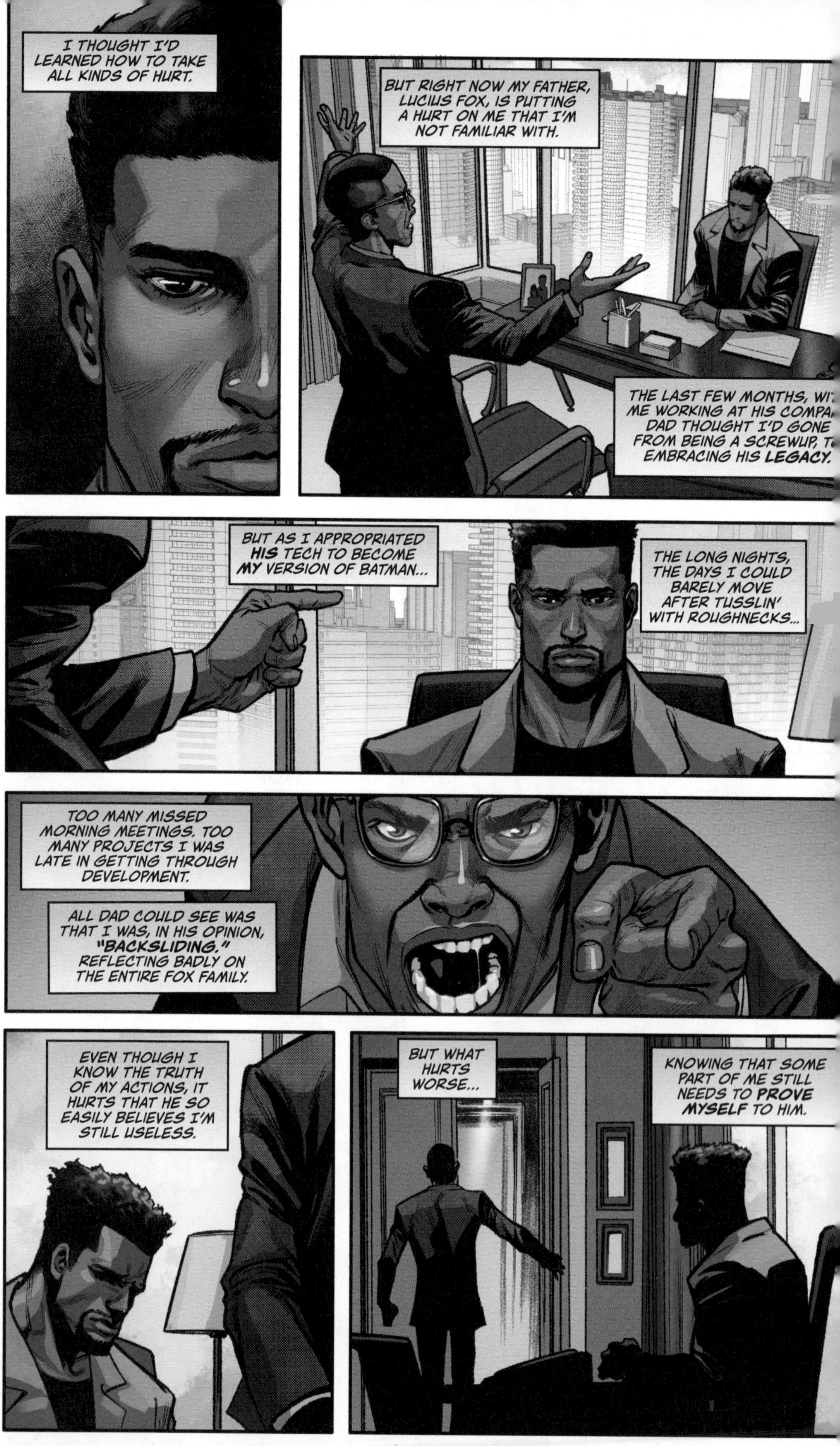

I THOUGHT I'D LEARNED HOW TO TAKE ALL KINDS OF HURT.
BUT RIGHT NOW MY FATHER, LUCIUS FOX, IS PUTTING A HURT ON ME THAT I'M NOT FAMILIAR WITH.
THE LAST FEW MONTHS, WI
ME WORKING AT HIS COMPA
DAD THOUGHT I'D GONE
FROM BEING A SCREWUP, T
EMBRACING HIS LEGACY.
BUT AS I APPROPRIATED HIS TECH TO BECOME MY VERSION OF BATMAN...
THE LONG NIGHTS, THE DAYS I COULD BARELY MOVE AFTER TUSSLIN' WITH ROUGHNECKS...
TOO MANY MISSED MORNING MEETINGS. TOO MANY PROJECTS I WAS LATE IN GETTING THROUGH DEVELOPMENT.
ALL DAD COULD SEE WAS THAT I WAS, IN HIS OPINION, "BACKSLIDING." REFLECTING BADLY ON THE ENTIRE FOX FAMILY.
EVEN THOUGH I KNOW THE TRUTH OF MY ACTIONS, IT HURTS THAT HE SO EASILY BELIEVES I'M STILL USELESS.
BUT WHAT HURTS WORSE...
KNOWING THAT SOME PART OF ME STILL NEEDS TO PROVE MYSELF TO HIM.

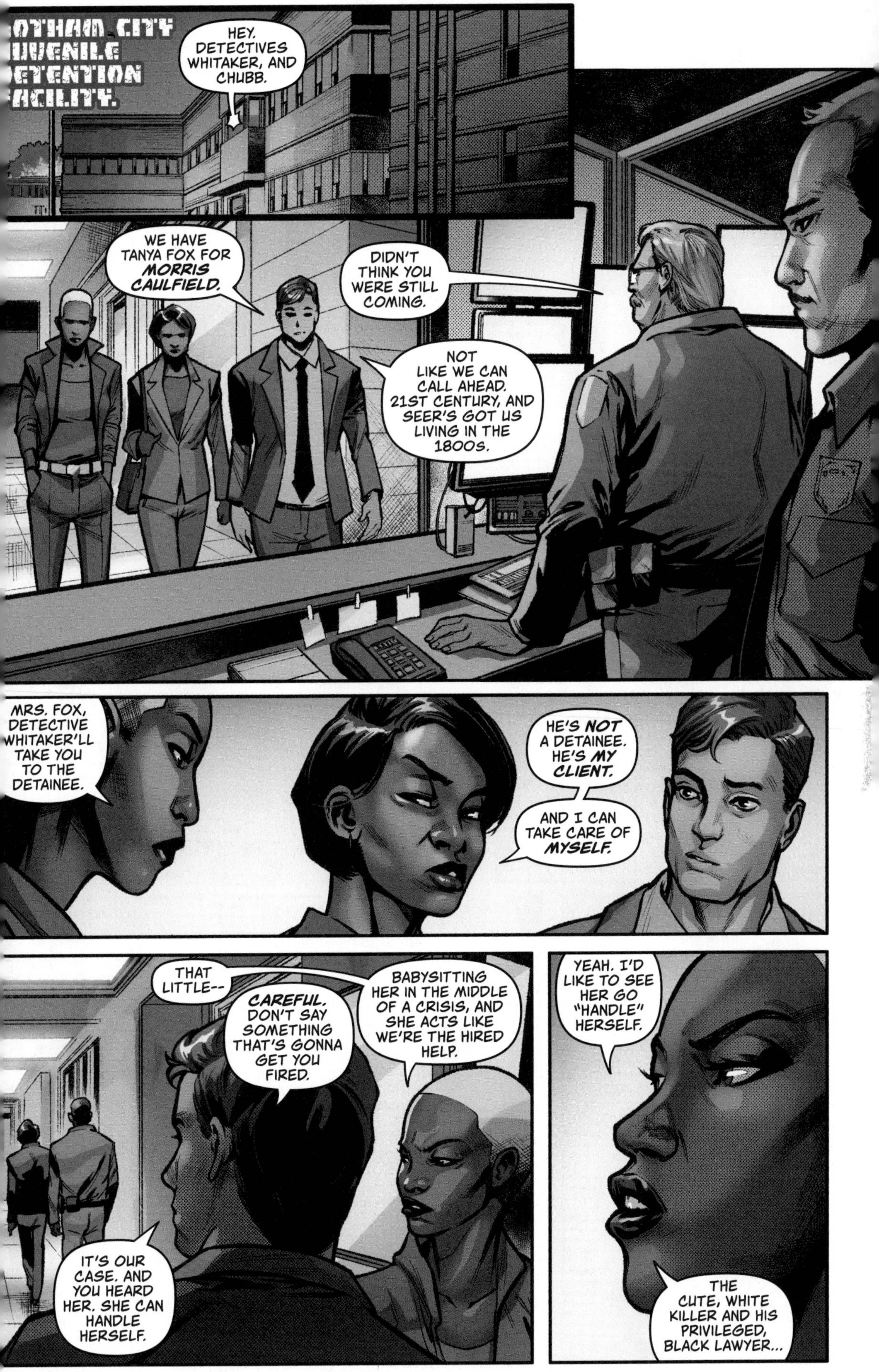

OTHAM CITY
UVENILE
ETENTION
ACILITY.
HEY. DETECTIVES WHITAKER, AND CHUBB.
WE HAVE TANYA FOX FOR MORRIS CAULFIELD.
DIDN'T THINK YOU WERE STILL COMING.
NOT LIKE WE CAN CALL AHEAD. 21ST CENTURY, AND SEER'S GOT US LIVING IN THE 1800S.
MRS. FOX, DETECTIVE WHITAKER'LL TAKE YOU TO THE DETAINEE.
HE'S NOT A DETAINEE. HE'S MY CLIENT.
AND I CAN TAKE CARE OF MYSELF.
THAT LITTLE--
BABYSITTING HER IN THE MIDDLE OF A CRISIS, AND SHE ACTS LIKE WE'RE THE HIRED HELP.
CAREFUL. DON'T SAY SOMETHING THAT'S GONNA GET YOU FIRED.
IT'S OUR CASE. AND YOU HEARD HER. SHE CAN HANDLE HERSELF.
YEAH. I'D LIKE TO SEE HER GO "HANDLE" HERSELF.
THE CUTE, WHITE KILLER AND HIS PRIVILEGED, BLACK LAWYER...

"THEY DESERVE EACH OTHER."

MORRIS...? MY NAME IS *TANYA FOX.* I'M YOUR NEW LAWYER.

MY FAMILY CAN'T AFFORD A LAWYER.

WHAT I'M DOING...IT'S CALLED PRO BONO PUBLICO. I'M WORKING FOR *FREE.*

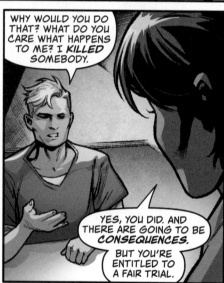

WHY WOULD YOU DO THAT? WHAT DO YOU CARE WHAT HAPPENS TO ME? I *KILLED* SOMEBODY.

YES, YOU DID. AND THERE ARE GOING TO BE *CONSEQUENCES.*

BUT YOU'RE ENTITLED TO A FAIR TRIAL.

AND AS TO WHAT HAPPENED...

YOU'RE A YOUNG MAN, MORRIS. A *VERY* YOUNG MAN. IF YOU WERE COERCED INTO KILLING *ANARKY*--

YOU THINK I'M STUPID? YOU THINK PEOPLE USED ME?

THE MASKS, THE MAGISTRATE... THEY'RE EVIL.

SEER SAID I'M SPECIAL. SPECIAL PEOPLE HAVE TO PROTECT THE REST OF YOU FROM THE HIDDEN AGENDA.

I AGREE THAT THE MASKS AND THE MAGISTRATE ARE BOTH EXTREME. BUT JUST BECAUSE SOMEONE TELLS YOU YOU'RE SPECIAL...

THAT DOESN'T GIVE YOU LICENSE TO MEET VIOLENCE WITH VIOLENCE.

HOW DO *YOU* KNOW? HAVE YOU EVER HAD TO?

I...

WHAT THE HELL...

BOOM

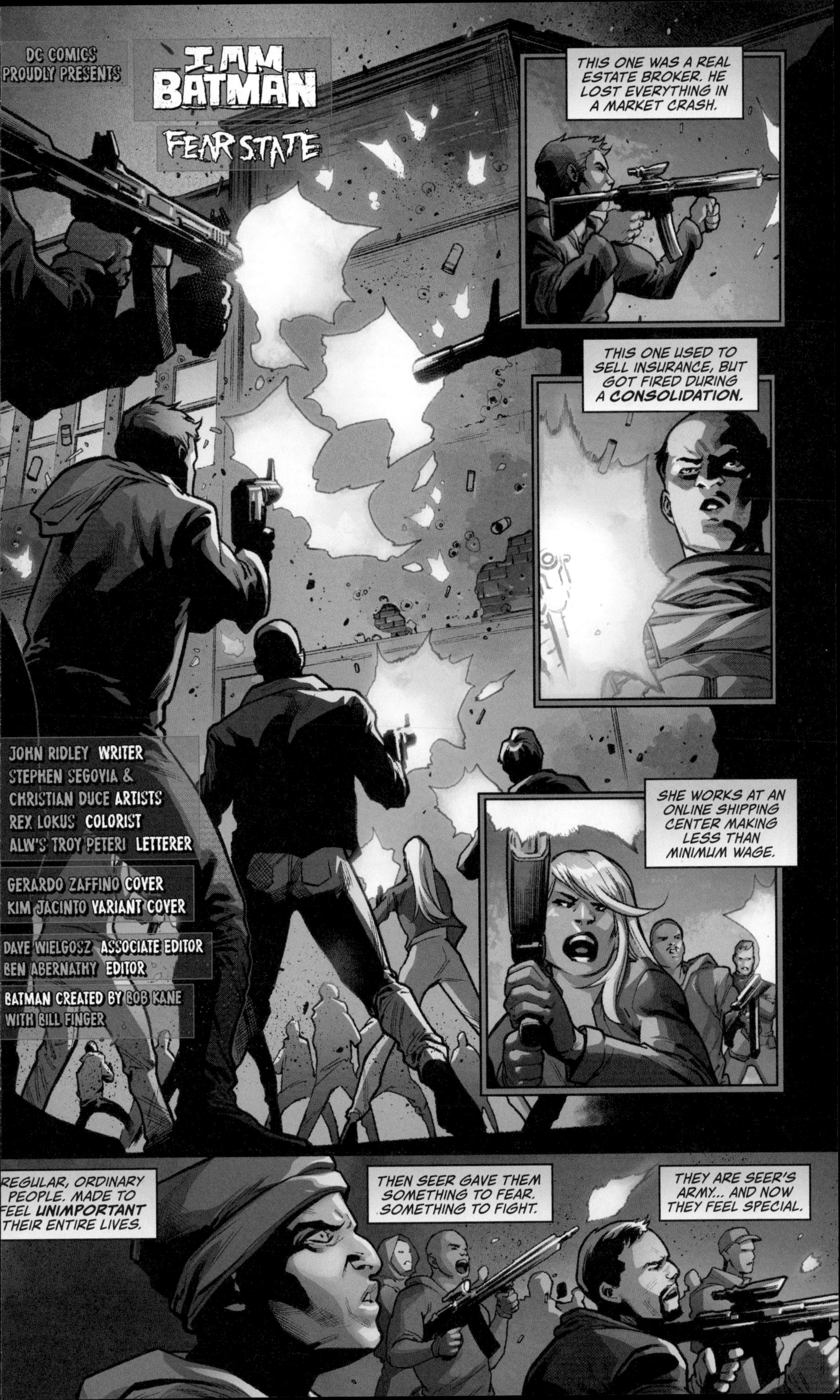
DC COMICS PROUDLY PRESENTS
I AM BATMAN
FEAR STATE
THIS ONE WAS A REAL ESTATE BROKER. HE LOST EVERYTHING IN A MARKET CRASH.
THIS ONE USED TO SELL INSURANCE, BUT GOT FIRED DURING A **CONSOLIDATION.**
SHE WORKS AT AN ONLINE SHIPPING CENTER MAKING LESS THAN MINIMUM WAGE.
JOHN RIDLEY WRITER
STEPHEN SEGOVIA & CHRISTIAN DUCE ARTISTS
REX LOKUS COLORIST
ALW'S TROY PETERI LETTERER
GERARDO ZAFFINO COVER
KIM JACINTO VARIANT COVER
DAVE WIELGOSZ ASSOCIATE EDITOR
BEN ABERNATHY EDITOR
BATMAN CREATED BY BOB KANE WITH BILL FINGER
REGULAR, ORDINARY PEOPLE. MADE TO FEEL **UNIMPORTANT** THEIR ENTIRE LIVES.
THEN SEER GAVE THEM SOMETHING TO FEAR. SOMETHING TO FIGHT.
THEY ARE SEER'S ARMY... AND NOW THEY FEEL SPECIAL.

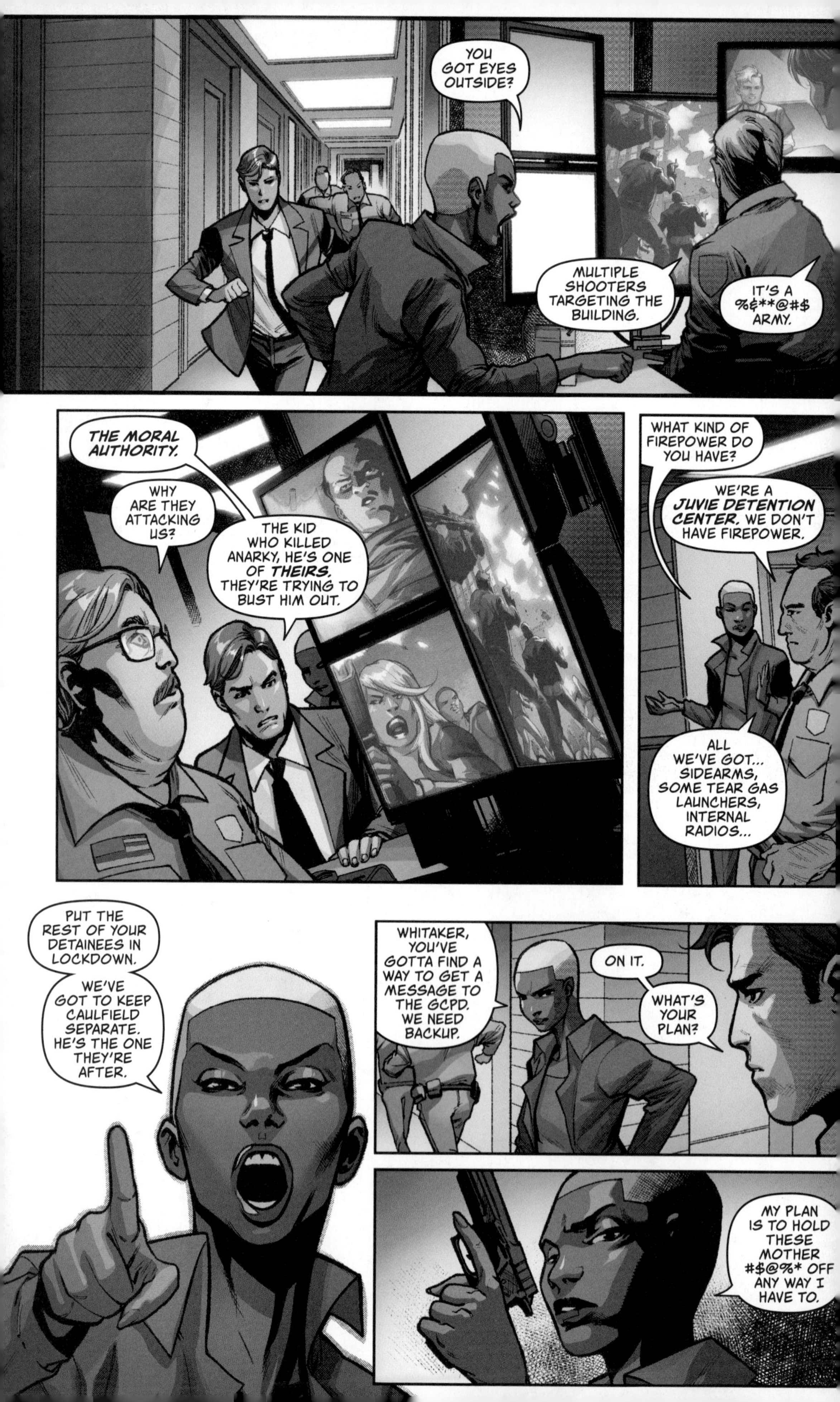
YOU GOT EYES OUTSIDE?
MULTIPLE SHOOTERS TARGETING THE BUILDING.
IT'S A %$**@#$ ARMY.
THE MORAL AUTHORITY.
WHY ARE THEY ATTACKING US?
THE KID WHO KILLED ANARKY, HE'S ONE OF THEIRS. THEY'RE TRYING TO BUST HIM OUT.
WHAT KIND OF FIREPOWER DO YOU HAVE?
WE'RE A JUVIE DETENTION CENTER. WE DON'T HAVE FIREPOWER.
ALL WE'VE GOT... SIDEARMS, SOME TEAR GAS LAUNCHERS, INTERNAL RADIOS...
PUT THE REST OF YOUR DETAINEES IN LOCKDOWN.
WE'VE GOT TO KEEP CAULFIELD SEPARATE. HE'S THE ONE THEY'RE AFTER.
WHITAKER, YOU'VE GOTTA FIND A WAY TO GET A MESSAGE TO THE GCPD. WE NEED BACKUP.
ON IT.
WHAT'S YOUR PLAN?
MY PLAN IS TO HOLD THESE MOTHER #$@%* OFF ANY WAY I HAVE TO.

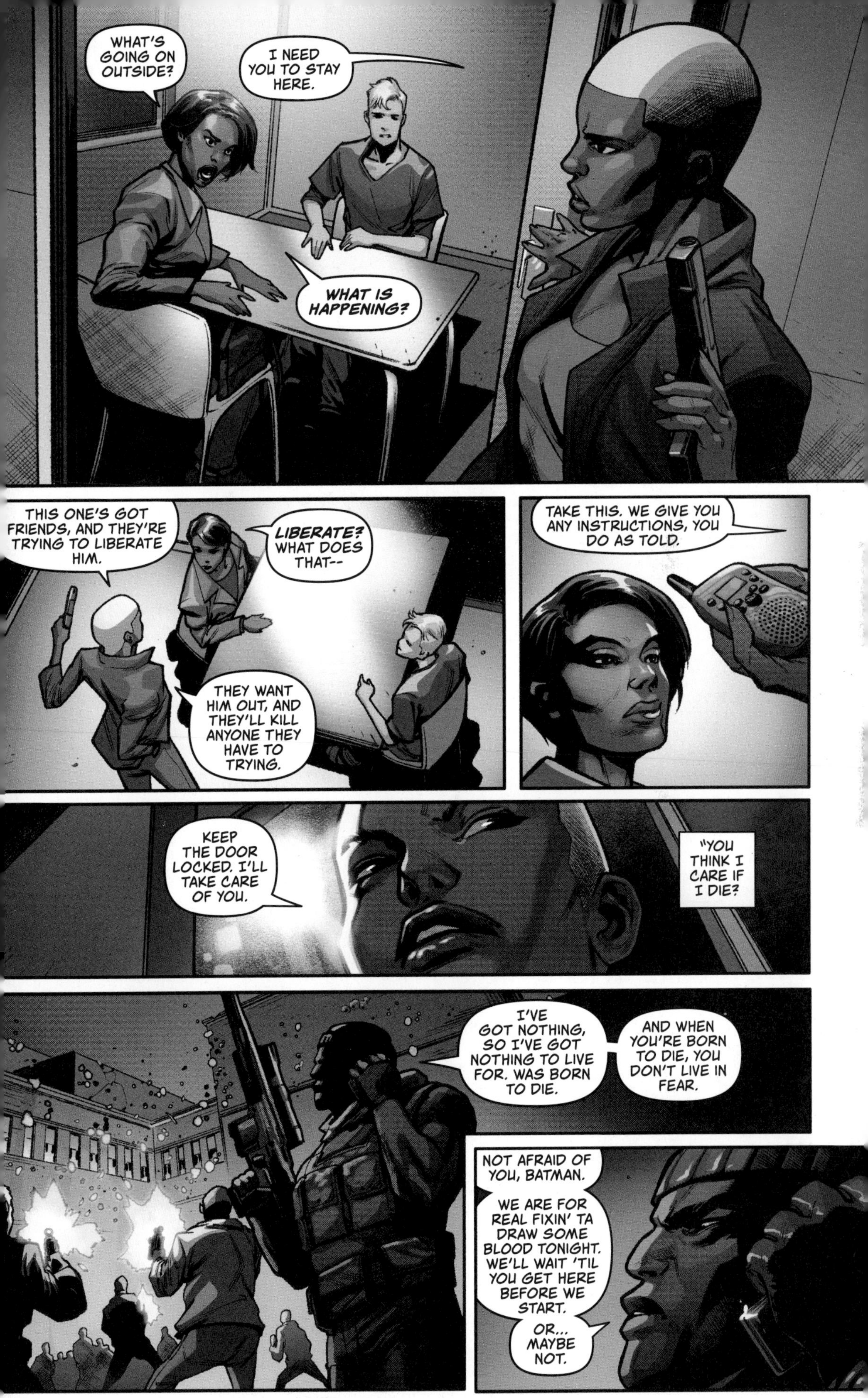
WHAT'S GOING ON OUTSIDE?
I NEED YOU TO STAY HERE.
WHAT IS HAPPENING?
THIS ONE'S GOT FRIENDS, AND THEY'RE TRYING TO LIBERATE HIM.
LIBERATE? WHAT DOES THAT--
THEY WANT HIM OUT, AND THEY'LL KILL ANYONE THEY HAVE TO TRYING.
TAKE THIS. WE GIVE YOU ANY INSTRUCTIONS, YOU DO AS TOLD.
KEEP THE DOOR LOCKED. I'LL TAKE CARE OF YOU.
"YOU THINK I CARE IF I DIE?
I'VE GOT NOTHING, SO I'VE GOT NOTHING TO LIVE FOR. WAS BORN TO DIE.
AND WHEN YOU'RE BORN TO DIE, YOU DON'T LIVE IN FEAR.
NOT AFRAID OF YOU, BATMAN.
WE ARE FOR REAL FIXIN' TA DRAW SOME BLOOD TONIGHT. WE'LL WAIT 'TIL YOU GET HERE BEFORE WE START.
OR... MAYBE NOT.

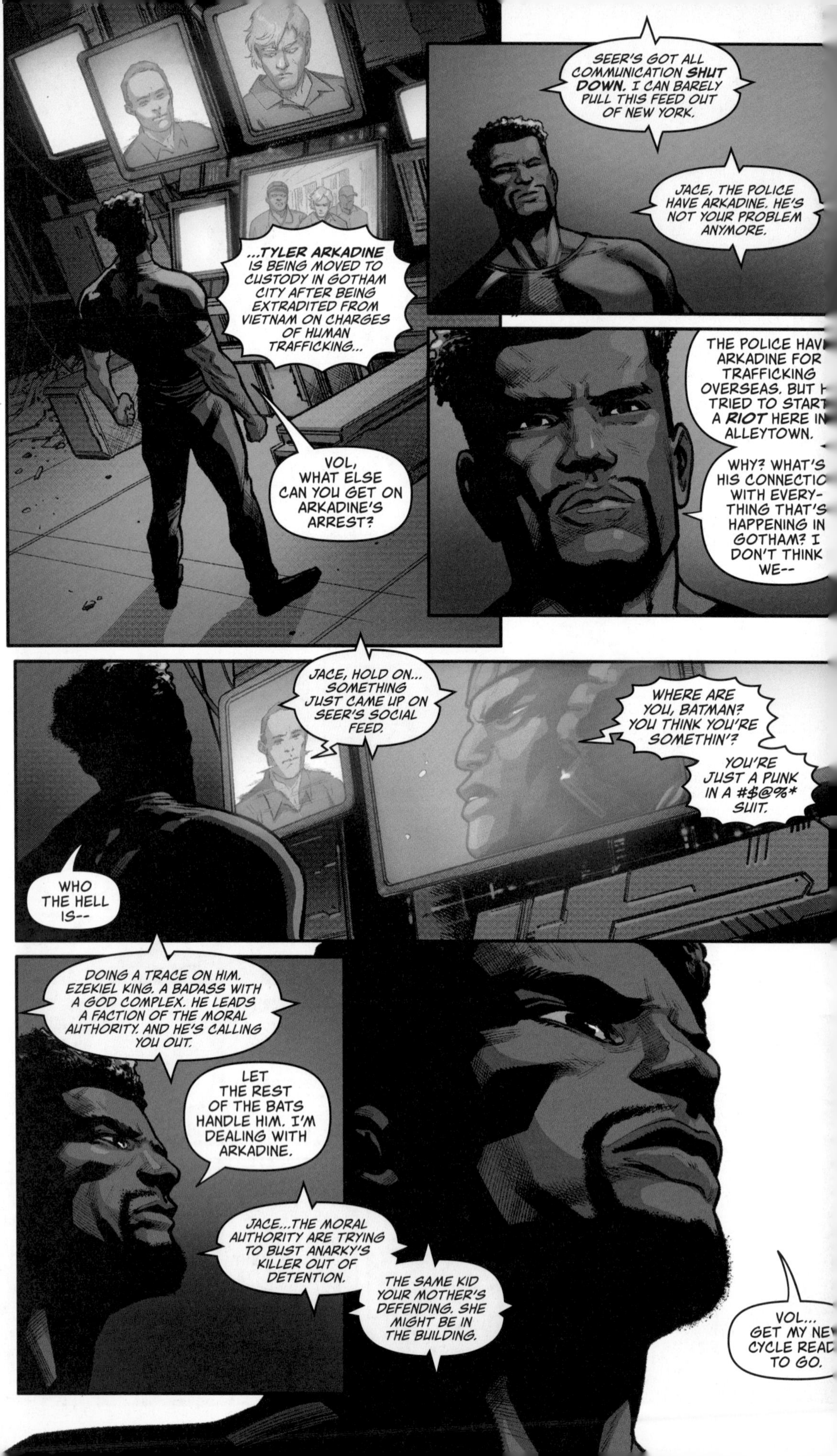
...TYLER ARKADINE IS BEING MOVED TO CUSTODY IN GOTHAM CITY AFTER BEING EXTRADITED FROM VIETNAM ON CHARGES OF HUMAN TRAFFICKING...
VOL, WHAT ELSE CAN YOU GET ON ARKADINE'S ARREST?
SEER'S GOT ALL COMMUNICATION SHUT DOWN. I CAN BARELY PULL THIS FEED OUT OF NEW YORK.
JACE, THE POLICE HAVE ARKADINE. HE'S NOT YOUR PROBLEM ANYMORE.
THE POLICE HAV ARKADINE FOR TRAFFICKING OVERSEAS. BUT H TRIED TO START A RIOT HERE IN ALLEYTOWN.
WHY? WHAT'S HIS CONNECTIO WITH EVERY-THING THAT'S HAPPENING IN GOTHAM? I DON'T THINK WE--
JACE, HOLD ON... SOMETHING JUST CAME UP ON SEER'S SOCIAL FEED.
WHERE ARE YOU, BATMAN? YOU THINK YOU'RE SOMETHIN'?
YOU'RE JUST A PUNK IN A #$@%* SUIT.
WHO THE HELL IS--
DOING A TRACE ON HIM. EZEKIEL KING. A BADASS WITH A GOD COMPLEX. HE LEADS A FACTION OF THE MORAL AUTHORITY. AND HE'S CALLING YOU OUT.
LET THE REST OF THE BATS HANDLE HIM. I'M DEALING WITH ARKADINE.
JACE...THE MORAL AUTHORITY ARE TRYING TO BUST ANARKY'S KILLER OUT OF DETENTION.
THE SAME KID YOUR MOTHER'S DEFENDING. SHE MIGHT BE IN THE BUILDING.
VOL... GET MY NE CYCLE READ TO GO.

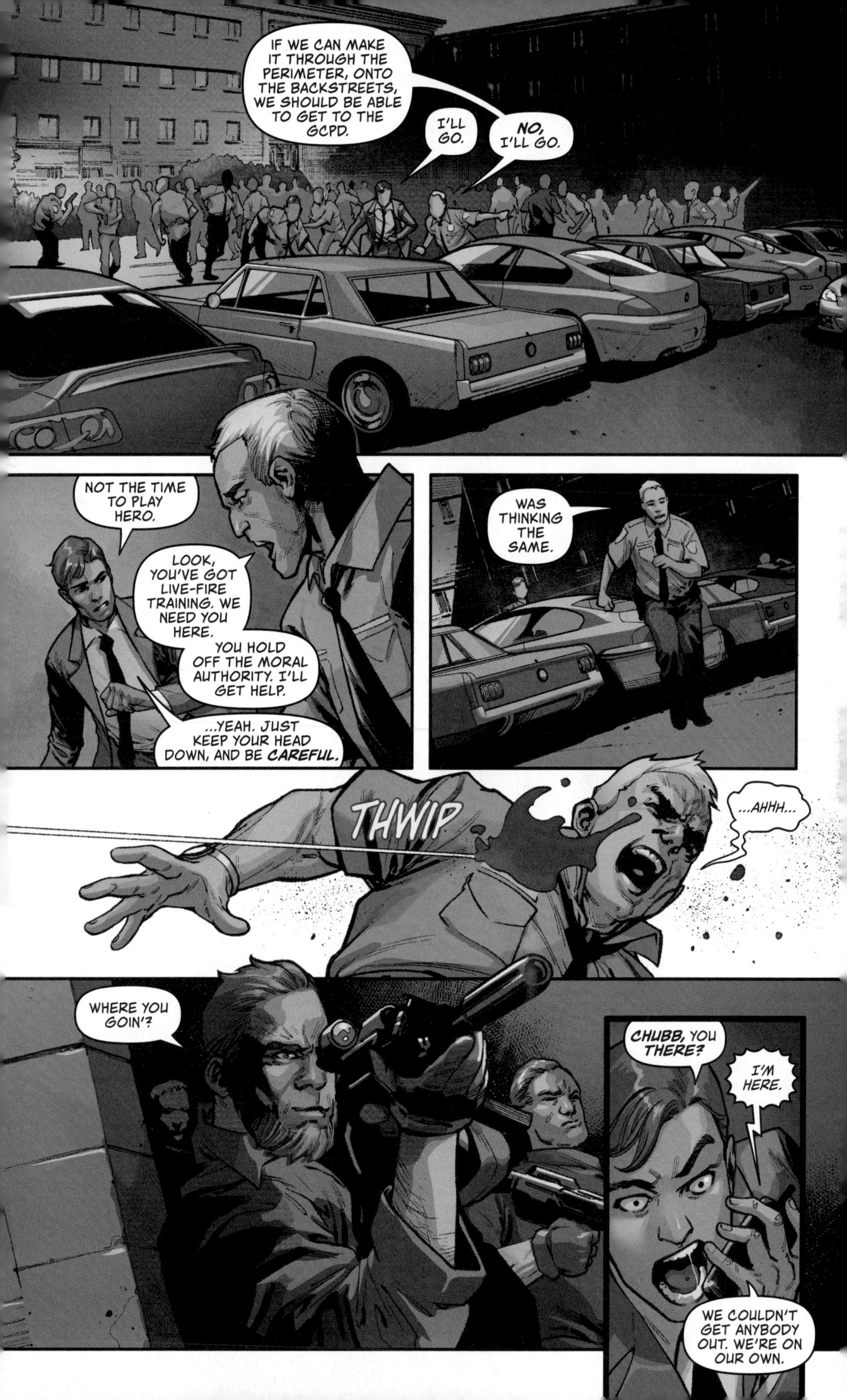
IF WE CAN MAKE IT THROUGH THE PERIMETER, ONTO THE BACKSTREETS, WE SHOULD BE ABLE TO GET TO THE GCPD.
I'LL GO.
NO, I'LL GO.
NOT THE TIME TO PLAY HERO.
LOOK, YOU'VE GOT LIVE-FIRE TRAINING. WE NEED YOU HERE.
YOU HOLD OFF THE MORAL AUTHORITY. I'LL GET HELP.
...YEAH. JUST KEEP YOUR HEAD DOWN, AND BE CAREFUL.
WAS THINKING THE SAME.
THWIP
...AHHH...
WHERE YOU GOIN'?
CHUBB, YOU THERE?
I'M HERE.
WE COULDN'T GET ANYBODY OUT. WE'RE ON OUR OWN.

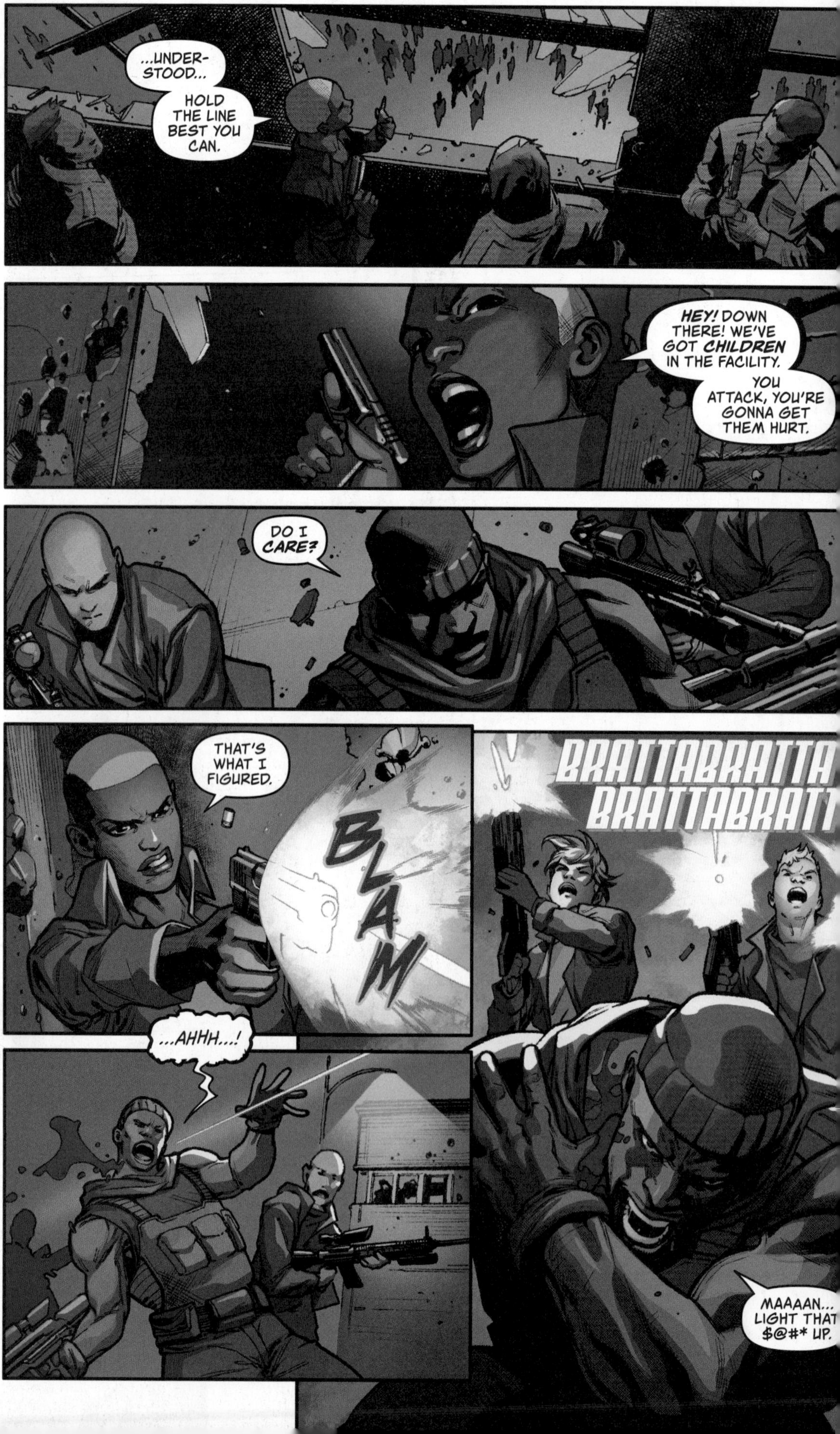

...UNDER-STOOD...
HOLD THE LINE BEST YOU CAN.
HEY! DOWN THERE! WE'VE GOT CHILDREN IN THE FACILITY.
YOU ATTACK, YOU'RE GONNA GET THEM HURT.
DO I CARE?
THAT'S WHAT I FIGURED.
BLAM
BRATTABRATTA
BRATTABRATT
...AHHH...!
MAAAAN... LIGHT THAT $@#* UP.

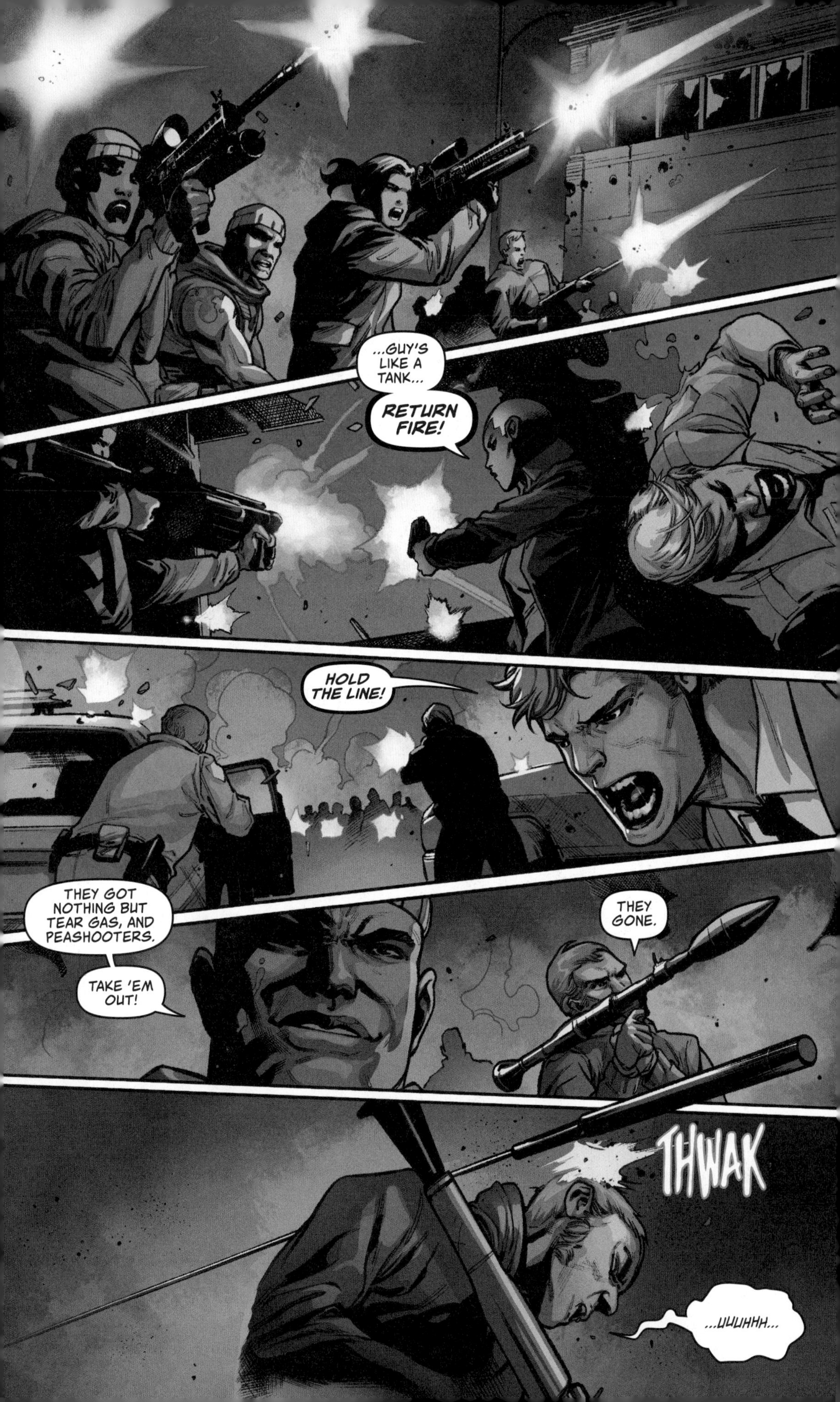
...GUY'S LIKE A TANK...
RETURN FIRE!
HOLD THE LINE!
THEY GOT NOTHING BUT TEAR GAS, AND PEASHOOTERS.
TAKE 'EM OUT!
THEY GONE.
THWAK
...UUUHHH...

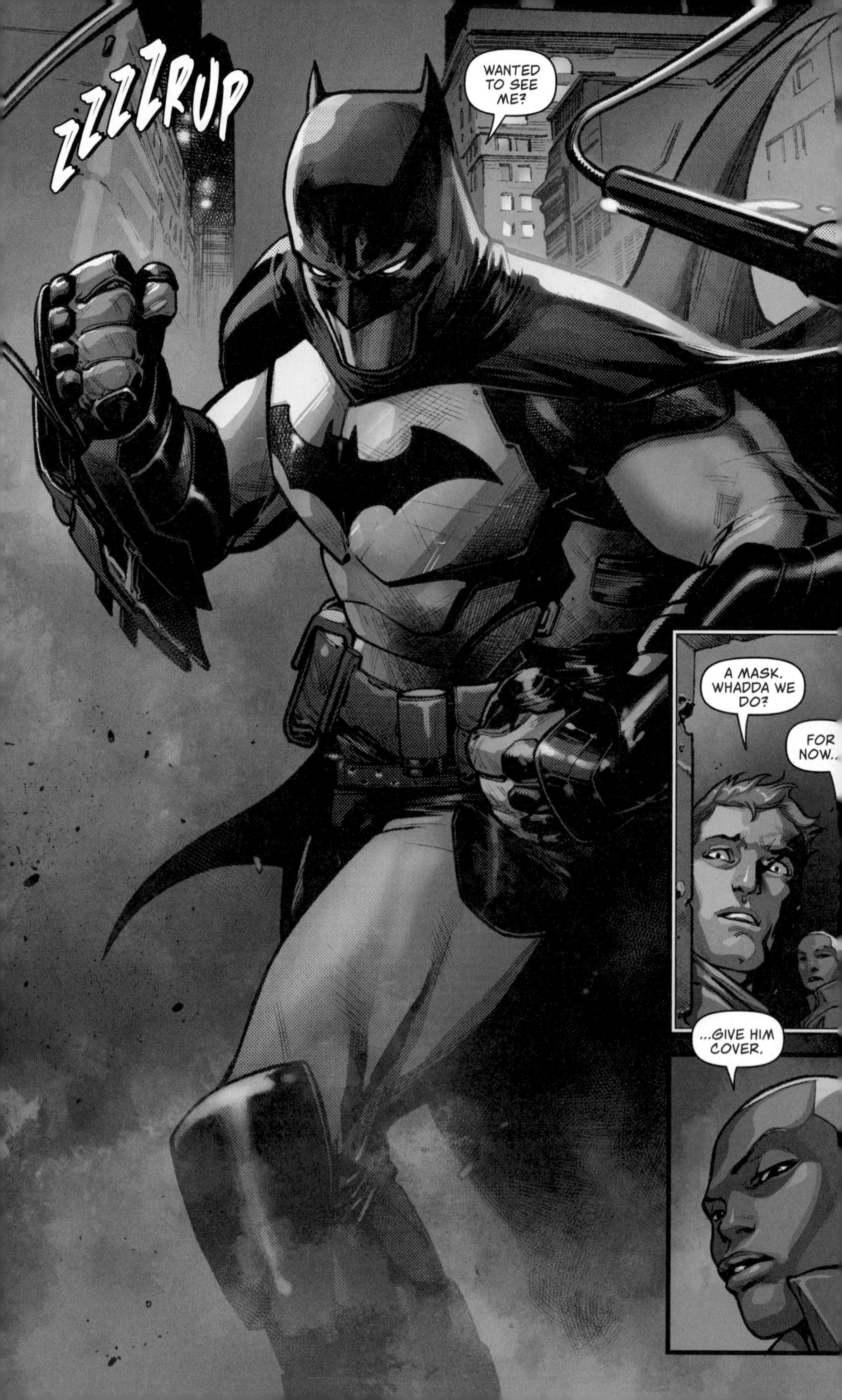
ZZZZZRUP
WANTED TO SEE ME?
A MASK. WHADDA WE DO?
FOR NOW...
...GIVE HIM COVER.

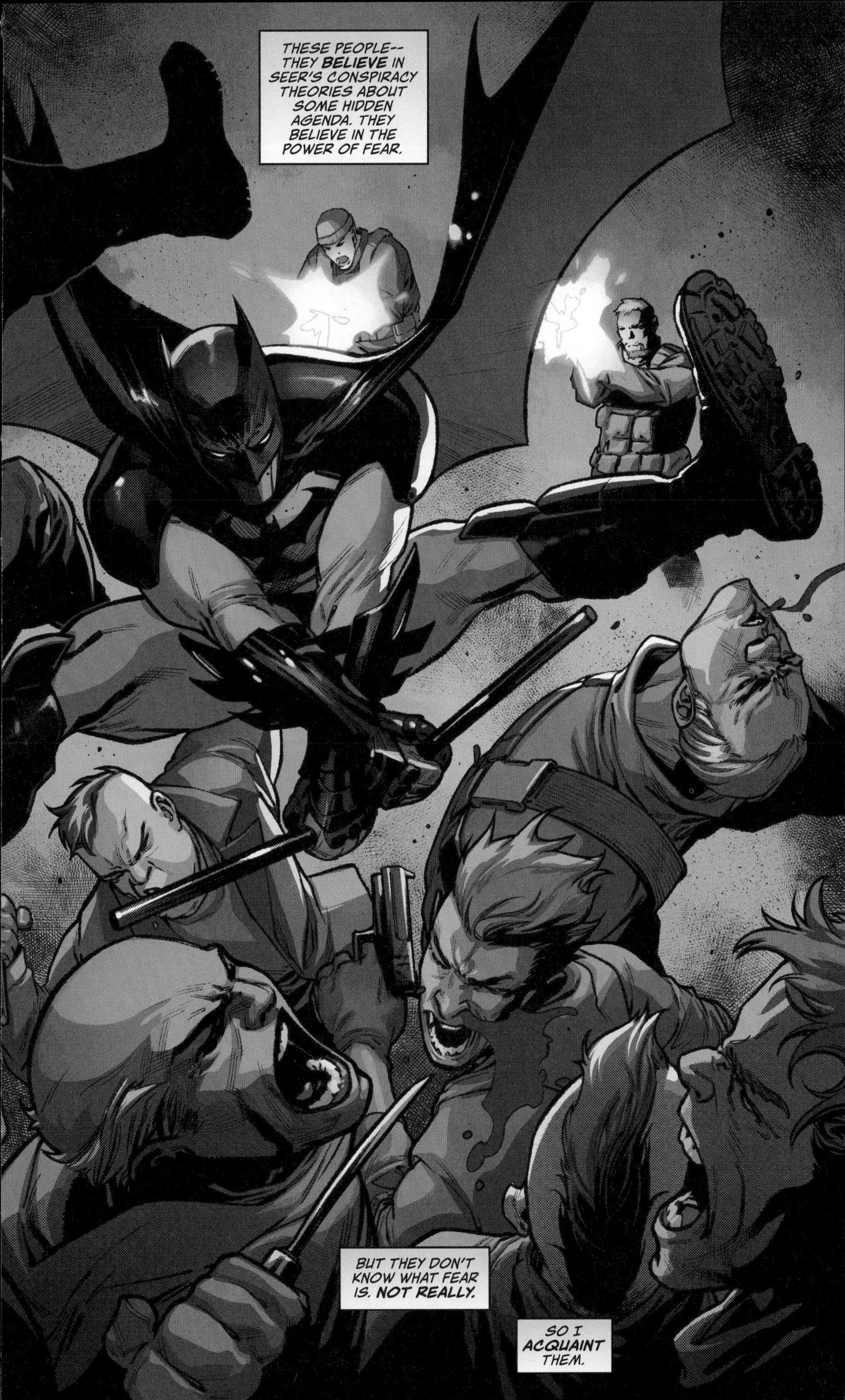

THESE PEOPLE-- THEY **BELIEVE** IN SEER'S CONSPIRACY THEORIES ABOUT SOME HIDDEN AGENDA. THEY BELIEVE IN THE POWER OF FEAR.
BUT THEY DON'T KNOW WHAT FEAR IS. **NOT REALLY.**
SO I **ACQUAINT** THEM.

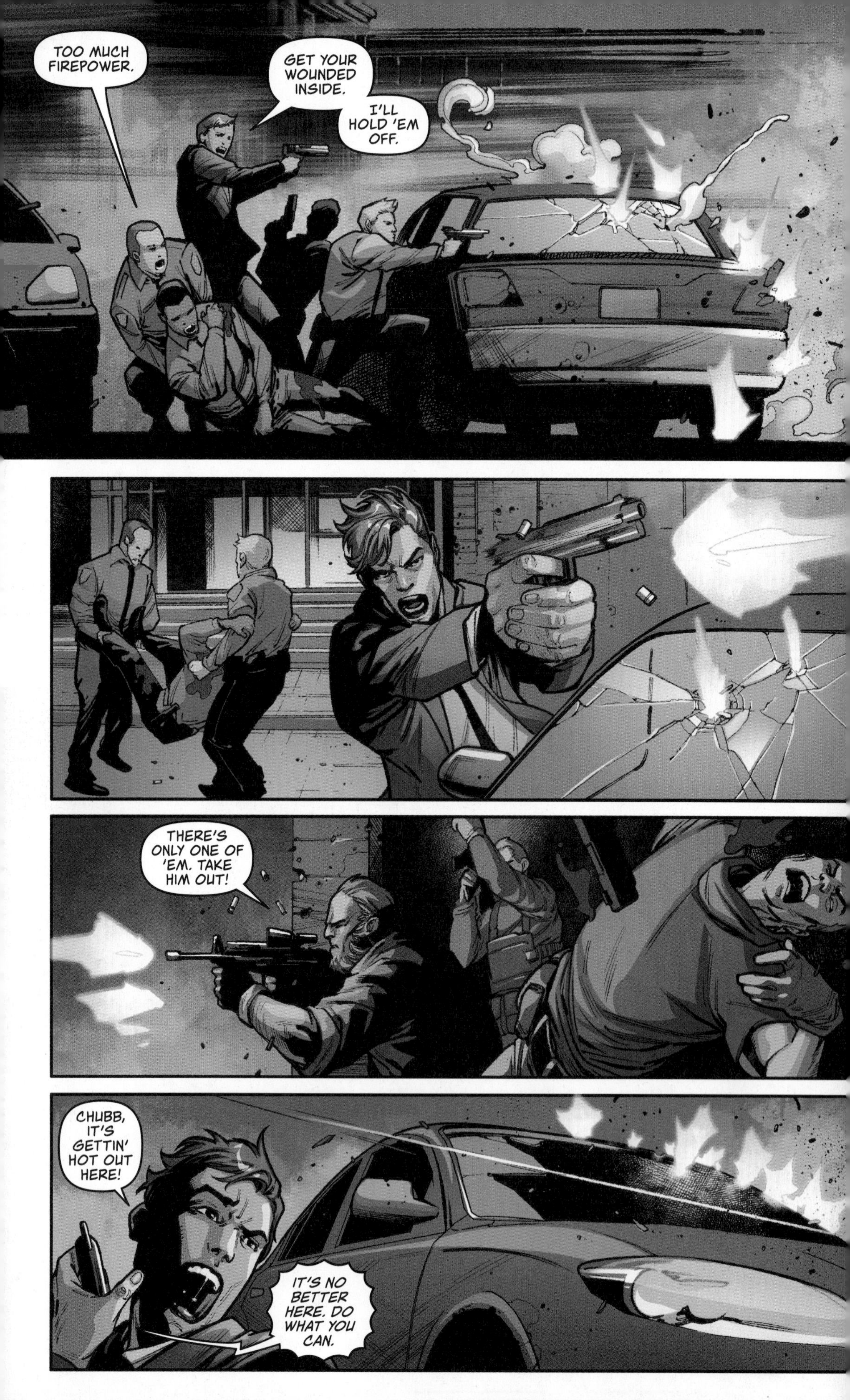
TOO MUCH FIREPOWER.
GET YOUR WOUNDED INSIDE.
I'LL HOLD 'EM OFF.
THERE'S ONLY ONE OF 'EM. TAKE HIM OUT!
CHUBB, IT'S GETTIN' HOT OUT HERE!
IT'S NO BETTER HERE. DO WHAT YOU CAN.

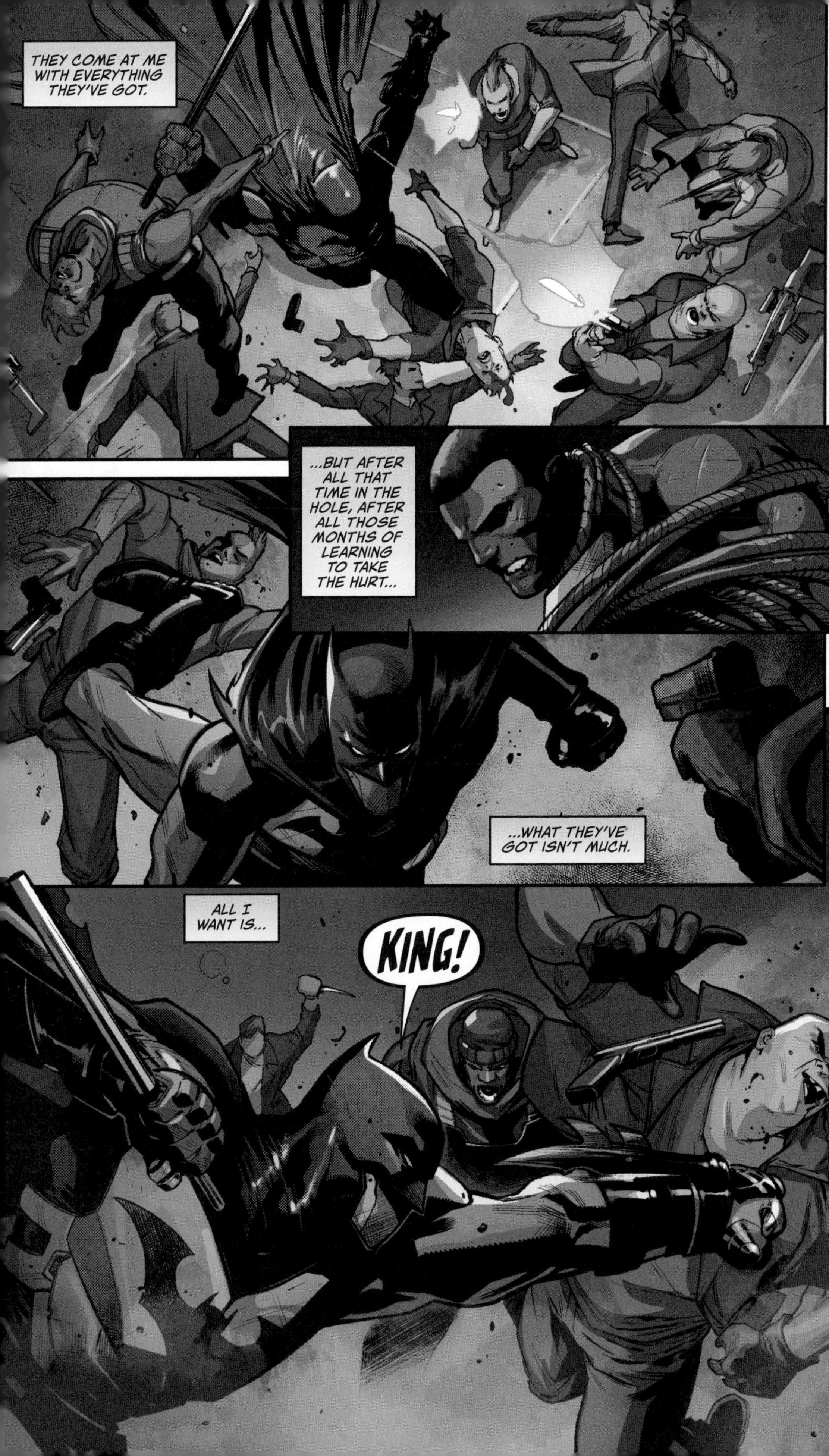
THEY COME AT ME WITH EVERYTHING THEY'VE GOT.
...BUT AFTER ALL THAT TIME IN THE HOLE, AFTER ALL THOSE MONTHS OF LEARNING TO TAKE THE HURT...
...WHAT THEY'VE GOT ISN'T MUCH.
ALL I WANT IS...
KING!

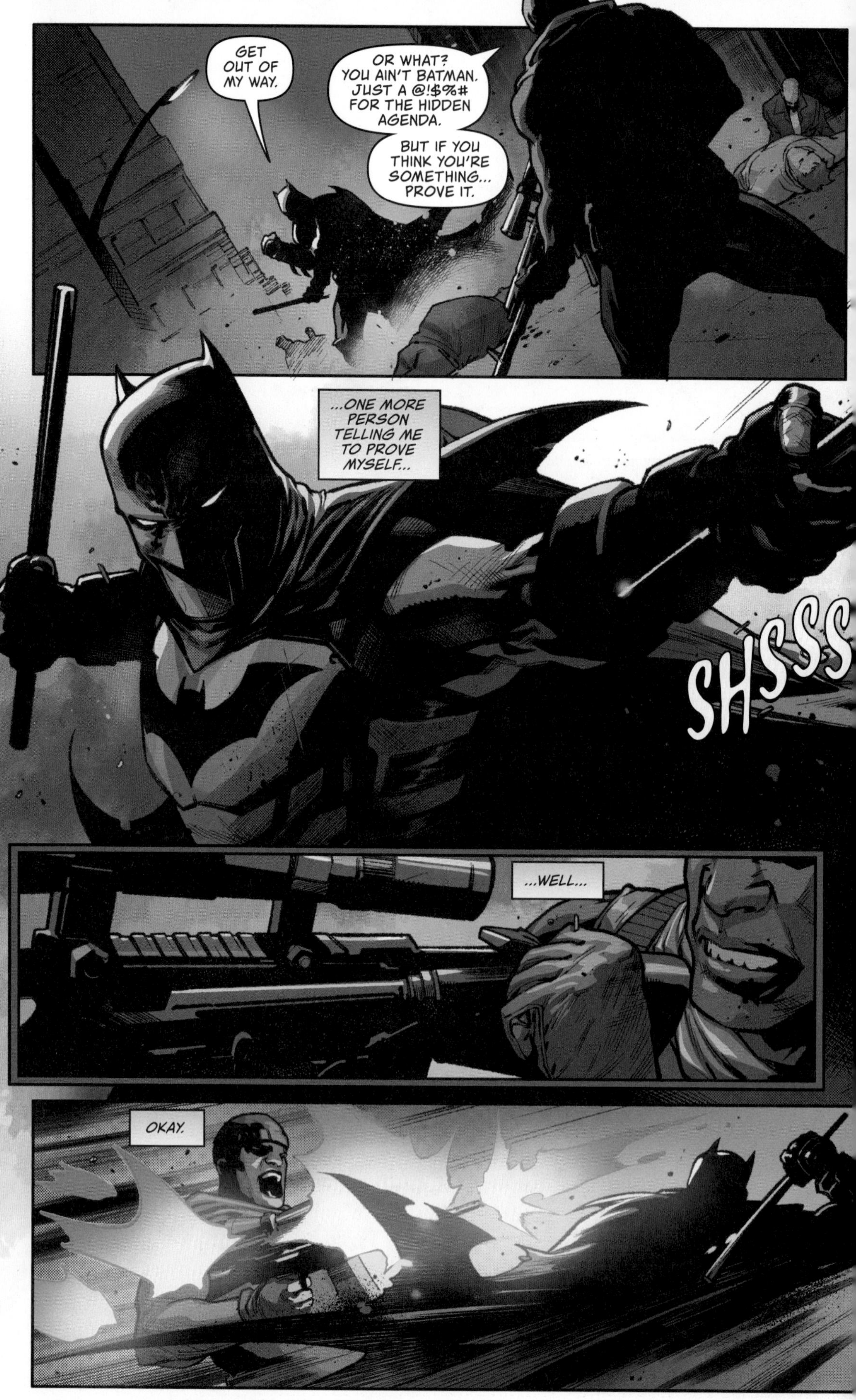
GET OUT OF MY WAY.
OR WHAT? YOU AIN'T BATMAN. JUST A @!$%# FOR THE HIDDEN AGENDA.
BUT IF YOU THINK YOU'RE SOMETHING... PROVE IT.
...ONE MORE PERSON TELLING ME TO PROVE MYSELF...
SHSSS
...WELL...
OKAY.

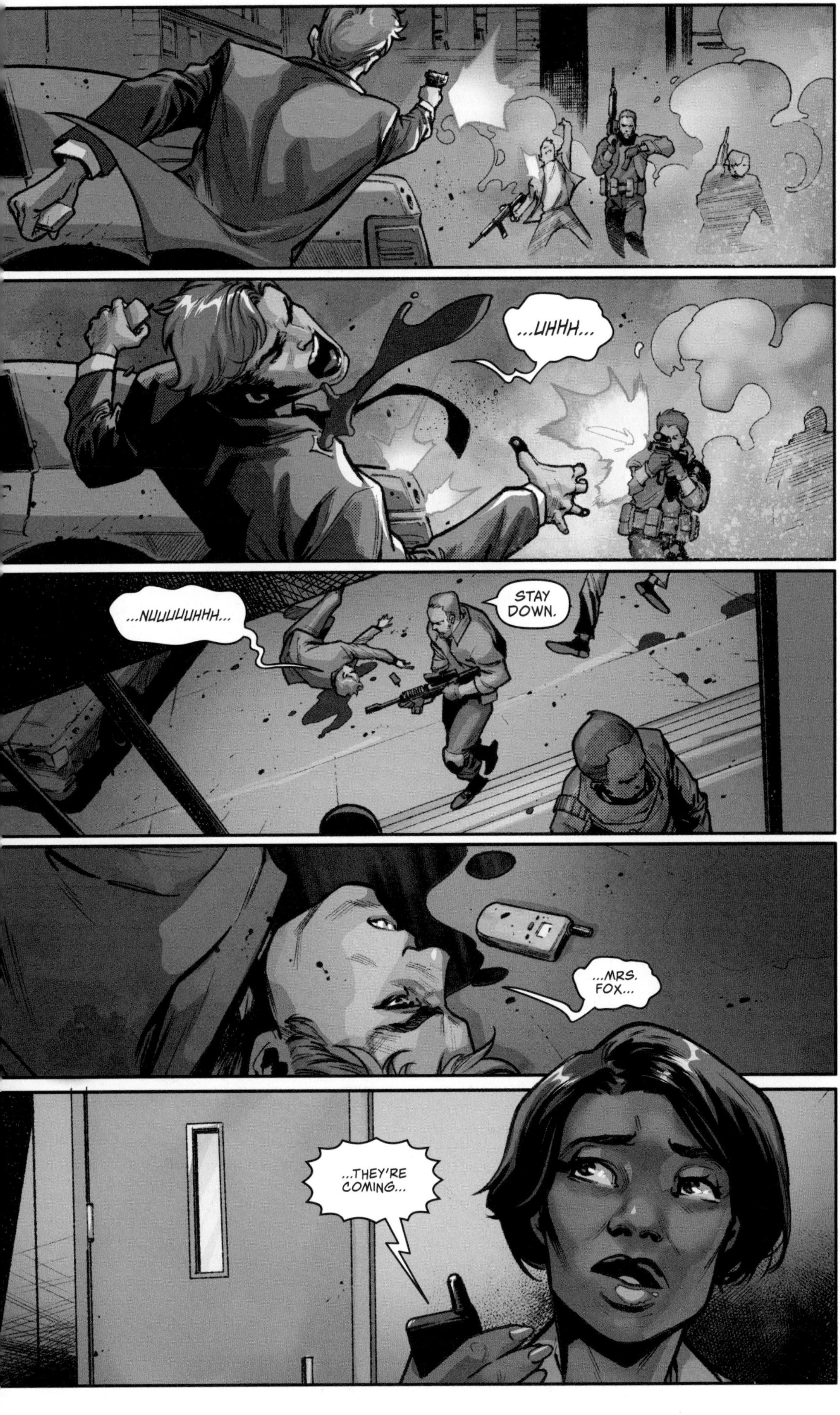
...UHHH...
...NUUUUUHHH...
STAY DOWN.
...MRS. FOX...
...THEY'RE COMING...

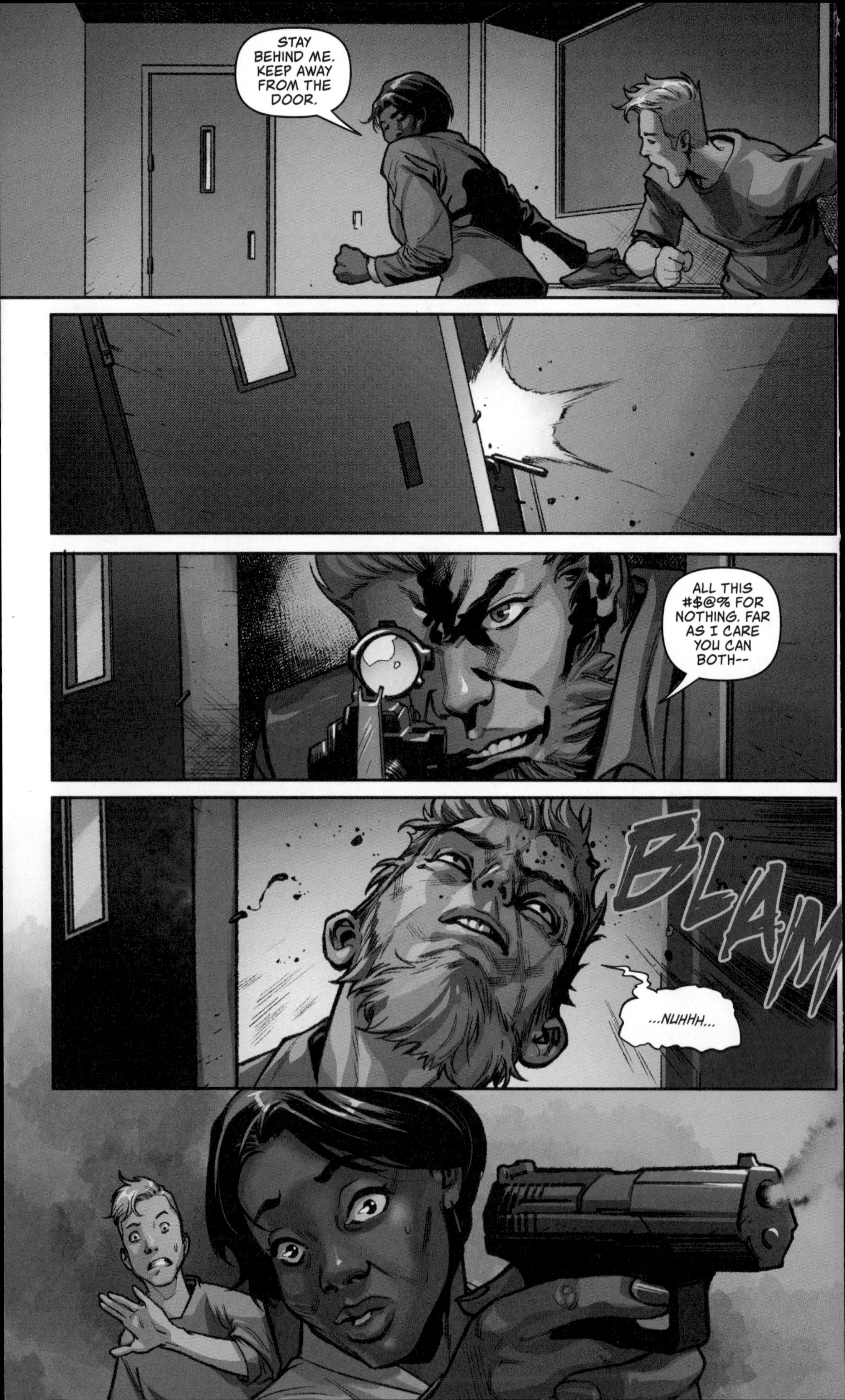
STAY BEHIND ME. KEEP AWAY FROM THE DOOR.
ALL THIS #$@% FOR NOTHING. FAR AS I CARE YOU CAN BOTH--
BLAM
...NUHHH...

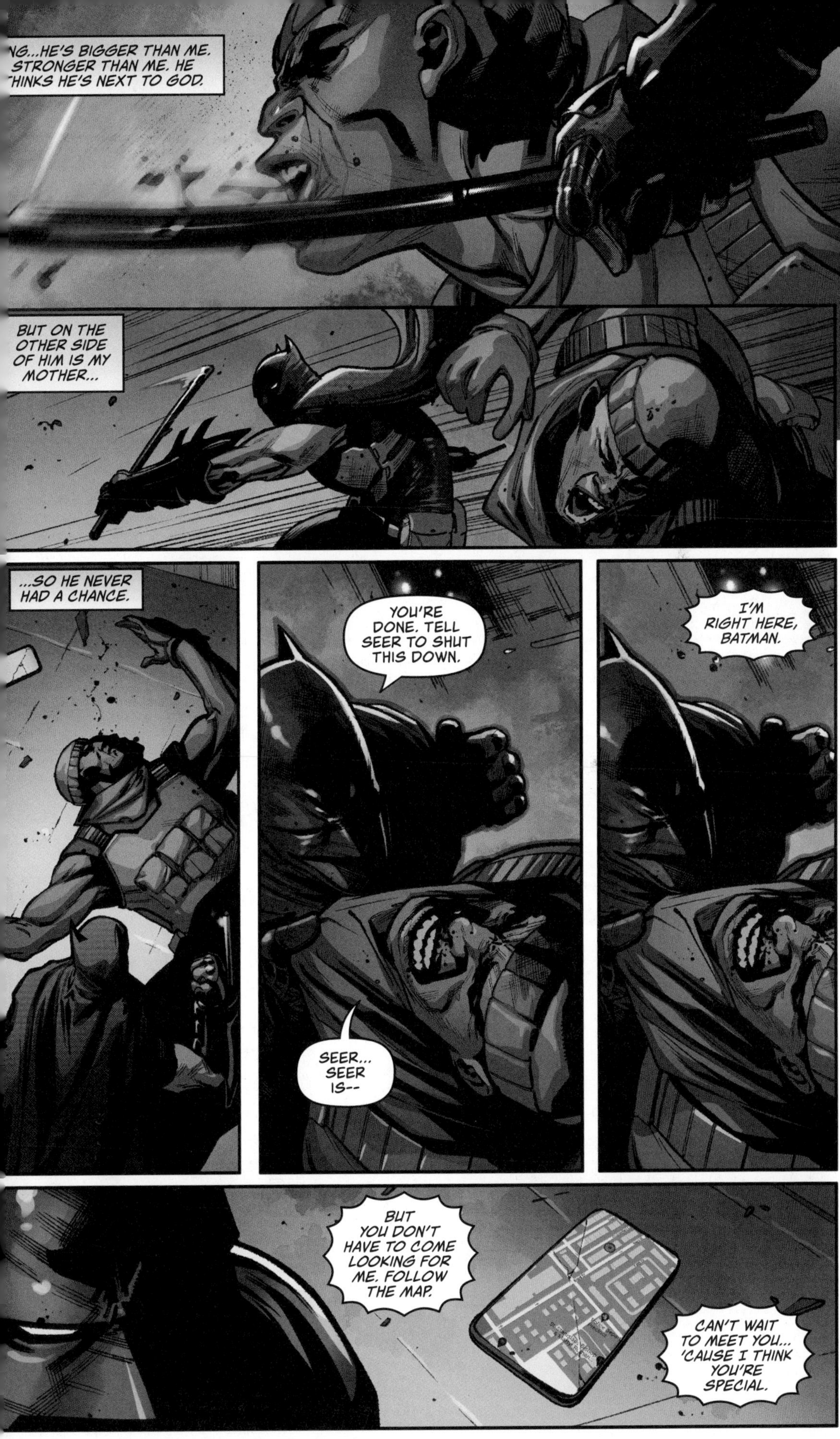

NG...HE'S BIGGER THAN ME. STRONGER THAN ME. HE THINKS HE'S NEXT TO GOD.
BUT ON THE OTHER SIDE OF HIM IS MY MOTHER...
...SO HE NEVER HAD A CHANCE.
YOU'RE DONE. TELL SEER TO SHUT THIS DOWN.
SEER... SEER IS--
I'M RIGHT HERE, BATMAN.
BUT YOU DON'T HAVE TO COME LOOKING FOR ME. FOLLOW THE MAP.
CAN'T WAIT TO MEET YOU... 'CAUSE I THINK YOU'RE SPECIAL.

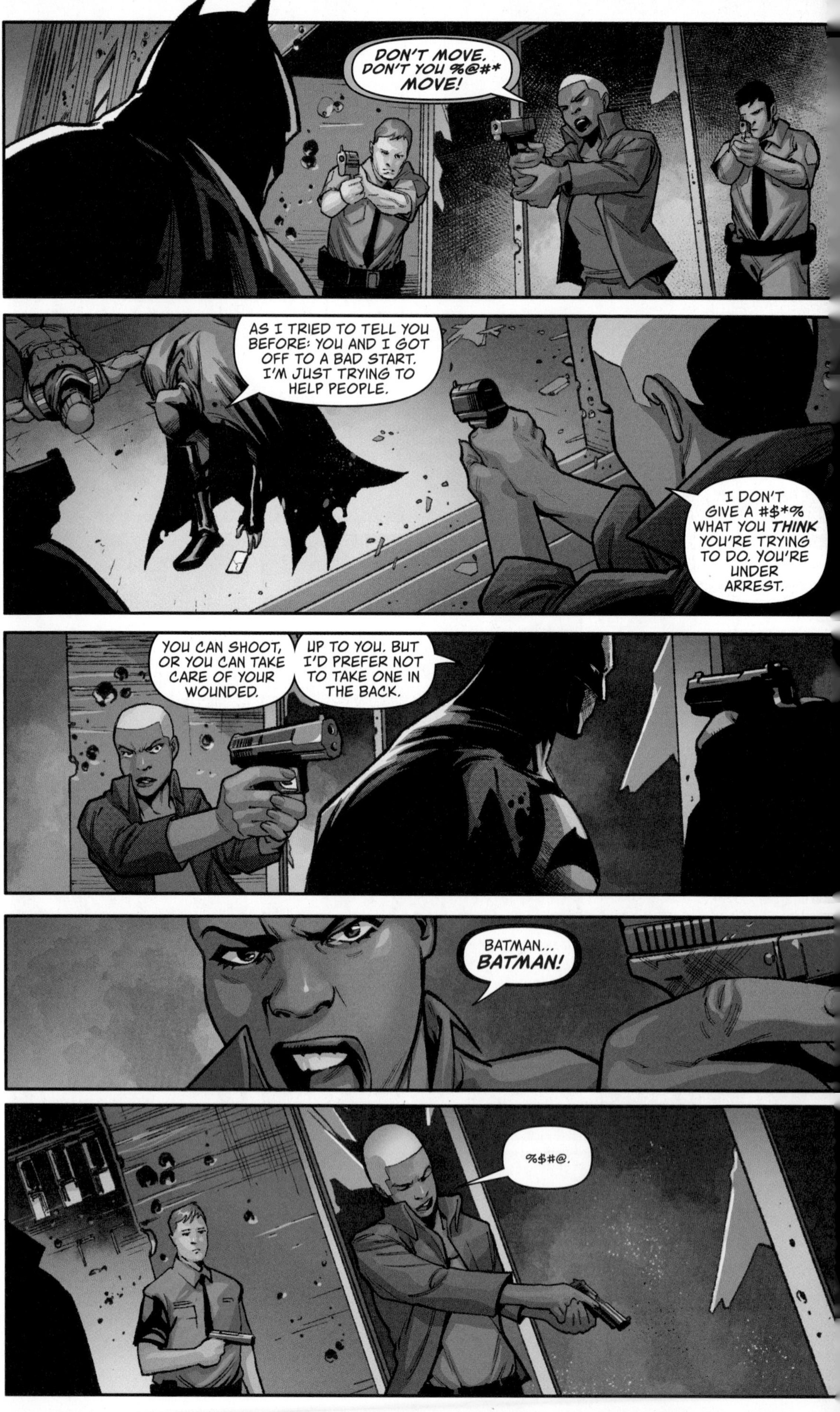
DON'T MOVE. DON'T YOU %@#* MOVE!
AS I TRIED TO TELL YOU BEFORE: YOU AND I GOT OFF TO A BAD START. I'M JUST TRYING TO HELP PEOPLE.
I DON'T GIVE A #$*% WHAT YOU THINK YOU'RE TRYING TO DO. YOU'RE UNDER ARREST.
YOU CAN SHOOT, OR YOU CAN TAKE CARE OF YOUR WOUNDED.
UP TO YOU. BUT I'D PREFER NOT TO TAKE ONE IN THE BACK.
BATMAN... BATMAN!
%$#@.

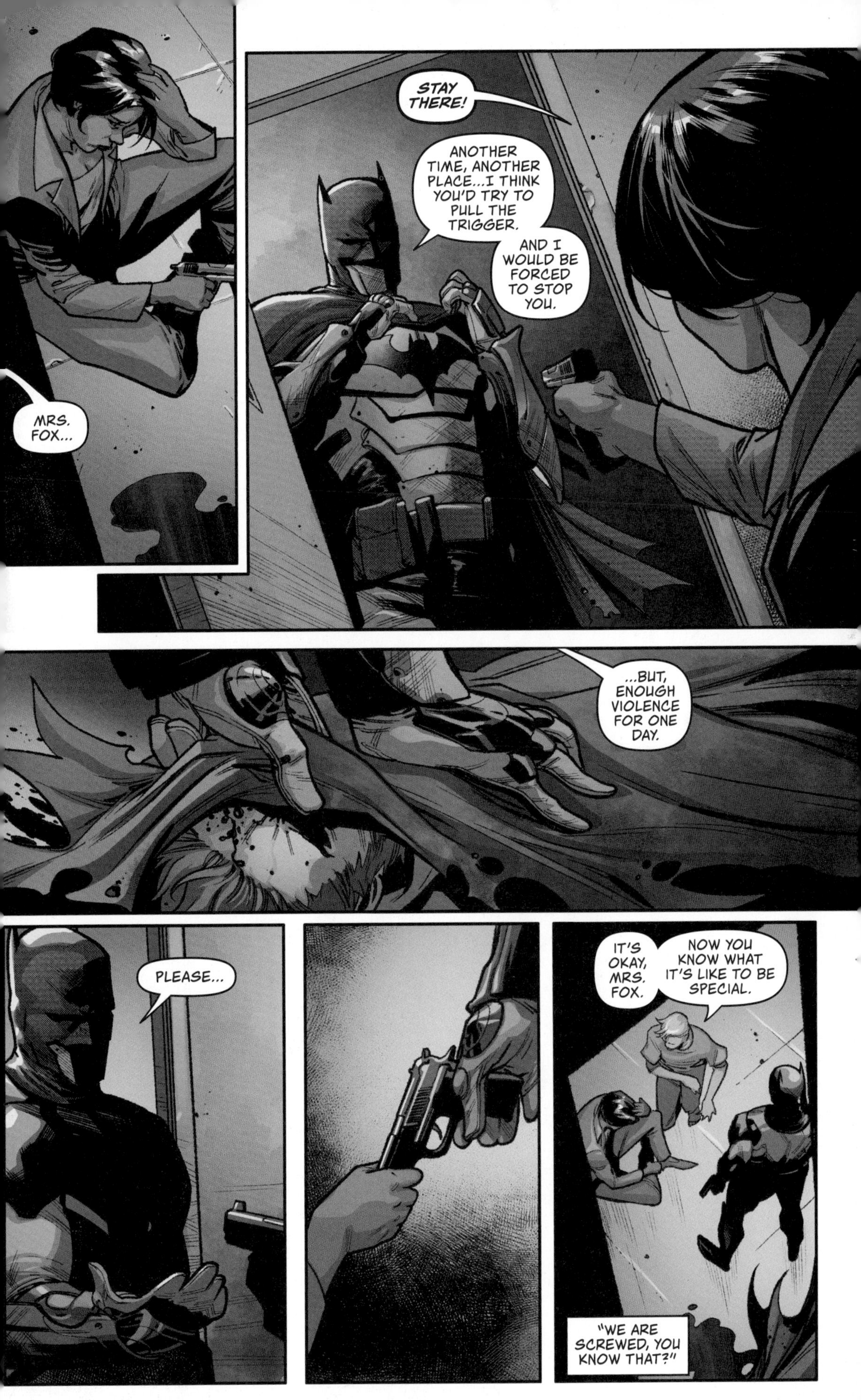
STAY THERE!
ANOTHER TIME, ANOTHER PLACE...I THINK YOU'D TRY TO PULL THE TRIGGER.
AND I WOULD BE FORCED TO STOP YOU.
MRS. FOX...
...BUT, ENOUGH VIOLENCE FOR ONE DAY.
PLEASE...
IT'S OKAY, MRS. FOX.
NOW YOU KNOW WHAT IT'S LIKE TO BE SPECIAL.
"WE ARE SCREWED, YOU KNOW THAT?"

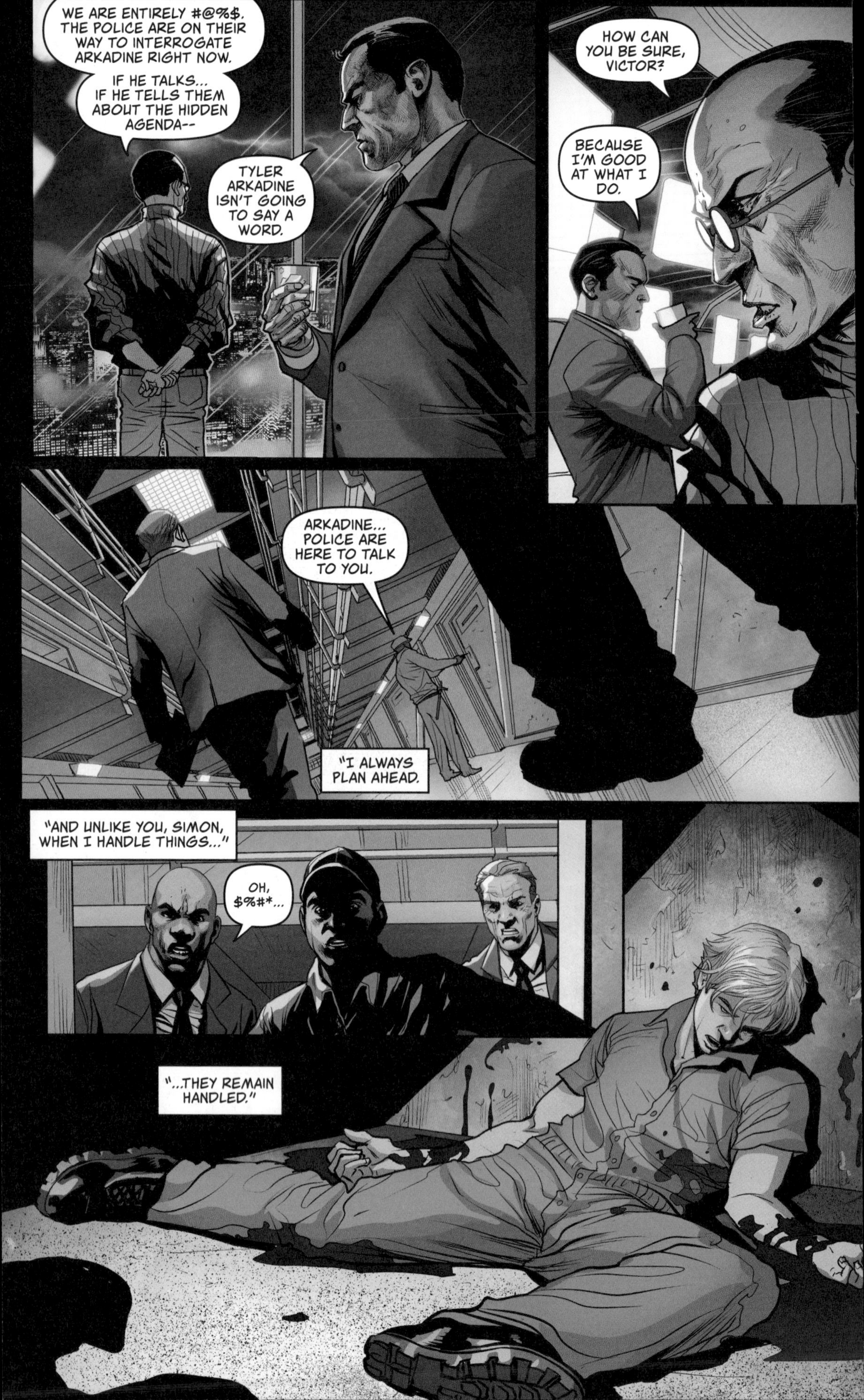
WE ARE ENTIRELY #@%$. THE POLICE ARE ON THEIR WAY TO INTERROGATE ARKADINE RIGHT NOW.
IF HE TALKS... IF HE TELLS THEM ABOUT THE HIDDEN AGENDA--
TYLER ARKADINE ISN'T GOING TO SAY A WORD.
HOW CAN YOU BE SURE, VICTOR?
BECAUSE I'M GOOD AT WHAT I DO.
ARKADINE... POLICE ARE HERE TO TALK TO YOU.
"I ALWAYS PLAN AHEAD.
"AND UNLIKE YOU, SIMON, WHEN I HANDLE THINGS..."
OH, $%#*...
"...THEY REMAIN HANDLED."

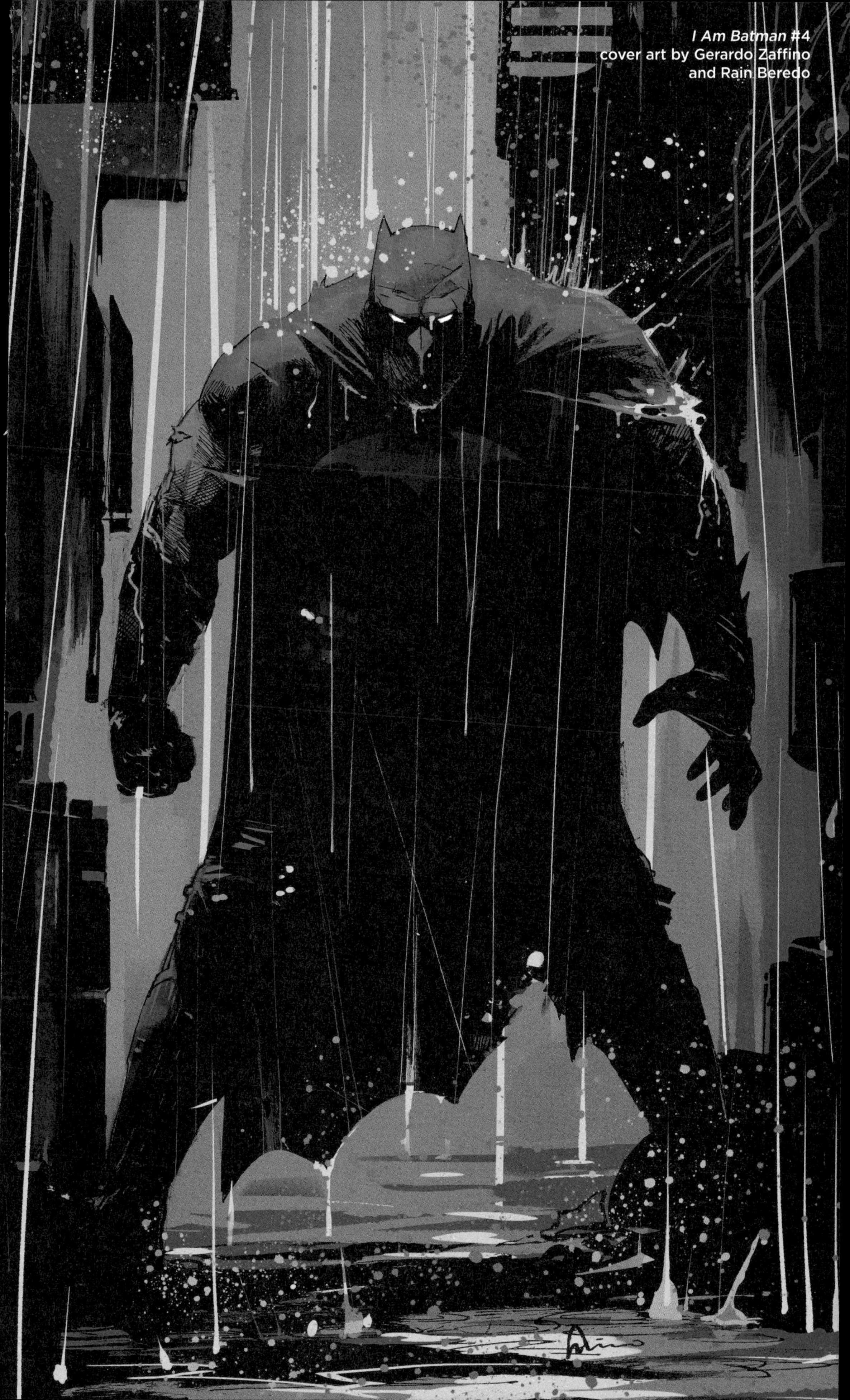

I Am Batman #4
cover art by Gerardo Zaffino
and Rain Beredo

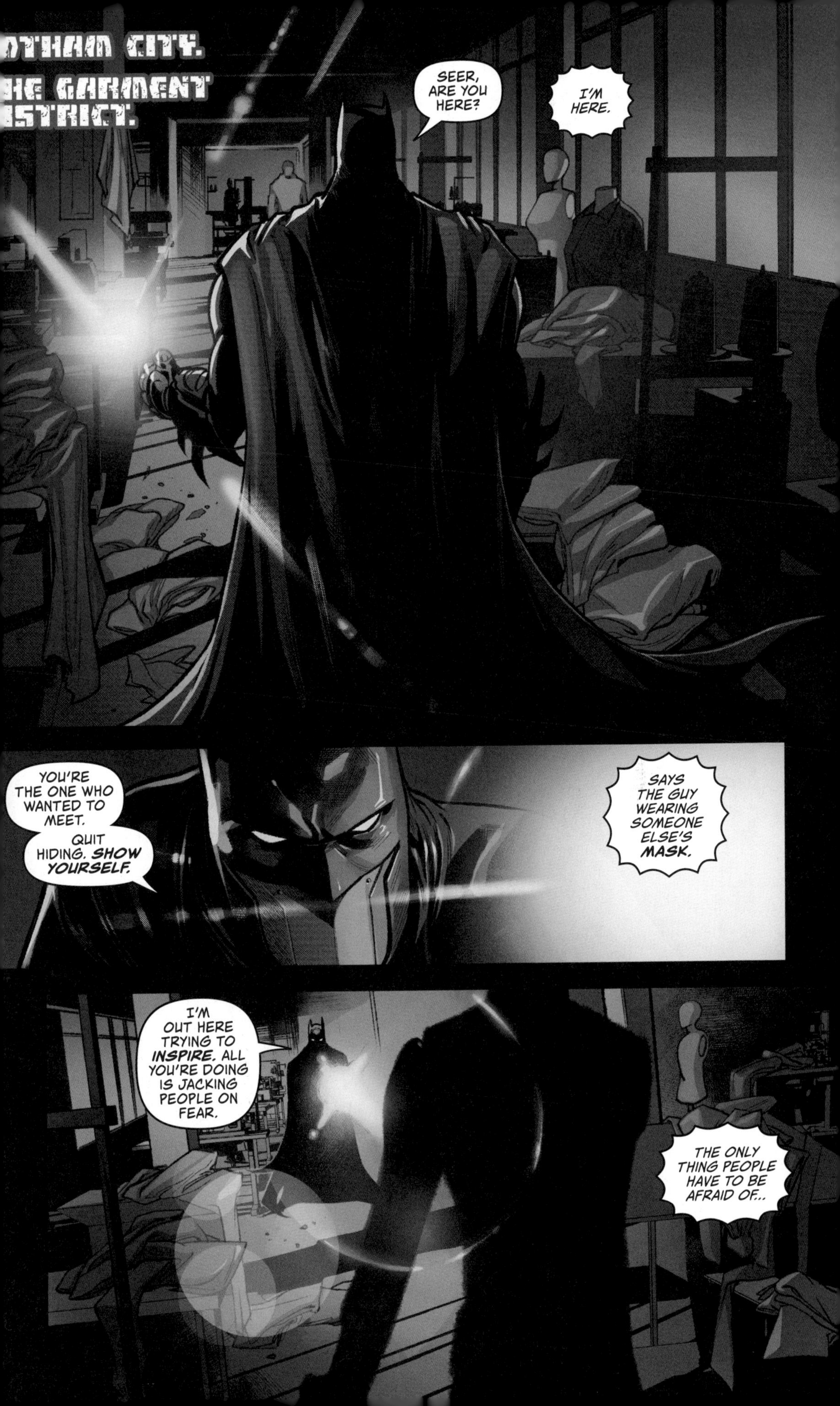
OTHAM CITY.
HE GARMENT
ISTRICT.
SEER, ARE YOU HERE?
I'M HERE.
YOU'RE THE ONE WHO WANTED TO MEET.
QUIT HIDING. SHOW YOURSELF.
SAYS THE GUY WEARING SOMEONE ELSE'S MASK.
I'M OUT HERE TRYING TO INSPIRE. ALL YOU'RE DOING IS JACKING PEOPLE ON FEAR.
THE ONLY THING PEOPLE HAVE TO BE AFRAID OF...

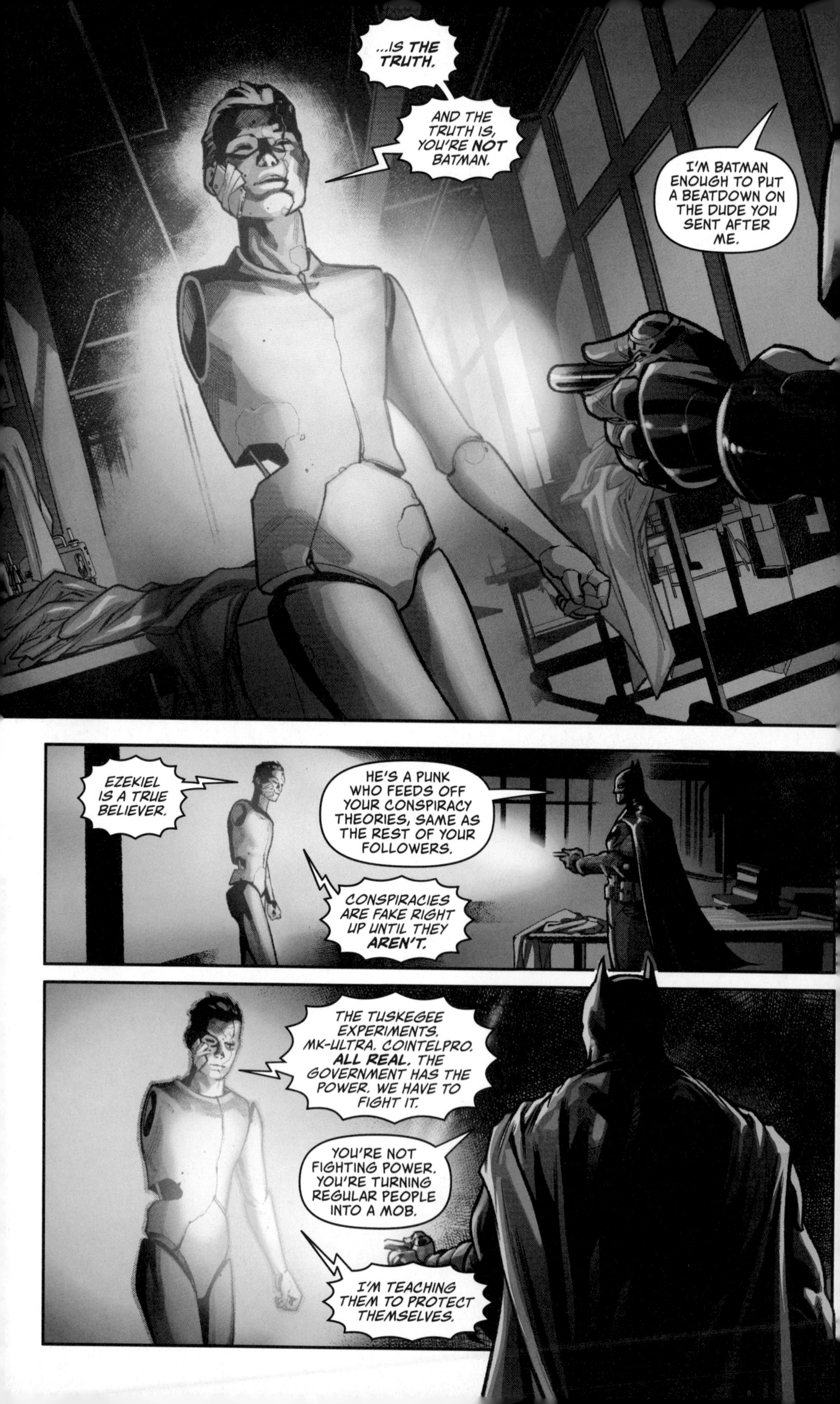
...IS THE TRUTH.
AND THE TRUTH IS, YOU'RE NOT BATMAN.
I'M BATMAN ENOUGH TO PUT A BEATDOWN ON THE DUDE YOU SENT AFTER ME.
EZEKIEL IS A TRUE BELIEVER.
HE'S A PUNK WHO FEEDS OFF YOUR CONSPIRACY THEORIES, SAME AS THE REST OF YOUR FOLLOWERS.
CONSPIRACIES ARE FAKE RIGHT UP UNTIL THEY AREN'T.
THE TUSKEGEE EXPERIMENTS. MK-ULTRA. COINTELPRO. ALL REAL. THE GOVERNMENT HAS THE POWER. WE HAVE TO FIGHT IT.
YOU'RE NOT FIGHTING POWER. YOU'RE TURNING REGULAR PEOPLE INTO A MOB.
I'M TEACHING THEM TO PROTECT THEMSELVES.

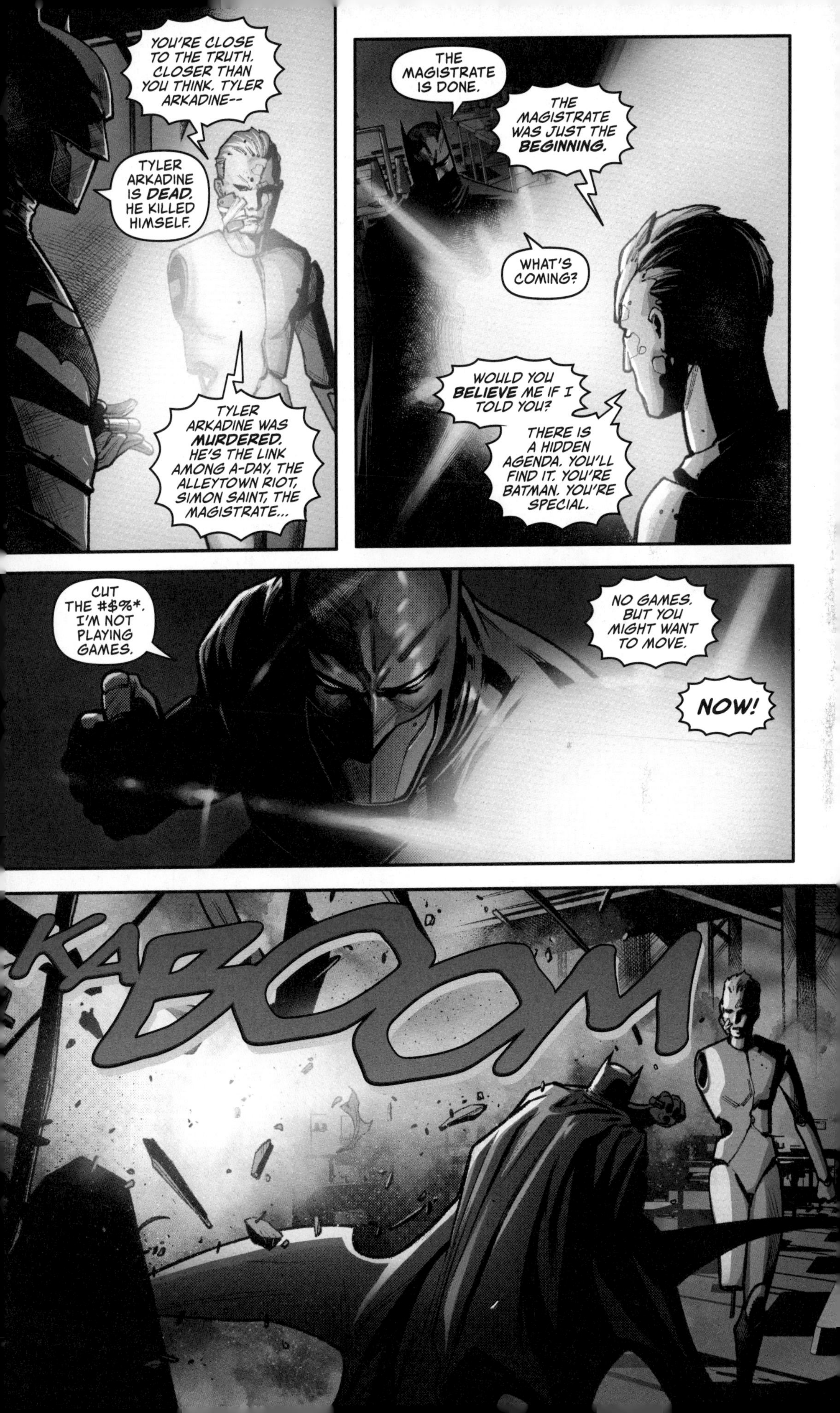
YOU'RE CLOSE TO THE TRUTH. CLOSER THAN YOU THINK. TYLER ARKADINE--
TYLER ARKADINE IS DEAD. HE KILLED HIMSELF.
TYLER ARKADINE WAS MURDERED. HE'S THE LINK AMONG A-DAY, THE ALLEYTOWN RIOT, SIMON SAINT, THE MAGISTRATE...
THE MAGISTRATE IS DONE.
THE MAGISTRATE WAS JUST THE BEGINNING.
WHAT'S COMING?
WOULD YOU BELIEVE ME IF I TOLD YOU?
THERE IS A HIDDEN AGENDA. YOU'LL FIND IT. YOU'RE BATMAN. YOU'RE SPECIAL.
CUT THE #$%*. I'M NOT PLAYING GAMES.
NO GAMES. BUT YOU MIGHT WANT TO MOVE.
NOW!
KABOOM

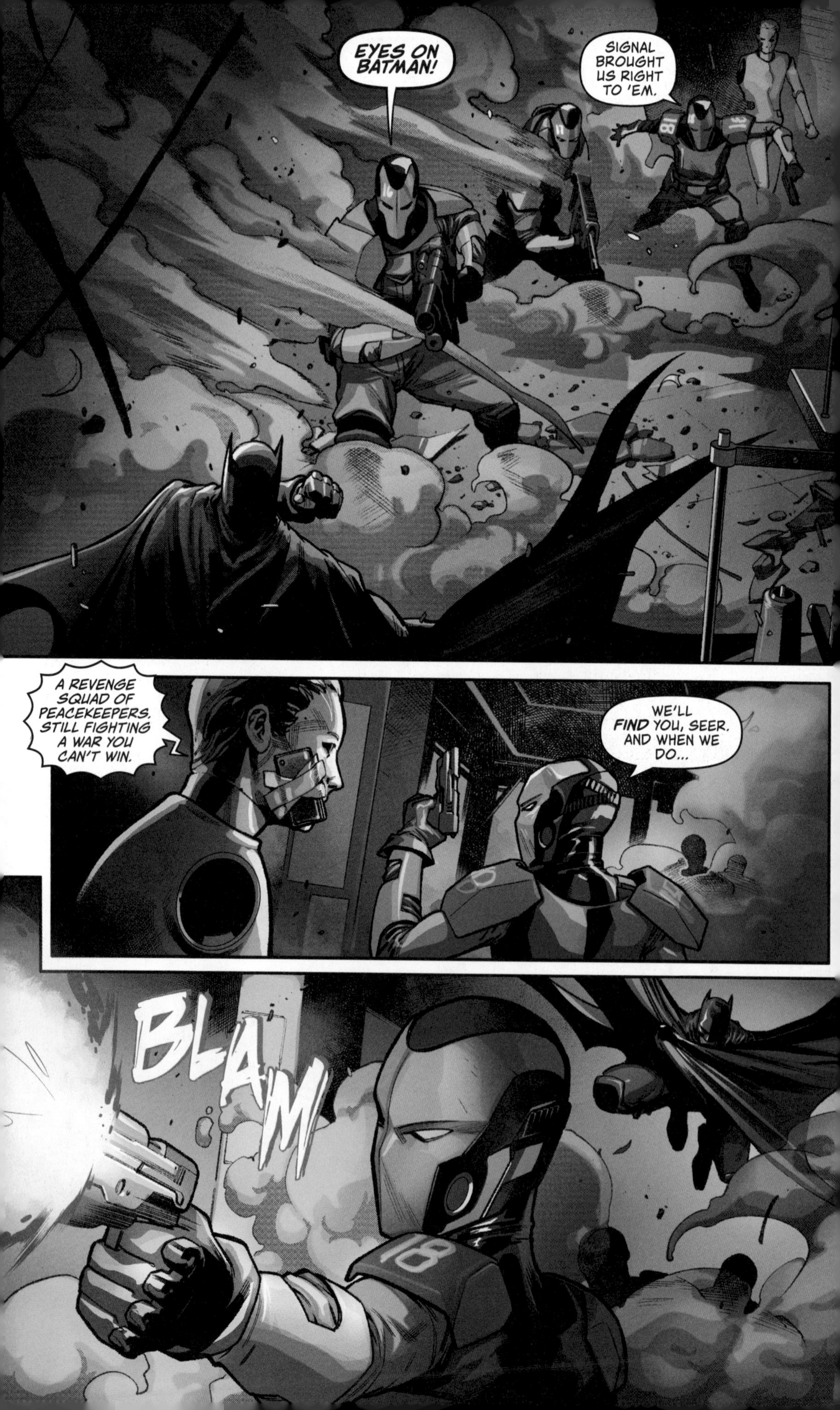
EYES ON BATMAN!
SIGNAL BROUGHT US RIGHT TO 'EM.
A REVENGE SQUAD OF PEACEKEEPERS. STILL FIGHTING A WAR YOU CAN'T WIN.
WE'LL FIND YOU, SEER. AND WHEN WE DO...
BLAM

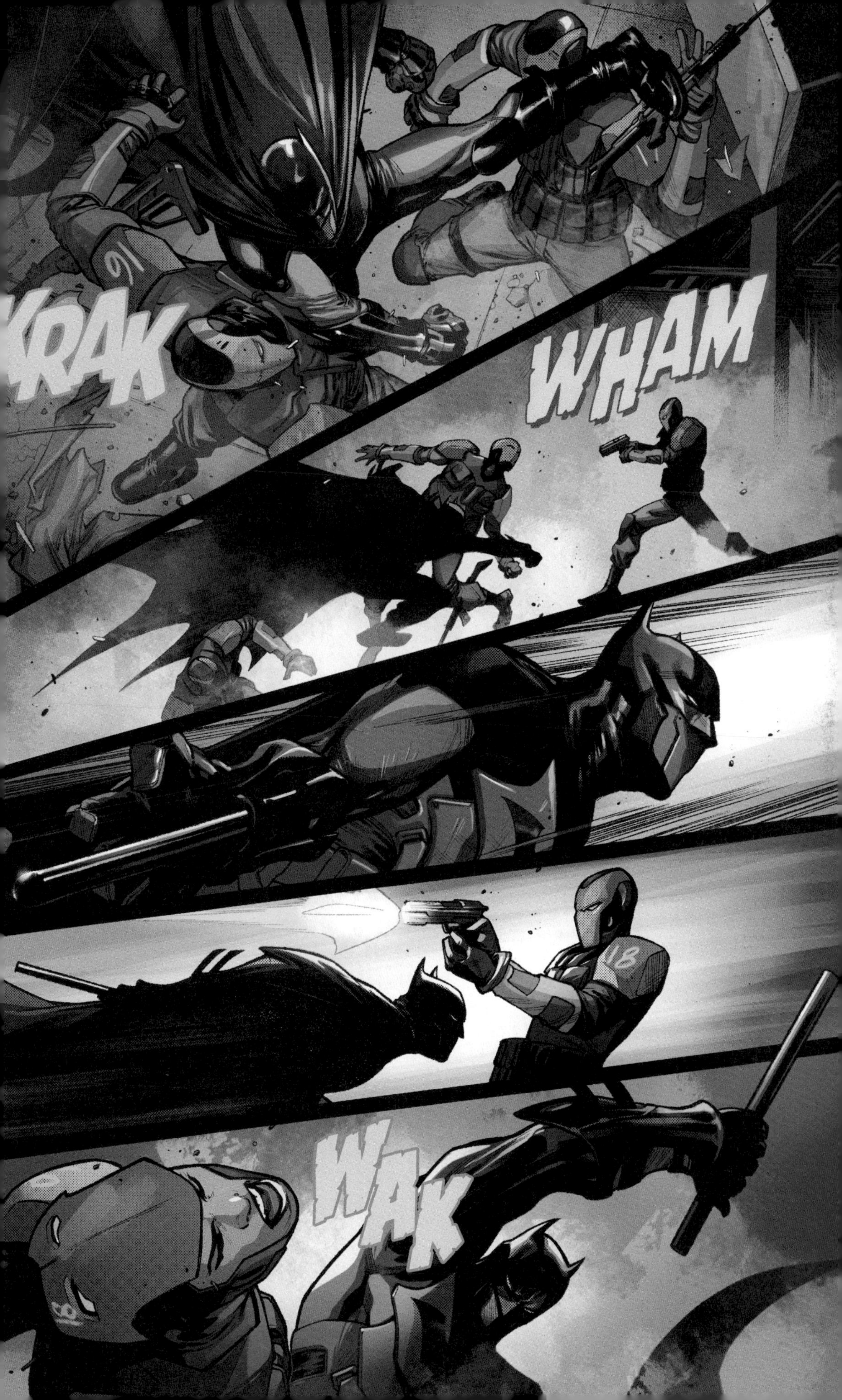
KRAK
WHAM
WAK

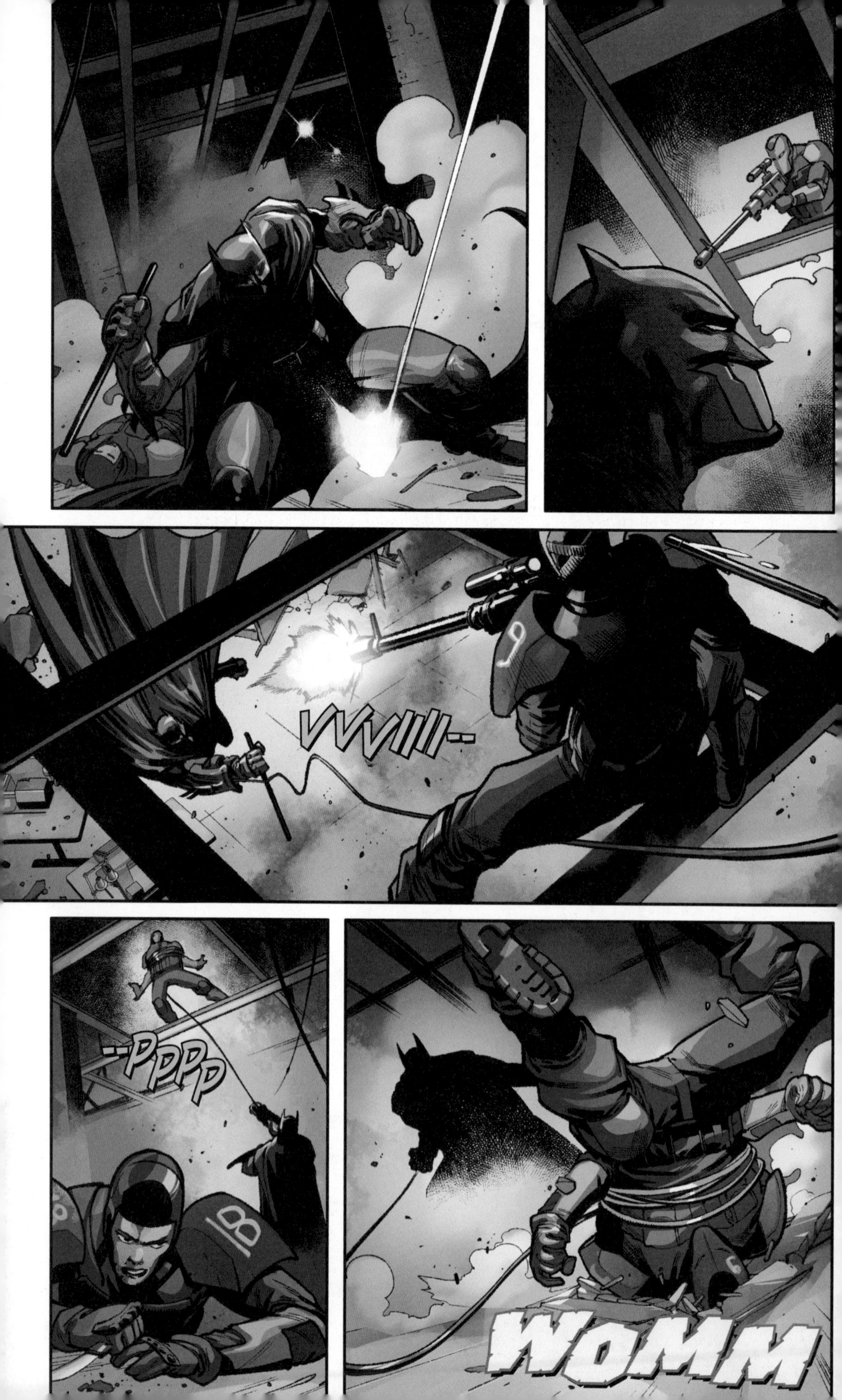

VVVIIII--
--PPPP
WOMM

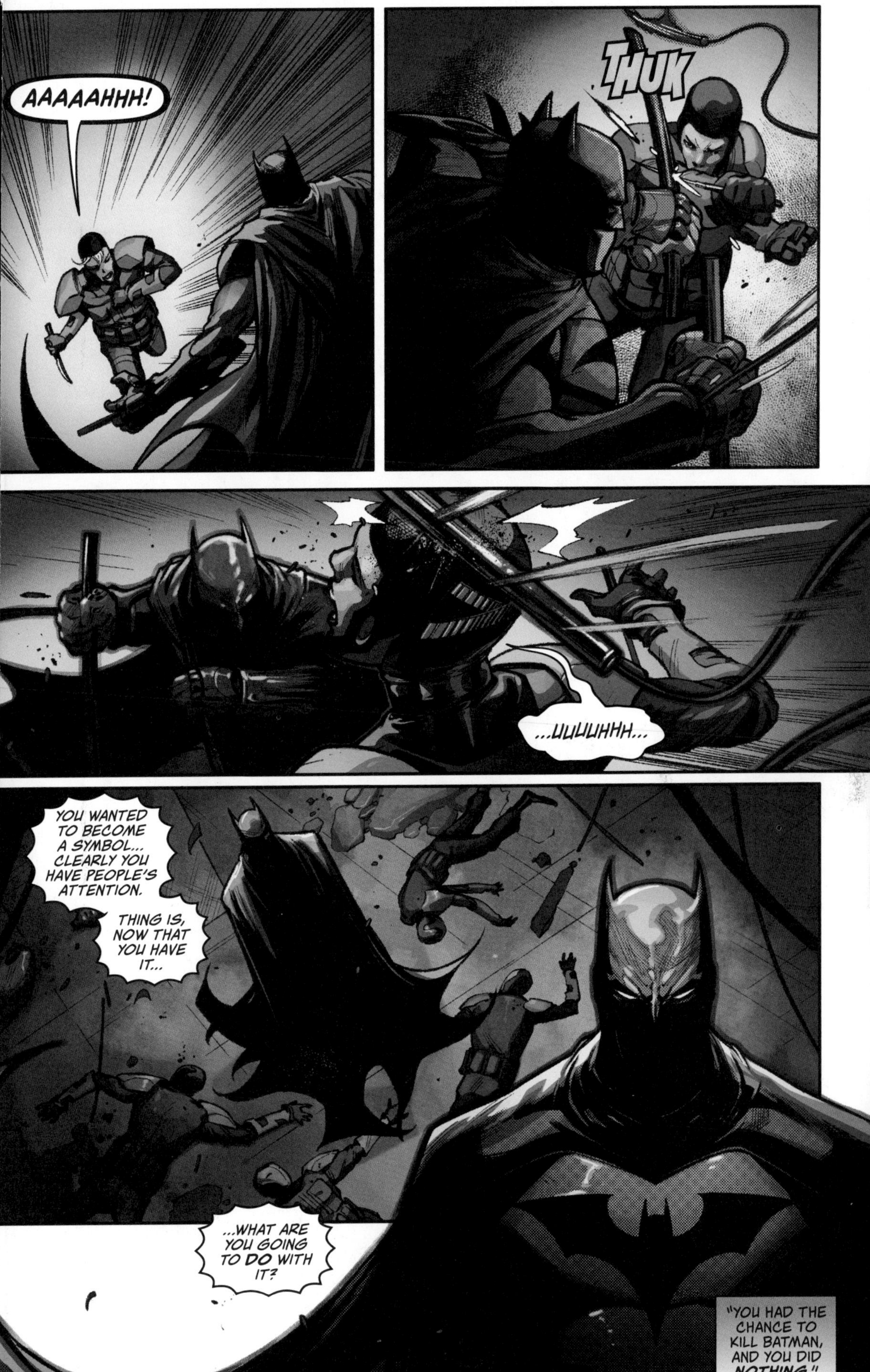
AAAAAHHH!
THUK
...UUUUHHH...
YOU WANTED TO BECOME A SYMBOL... CLEARLY YOU HAVE PEOPLE'S ATTENTION.
THING IS, NOW THAT YOU HAVE IT...
...WHAT ARE YOU GOING TO DO WITH IT?
"YOU HAD THE CHANCE TO KILL BATMAN, AND YOU DID NOTHING."

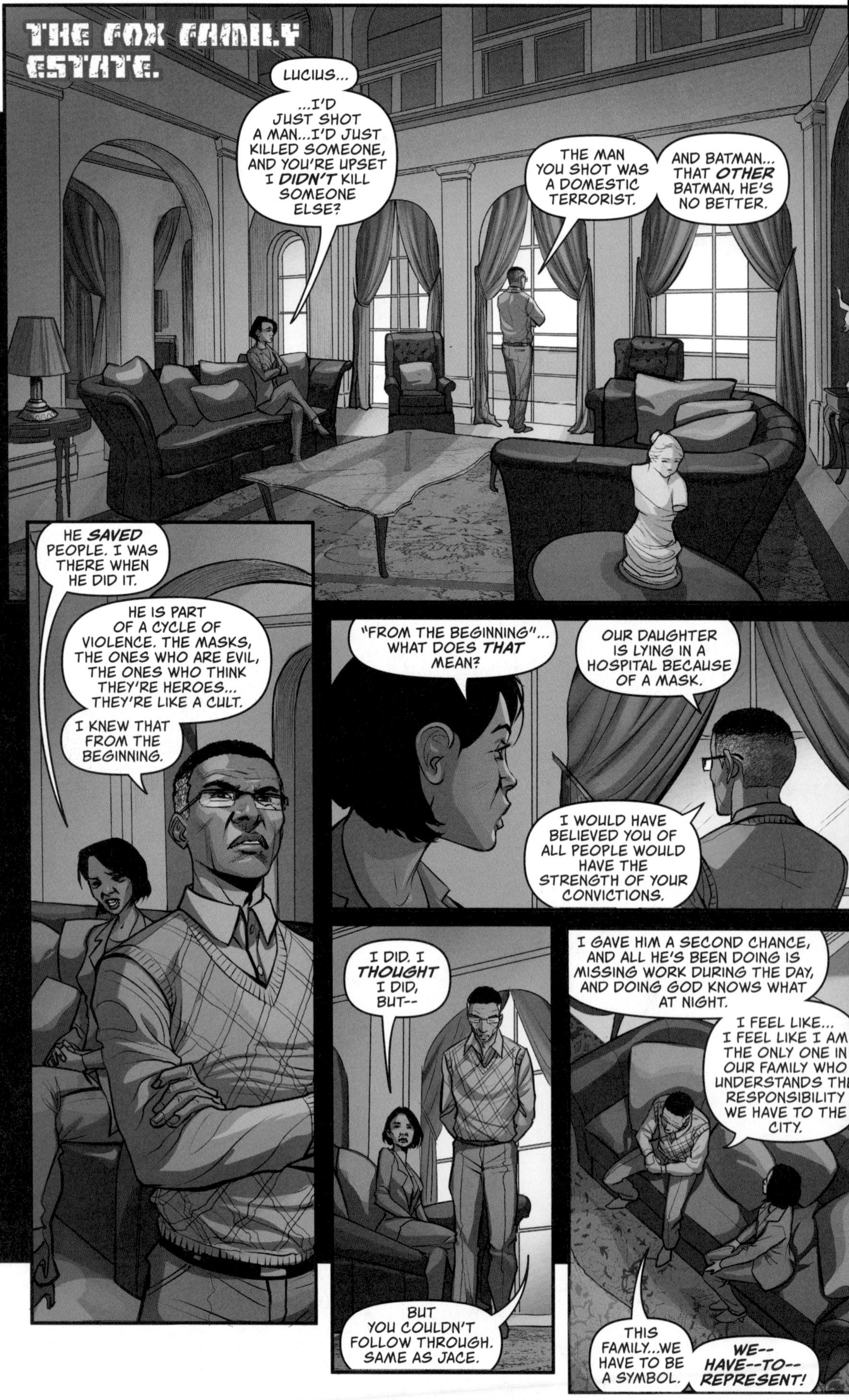
THE FOX FAMILY ESTATE.
LUCIUS...
...I'D JUST SHOT A MAN...I'D JUST KILLED SOMEONE, AND YOU'RE UPSET I DIDN'T KILL SOMEONE ELSE?
THE MAN YOU SHOT WAS A DOMESTIC TERRORIST.
AND BATMAN... THAT OTHER BATMAN, HE'S NO BETTER.
HE SAVED PEOPLE. I WAS THERE WHEN HE DID IT.
HE IS PART OF A CYCLE OF VIOLENCE. THE MASKS, THE ONES WHO ARE EVIL, THE ONES WHO THINK THEY'RE HEROES... THEY'RE LIKE A CULT.
I KNEW THAT FROM THE BEGINNING.
"FROM THE BEGINNING"... WHAT DOES THAT MEAN?
OUR DAUGHTER IS LYING IN A HOSPITAL BECAUSE OF A MASK.
I WOULD HAVE BELIEVED YOU OF ALL PEOPLE WOULD HAVE THE STRENGTH OF YOUR CONVICTIONS.
I DID. I THOUGHT I DID, BUT--
BUT YOU COULDN'T FOLLOW THROUGH. SAME AS JACE.
I GAVE HIM A SECOND CHANCE, AND ALL HE'S BEEN DOING IS MISSING WORK DURING THE DAY, AND DOING GOD KNOWS WHAT AT NIGHT.
I FEEL LIKE... I FEEL LIKE I AM THE ONLY ONE IN OUR FAMILY WHO UNDERSTANDS THE RESPONSIBILITY WE HAVE TO THE CITY.
THIS FAMILY...WE HAVE TO BE A SYMBOL.
WE--HAVE--TO--REPRESENT!

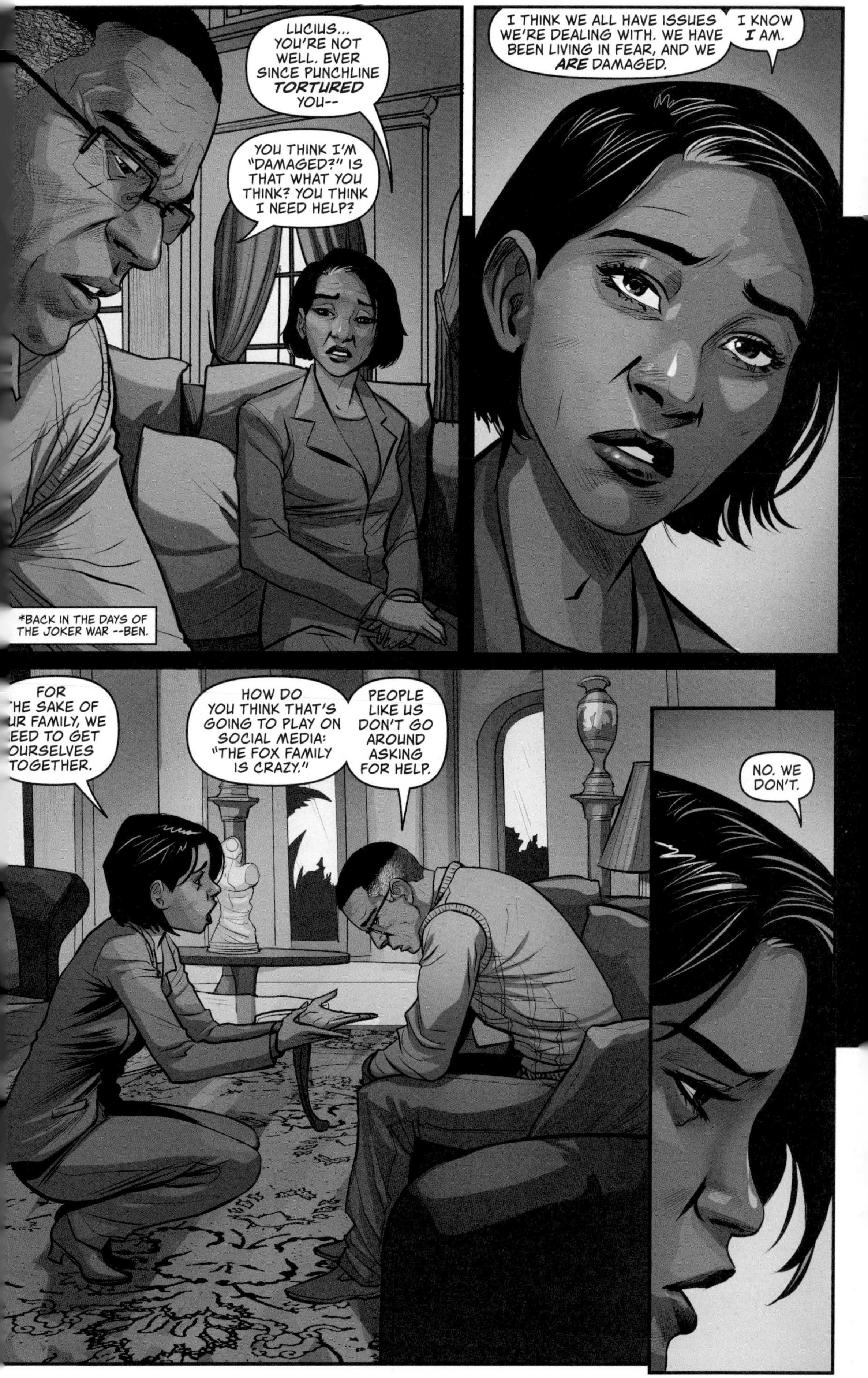
LUCIUS... YOU'RE NOT WELL. EVER SINCE PUNCHLINE TORTURED YOU--
YOU THINK I'M "DAMAGED?" IS THAT WHAT YOU THINK? YOU THINK I NEED HELP?
*BACK IN THE DAYS OF THE JOKER WAR --BEN.
I THINK WE ALL HAVE ISSUES WE'RE DEALING WITH. WE HAVE BEEN LIVING IN FEAR, AND WE ARE DAMAGED.
I KNOW I AM.
FOR HE SAKE OF UR FAMILY, WE EED TO GET OURSELVES TOGETHER.
HOW DO YOU THINK THAT'S GOING TO PLAY ON SOCIAL MEDIA: "THE FOX FAMILY IS CRAZY."
PEOPLE LIKE US DON'T GO AROUND ASKING FOR HELP.
NO. WE DON'T.

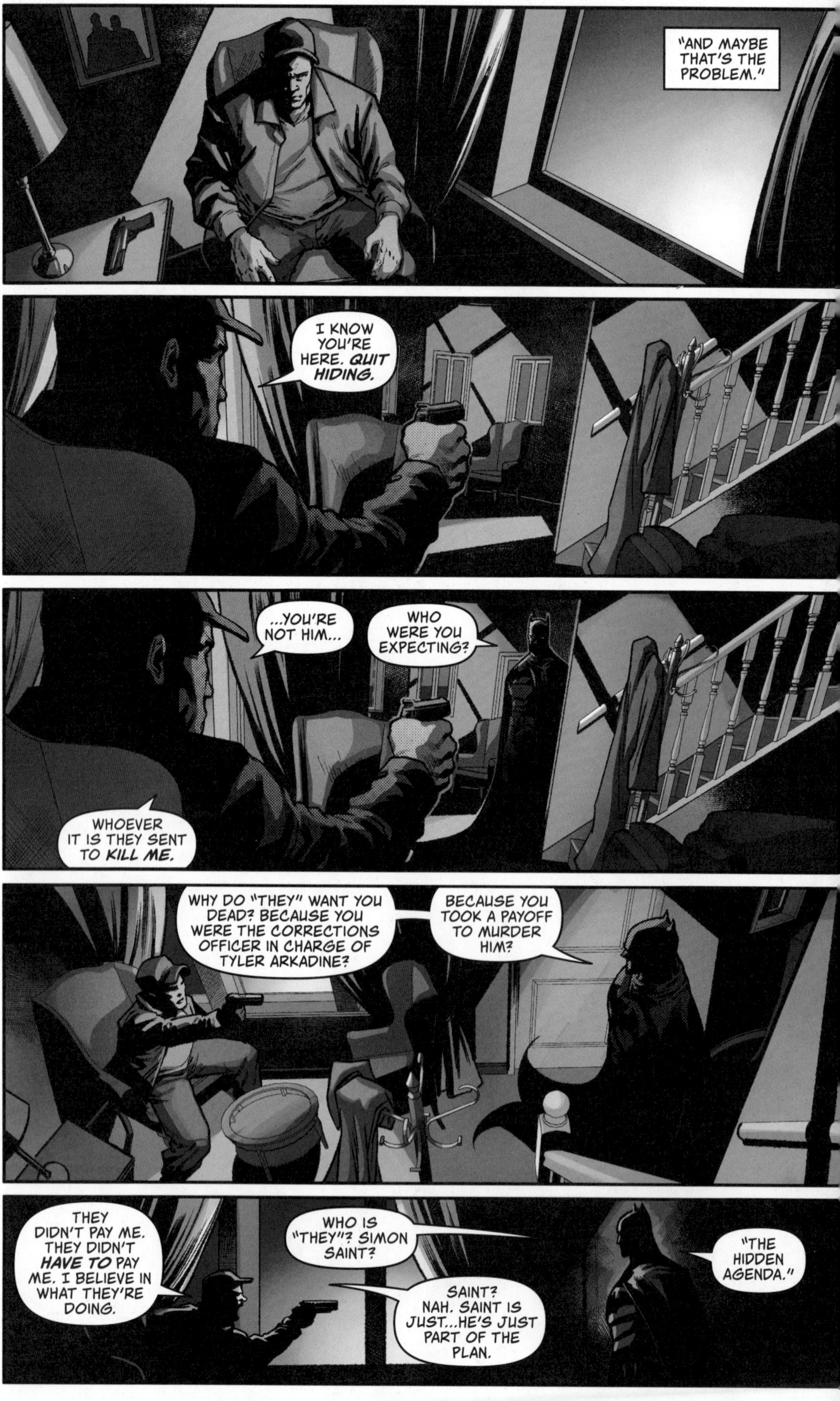
"AND MAYBE THAT'S THE PROBLEM."
I KNOW YOU'RE HERE. QUIT HIDING.
...YOU'RE NOT HIM...
WHO WERE YOU EXPECTING?
WHOEVER IT IS THEY SENT TO KILL ME.
WHY DO "THEY" WANT YOU DEAD? BECAUSE YOU WERE THE CORRECTIONS OFFICER IN CHARGE OF TYLER ARKADINE?
BECAUSE YOU TOOK A PAYOFF TO MURDER HIM?
THEY DIDN'T PAY ME. THEY DIDN'T HAVE TO PAY ME. I BELIEVE IN WHAT THEY'RE DOING.
WHO IS "THEY"? SIMON SAINT?
SAINT? NAH. SAINT IS JUST...HE'S JUST PART OF THE PLAN.
"THE HIDDEN AGENDA."

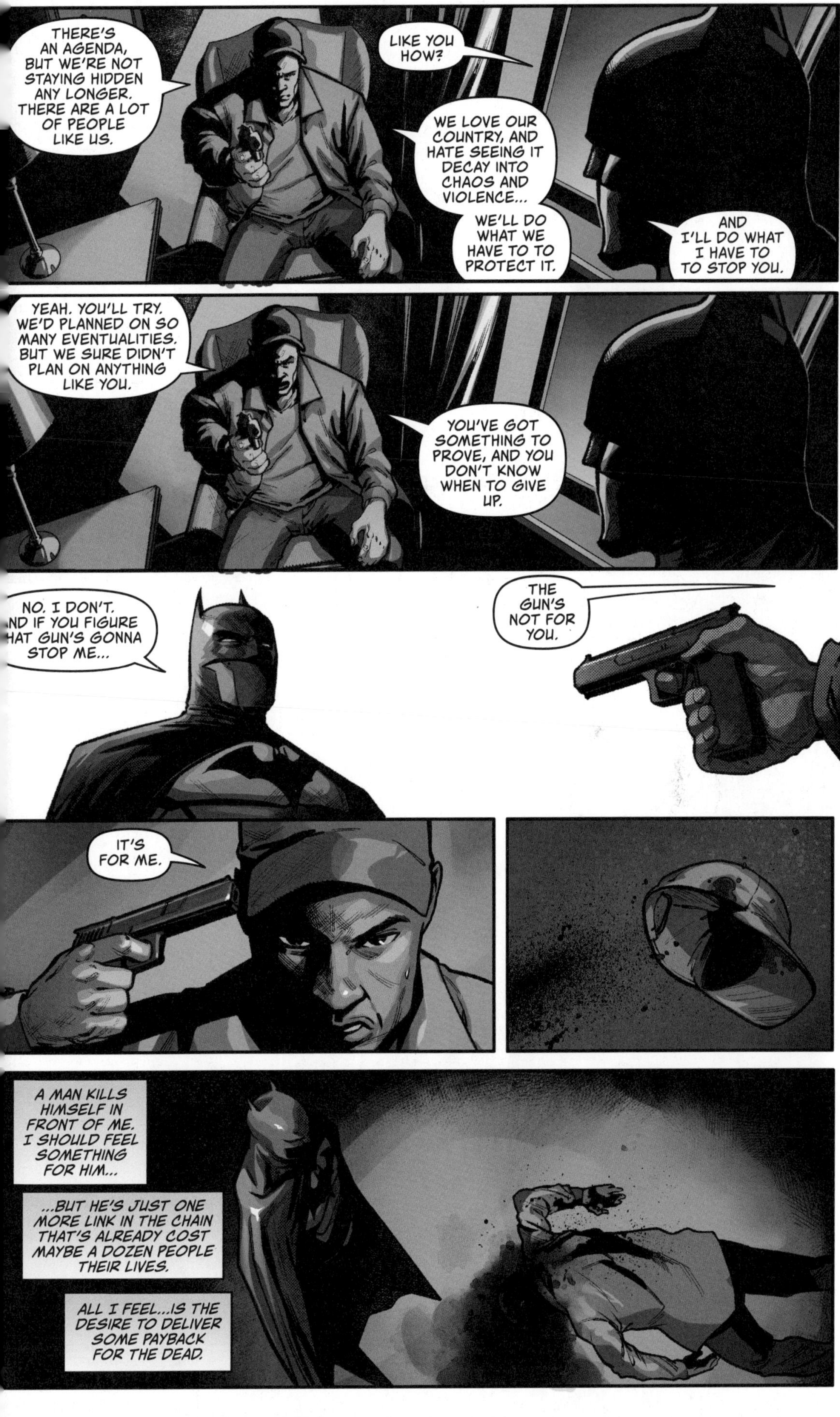
THERE'S AN AGENDA, BUT WE'RE NOT STAYING HIDDEN ANY LONGER. THERE ARE A LOT OF PEOPLE LIKE US.
LIKE YOU HOW?
WE LOVE OUR COUNTRY, AND HATE SEEING IT DECAY INTO CHAOS AND VIOLENCE...
WE'LL DO WHAT WE HAVE TO TO PROTECT IT.
AND I'LL DO WHAT I HAVE TO TO STOP YOU.
YEAH. YOU'LL TRY. WE'D PLANNED ON SO MANY EVENTUALITIES. BUT WE SURE DIDN'T PLAN ON ANYTHING LIKE YOU.
YOU'VE GOT SOMETHING TO PROVE, AND YOU DON'T KNOW WHEN TO GIVE UP.
NO. I DON'T. ND IF YOU FIGURE HAT GUN'S GONNA STOP ME...
THE GUN'S NOT FOR YOU.
IT'S FOR ME.
A MAN KILLS HIMSELF IN FRONT OF ME. I SHOULD FEEL SOMETHING FOR HIM...
...BUT HE'S JUST ONE MORE LINK IN THE CHAIN THAT'S ALREADY COST MAYBE A DOZEN PEOPLE THEIR LIVES.
ALL I FEEL...IS THE DESIRE TO DELIVER SOME PAYBACK FOR THE DEAD.

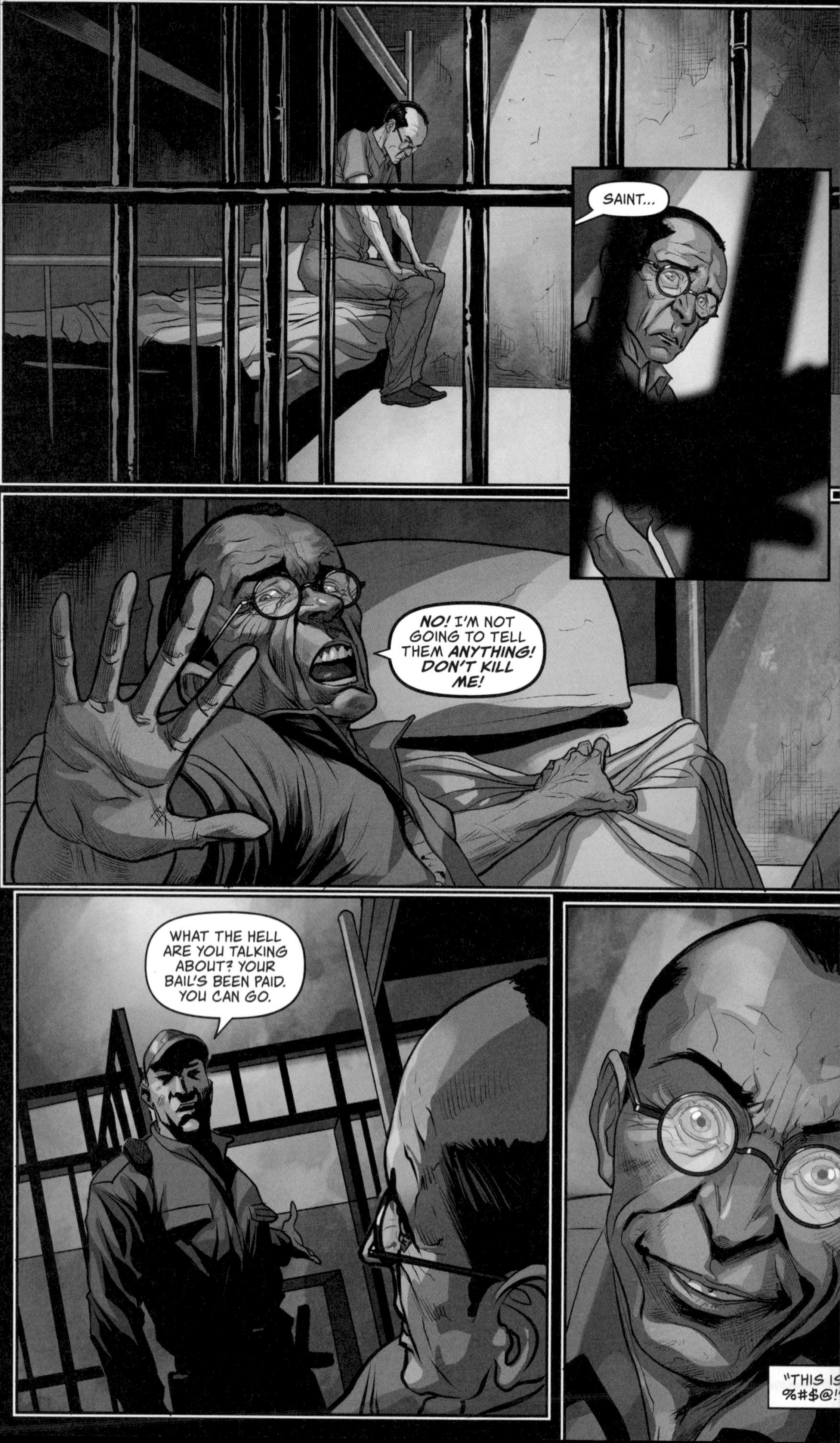
SAINT...
NO! I'M NOT GOING TO TELL THEM ANYTHING! DON'T KILL ME!
WHAT THE HELL ARE YOU TALKING ABOUT? YOUR BAIL'S BEEN PAID. YOU CAN GO.
"THIS IS
%#$@!

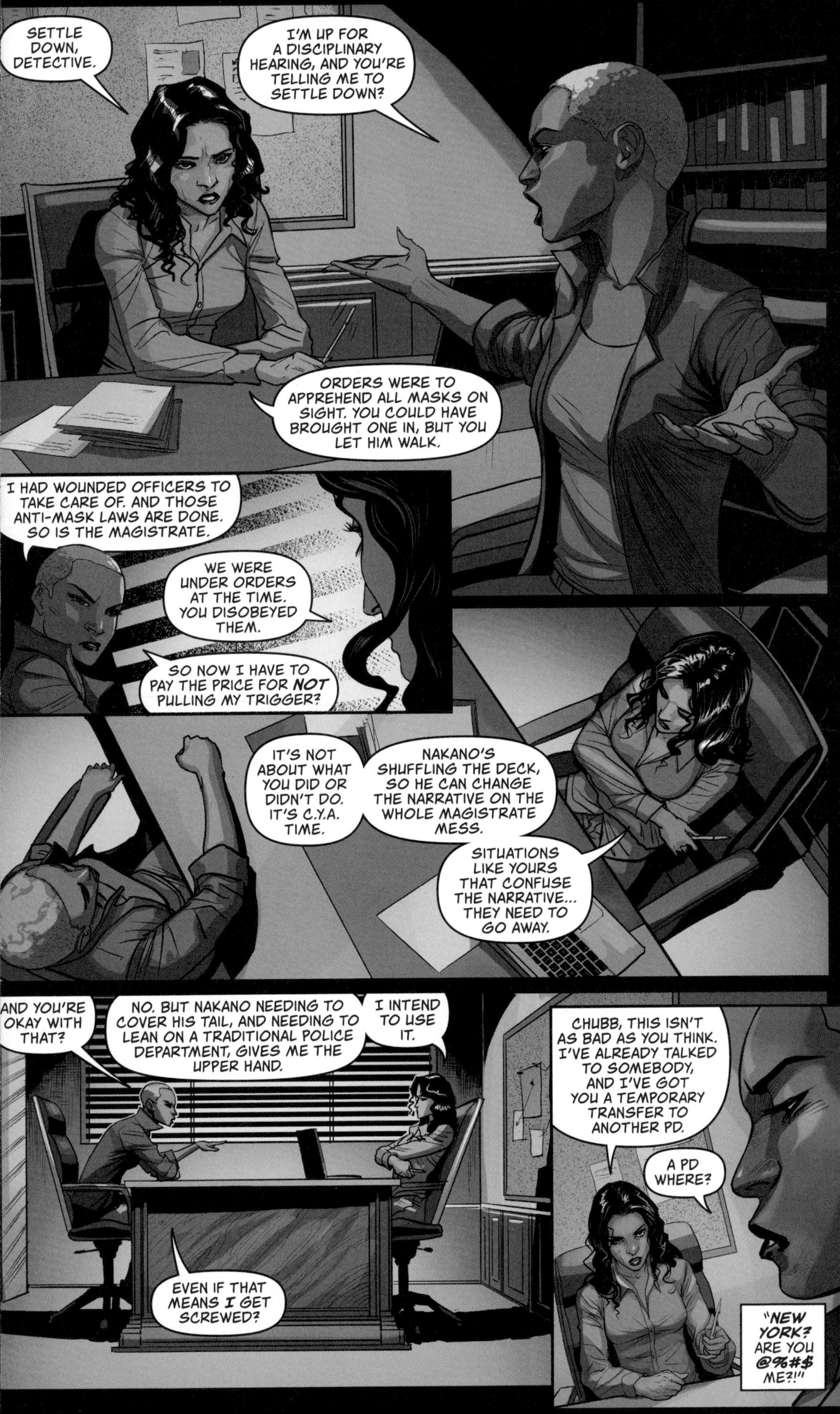
SETTLE DOWN, DETECTIVE.
I'M UP FOR A DISCIPLINARY HEARING, AND YOU'RE TELLING ME TO SETTLE DOWN?
ORDERS WERE TO APPREHEND ALL MASKS ON SIGHT. YOU COULD HAVE BROUGHT ONE IN, BUT YOU LET HIM WALK.
I HAD WOUNDED OFFICERS TO TAKE CARE OF. AND THOSE ANTI-MASK LAWS ARE DONE. SO IS THE MAGISTRATE.
WE WERE UNDER ORDERS AT THE TIME. YOU DISOBEYED THEM.
SO NOW I HAVE TO PAY THE PRICE FOR NOT PULLING MY TRIGGER?
IT'S NOT ABOUT WHAT YOU DID OR DIDN'T DO. IT'S C.Y.A. TIME.
NAKANO'S SHUFFLING THE DECK, SO HE CAN CHANGE THE NARRATIVE ON THE WHOLE MAGISTRATE MESS.
SITUATIONS LIKE YOURS THAT CONFUSE THE NARRATIVE... THEY NEED TO GO AWAY.
AND YOU'RE OKAY WITH THAT?
NO. BUT NAKANO NEEDING TO COVER HIS TAIL, AND NEEDING TO LEAN ON A TRADITIONAL POLICE DEPARTMENT, GIVES ME THE UPPER HAND.
I INTEND TO USE IT.
EVEN IF THAT MEANS I GET SCREWED?
CHUBB, THIS ISN'T AS BAD AS YOU THINK. I'VE ALREADY TALKED TO SOMEBODY, AND I'VE GOT YOU A TEMPORARY TRANSFER TO ANOTHER PD.
A PD WHERE?
"NEW YORK? ARE YOU @%#$ ME?!"

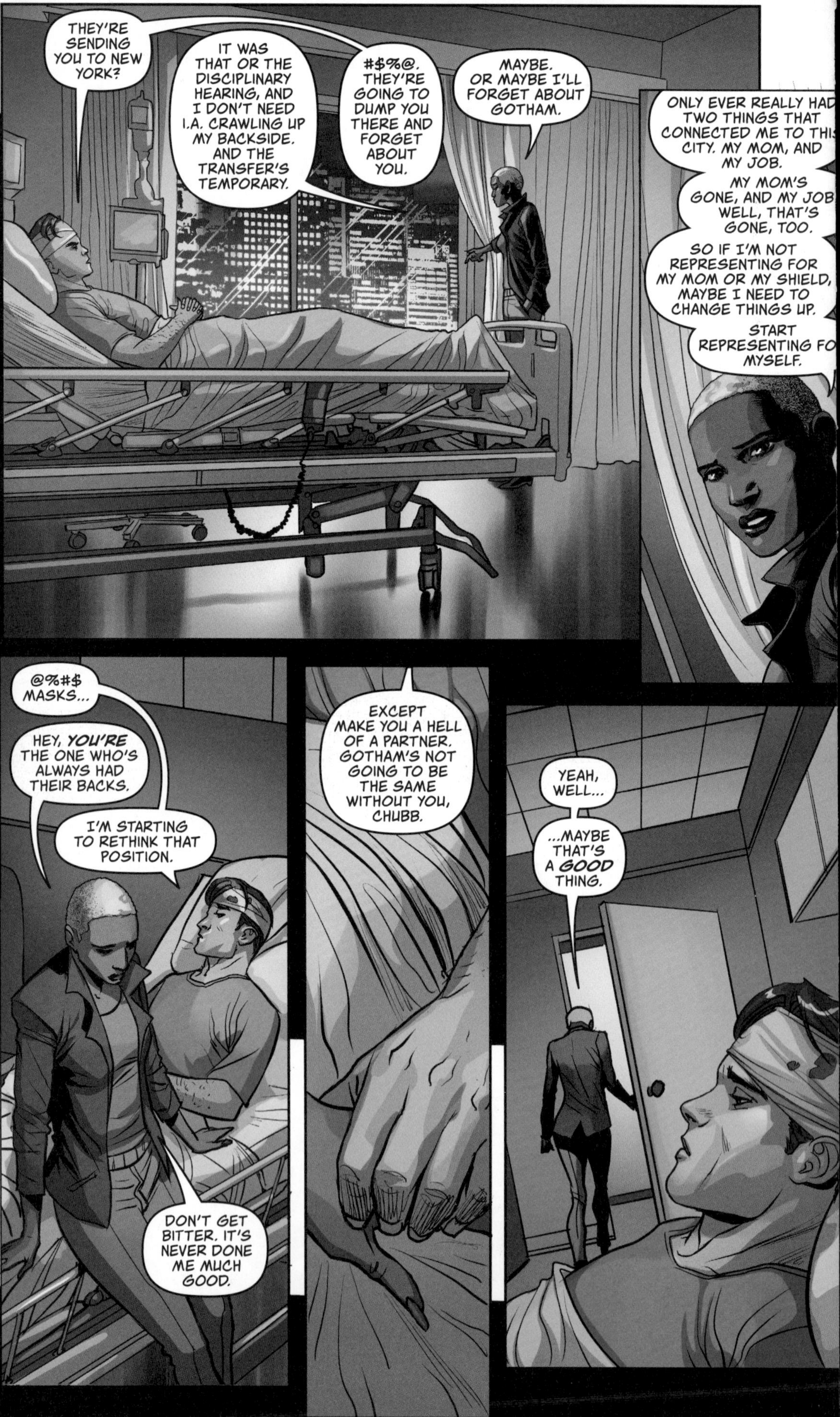
THEY'RE SENDING YOU TO NEW YORK?
IT WAS THAT OR THE DISCIPLINARY HEARING, AND I DON'T NEED I.A. CRAWLING UP MY BACKSIDE. AND THE TRANSFER'S TEMPORARY.
#$%@. THEY'RE GOING TO DUMP YOU THERE AND FORGET ABOUT YOU.
MAYBE. OR MAYBE I'LL FORGET ABOUT GOTHAM.
ONLY EVER REALLY HAD TWO THINGS THAT CONNECTED ME TO THI CITY. MY MOM, AND MY JOB.
MY MOM'S GONE, AND MY JOB WELL, THAT'S GONE, TOO.
SO IF I'M NOT REPRESENTING FOR MY MOM OR MY SHIELD, MAYBE I NEED TO CHANGE THINGS UP.
START REPRESENTING FO MYSELF.
@%#$ MASKS...
HEY, ***YOU'RE*** THE ONE WHO'S ALWAYS HAD THEIR BACKS.
I'M STARTING TO RETHINK THAT POSITION.
DON'T GET BITTER. IT'S NEVER DONE ME MUCH GOOD.
EXCEPT MAKE YOU A HELL OF A PARTNER. GOTHAM'S NOT GOING TO BE THE SAME WITHOUT YOU, CHUBB.
YEAH, WELL...
...MAYBE THAT'S A ***GOOD*** THING.

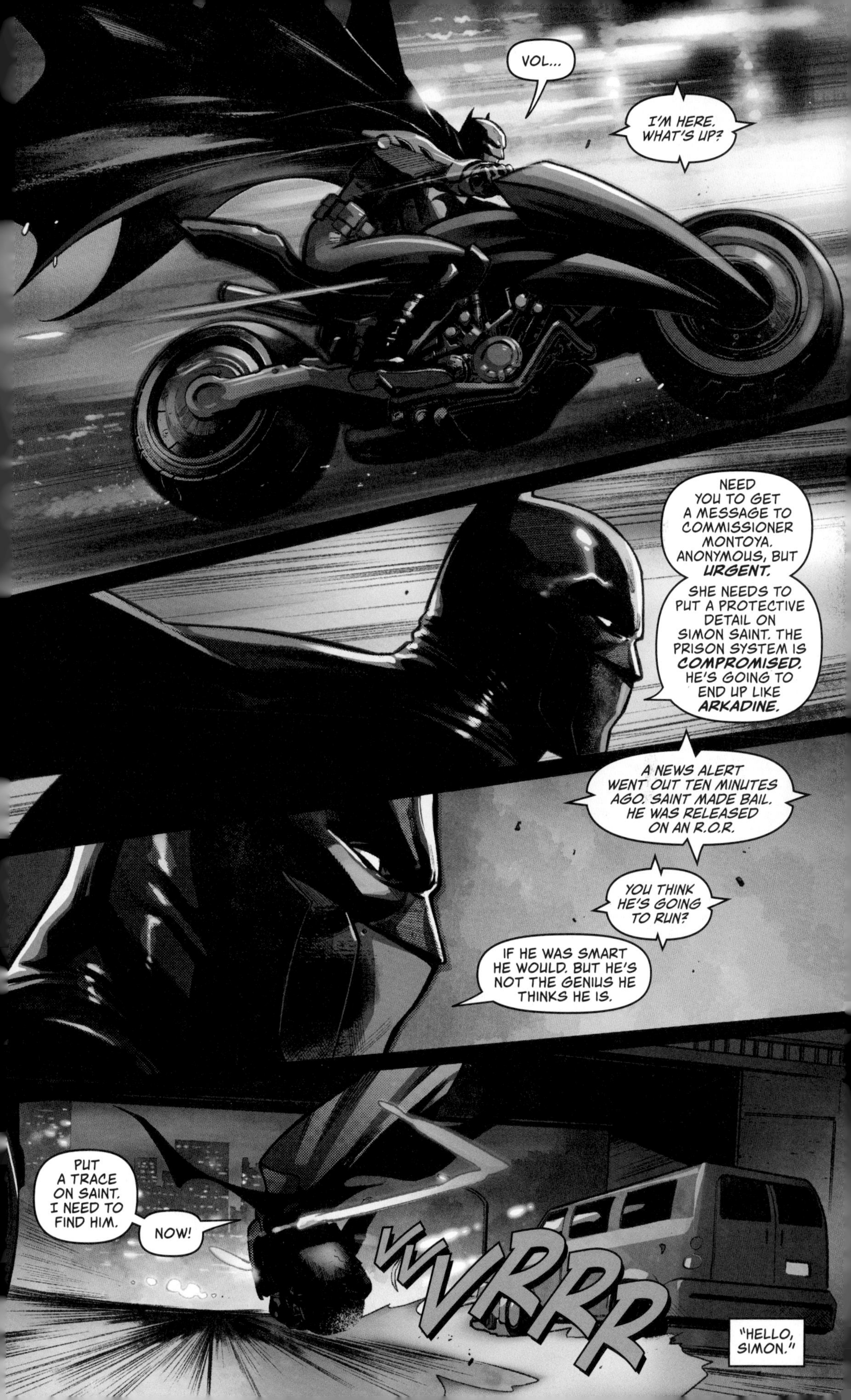
VOL...
I'M HERE. WHAT'S UP?
NEED YOU TO GET A MESSAGE TO COMMISSIONER MONTOYA. ANONYMOUS, BUT URGENT.
SHE NEEDS TO PUT A PROTECTIVE DETAIL ON SIMON SAINT. THE PRISON SYSTEM IS COMPROMISED. HE'S GOING TO END UP LIKE ARKADINE.
A NEWS ALERT WENT OUT TEN MINUTES AGO. SAINT MADE BAIL. HE WAS RELEASED ON AN R.O.R.
YOU THINK HE'S GOING TO RUN?
IF HE WAS SMART HE WOULD. BUT HE'S NOT THE GENIUS HE THINKS HE IS.
PUT A TRACE ON SAINT. I NEED TO FIND HIM.
NOW!
VVVRRRR
"HELLO, SIMON."

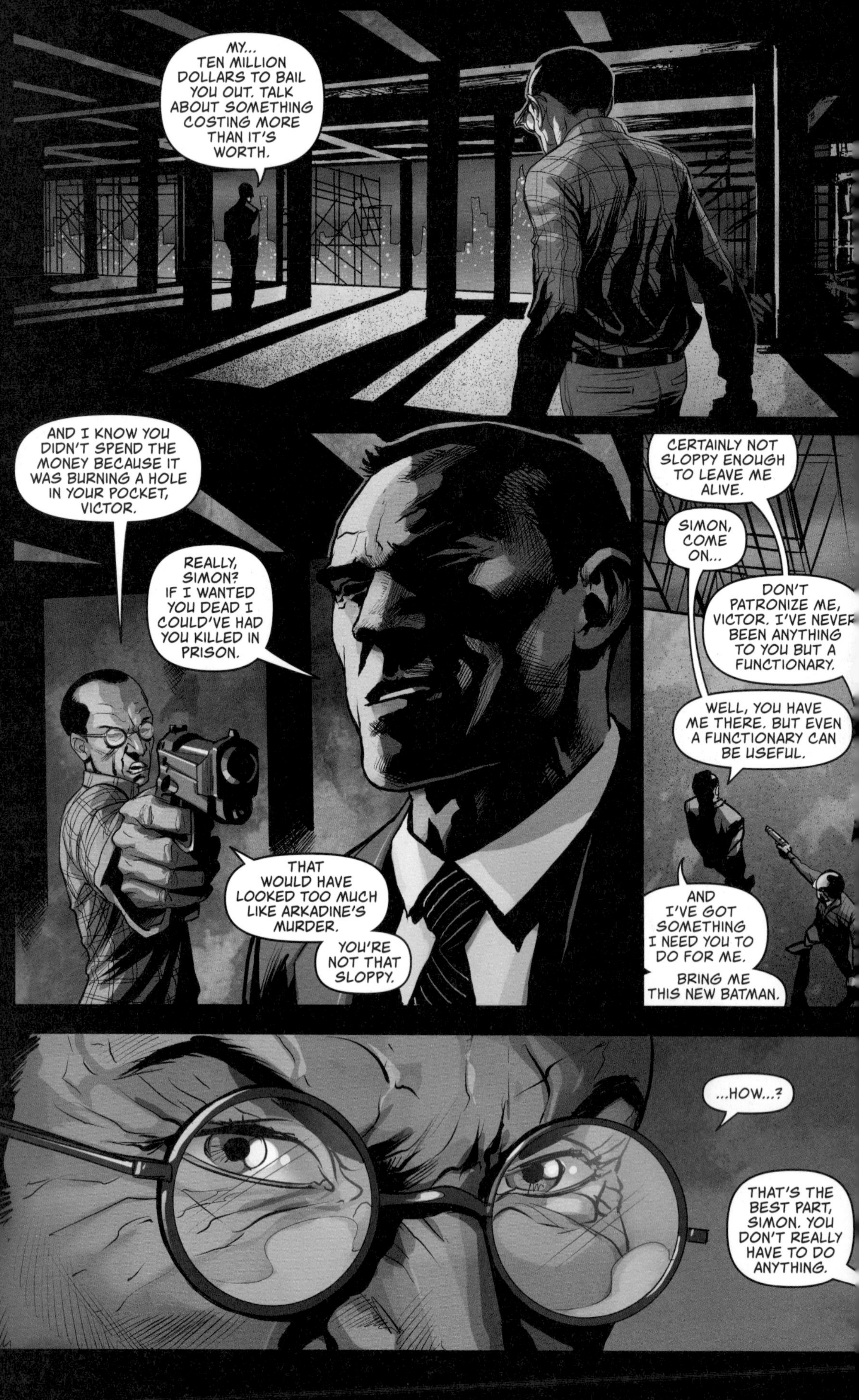
MY... TEN MILLION DOLLARS TO BAIL YOU OUT. TALK ABOUT SOMETHING COSTING MORE THAN IT'S WORTH.
AND I KNOW YOU DIDN'T SPEND THE MONEY BECAUSE IT WAS BURNING A HOLE IN YOUR POCKET, VICTOR.
REALLY, SIMON? IF I WANTED YOU DEAD I COULD'VE HAD YOU KILLED IN PRISON.
THAT WOULD HAVE LOOKED TOO MUCH LIKE ARKADINE'S MURDER.
YOU'RE NOT THAT SLOPPY.
CERTAINLY NOT SLOPPY ENOUGH TO LEAVE ME ALIVE.
SIMON, COME ON...
DON'T PATRONIZE ME, VICTOR. I'VE NEVER BEEN ANYTHING TO YOU BUT A FUNCTIONARY.
WELL, YOU HAVE ME THERE. BUT EVEN A FUNCTIONARY CAN BE USEFUL.
AND I'VE GOT SOMETHING I NEED YOU TO DO FOR ME.
BRING ME THIS NEW BATMAN.
...HOW...?
THAT'S THE BEST PART, SIMON. YOU DON'T REALLY HAVE TO DO ANYTHING.

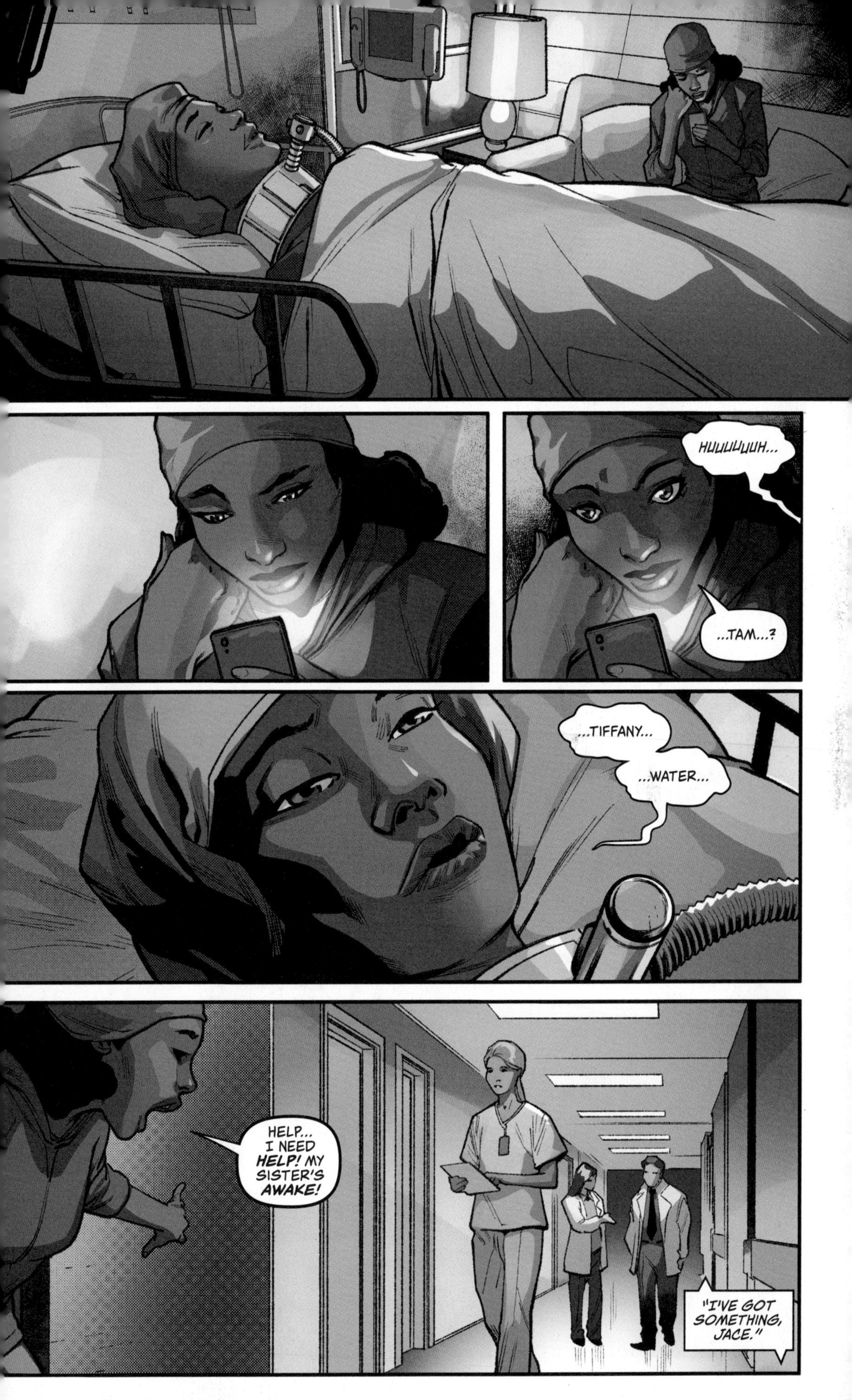
HUUUUUUH...
...TAM...?
...TIFFANY...
...WATER...
HELP... I NEED HELP! MY SISTER'S AWAKE!
"I'VE GOT SOMETHING, JACE."

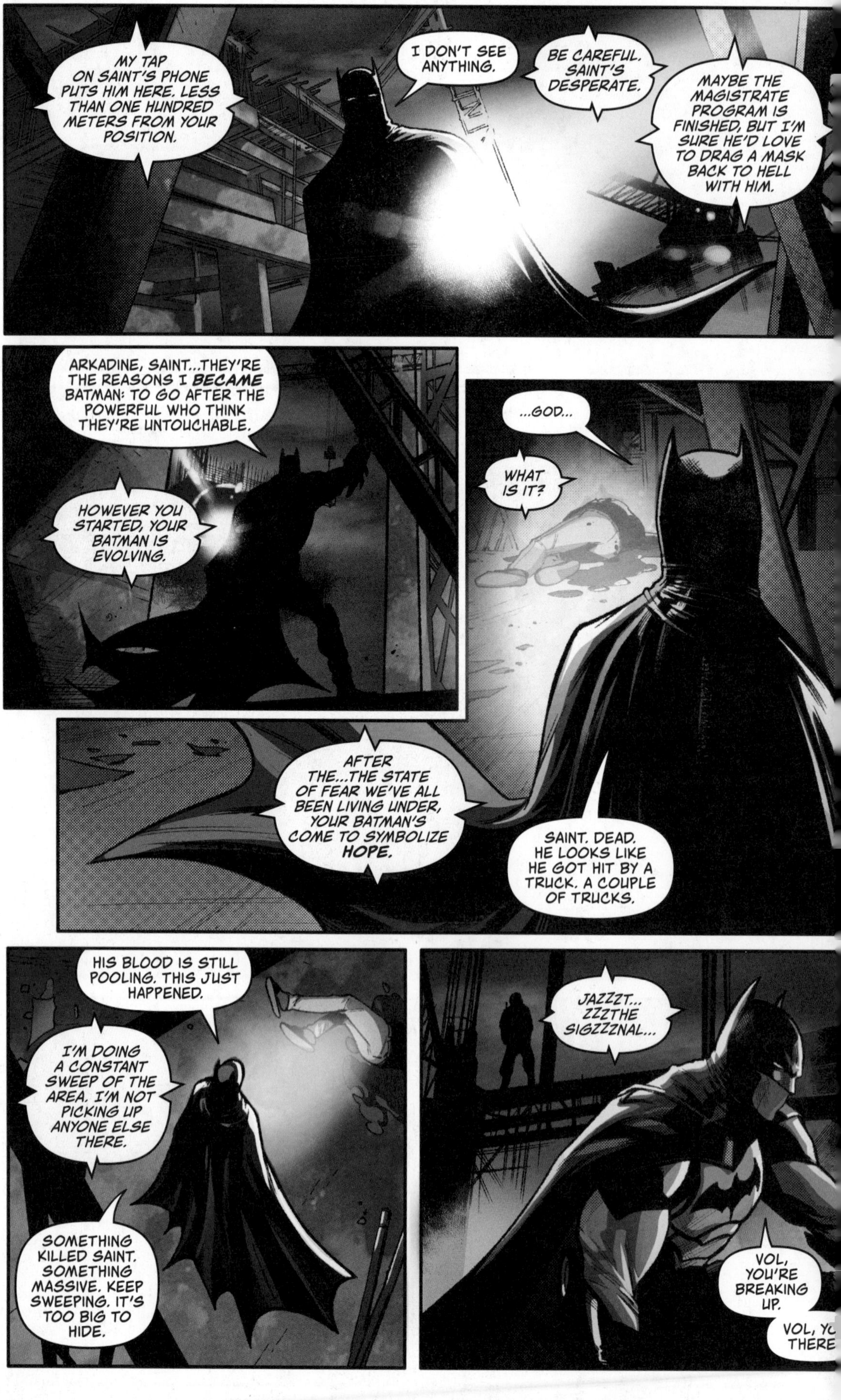
MY TAP ON SAINT'S PHONE PUTS HIM HERE. LESS THAN ONE HUNDRED METERS FROM YOUR POSITION.
I DON'T SEE ANYTHING.
BE CAREFUL. SAINT'S DESPERATE.
MAYBE THE MAGISTRATE PROGRAM IS FINISHED, BUT I'M SURE HE'D LOVE TO DRAG A MASK BACK TO HELL WITH HIM.
ARKADINE, SAINT...THEY'RE THE REASONS I BECAME BATMAN: TO GO AFTER THE POWERFUL WHO THINK THEY'RE UNTOUCHABLE.
HOWEVER YOU STARTED, YOUR BATMAN IS EVOLVING.
...GOD...
WHAT IS IT?
AFTER THE...THE STATE OF FEAR WE'VE ALL BEEN LIVING UNDER, YOUR BATMAN'S COME TO SYMBOLIZE HOPE.
SAINT. DEAD. HE LOOKS LIKE HE GOT HIT BY A TRUCK. A COUPLE OF TRUCKS.
HIS BLOOD IS STILL POOLING. THIS JUST HAPPENED.
I'M DOING A CONSTANT SWEEP OF THE AREA. I'M NOT PICKING UP ANYONE ELSE THERE.
SOMETHING KILLED SAINT. SOMETHING MASSIVE. KEEP SWEEPING. IT'S TOO BIG TO HIDE.
JAZZZT... ZZZTHE SIGZZZZNAL...
VOL, YOU'RE BREAKING UP.

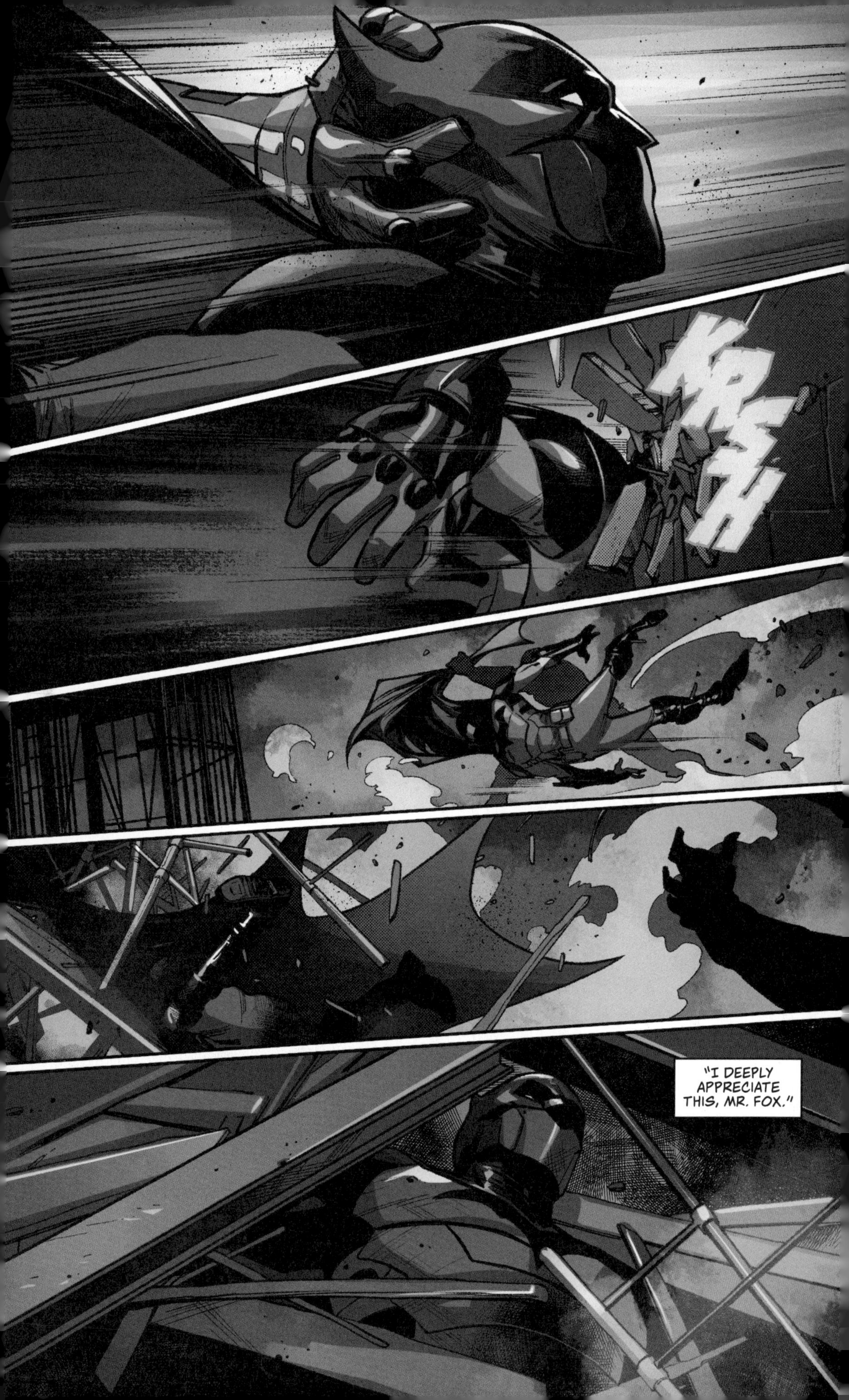
KRSSH
"I DEEPLY APPRECIATE THIS, MR. FOX."

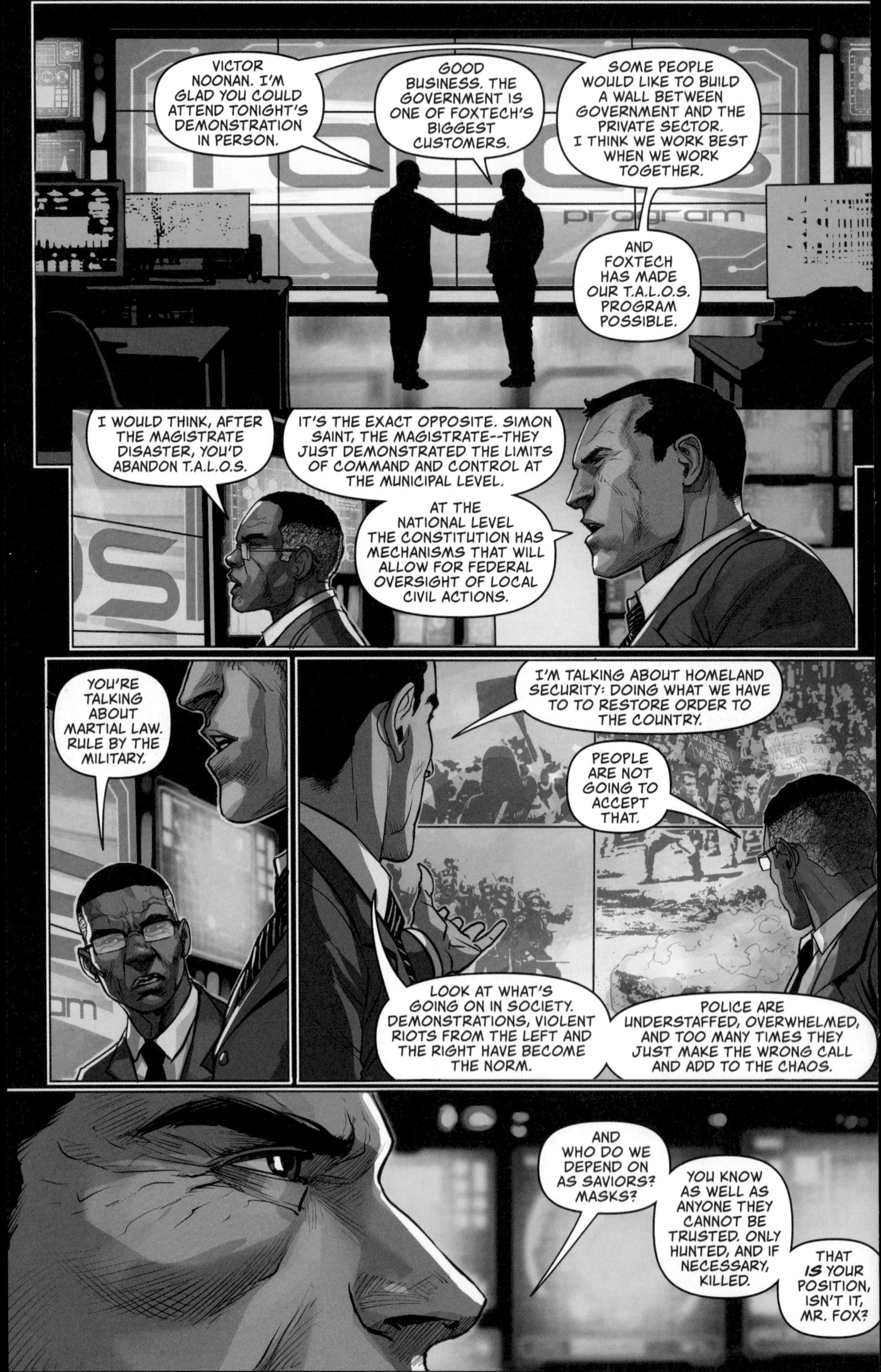
VICTOR NOONAN. I'M GLAD YOU COULD ATTEND TONIGHT'S DEMONSTRATION IN PERSON.
GOOD BUSINESS. THE GOVERNMENT IS ONE OF FOXTECH'S BIGGEST CUSTOMERS.
SOME PEOPLE WOULD LIKE TO BUILD A WALL BETWEEN GOVERNMENT AND THE PRIVATE SECTOR. I THINK WE WORK BEST WHEN WE WORK TOGETHER.
AND FOXTECH HAS MADE OUR T.A.L.O.S. PROGRAM POSSIBLE.
program
I WOULD THINK, AFTER THE MAGISTRATE DISASTER, YOU'D ABANDON T.A.L.O.S.
IT'S THE EXACT OPPOSITE. SIMON SAINT, THE MAGISTRATE--THEY JUST DEMONSTRATED THE LIMITS OF COMMAND AND CONTROL AT THE MUNICIPAL LEVEL.
AT THE NATIONAL LEVEL THE CONSTITUTION HAS MECHANISMS THAT WILL ALLOW FOR FEDERAL OVERSIGHT OF LOCAL CIVIL ACTIONS.
YOU'RE TALKING ABOUT MARTIAL LAW. RULE BY THE MILITARY.
I'M TALKING ABOUT HOMELAND SECURITY: DOING WHAT WE HAVE TO TO RESTORE ORDER TO THE COUNTRY.
PEOPLE ARE NOT GOING TO ACCEPT THAT.
LOOK AT WHAT'S GOING ON IN SOCIETY. DEMONSTRATIONS, VIOLENT RIOTS FROM THE LEFT AND THE RIGHT HAVE BECOME THE NORM.
POLICE ARE UNDERSTAFFED, OVERWHELMED, AND TOO MANY TIMES THEY JUST MAKE THE WRONG CALL AND ADD TO THE CHAOS.
AND WHO DO WE DEPEND ON AS SAVIORS? MASKS?
YOU KNOW AS WELL AS ANYONE THEY CANNOT BE TRUSTED. ONLY HUNTED, AND IF NECESSARY, KILLED.
THAT *IS* YOUR POSITION, ISN'T IT, MR. FOX?

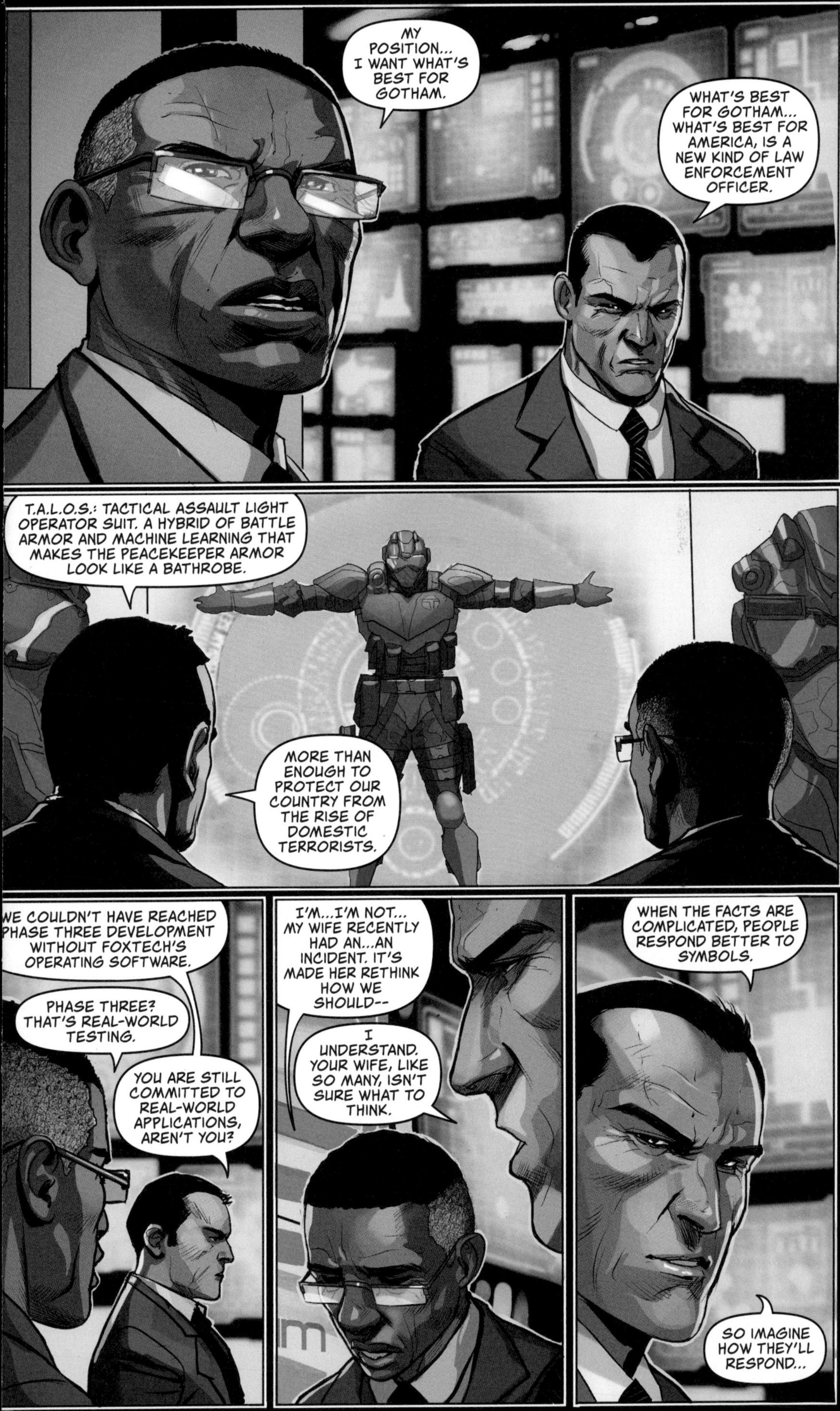

MY POSITION... I WANT WHAT'S BEST FOR GOTHAM.
WHAT'S BEST FOR GOTHAM... WHAT'S BEST FOR AMERICA, IS A NEW KIND OF LAW ENFORCEMENT OFFICER.
T.A.L.O.S.: TACTICAL ASSAULT LIGHT OPERATOR SUIT. A HYBRID OF BATTLE ARMOR AND MACHINE LEARNING THAT MAKES THE PEACEKEEPER ARMOR LOOK LIKE A BATHROBE.
MORE THAN ENOUGH TO PROTECT OUR COUNTRY FROM THE RISE OF DOMESTIC TERRORISTS.
WE COULDN'T HAVE REACHED PHASE THREE DEVELOPMENT WITHOUT FOXTECH'S OPERATING SOFTWARE.
PHASE THREE? THAT'S REAL-WORLD TESTING.
YOU ARE STILL COMMITTED TO REAL-WORLD APPLICATIONS, AREN'T YOU?
I'M...I'M NOT... MY WIFE RECENTLY HAD AN...AN INCIDENT. IT'S MADE HER RETHINK HOW WE SHOULD--
I UNDERSTAND. YOUR WIFE, LIKE SO MANY, ISN'T SURE WHAT TO THINK.
WHEN THE FACTS ARE COMPLICATED, PEOPLE RESPOND BETTER TO SYMBOLS.
SO IMAGINE HOW THEY'LL RESPOND...

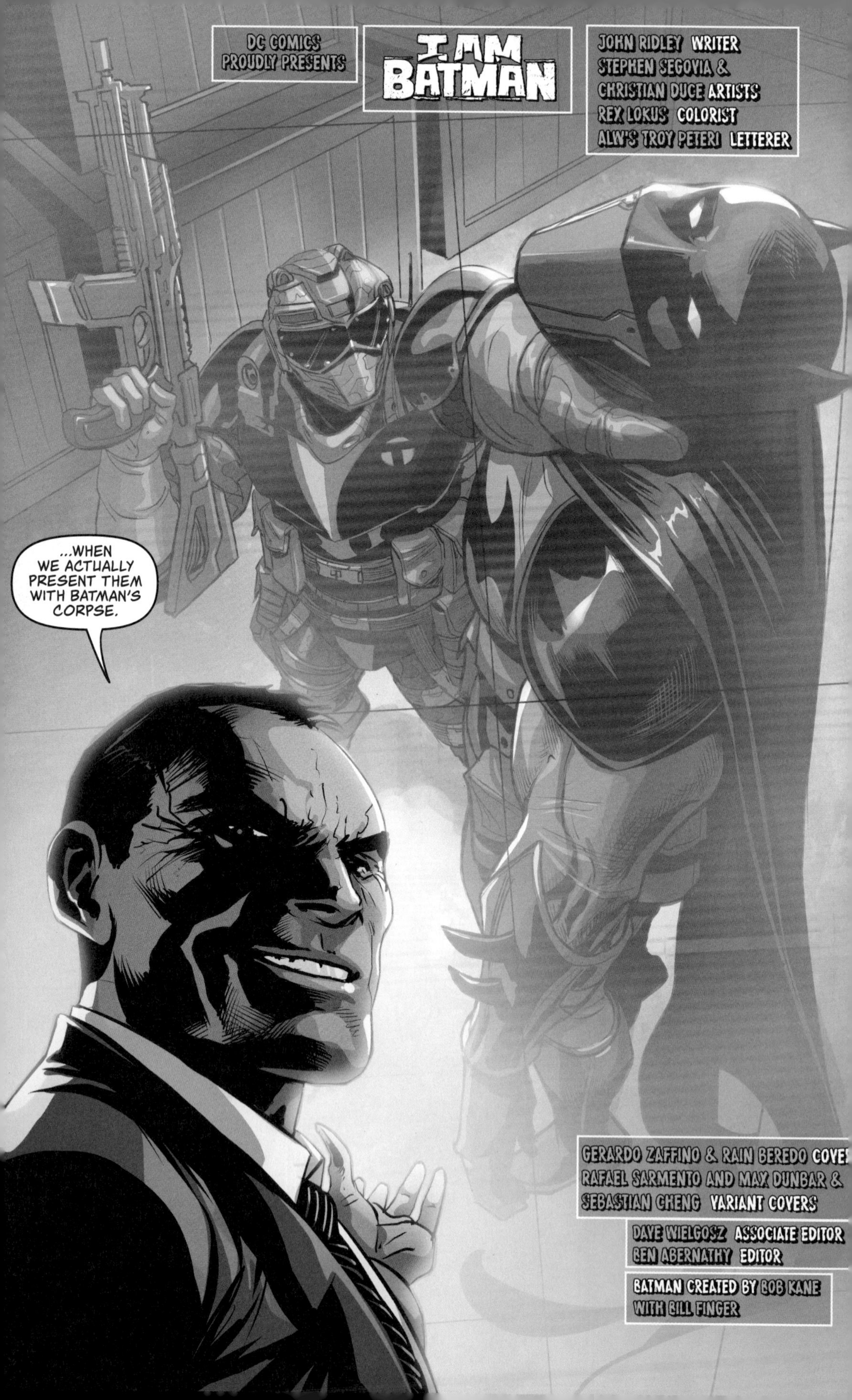
DC COMICS
PROUDLY PRESENTS
I AM
BATMAN
JOHN RIDLEY WRITER
STEPHEN SEGOVIA &
CHRISTIAN DUCE ARTISTS
REX LOKUS COLORIST
ALW'S TROY PETERI LETTERER
...WHEN WE ACTUALLY PRESENT THEM WITH BATMAN'S CORPSE.
GERARDO ZAFFINO & RAIN BEREDO COVE
RAFAEL SARMENTO AND MAX DUNBAR &
SEBASTIAN CHENG VARIANT COVERS
DAVE WIELGOSZ ASSOCIATE EDITOR
BEN ABERNATHY EDITOR
BATMAN CREATED BY BOB KANE
WITH BILL FINGER

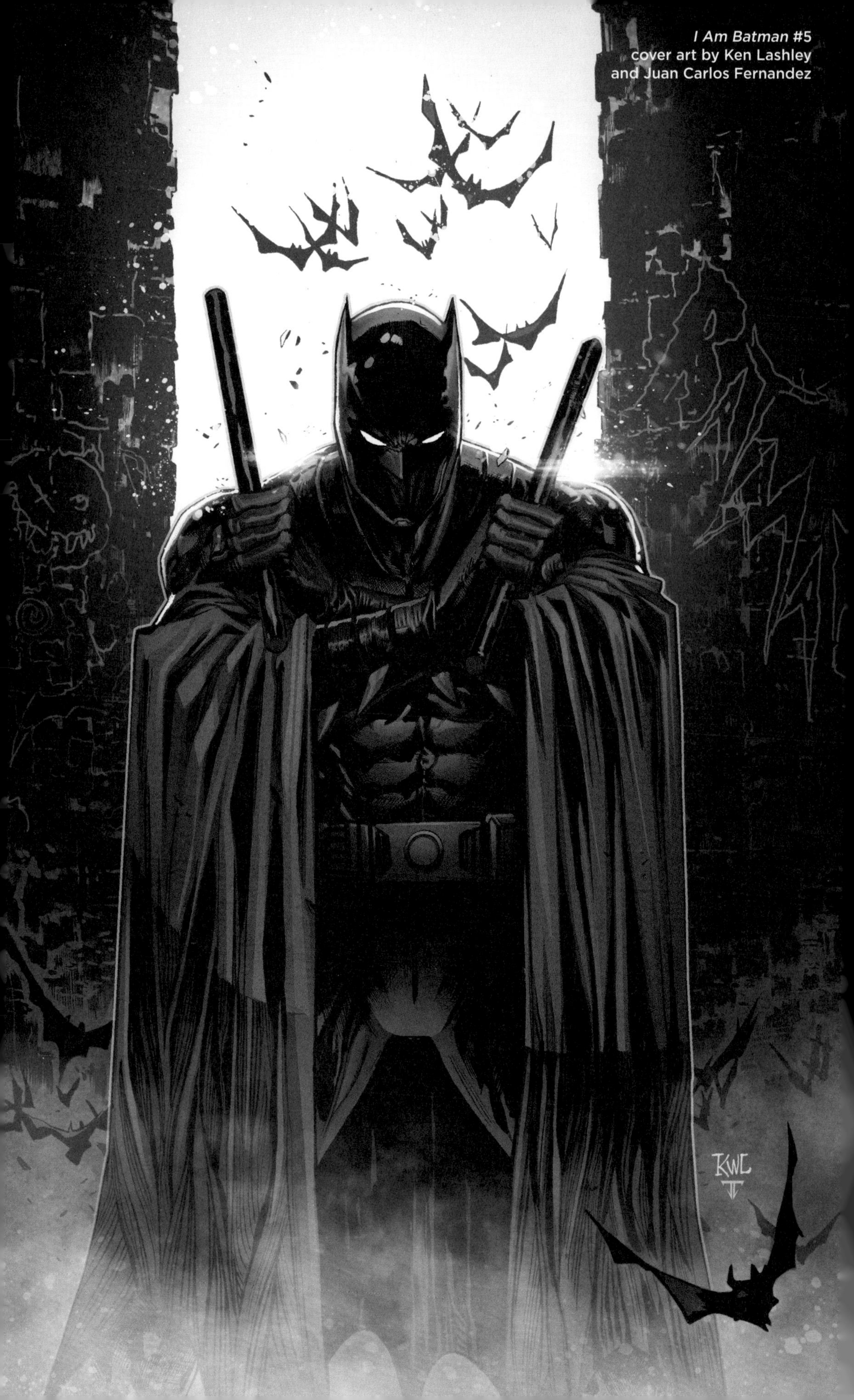

I Am Batman #5
cover art by Ken Lashley
and Juan Carlos Fernandez

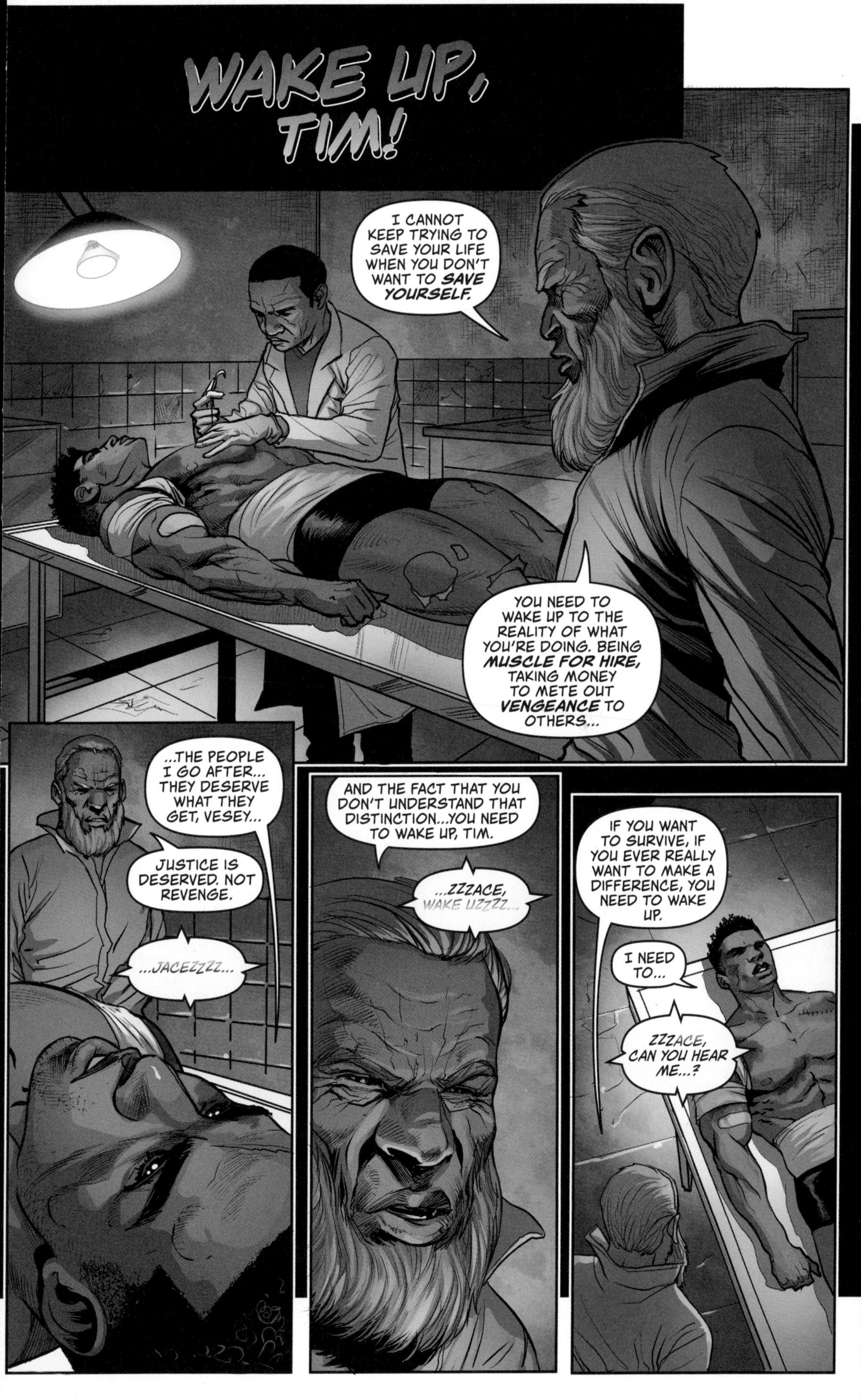
WAKE UP, TIM!
I CANNOT KEEP TRYING TO SAVE YOUR LIFE WHEN YOU DON'T WANT TO SAVE YOURSELF.
YOU NEED TO WAKE UP TO THE REALITY OF WHAT YOU'RE DOING. BEING MUSCLE FOR HIRE, TAKING MONEY TO METE OUT VENGEANCE TO OTHERS...
...THE PEOPLE I GO AFTER... THEY DESERVE WHAT THEY GET, VESEY...
JUSTICE IS DESERVED. NOT REVENGE.
...JACEZZZZ...
AND THE FACT THAT YOU DON'T UNDERSTAND THAT DISTINCTION...YOU NEED TO WAKE UP, TIM.
...ZZZACE, WAKE UZZZZ...
IF YOU WANT TO SURVIVE, IF YOU EVER REALLY WANT TO MAKE A DIFFERENCE, YOU NEED TO WAKE UP.
I NEED TO...
ZZZACE, CAN YOU HEAR ME...?

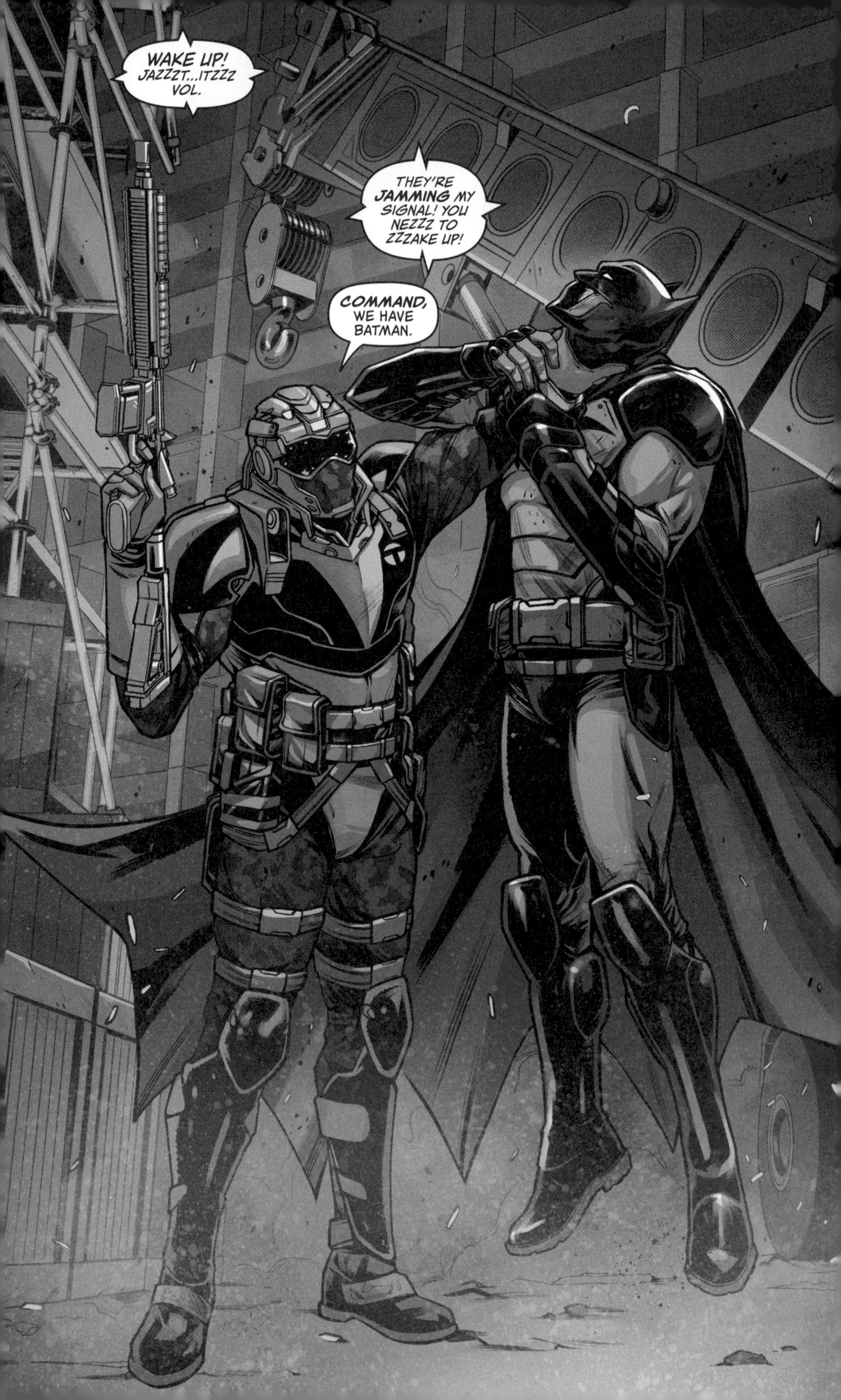

WAKE UP! JAZZZT...ITZZZ VOL.
THEY'RE JAMMING MY SIGNAL! YOU NEZZZ TO ZZZAKE UP!
COMMAND, WE HAVE BATMAN.

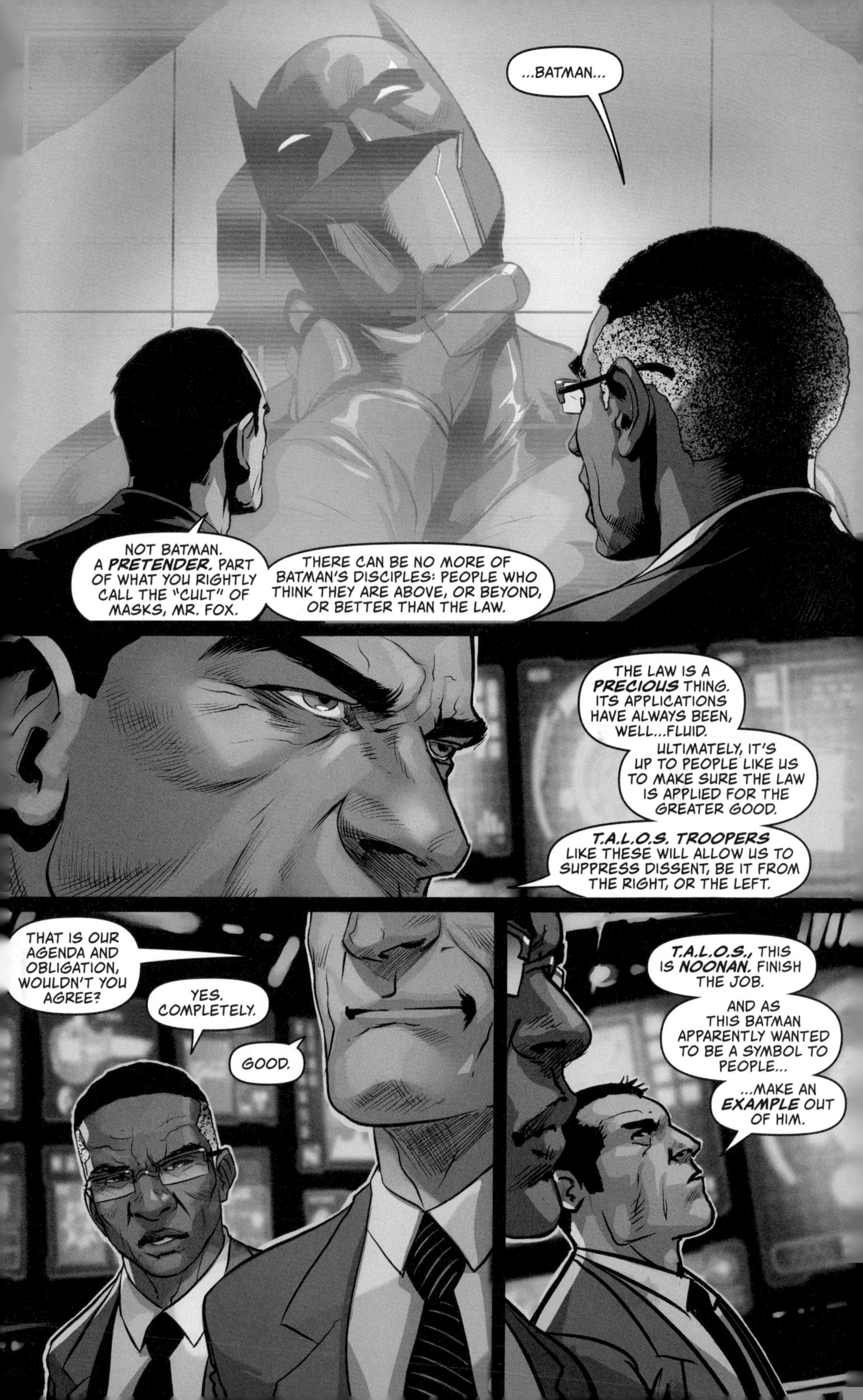
...BATMAN...
NOT BATMAN. A PRETENDER. PART OF WHAT YOU RIGHTLY CALL THE "CULT" OF MASKS, MR. FOX.
THERE CAN BE NO MORE OF BATMAN'S DISCIPLES: PEOPLE WHO THINK THEY ARE ABOVE, OR BEYOND, OR BETTER THAN THE LAW.
THE LAW IS A PRECIOUS THING. ITS APPLICATIONS HAVE ALWAYS BEEN, WELL...FLUID.
ULTIMATELY, IT'S UP TO PEOPLE LIKE US TO MAKE SURE THE LAW IS APPLIED FOR THE GREATER GOOD.
T.A.L.O.S. TROOPERS LIKE THESE WILL ALLOW US TO SUPPRESS DISSENT, BE IT FROM THE RIGHT, OR THE LEFT.
THAT IS OUR AGENDA AND OBLIGATION, WOULDN'T YOU AGREE?
YES. COMPLETELY.
GOOD.
T.A.L.O.S., THIS IS NOONAN. FINISH THE JOB.
AND AS THIS BATMAN APPARENTLY WANTED TO BE A SYMBOL TO PEOPLE...
...MAKE AN EXAMPLE OUT OF HIM.

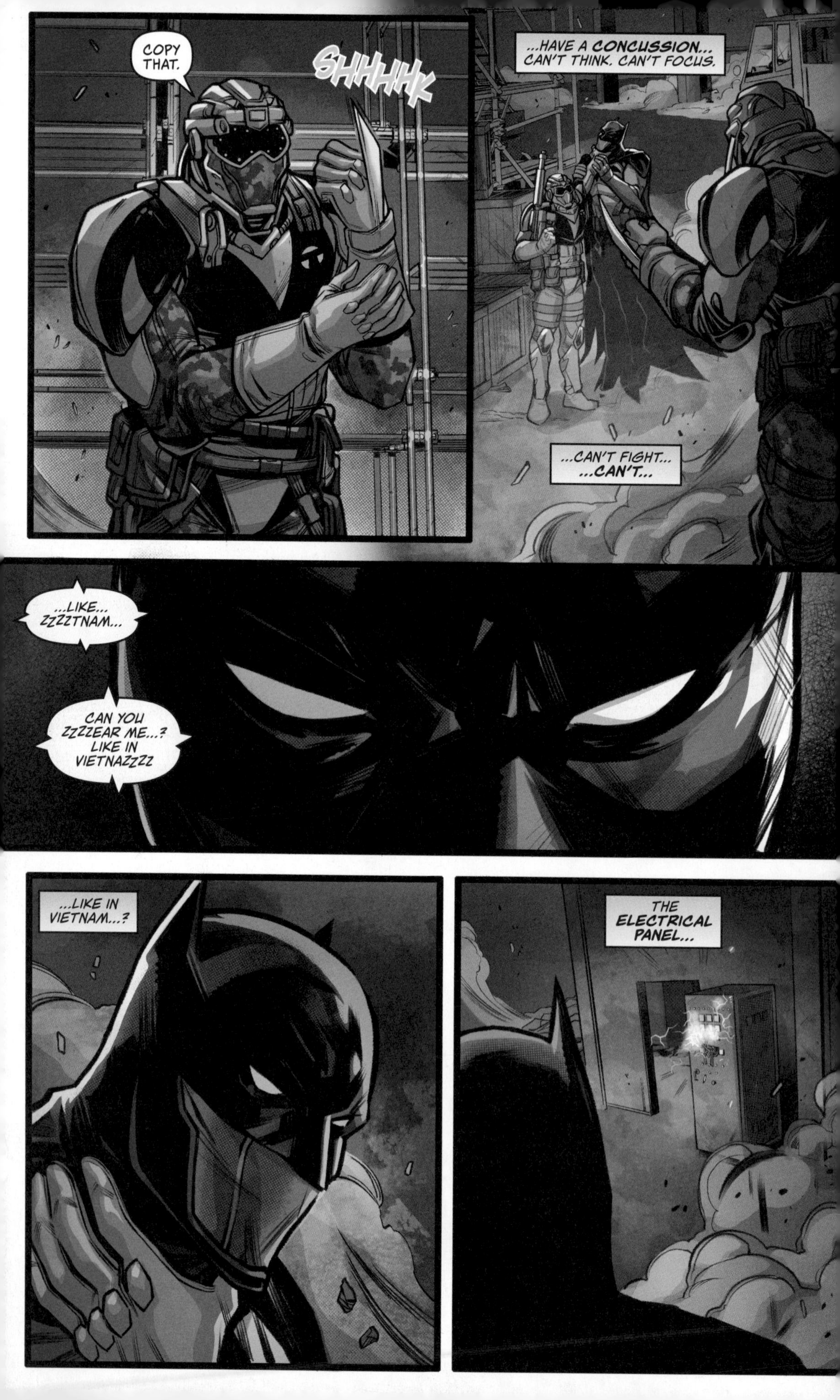
COPY THAT.
SHHHHK
...HAVE A CONCUSSION... CAN'T THINK. CAN'T FOCUS.
...CAN'T FIGHT... ...CAN'T...
...LIKE... ZZZZTNAM...
CAN YOU ZZZZEAR ME...? LIKE IN VIETNAZZZZ
...LIKE IN VIETNAM...?
THE ELECTRICAL PANEL...

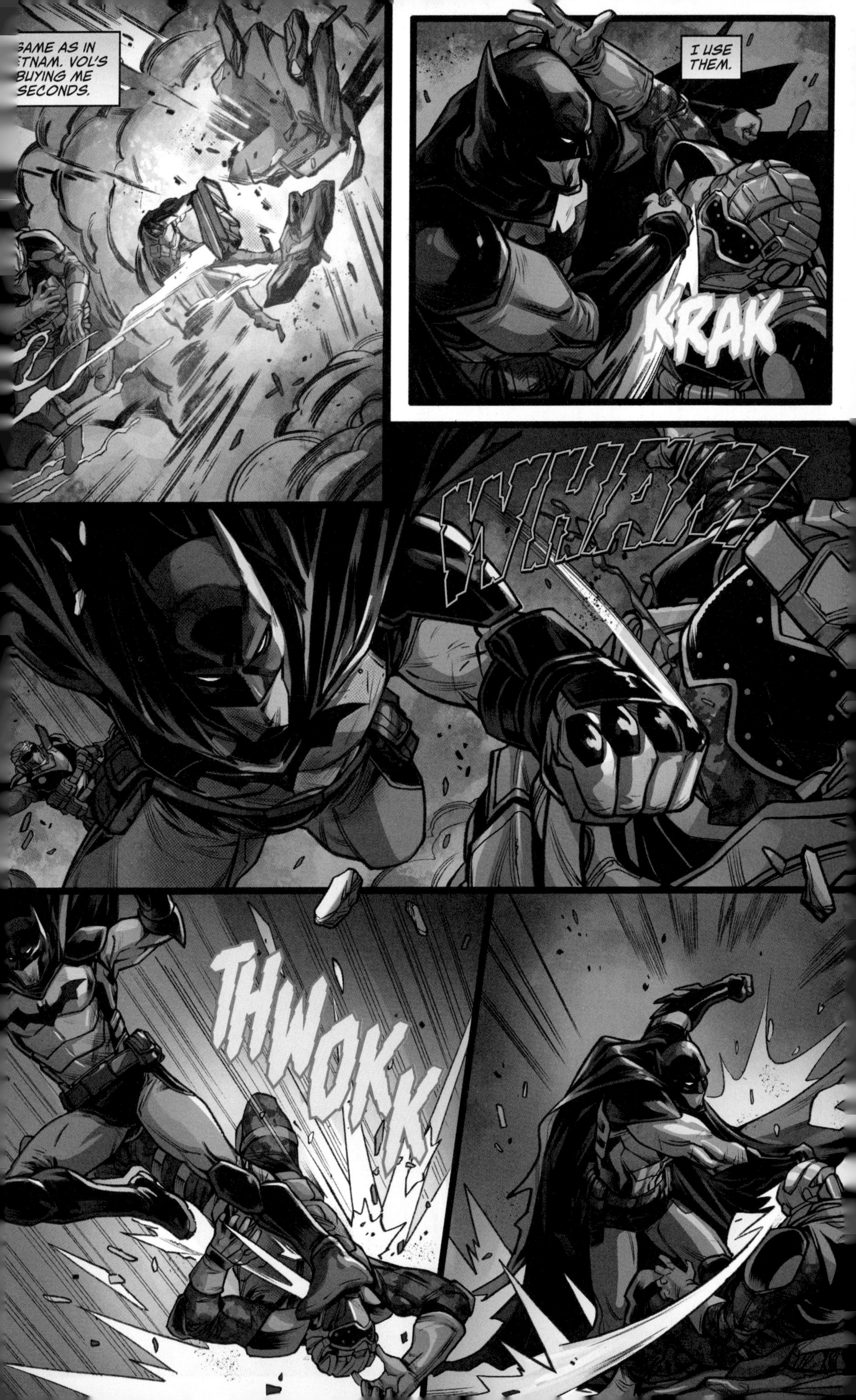
SAME AS IN
ETNAM. VOL'S
BUYING ME
SECONDS.
I USE
THEM.
KRAK
WHAM
THWOKK

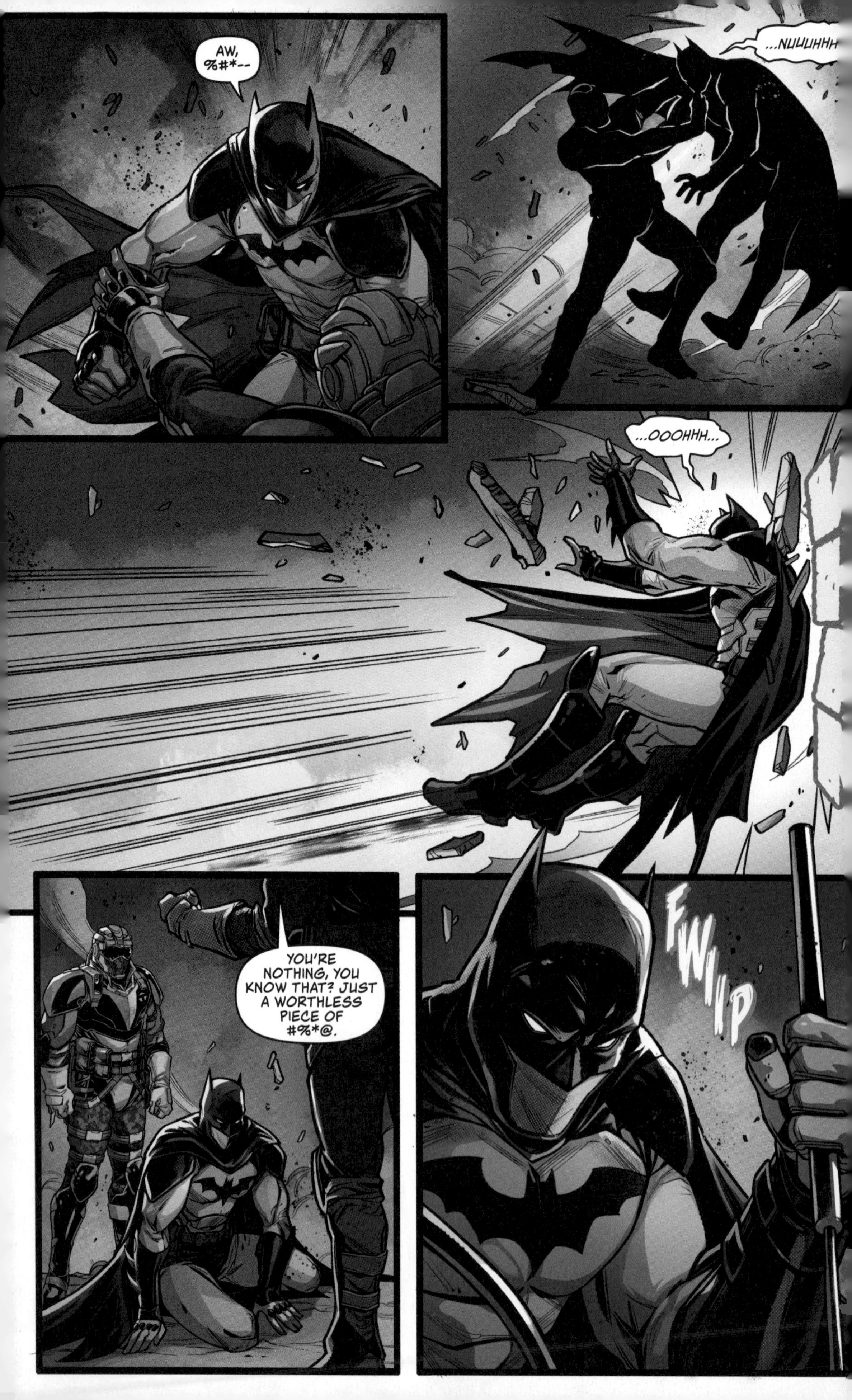
AW, %#*--
...NUUUHHH
...OOOHHH...
YOU'RE NOTHING, YOU KNOW THAT? JUST A WORTHLESS PIECE OF #%*@.
FWIIIP

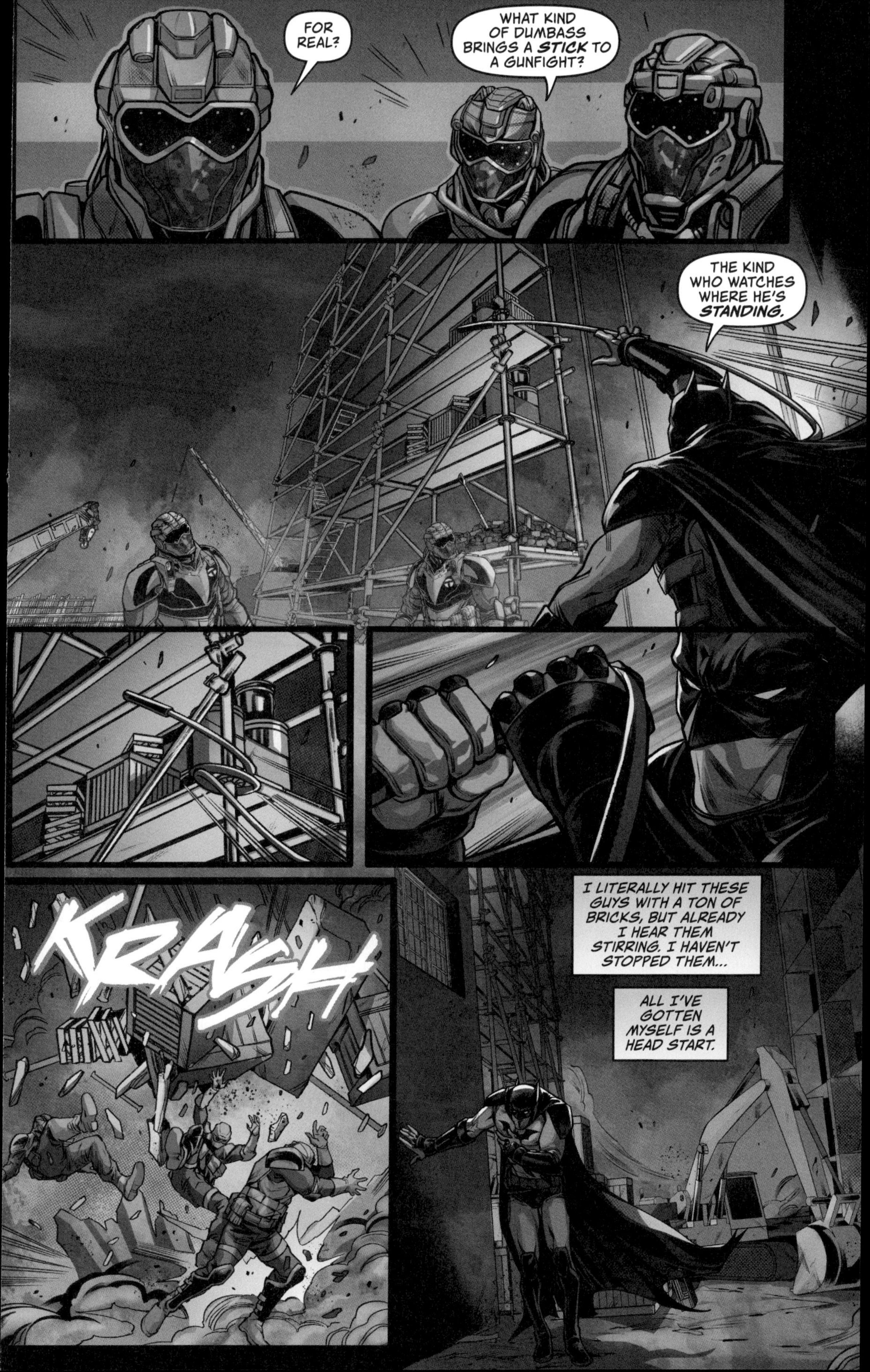
FOR REAL?
WHAT KIND OF DUMBASS BRINGS A STICK TO A GUNFIGHT?
THE KIND WHO WATCHES WHERE HE'S STANDING.
KRASH
I LITERALLY HIT THESE GUYS WITH A TON OF BRICKS, BUT ALREADY I HEAR THEM STIRRING. I HAVEN'T STOPPED THEM...
ALL I'VE GOTTEN MYSELF IS A HEAD START.

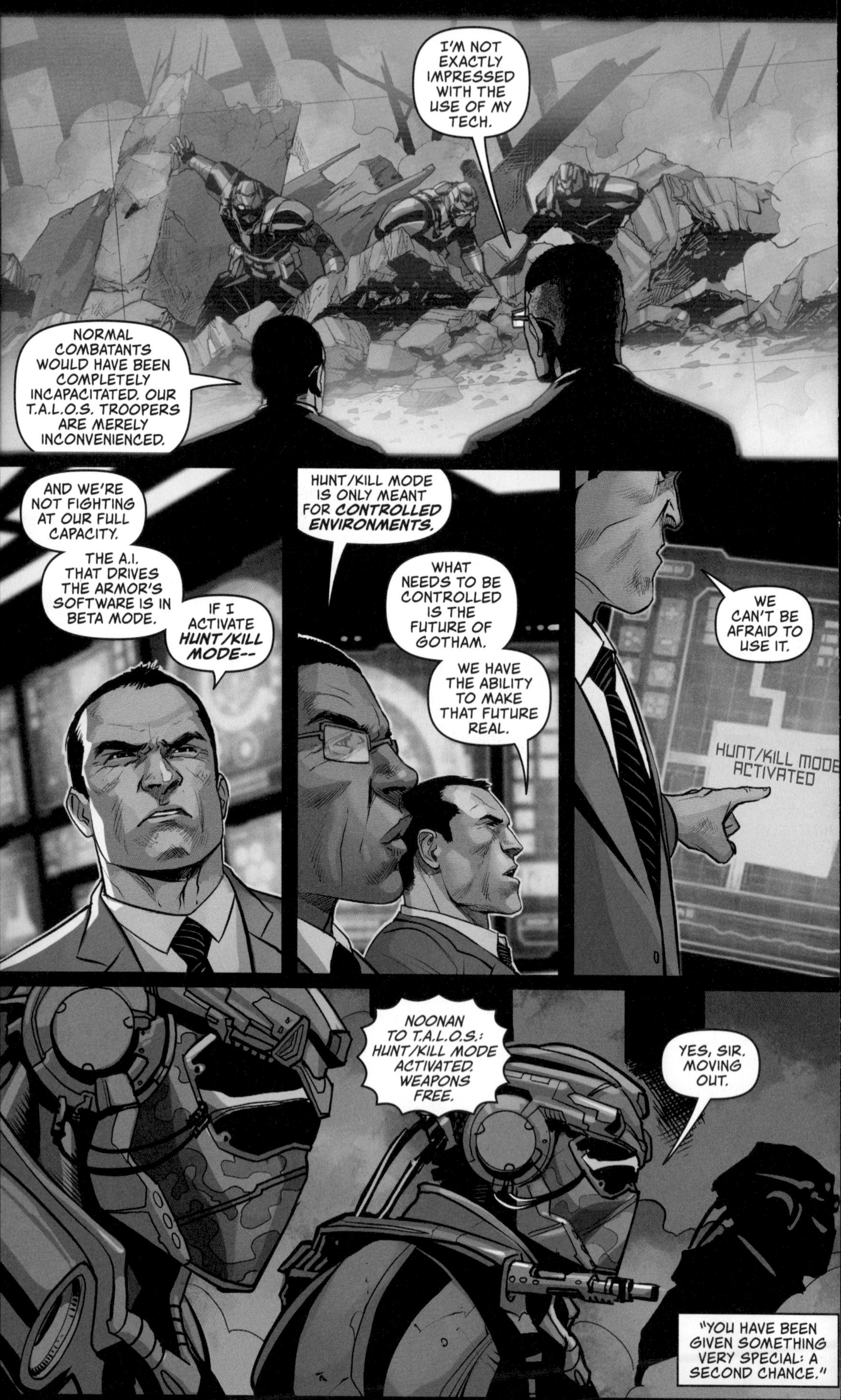
I'M NOT EXACTLY IMPRESSED WITH THE USE OF MY TECH.
NORMAL COMBATANTS WOULD HAVE BEEN COMPLETELY INCAPACITATED. OUR T.A.L.O.S. TROOPERS ARE MERELY INCONVENIENCED.
AND WE'RE NOT FIGHTING AT OUR FULL CAPACITY.
THE A.I. THAT DRIVES THE ARMOR'S SOFTWARE IS IN BETA MODE.
IF I ACTIVATE ***HUNT/KILL MODE***--
HUNT/KILL MODE IS ONLY MEANT FOR ***CONTROLLED ENVIRONMENTS.***
WHAT NEEDS TO BE CONTROLLED IS THE FUTURE OF GOTHAM.
WE HAVE THE ABILITY TO MAKE THAT FUTURE REAL.
WE CAN'T BE AFRAID TO USE IT.
HUNT/KILL MODE ACTIVATED
NOONAN TO T.A.L.O.S.: HUNT/KILL MODE ACTIVATED. WEAPONS FREE.
YES, SIR. MOVING OUT.
"YOU HAVE BEEN GIVEN SOMETHING VERY SPECIAL: A SECOND CHANCE."

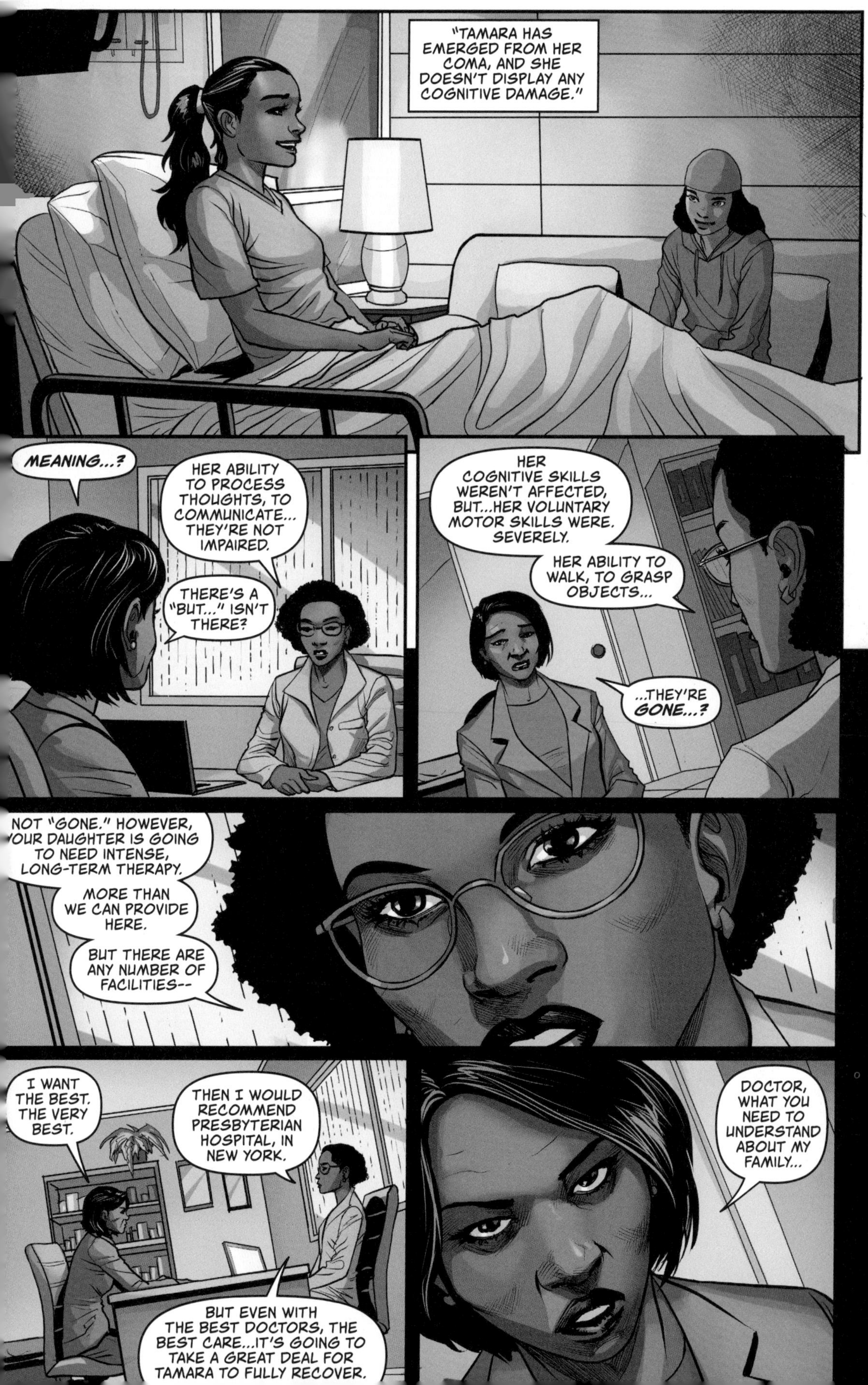
"TAMARA HAS EMERGED FROM HER COMA, AND SHE DOESN'T DISPLAY ANY COGNITIVE DAMAGE."
MEANING...?
HER ABILITY TO PROCESS THOUGHTS, TO COMMUNICATE... THEY'RE NOT IMPAIRED.
THERE'S A "BUT..." ISN'T THERE?
HER COGNITIVE SKILLS WEREN'T AFFECTED, BUT...HER VOLUNTARY MOTOR SKILLS WERE. SEVERELY.
HER ABILITY TO WALK, TO GRASP OBJECTS...
...THEY'RE GONE...?
NOT "GONE." HOWEVER, YOUR DAUGHTER IS GOING TO NEED INTENSE, LONG-TERM THERAPY.
MORE THAN WE CAN PROVIDE HERE.
BUT THERE ARE ANY NUMBER OF FACILITIES--
I WANT THE BEST. THE VERY BEST.
THEN I WOULD RECOMMEND PRESBYTERIAN HOSPITAL, IN NEW YORK.
BUT EVEN WITH THE BEST DOCTORS, THE BEST CARE...IT'S GOING TO TAKE A GREAT DEAL FOR TAMARA TO FULLY RECOVER.
DOCTOR, WHAT YOU NEED TO UNDERSTAND ABOUT MY FAMILY...

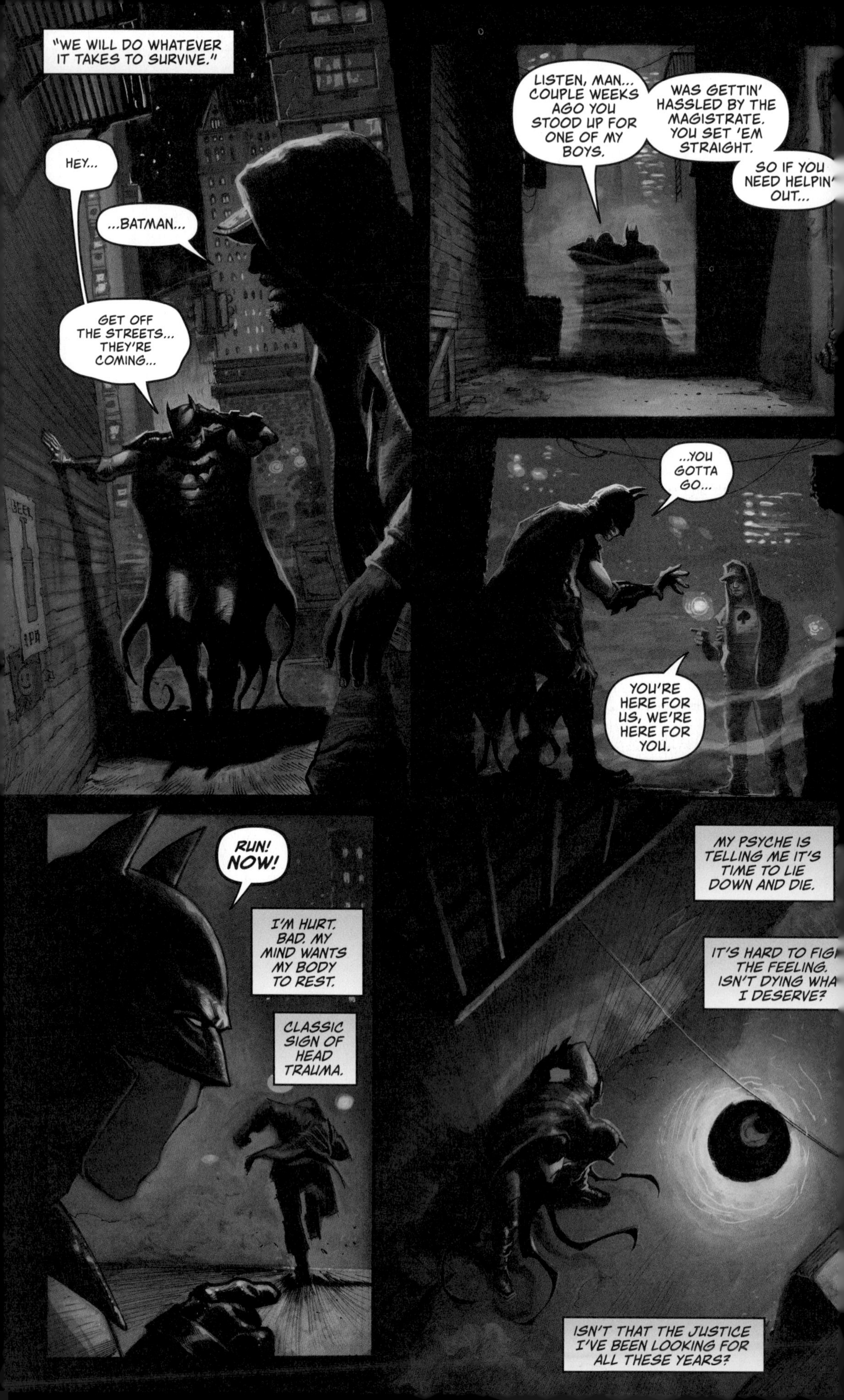
"WE WILL DO WHATEVER IT TAKES TO SURVIVE."
HEY...
...BATMAN...
GET OFF THE STREETS... THEY'RE COMING...
LISTEN, MAN... COUPLE WEEKS AGO YOU STOOD UP FOR ONE OF MY BOYS.
WAS GETTIN' HASSLED BY THE MAGISTRATE. YOU SET 'EM STRAIGHT.
SO IF YOU NEED HELPIN' OUT...
...YOU GOTTA GO...
YOU'RE HERE FOR US, WE'RE HERE FOR YOU.
RUN! NOW!
I'M HURT. BAD. MY MIND WANTS MY BODY TO REST.
CLASSIC SIGN OF HEAD TRAUMA.
MY PSYCHE IS TELLING ME IT'S TIME TO LIE DOWN AND DIE.
IT'S HARD TO FIG THE FEELING. ISN'T DYING WHA I DESERVE?
ISN'T THAT THE JUSTICE I'VE BEEN LOOKING FOR ALL THESE YEARS?

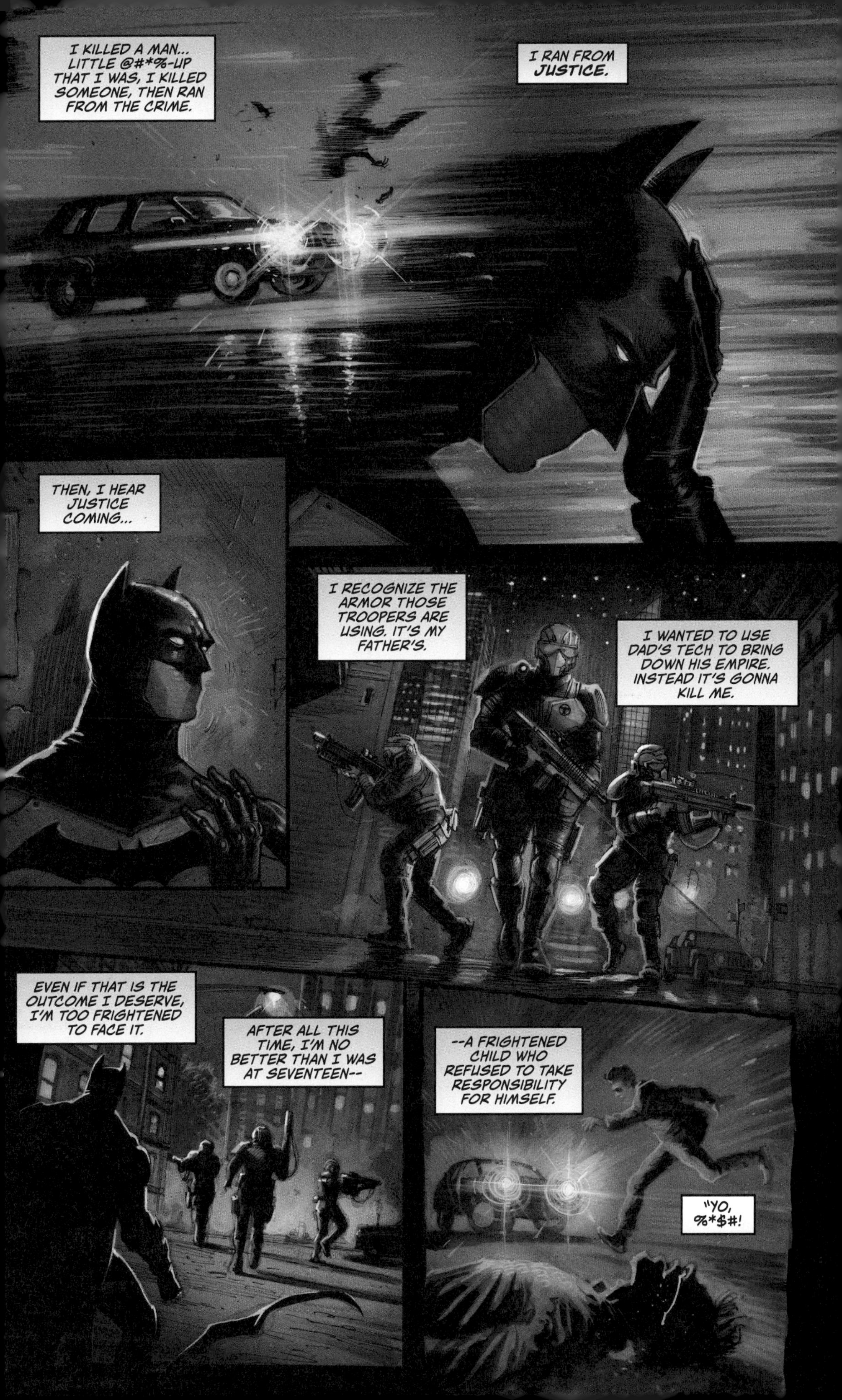

I KILLED A MAN... LITTLE @#*%-UP THAT I WAS, I KILLED SOMEONE, THEN RAN FROM THE CRIME.
I RAN FROM JUSTICE.
THEN, I HEAR JUSTICE COMING...
I RECOGNIZE THE ARMOR THOSE TROOPERS ARE USING. IT'S MY FATHER'S.
I WANTED TO USE DAD'S TECH TO BRING DOWN HIS EMPIRE. INSTEAD IT'S GONNA KILL ME.
EVEN IF THAT IS THE OUTCOME I DESERVE, I'M TOO FRIGHTENED TO FACE IT.
AFTER ALL THIS TIME, I'M NO BETTER THAN I WAS AT SEVENTEEN--
--A FRIGHTENED CHILD WHO REFUSED TO TAKE RESPONSIBILITY FOR HIMSELF.
"YO, %*$#!

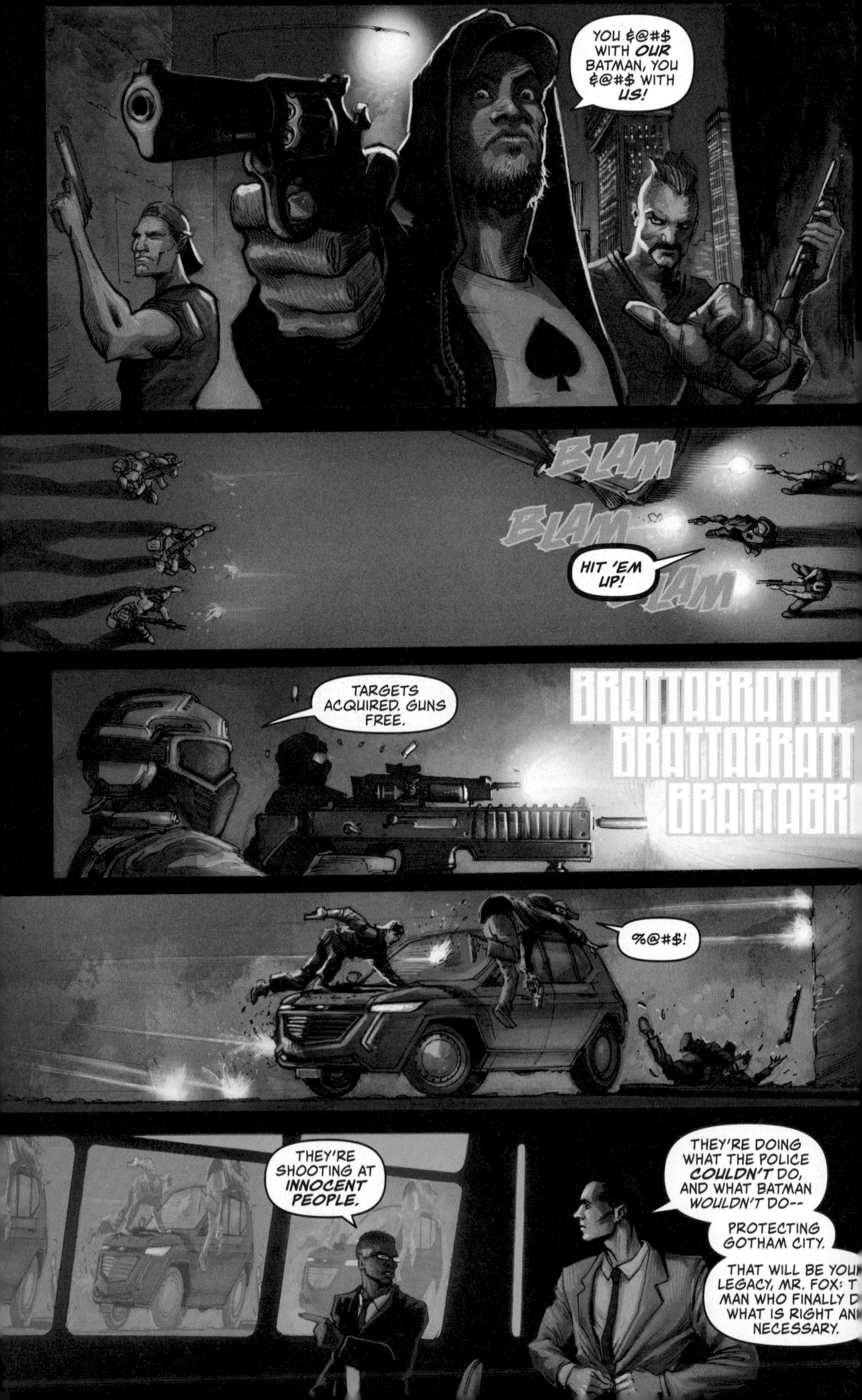
YOU &@#$ WITH OUR BATMAN, YOU &@#$ WITH US!
BLAM
BLAM
HIT 'EM UP!
TARGETS ACQUIRED. GUNS FREE.
%@#$!
THEY'RE SHOOTING AT INNOCENT PEOPLE.
THEY'RE DOING WHAT THE POLICE COULDN'T DO, AND WHAT BATMAN WOULDN'T DO--
PROTECTING GOTHAM CITY.

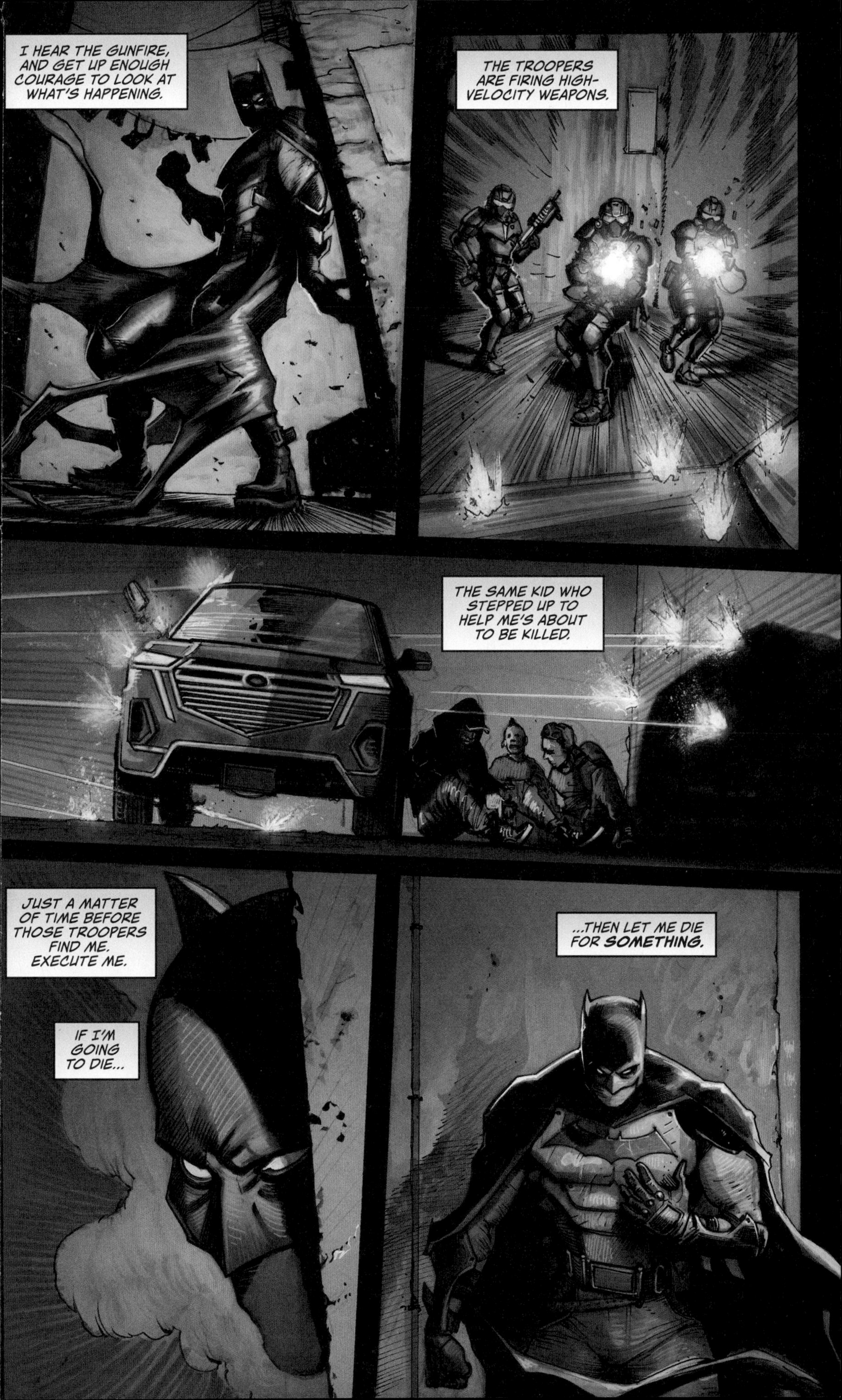
I HEAR THE GUNFIRE, AND GET UP ENOUGH COURAGE TO LOOK AT WHAT'S HAPPENING.
THE TROOPERS ARE FIRING HIGH-VELOCITY WEAPONS.
THE SAME KID WHO STEPPED UP TO HELP ME'S ABOUT TO BE KILLED.
JUST A MATTER OF TIME BEFORE THOSE TROOPERS FIND ME. EXECUTE ME.
IF I'M GOING TO DIE...
...THEN LET ME DIE FOR SOMETHING.

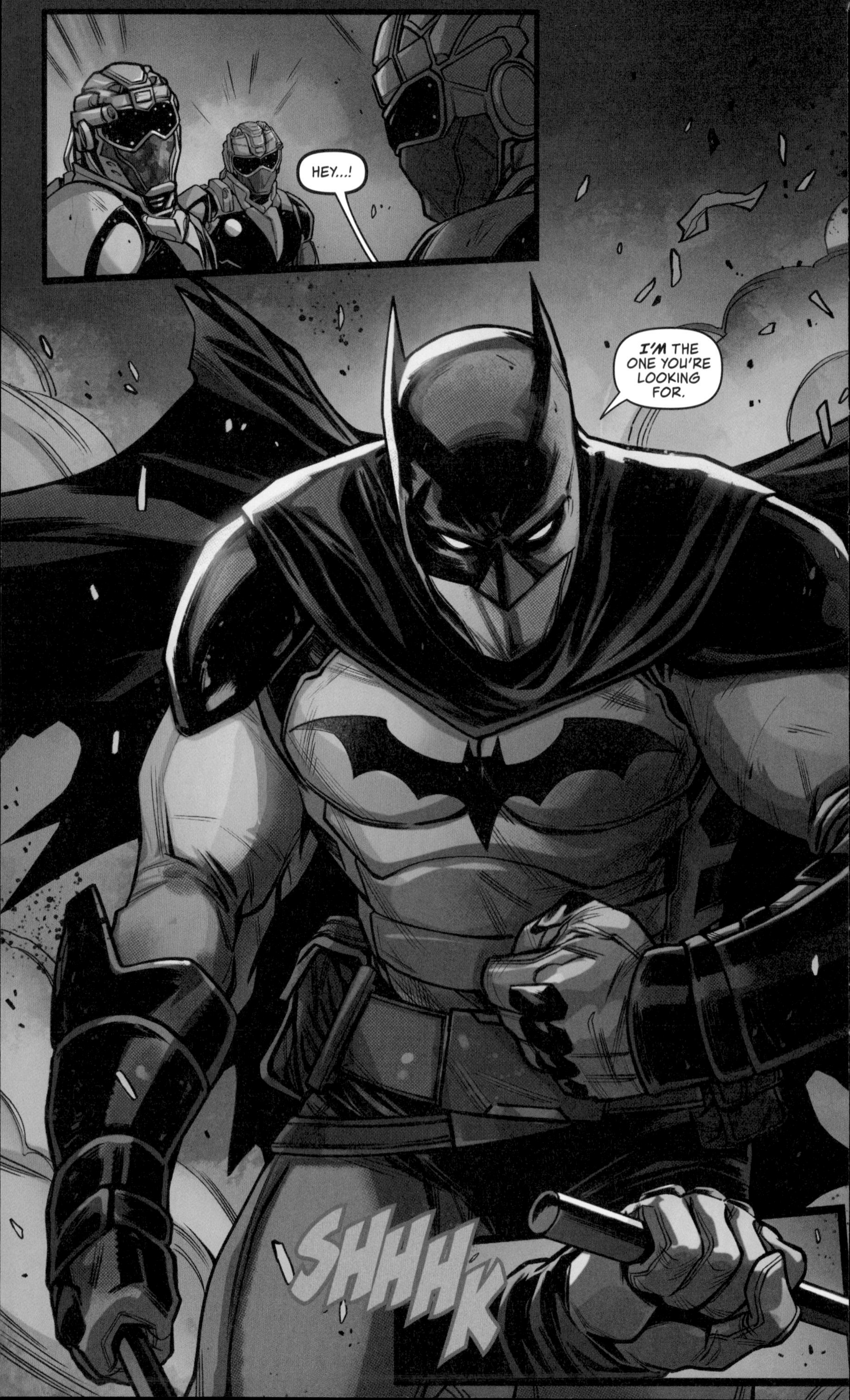
HEY...!
I'M THE ONE YOU'RE LOOKING FOR.
SHHHK

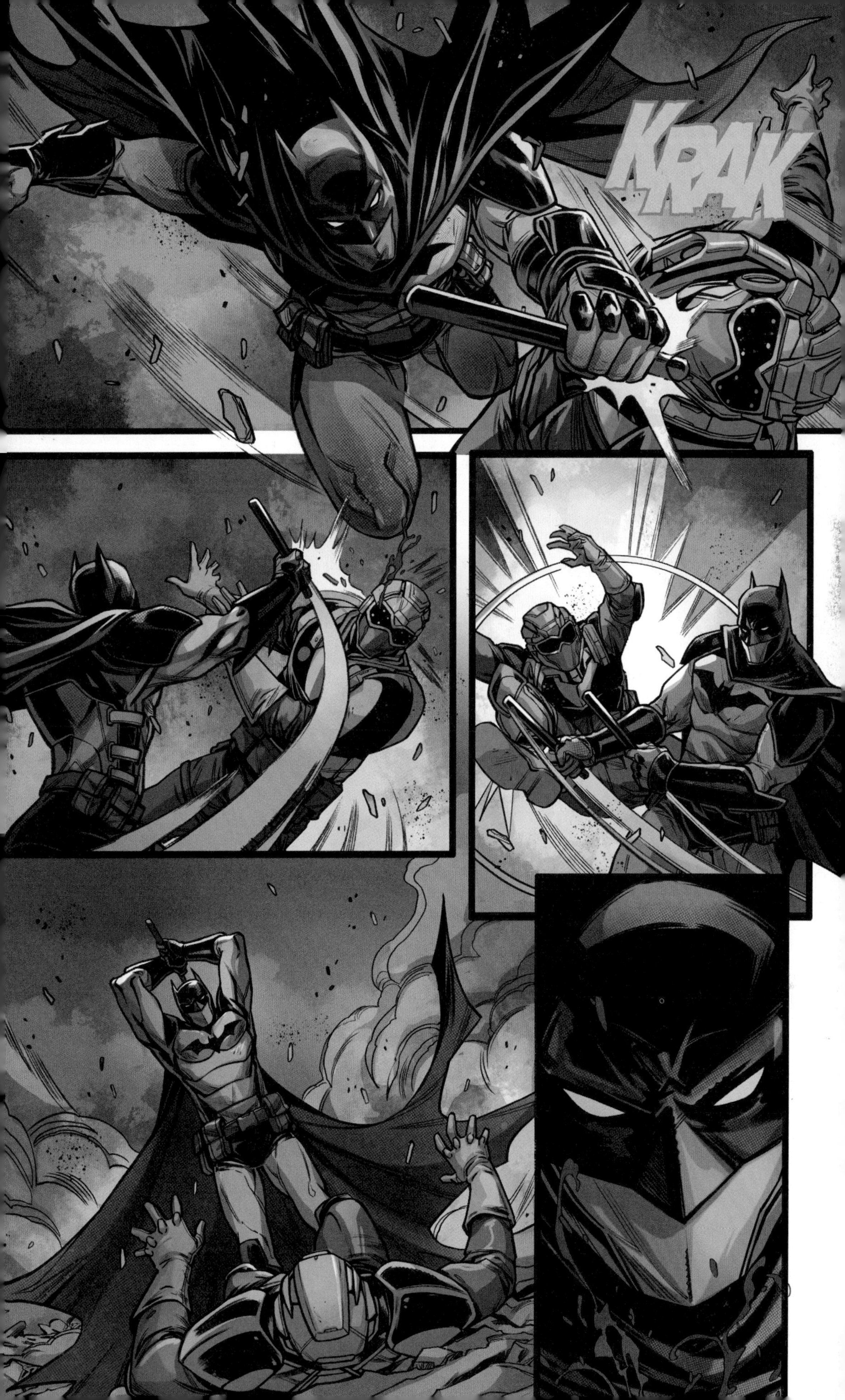
KRAK

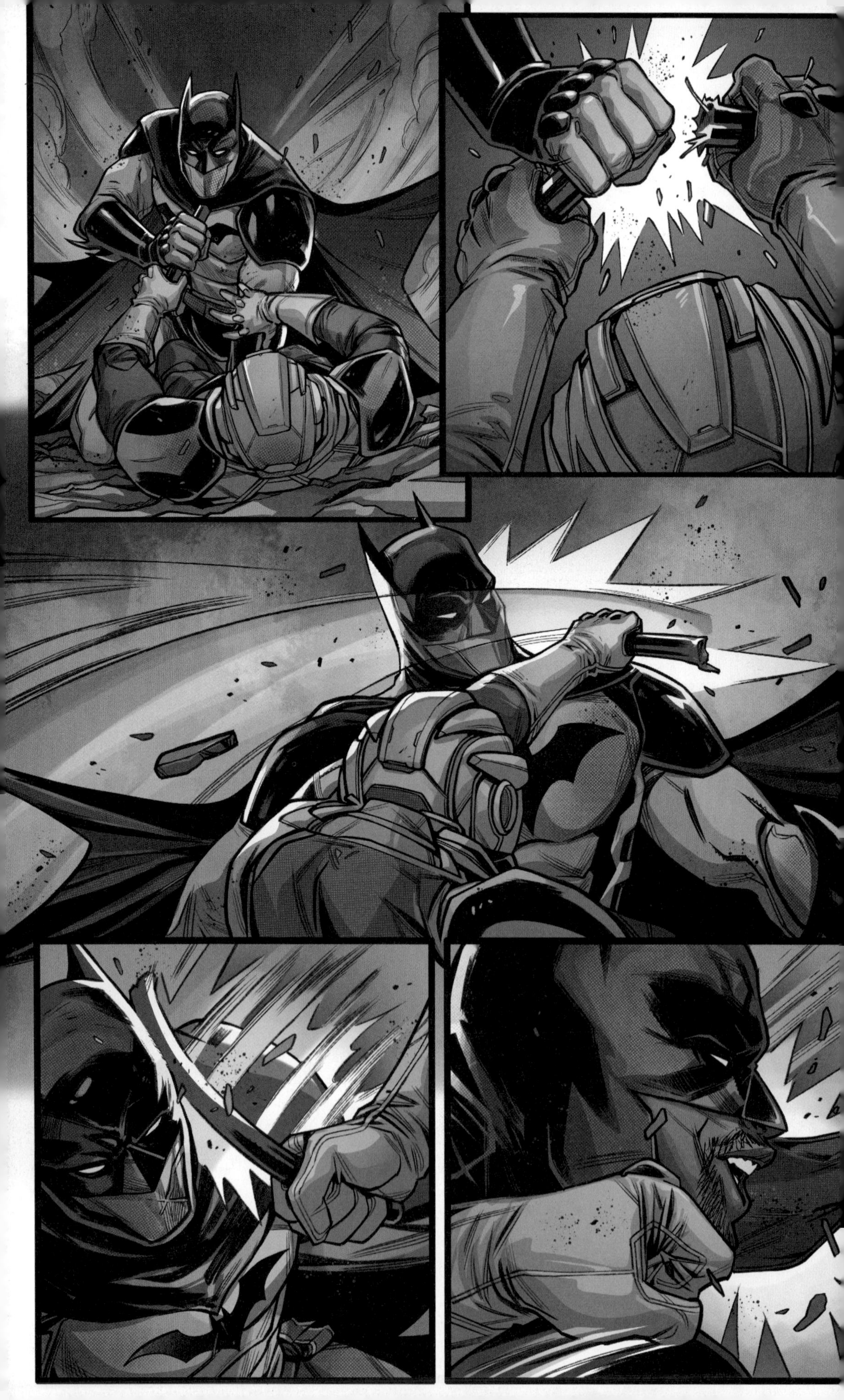

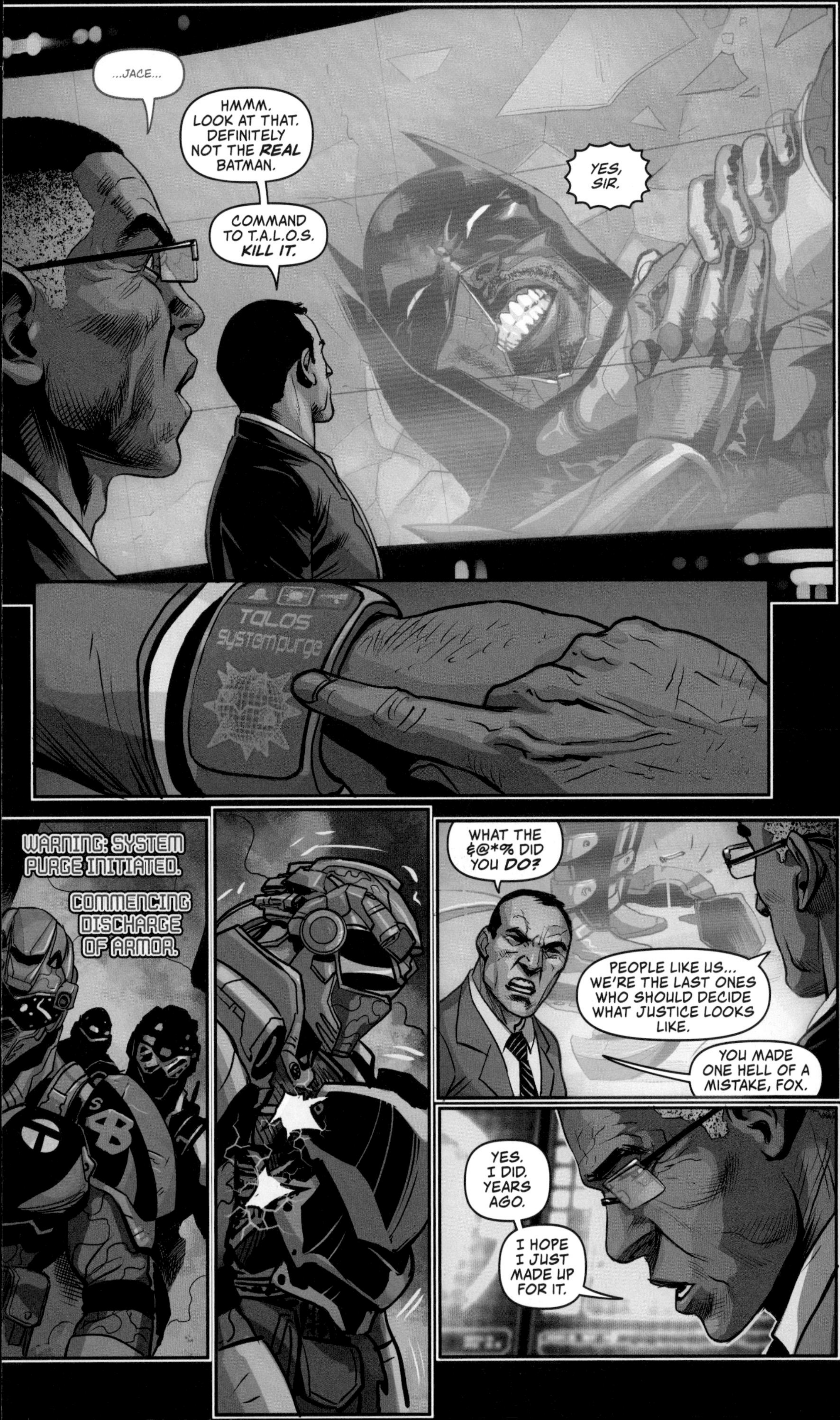
...JACE...
HMMM. LOOK AT THAT. DEFINITELY NOT THE *REAL* BATMAN.
COMMAND TO T.A.L.O.S. *KILL IT.*
YES, SIR.
TALOS
systempurge
WARNING: SYSTEM PURGE INITIATED.
COMMENCING DISCHARGE OF ARMOR.
WHAT THE $@*% DID YOU *DO?*
PEOPLE LIKE US... WE'RE THE LAST ONES WHO SHOULD DECIDE WHAT JUSTICE LOOKS LIKE.
YOU MADE ONE HELL OF A MISTAKE, FOX.
YES. I DID, YEARS AGO.
I HOPE I JUST MADE UP FOR IT.

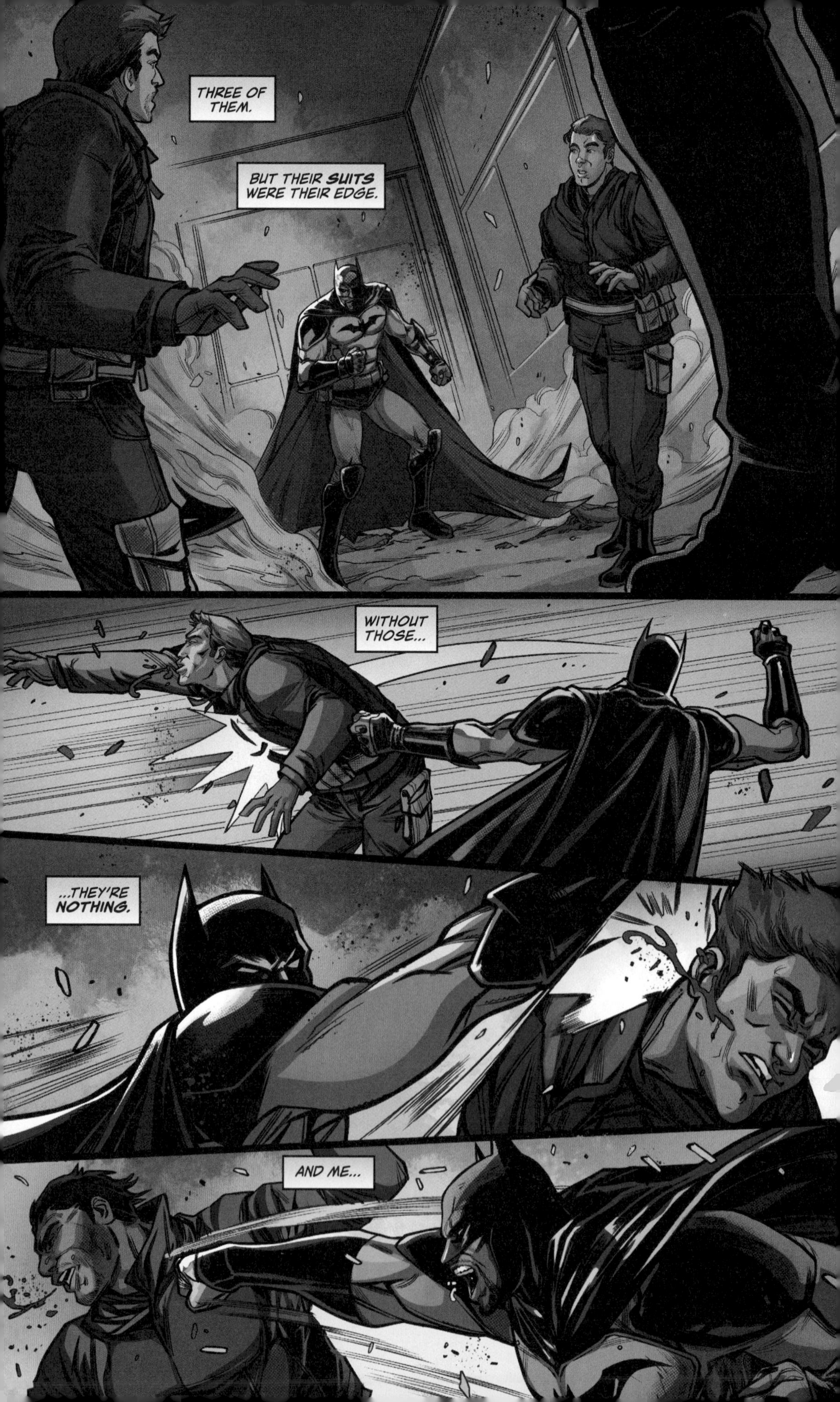

THREE OF THEM.
BUT THEIR SUITS WERE THEIR EDGE.
WITHOUT THOSE...
...THEY'RE NOTHING.
AND ME...

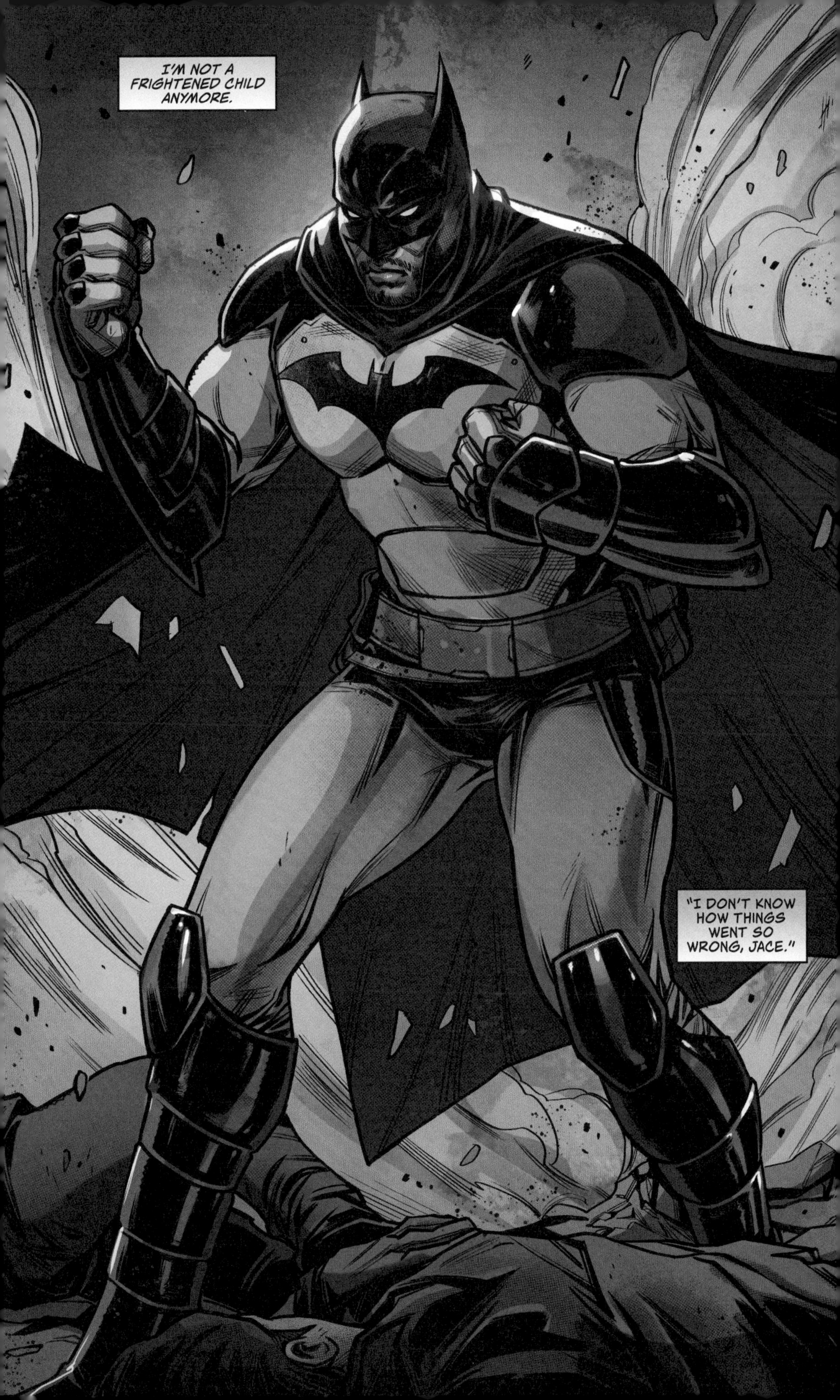
I'M NOT A FRIGHTENED CHILD ANYMORE.
"I DON'T KNOW HOW THINGS WENT SO WRONG, JACE."

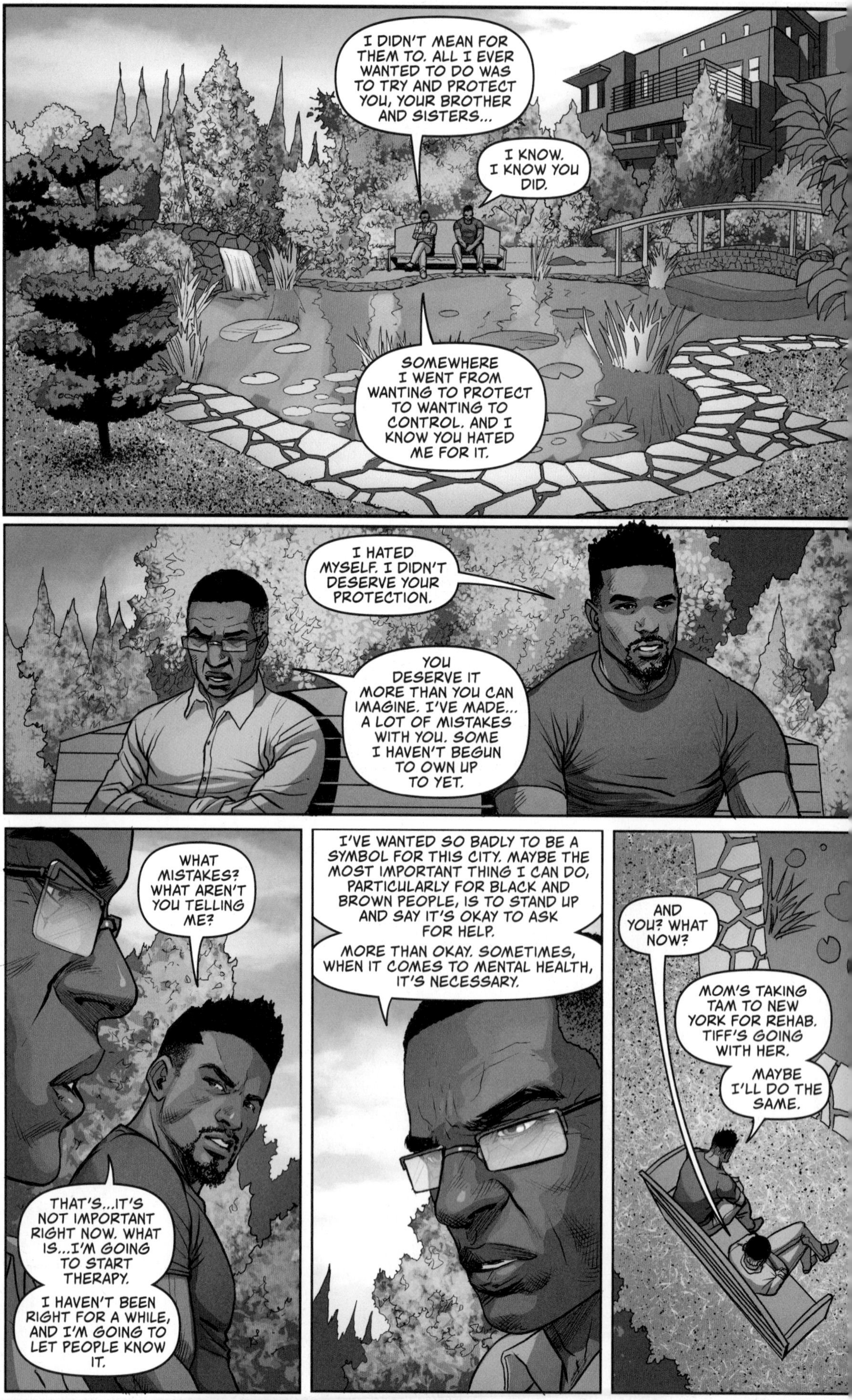
I DIDN'T MEAN FOR THEM TO. ALL I EVER WANTED TO DO WAS TO TRY AND PROTECT YOU, YOUR BROTHER AND SISTERS...
I KNOW. I KNOW YOU DID.
SOMEWHERE I WENT FROM WANTING TO PROTECT TO WANTING TO CONTROL. AND I KNOW YOU HATED ME FOR IT.
I HATED MYSELF. I DIDN'T DESERVE YOUR PROTECTION.
YOU DESERVE IT MORE THAN YOU CAN IMAGINE. I'VE MADE... A LOT OF MISTAKES WITH YOU. SOME I HAVEN'T BEGUN TO OWN UP TO YET.
WHAT MISTAKES? WHAT AREN'T YOU TELLING ME?
THAT'S...IT'S NOT IMPORTANT RIGHT NOW. WHAT IS...I'M GOING TO START THERAPY.
I HAVEN'T BEEN RIGHT FOR A WHILE, AND I'M GOING TO LET PEOPLE KNOW IT.
I'VE WANTED SO BADLY TO BE A SYMBOL FOR THIS CITY. MAYBE THE MOST IMPORTANT THING I CAN DO, PARTICULARLY FOR BLACK AND BROWN PEOPLE, IS TO STAND UP AND SAY IT'S OKAY TO ASK FOR HELP.
MORE THAN OKAY. SOMETIMES, WHEN IT COMES TO MENTAL HEALTH, IT'S NECESSARY.
AND YOU? WHAT NOW?
MOM'S TAKING TAM TO NEW YORK FOR REHAB. TIFF'S GOING WITH HER.
MAYBE I'LL DO THE SAME.

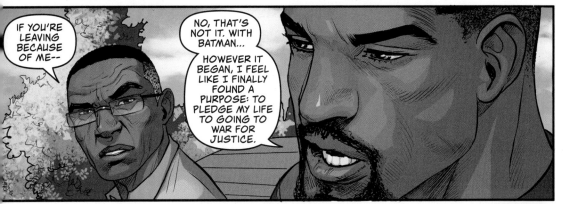

IF YOU'RE LEAVING BECAUSE OF ME--

NO, THAT'S NOT IT. WITH BATMAN...

HOWEVER IT BEGAN, I FEEL LIKE I FINALLY FOUND A PURPOSE: TO PLEDGE MY LIFE TO GOING TO WAR FOR JUSTICE.

THE, UH... THE *OTHER* BATMAN ONCE SAID THE SAME THING.

YEAH, WELL... THAT'S PART OF THE PROBLEM. AS LONG AS I'M IN GOTHAM, I'LL ALWAYS BE THE *OTHER* BATMAN, OR *REPLACEMENT* BATMAN, OR *SUBSTITUTE* BATMAN.

BUT THE TRUTH IS--

THE TRUTH IS *YOU ARE* BATMAN. SO...DO ME ONE FAVOR--

DITCH THAT FACEPLATE.

THE FACEPLATE? WHY?

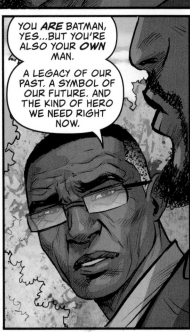

YOU *ARE* BATMAN, YES...BUT YOU'RE ALSO YOUR *OWN* MAN.

A LEGACY OF OUR PAST. A SYMBOL OF OUR FUTURE. AND THE KIND OF HERO WE NEED RIGHT NOW.

NEVER BE AFRAID TO SHOW PEOPLE WHO YOU ARE. TAKE PRIDE IN THE FACT THAT YOU INSPIRE. AND ABOVE EVERYTHING ELSE, MY SON...

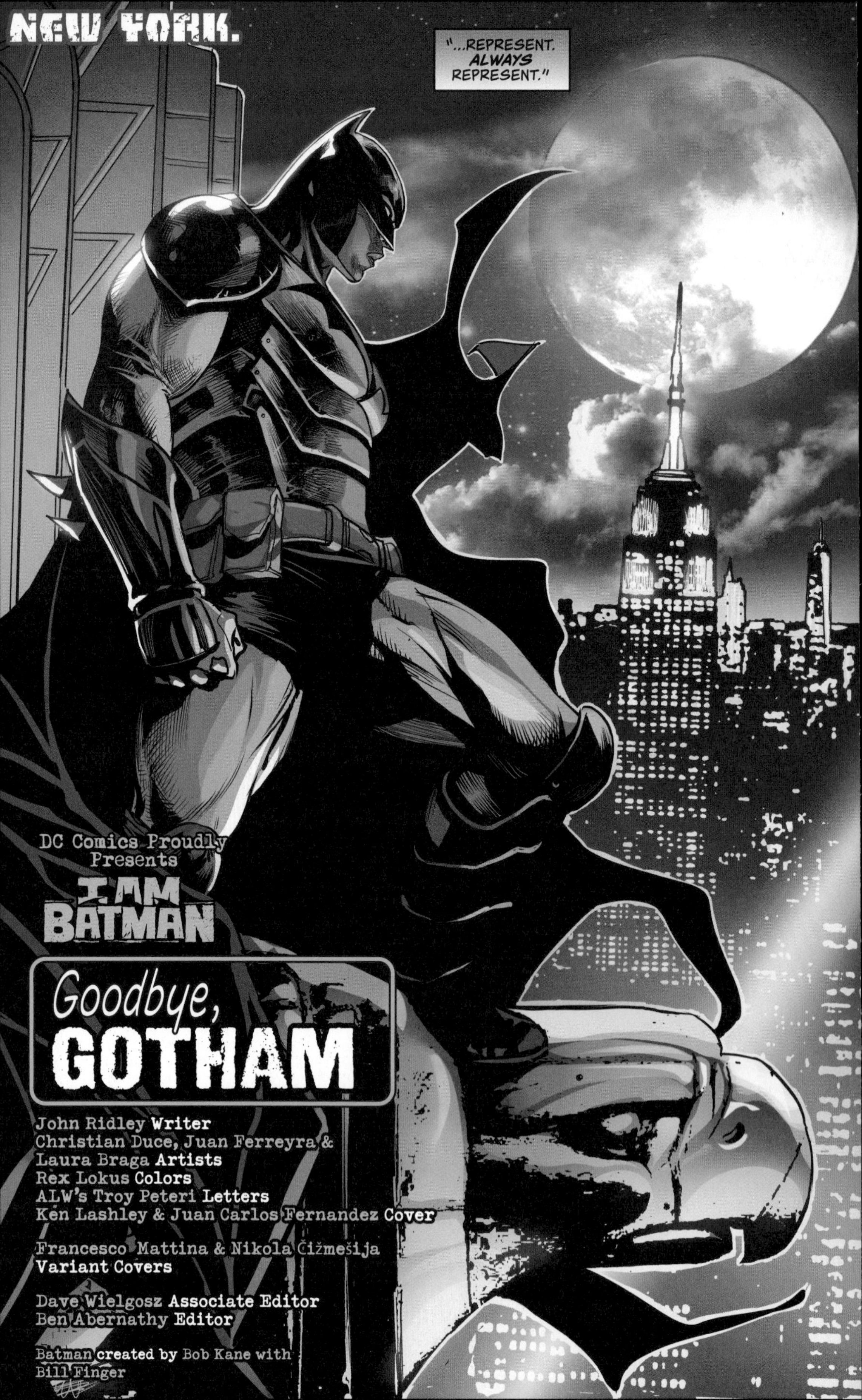
NEW YORK.
"...REPRESENT. ALWAYS REPRESENT."
DC Comics Proudly Presents
I AM BATMAN
Goodbye, GOTHAM
John Ridley Writer
Christian Duce, Juan Ferreyra & Laura Braga Artists
Rex Lokus Colors
ALW's Troy Peteri Letters
Ken Lashley & Juan Carlos Fernandez Cover
Francesco Mattina & Nikola Čižmešija Variant Covers
Dave Wielgosz Associate Editor
Ben Abernathy Editor
Batman created by Bob Kane with Bill Finger

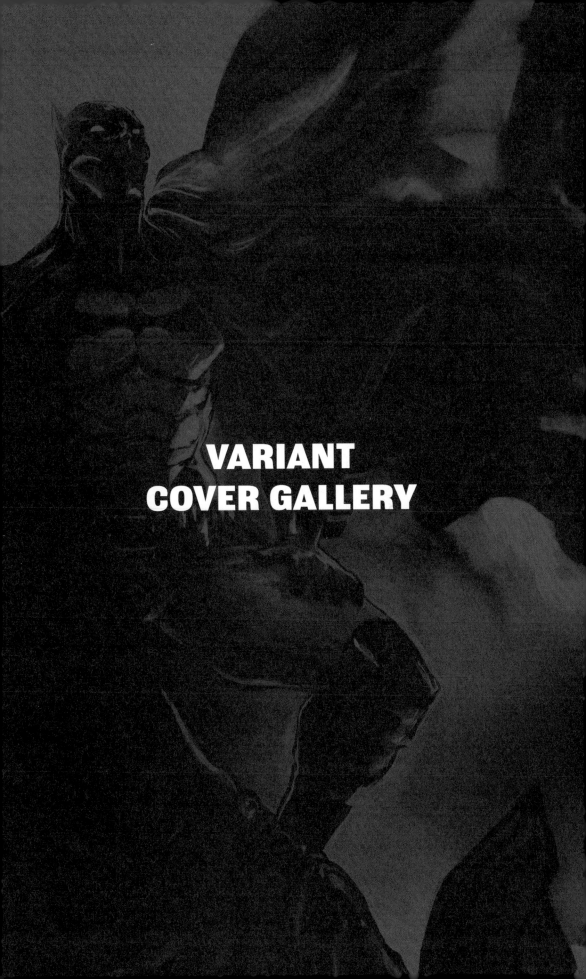

VARIANT
COVER GALLERY

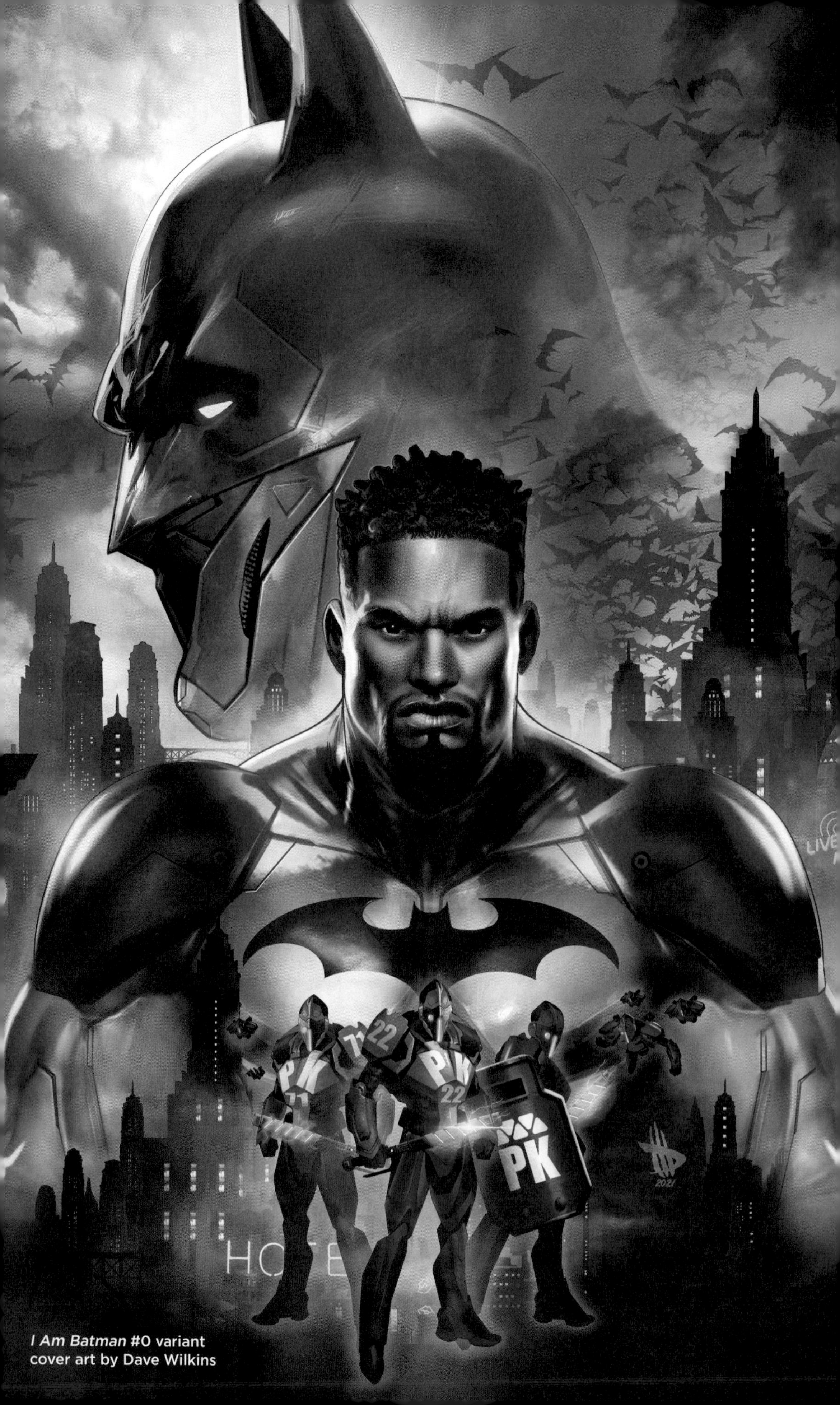
PK
71
22
PK
22
PK
2021

I Am Batman #0 variant
cover art by Dave Wilkins

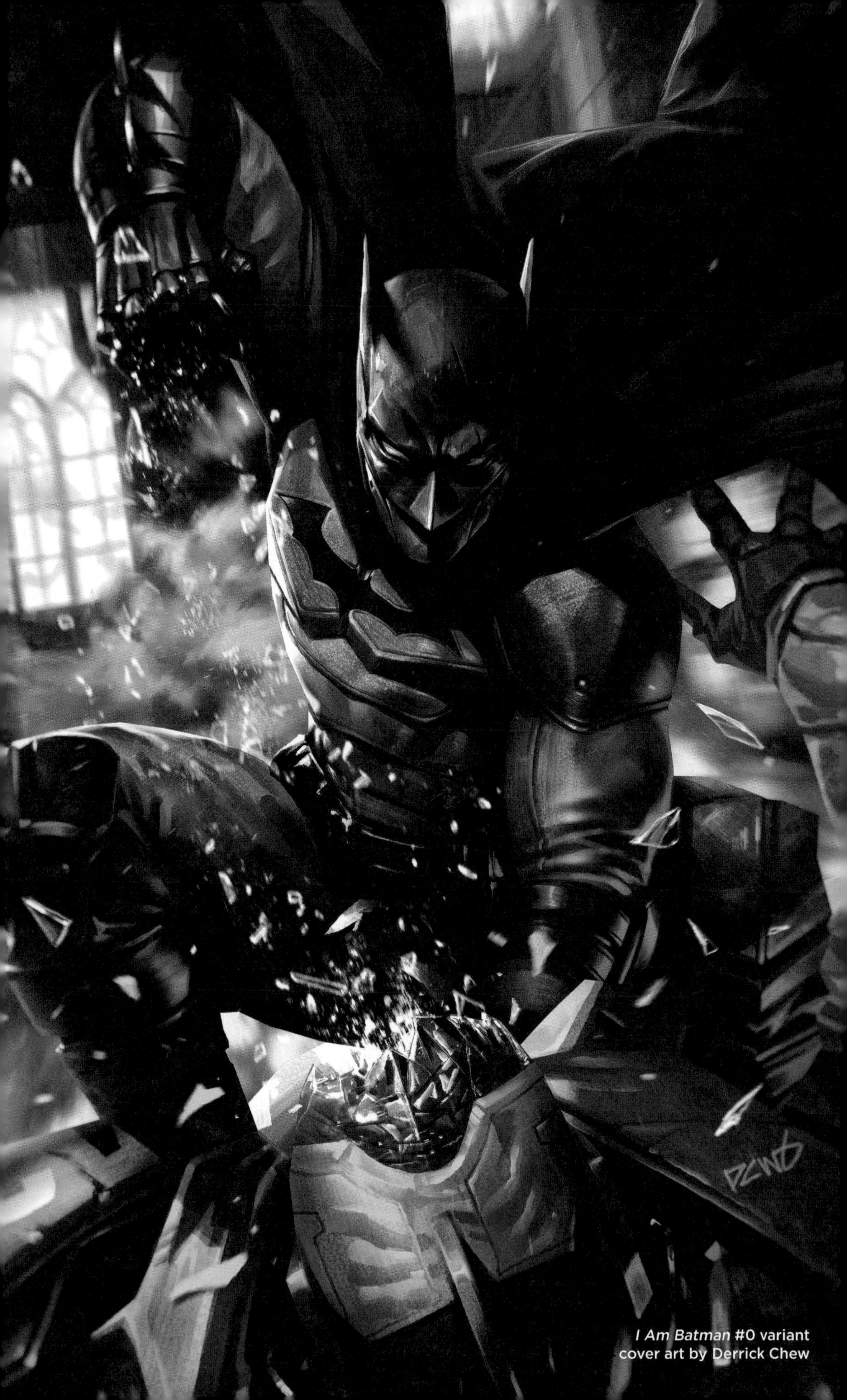

I Am Batman #0 variant
cover art by Derrick Chew

I Am Batman #0 variant
cover art by Riccardo Federici

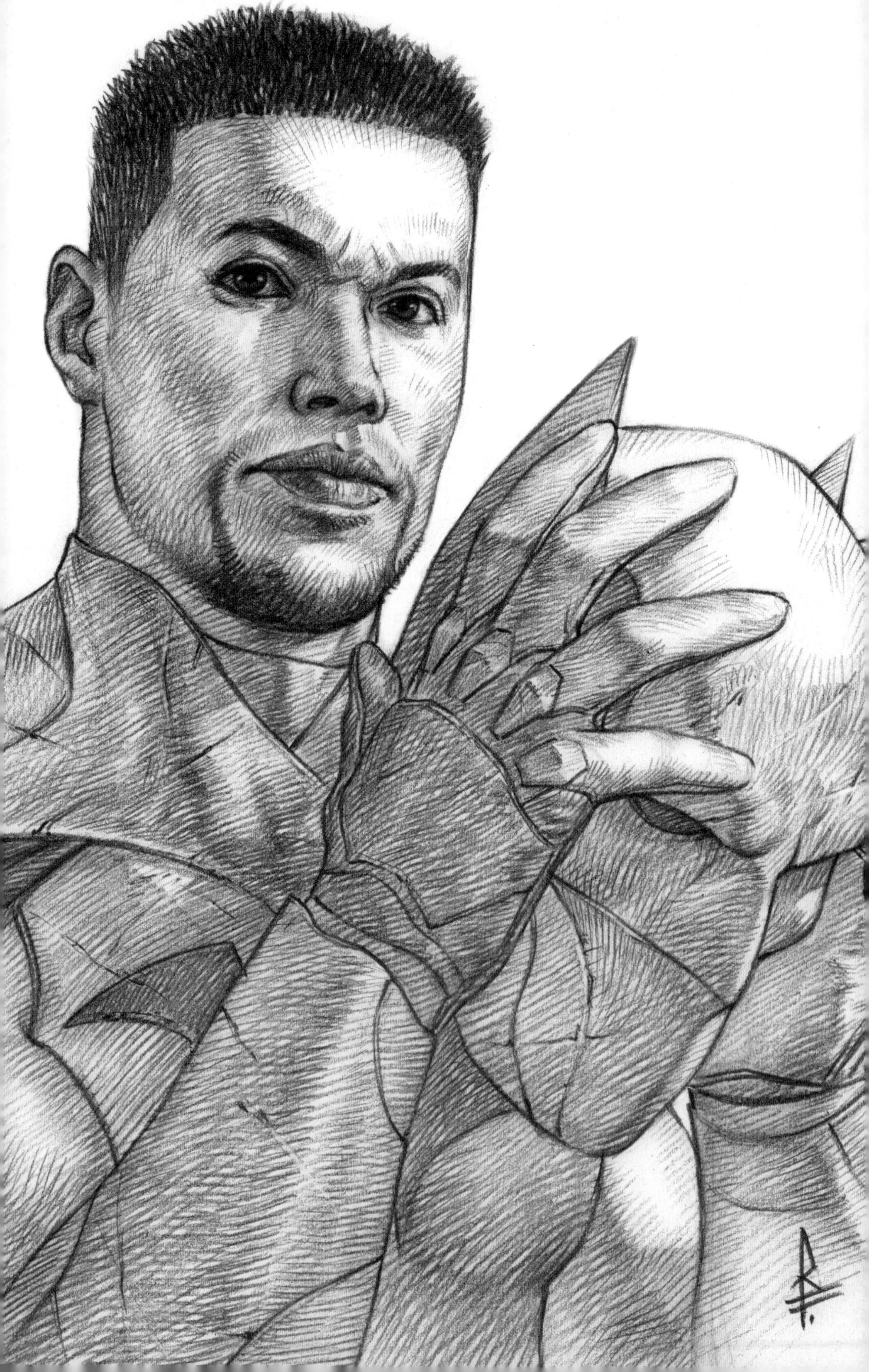

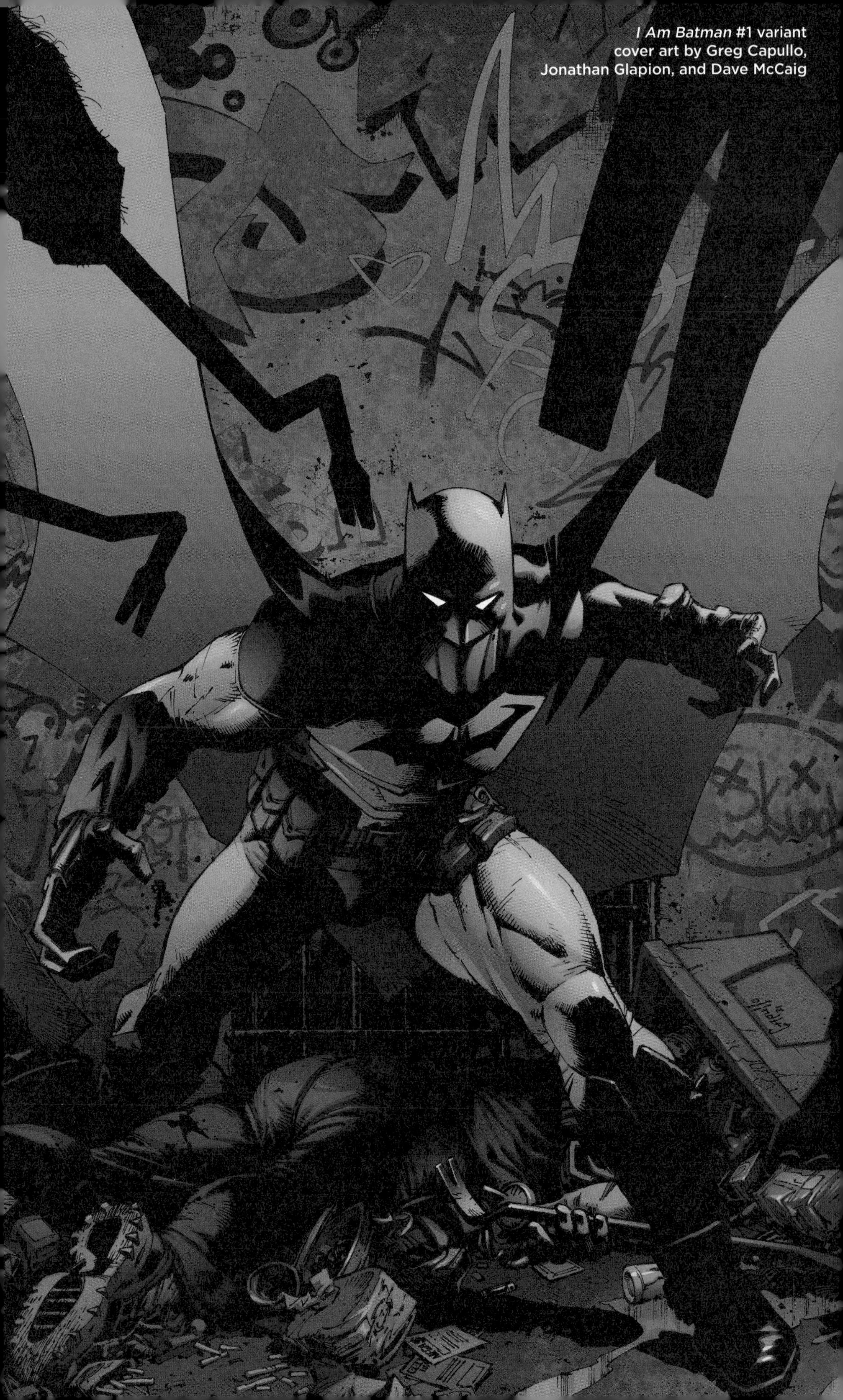

I Am Batman #1 variant cover art by Greg Capullo, Jonathan Glapion, and Dave McCaig

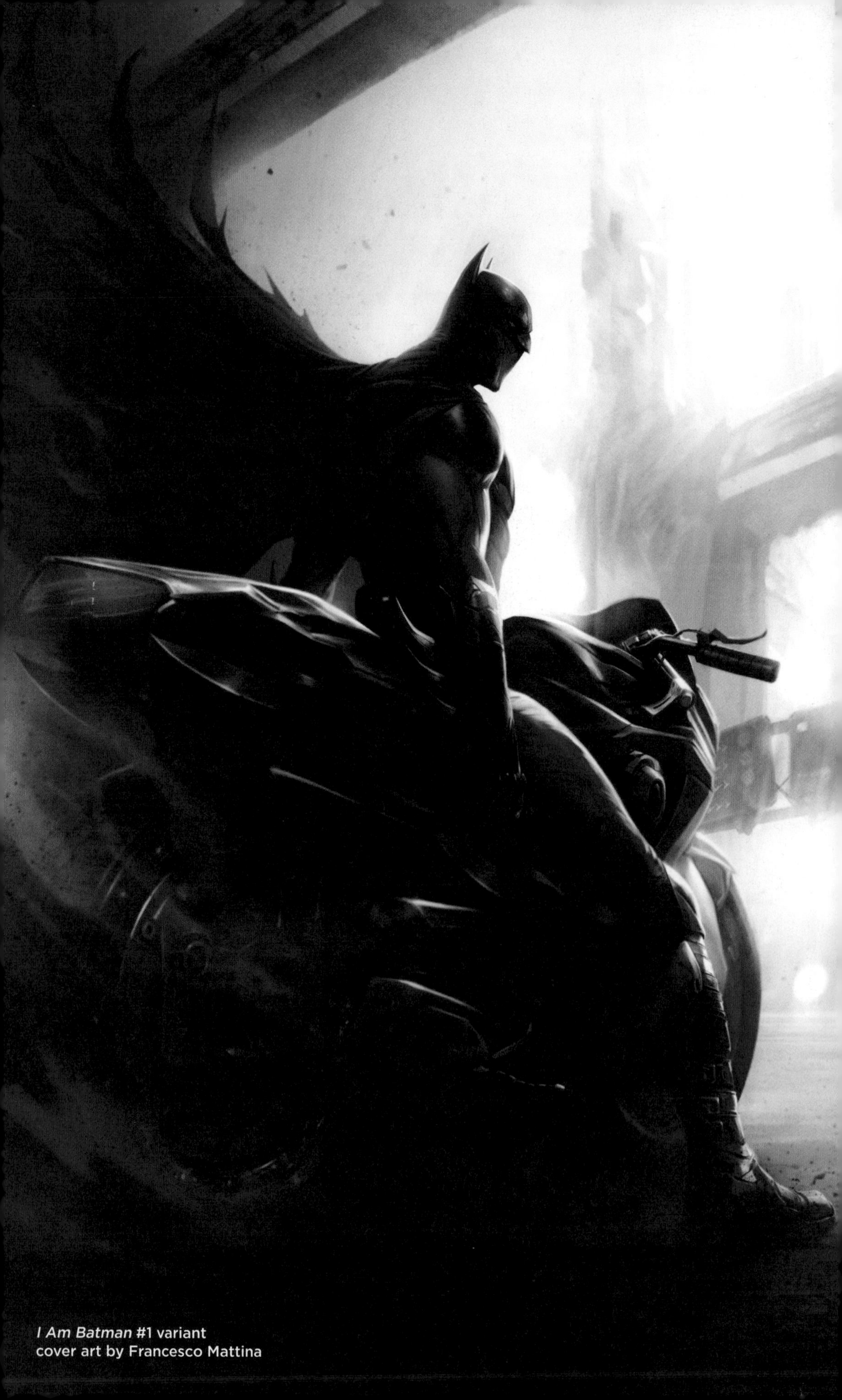

I Am Batman #1 variant
cover art by Francesco Mattina

WANTED

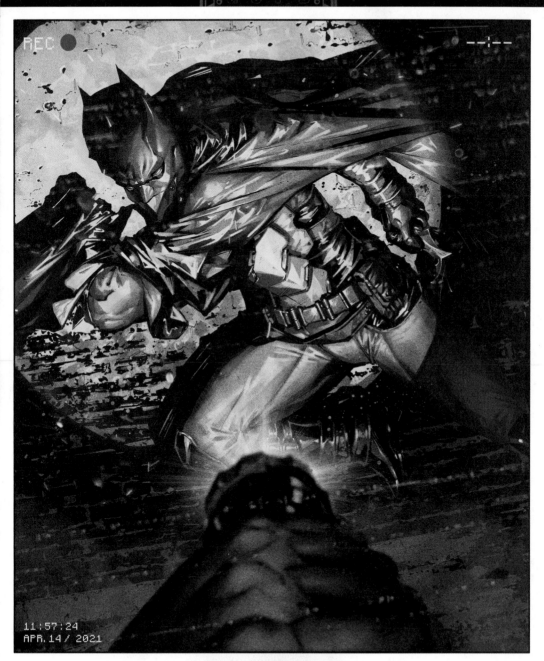

BATMAN

KNOWN ACCOMPLICES—JOHN RIDLEY, OLIVIER COIPEL, ALEX SINCLAIR
CONSIDERED ARMED AND EXTREMELY DANGEROUS
IMMEDIATELY CONTACT THE GCPD OR THE MAGISTRATE

GOTHAM
CITY
POLICE
DEPARTMENT

I Am Batman #1 variant
cover art by Kael Ngu

I Am Batman #1 variant
cover art by Gabriele Dell'Otto

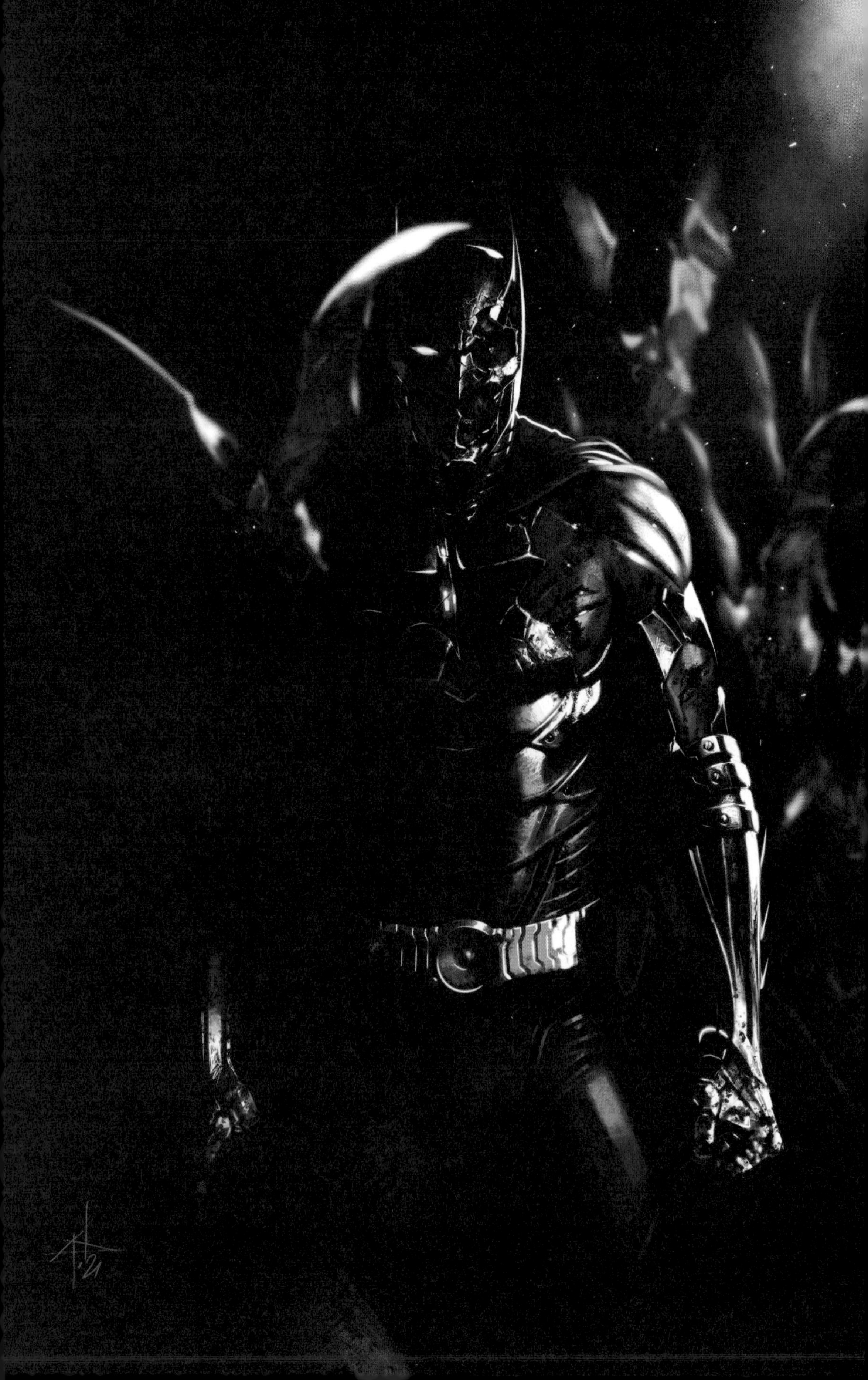

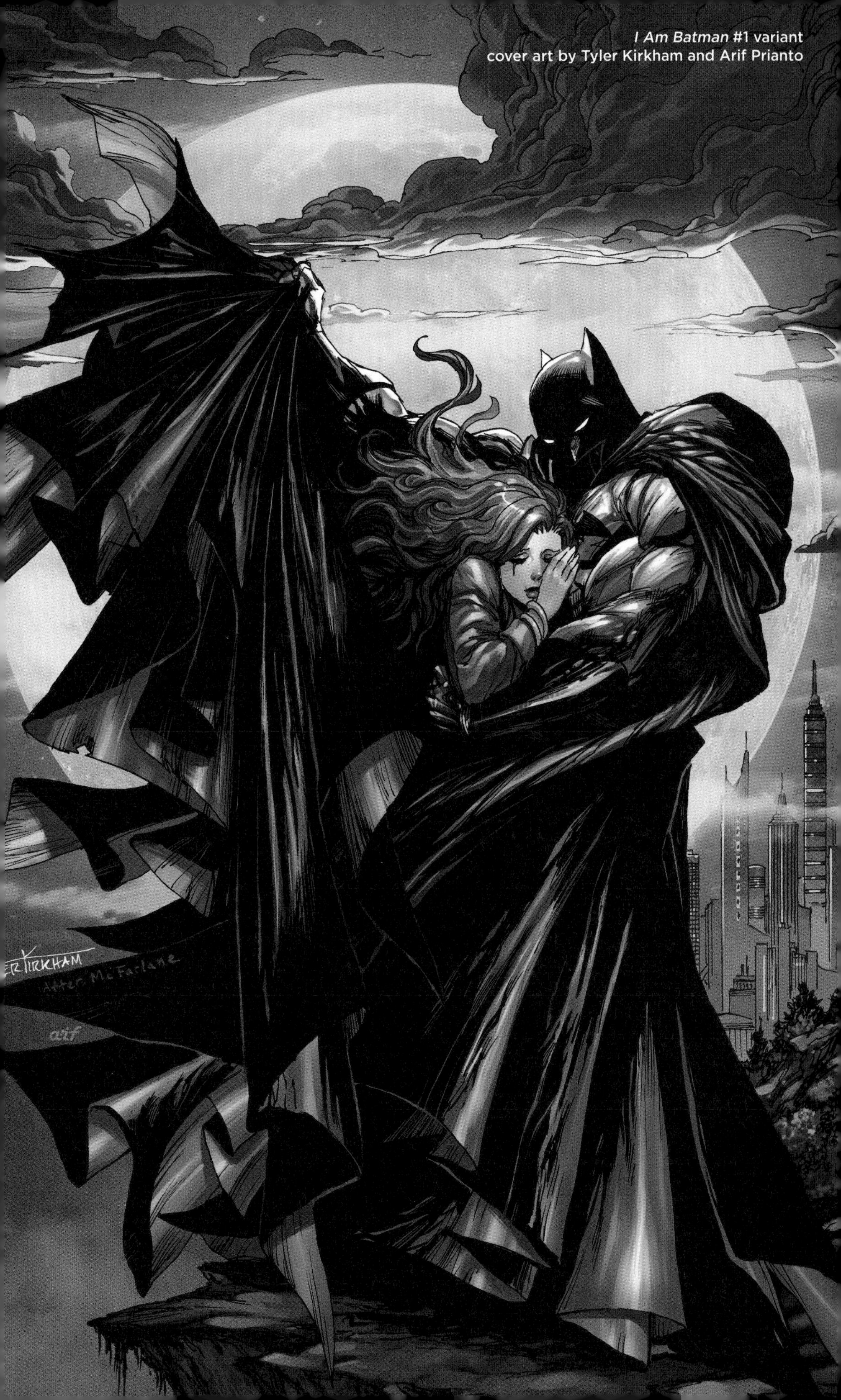
After McFarlane
arif

I Am Batman #1 variant
cover art by Tyler Kirkham and Arif Prianto

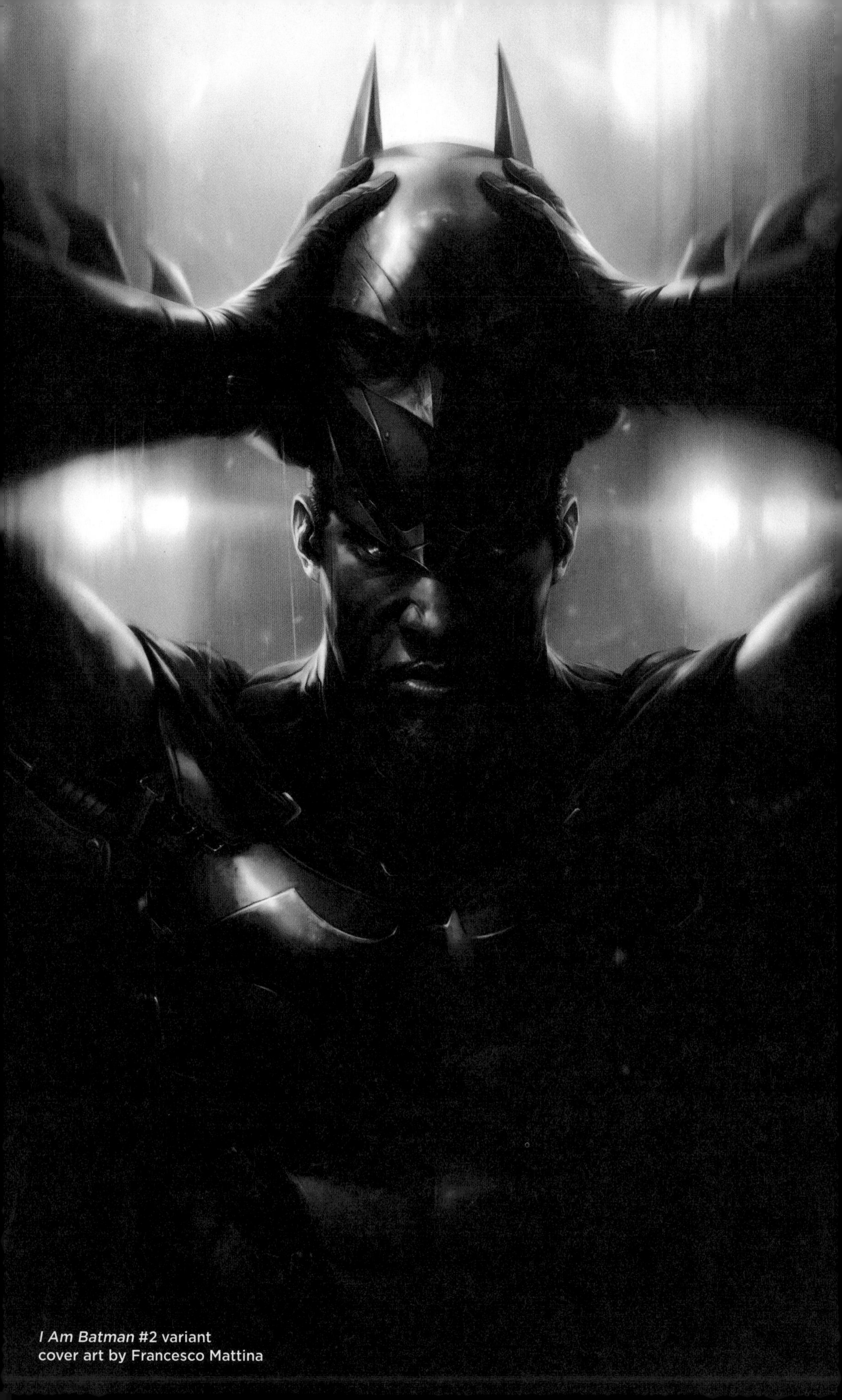

I Am Batman #2 variant
cover art by Francesco Mattina

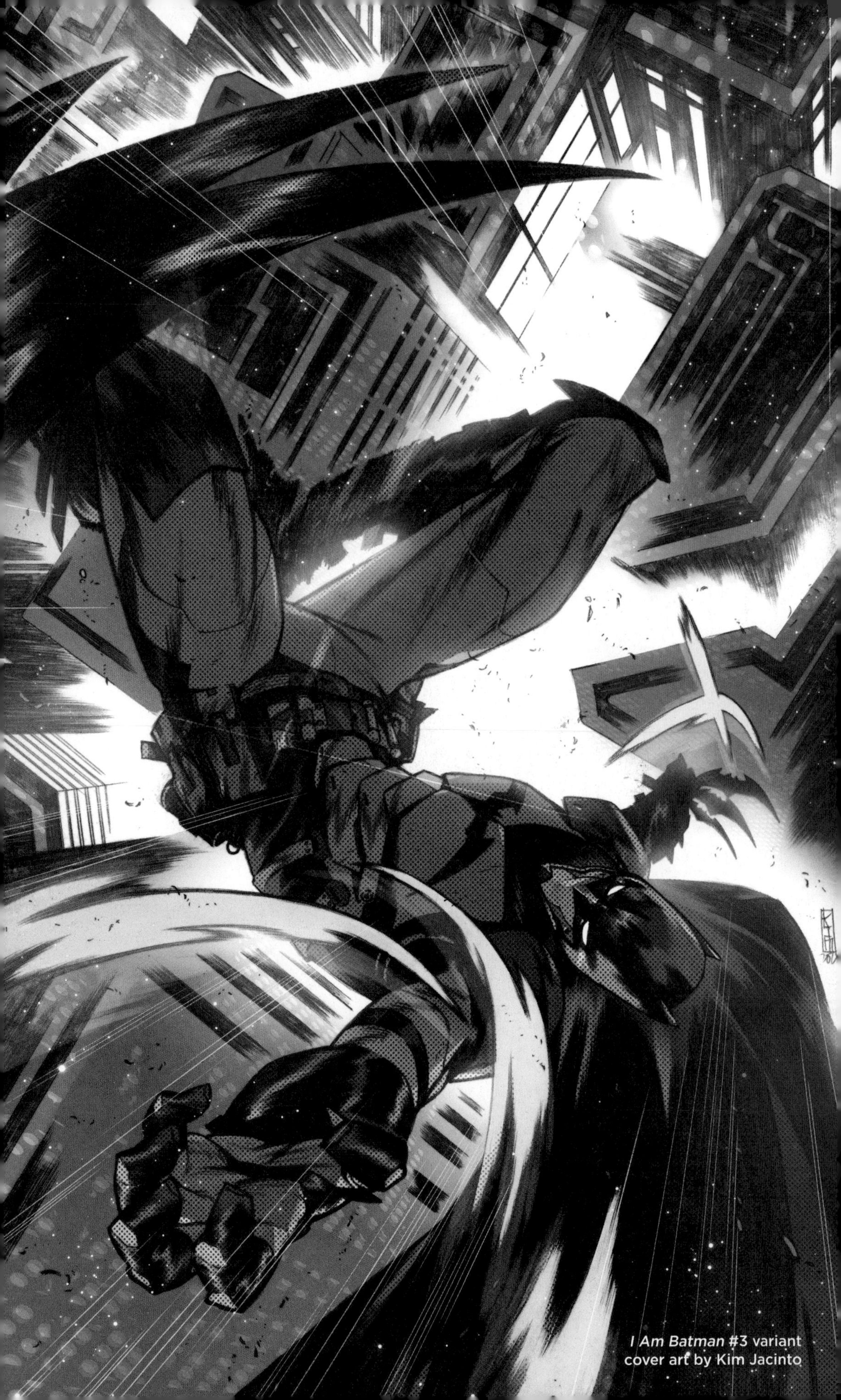

I Am Batman #3 variant
cover art by Kim Jacinto

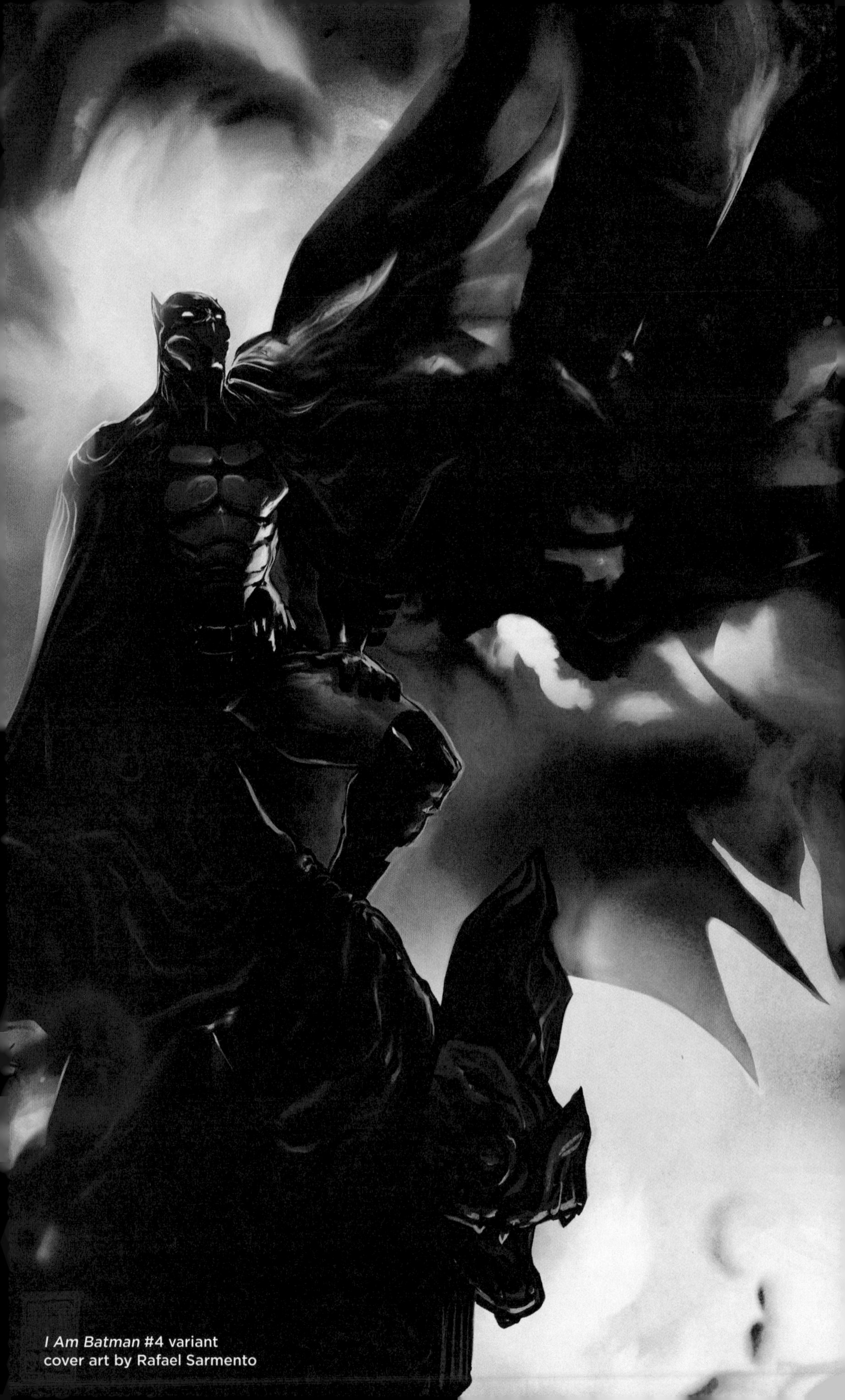

I Am Batman #4 variant
cover art by Rafael Sarmento

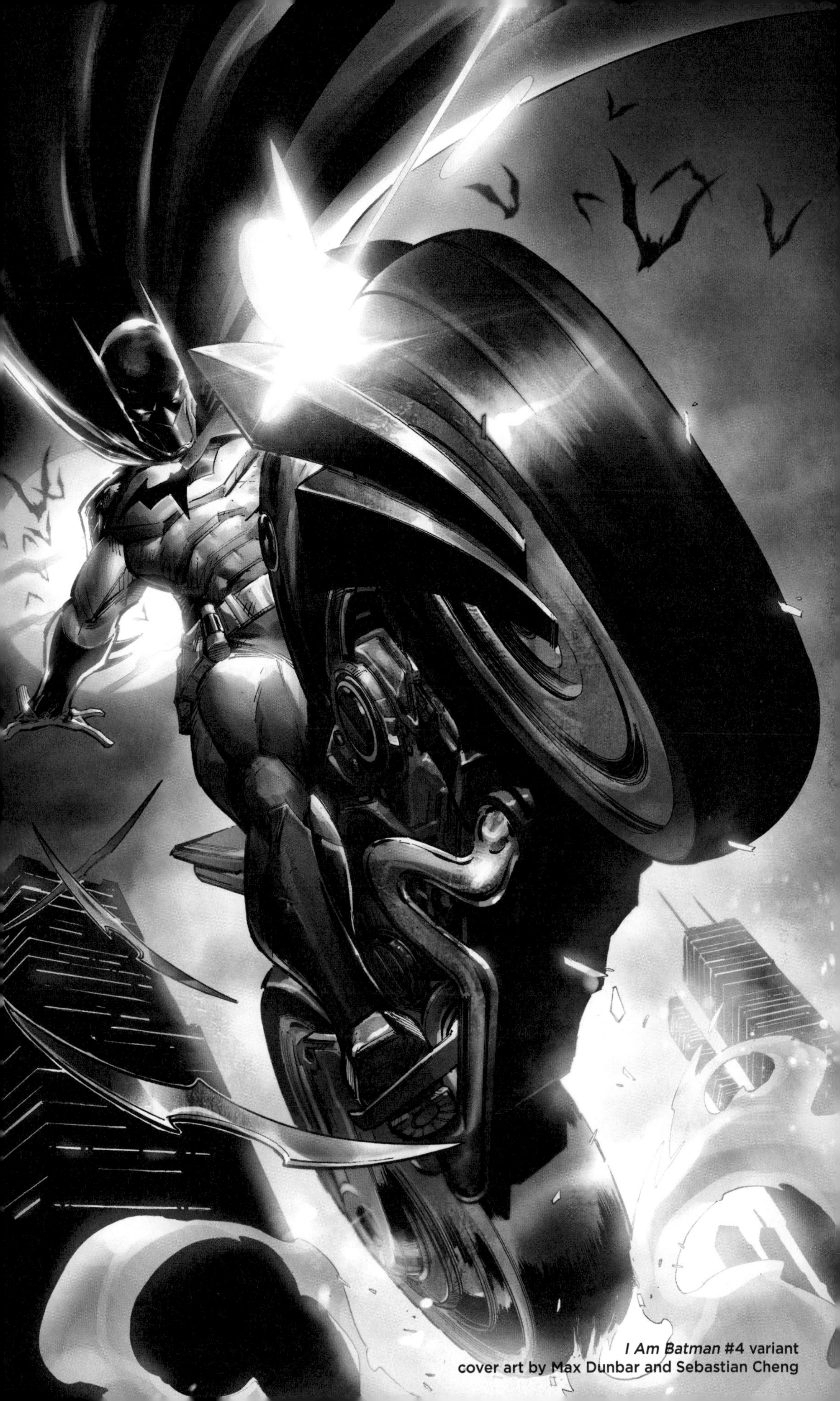

I Am Batman #4 variant
cover art by Max Dunbar and Sebastian Cheng

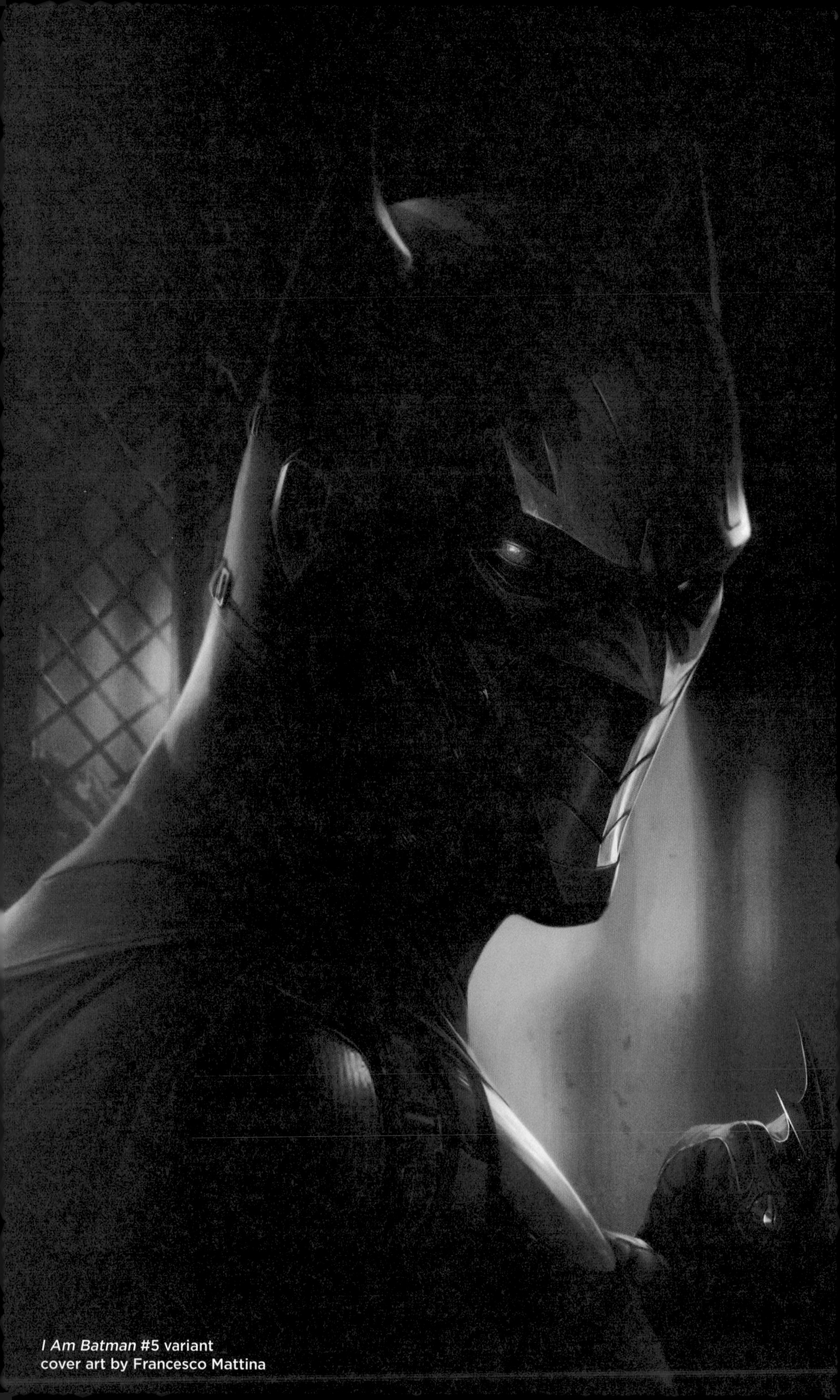

I Am Batman #5 variant
cover art by Francesco Mattina

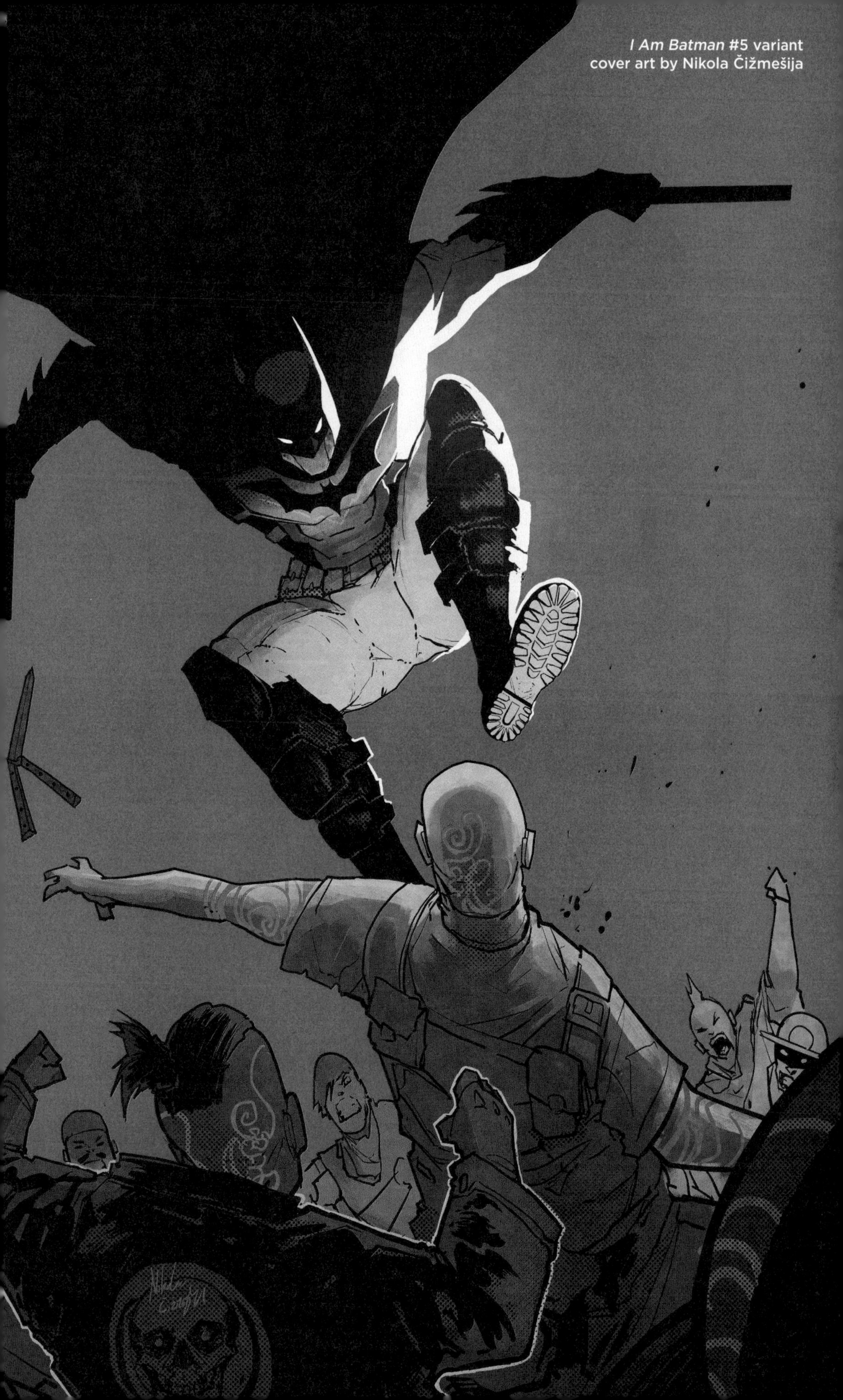

I Am Batman #5 variant
cover art by Nikola Čižmešija

Character designs by Olivier Coipel

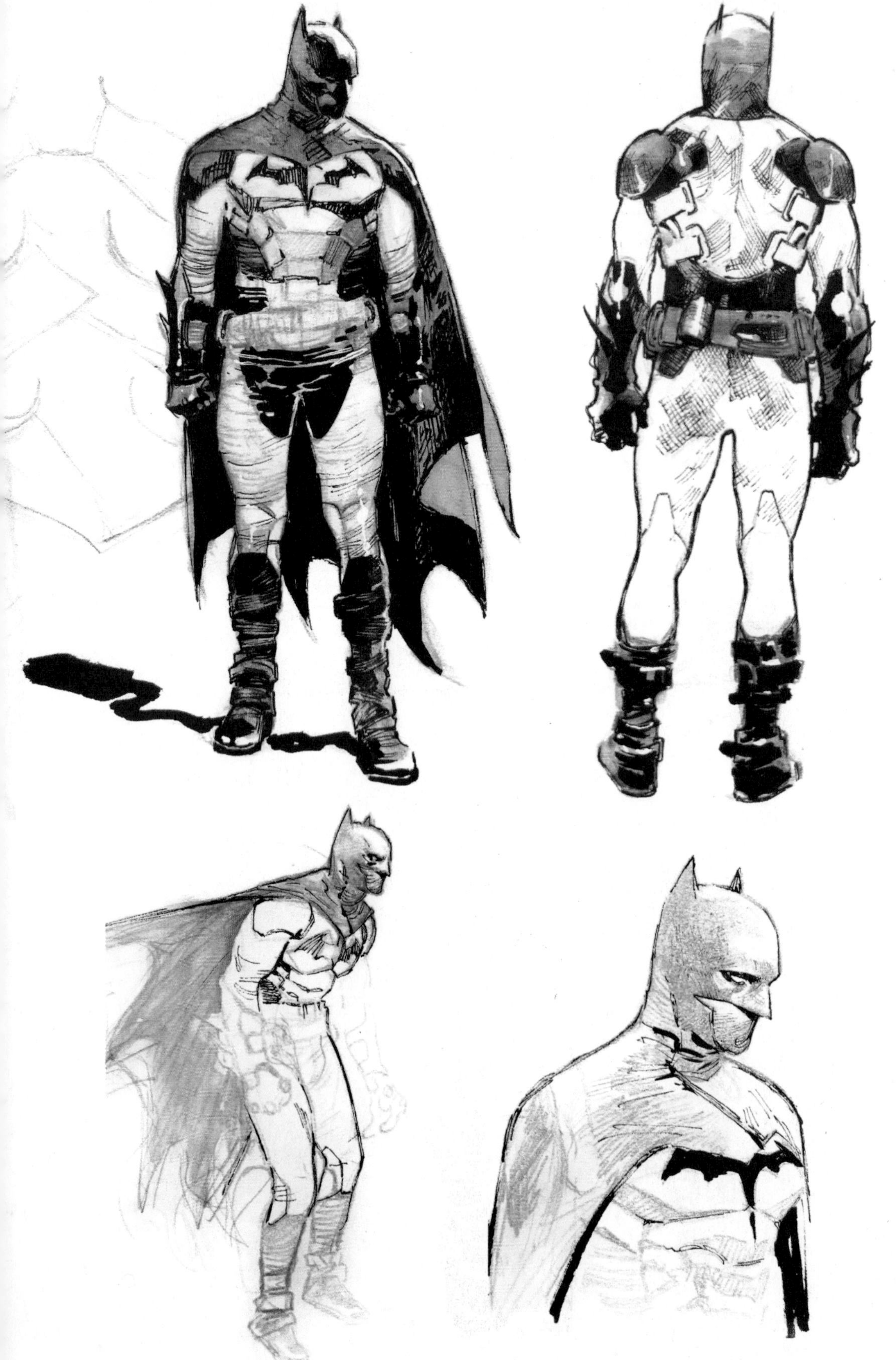

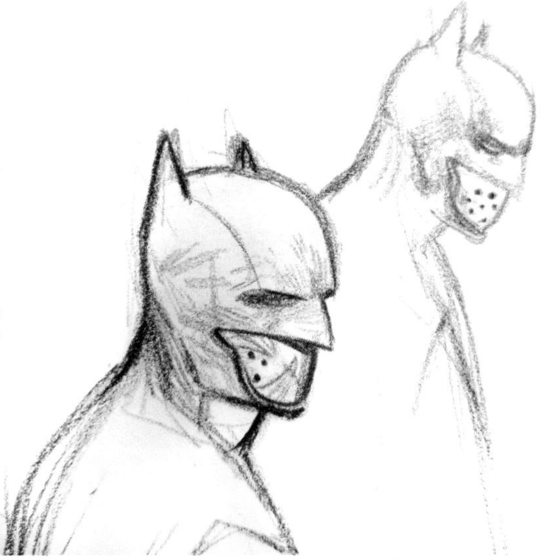

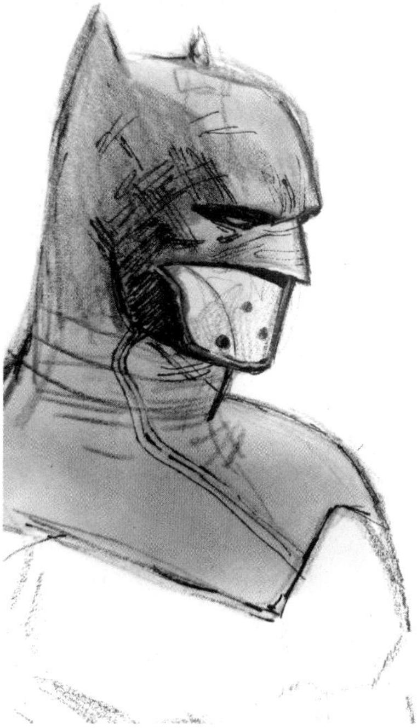

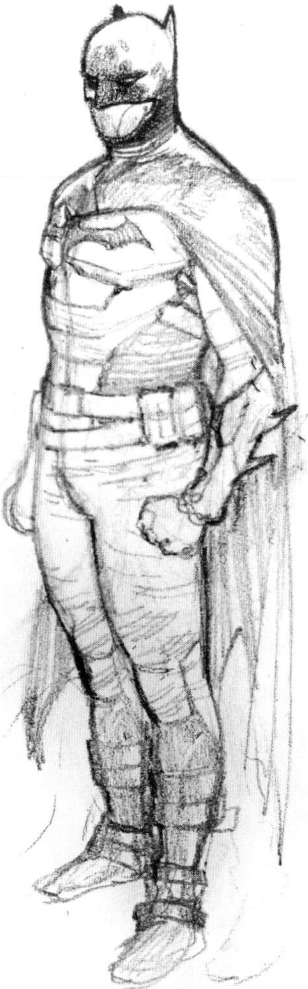

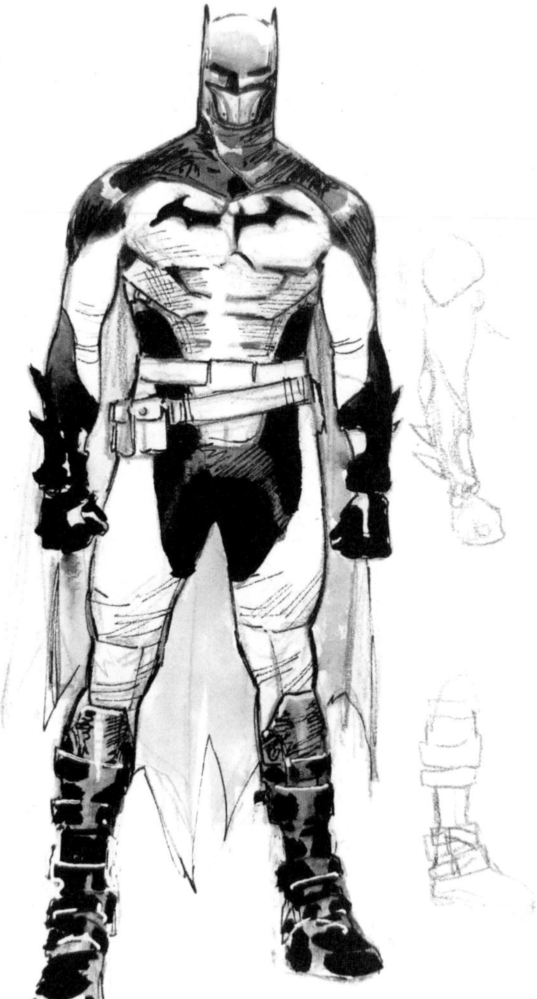

YOU THINK YOU KNOW WHAT HAPPENED.
BUT YOU HAVEN'T HEARD THEIR STORIES.

THE
OTHER
HISTORY
OF THE DC UNIVERSE

Written by Academy Award winner
JOHN RIDLEY

Art by
GIUSEPPE CAMUNCOLI AND **ANDREA CUCCHI**

A graphic novel collection of the acclaimed series

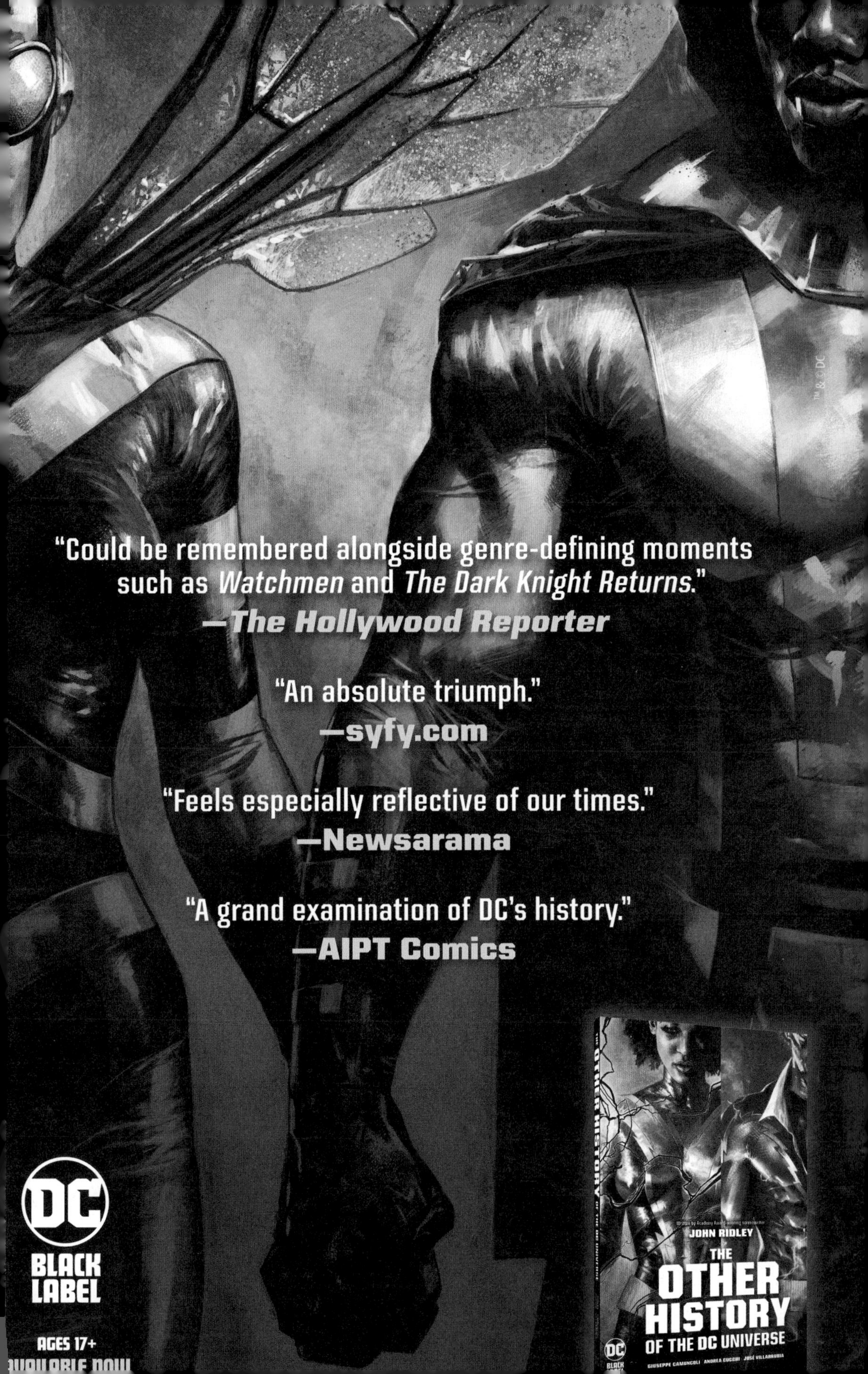

"Could be remembered alongside genre-defining moments such as *Watchmen* and *The Dark Knight Returns*."
—*The Hollywood Reporter*

"An absolute triumph."
—syfy.com

"Feels especially reflective of our times."
—Newsarama

"A grand examination of DC's history."
—AIPT Comics

JOHN RIDLEY

THE OTHER HISTORY OF THE DC UNIVERSE

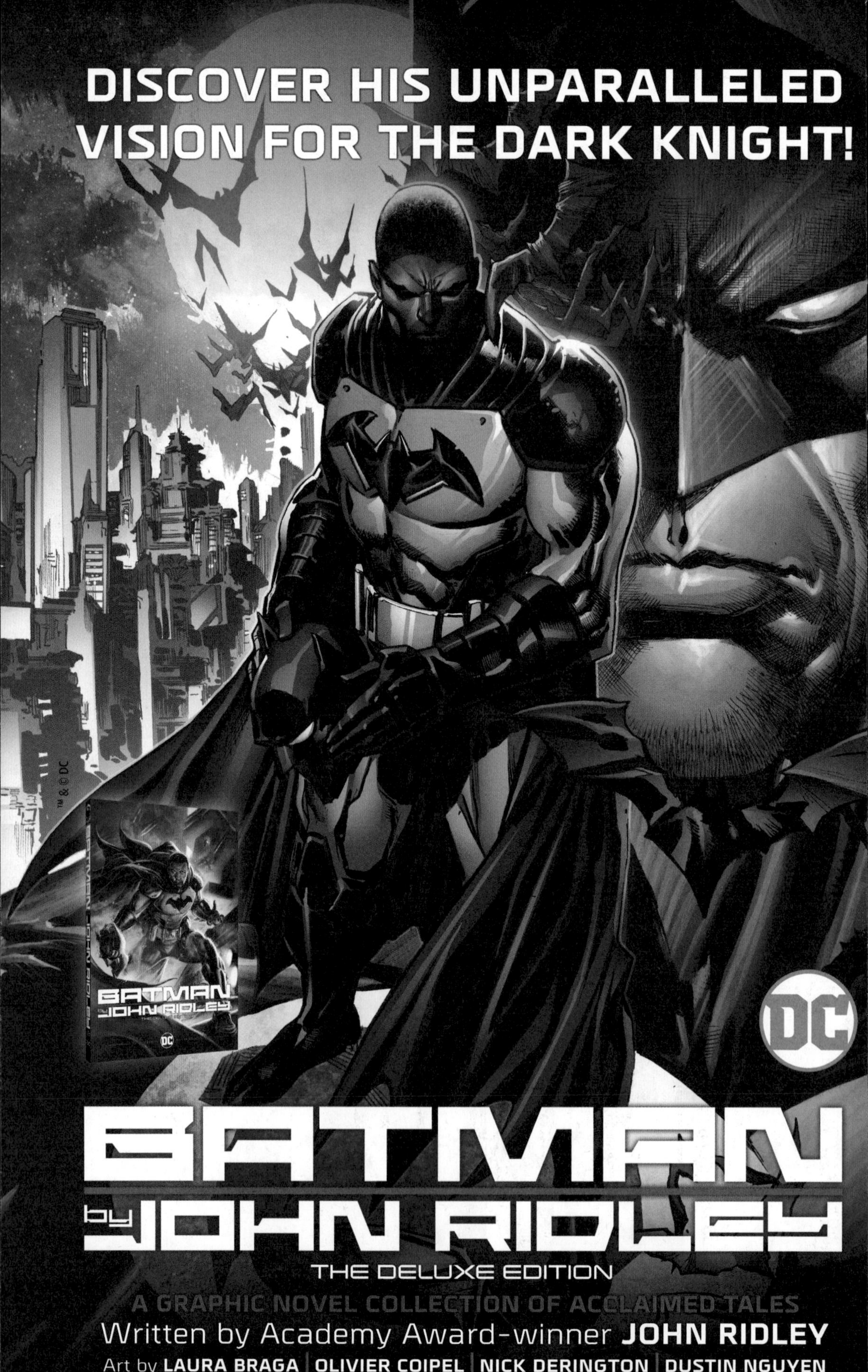

DISCOVER HIS UNPARALLELED VISION FOR THE DARK KNIGHT!
TM & © DC
BATMAN by JOHN RIDLEY
DC
BATMAN
by JOHN RIDLEY
THE DELUXE EDITION
A GRAPHIC NOVEL COLLECTION OF ACCLAIMED TALES
Written by Academy Award-winner JOHN RIDLEY
Art by LAURA BRAGA | OLIVIER COIPEL | NICK DERINGTON | DUSTIN NGUYEN

Pine River Library
395 Bayfield Center Dr.
P.O. Box 227
Bayfield, CO 81122
(970) 884-2222
www.prlibrary.org